Atlas of
ANCIENT
AMERICA

Editor Graham Speake
Art Editor Andrew
   Lawson
Map editors Nicholas
   Harris, Zoë Goodwin
Text editor Robert
   Peberdy
Index Ann Barrett
Design Adrian Hodgkins
Production Clive Sparling

 AN EQUINOX BOOK

Published in North America by
Facts On File, Inc., 460 Park
Avenue South, New York, N.Y.
10016

Published in Great Britain by
Facts On File Ltd, Collins Street,
Oxford, England OX4 1XJ

Planned and produced by
Equinox (Oxford) Ltd, Littlegate
House, St Ebbe's Street, Oxford,
England OX1 1SQ

**Library of Congress
Cataloging in Publication Data**
Main entry under title:
Atlas of ancient America.
Includes index.
1. Indians-Antiquities.
2. America-Antiquities. I. Coe,
Michael D. II. Benson, Elizabeth
P. III. Snow, Dean R., 1940-
E61.A88 1986   970   84-25999
ISBN 0-8160-1199-0

**British Library Cataloguing in
Publication Data**
Coe, Michael D.
The cultural atlas of ancient
America.
(Cultural atlas series)
1. America—History—To 1810
I. Title II. Snow, Dean R. III.
Benson, Elizabeth P. IV. Series
970.01   E58

Origination by Scantrans,
Singapore

Maps drawn and originated by
Lovell Johns Ltd, Oxford; Alan
Mais, Hornchurch; Location Map
Services, Fleet.

Filmset by
Hourds Typographica, Stafford.
Printed in Portugal by Printer
Portuguesa

Atlas of ANCIENT AMERICA

by Michael Coe, Dean Snow
and Elizabeth Benson

Facts On File Publications
New York, New York • Oxford, England

CONTENTS

Frontispiece Hunters and raiders depicted on two Maya vases. The naked man has been captured and is being led away for sacrifice by decapitation.

Special Features

Site Features

List of Maps

CHRONOLOGICAL TABLE

	20 000	10 000	9000	8000	7000	6000	5000	4000	3000	2000	MILLENNIA 1000 BC	CENTURIES 0 AD 100

PANAMERICA

UPPER LITHIC (Alaska)

LOWER LITHIC   MIDDLE LITHIC   ARCHAIC (adaptation of Indian bands to restricted environments)

(N. America) Clovis   Folsom   Lanceolate point tradition

c. 10 000 BC points and scrapers, ●
El Jobo, Venezuela

● Extinction of many large animals c. 10 000–8000 BC

Olmec head, La Venta c. 900–400 BC

Folsom point c. 9000 BC

Valdivia figurine
c. 3000–1800 BC

NORTH AMERICA

Eskimo cultures Stage I   Eskimo Stage III

Eskimo cultures Stage II   Eskimo cultures Stage IV

Eastern Woodlands

Eastern Woodlands

Great Plains

Southwest   prehistoric traditions

Southwest

Emergence of California tribes

Northwest Coast   Archaic cultures established by 7700 BC

MESOAMERICA

ARCHAIC   EARLY FORMATIVE   LATE FORMATIVE

Maize in use by 5000 BC ●   Olmec   MIDDLE FORMAT

Teotihuacan

Ocós culture c. 1500 BC ●●   Izapan

Barra culture c. 1600 BC ●●

SOUTH AMERICA

Arawak migration to Antilles

Ceramics at Puerto Hormiga, Colombia c. 3000 BC ●   San Agustín

Las Vegas culture   Valdivia culture   Chorrera

INITIAL PERIOD   EARLY HORIZON

Chavín   Moche

Paracas   Nazca

Cotton cultivated by 3500 BC ●

Oldest known metalwork c. 1500 BC ●

300	400	500	600	700	800	900	1000	1100	1200	1300	1400	1500	1600	1700	1800	1900

Gunnbjörn sights Greenland 982 ● Norse settlements in Greenland

Leif Eirikson sights Vinland 986 ● Cabot discovers Newfoundland 1497 ● European settlements in N. America

Norse settlement at L'Anse aux Meadows, Newfoundland

Treaty of Tordesillas 1494 ● 1539 Hernando De Soto explores inland SE. N. America

Columbus reaches New World 1492 ● Spanish conquest and settlement of Mexico

Spanish conquest and settlement of Peru

Portuguese colonization of Brazil

Pampas Indians of Argentina exterminated 1880s

Moche pot c. 100–500 AD

Cliff Palace, Mesa Verde c. 1100

Lord Chac Zutz from Palenque 730 AD

Inca silver statuette

Eskimo cultures Stage V

Adena culture

Hopewell culture   Eastern Woodlands Mississippian culture

Eastern Woodlands local traditions   Southern cult Mississippi area

Plains Woodland period   Great Plains   Coalescent tradition

Great Plains   Plains Village period   ● Introduction of horse-mounted nomadism

Desert West and Southwest   Fremont culture

Southwest   Sinagua culture

Southwest   Hohokam tradition

Southwest   Mogollon tradition

Anasazi tradition

Mesa Verde cliff dwellings constructed

Californian cultures

Development of Northwest Coast Indian cultures

EARLY CLASSIC   LATE CLASSIC   EARLY POST-CLASSIC   LATE POST-CLASSIC

El Tajín

Toltec   Aztec

Monte Albán   c. 800   Collapse of Maya in Southern Lowlands   Oaxaca   Mixtec

Maya civilization ●

Ballgame in Antilles; new immigrants   New migrations and ceramic styles

gional Development period   Integration period

EARLY INTERMEDIATE PERIOD   MIDDLE HORIZON   LATE INTERMEDIATE PERIOD   LATE HORIZON

Sicán   Inca

Huari

Tiahuanaco   Chimú

9

PREFACE

On 12 October 1492 Columbus landed on a small island in the Bahamas, an event that changed the world in ways that neither the Europeans nor the native Americans could possibly have imagined. Two cultural traditions, which had developed for thousands of years without any knowledge of each other, were suddenly thrust into contact, and neither of them was ever the same again.

In those countries where a large Indian population still survives, there is no need to ask the question: why study American archaeology? The past is, quite visibly, part of the present. Elsewhere the cultures of ancient America are too often presented as curious but exotic, interesting perhaps, but irrelevant to the course of world history. This ignores the contribution of the American Indian to the world's food supply (international staples like maize, beans, potatoes and manioc/cassava), to medicine (quinine, coca, strychnine), and to the artistic heritage of the world in general. In the present century, with the rediscovery of ''primitive'' art by European painters and sculptors, the artifacts of native America—Olmec jades, Maya pots, Peruvian weaving, Haida masks—are valued as serious works of art, not merely as ethnographic curios. Artists like Henry Moore acknowledge a debt to Aztec and Toltec sculpture, and modern writers (including the Nobel prizewinner, Miguel Angel Asturias) draw their inspiration from native mythology.

This, of course, is a recent phenomenon but, from the moment of contact, America has always contributed to the mainstream of European intellectual life. The peoples discovered by the *conquistadores* were completely new, unaccounted for by the Bible or by the geographies of the known world. Somehow they had to be fitted into the scheme of things. Who were they? Where did they come from? Did they have souls? The discovery of a completely new continent, with a radically different set of social structures, raised a series of moral problems and at the same time provided a touchstone by which the institutions of Europe could be assessed. Some political philosophers saw the Indians as barbarians, untouched by Christianity or civilization; others, like Montaigne, Diderot and Rousseau, created the myth of the Noble Savage as a device to attack the European system of privilege and political oppression. The newly discovered lands provided a laboratory for social experiment, in the real world of the Jesuit missions in Paraguay but also in the fictional world of Sir Thomas More's *Utopia*.

The Americas played their part too in the development of archaeology as a science. By the early 18th century the more primitive of the American Indians were regarded as the living counterparts of the European tribes described by Greek and Roman authors. Prehistoric European stone axeheads were compared with those used by the Iroquois or the Tupinamba, and scholars formulated the idea of a Stone Age preceding the knowledge of bronze and iron. Other developmental schemes, also drawing on American evidence, argued for an age of hunting and gathering before the emergence of farming.

This same interest in the evolution of human behavior is at the heart of modern archaeology, and archaeologists are again asking universal questions, though of a very different kind. Was it overhunting that caused so many large mammals to become extinct around 10 000 years ago? How and why did farming replace foraging? What caused the first states to evolve in different parts of the world? Is cultural development governed by general laws, or is human behavior too complex to be explained in purely scientific terms? In examining these questions of global interest, the American evidence is crucial and the long isolation of America is an advantage. Any universal scheme based solely on Old World data can be tested by a simple question: did things happen the same way in the Americas?

There are good reasons, then, why this book is primarily about people and their behavior, the indigenous Americans and the rich variety of cultures they created. To appreciate this past variety, and to understand the Americas of today, there is a need for a book that offers an introduction to the hemisphere as a whole, that looks at *everything*, from the hunters of Tierra del Fuego in 10 000 BC to the splendid and civilized empires of the Aztec and Inca. Art and artifacts are a part of the story; so, too, are the important archaeological sites examined in the site features. But to understand these archaeological remains one must see them as they once were, and as the work of real people. The figures belong in a landscape—and that means maps. This book is, above all, an atlas set within a historical context, recreating the ever-changing landscape of the past in all its aspects, physical, cultural and political.

This is no longer a task for a single author. Today's archaeologists are specialists and, in the chapters that follow, the responsibilities are shared between Michael Coe (Parts One, Two and Four), Dean Snow (Parts One and Three) and Elizabeth Benson (Part Five). Each author has contributed to Part Six.

WARWICK BRAY

PART ONE
THE
NEW WORLD

The manner of their attire and painting them selues when they goe to their generall huntings, or at theire Solemne feasts.

ARCTIC OCEAN

The topography of the
Americas

Queen Elizabeth
Islands

Beaufort Sea

*Baffin
Bay*

GREENLAND
(Denmark)

70°

**Alaska
(US)**

Baffin
Island

Arctic Circle

MACKENZIE MTS

Davis Strait

*Great
Bear L*

ICELAND

Mt McKinley
6194 ▲

60°

ALASKA RANGE

Mackenzie

Anchorage

*Great
Slave L*

Hudson
Bay

COAST RANGE

Gulf of
Alaska

Athabasca L

CANADA

Labrador

Laurentian
Plateau

Newfoundland

50°

Vancouver

L Winnipeg

Winnipeg

L Superior

Gulf of
St Lawrence

SIERRA NEVADA

L Michigan

L Huron

Ottawa

Montréal

ROCKY MOUNTAINS

Great Plains

Missou

Toronto

L Ontario

New York

CASCADE RANGE

Great
Basin

Chicago

L Erie

40°

San Francisco

APPALACHIAN MTS

Mt Whitney
4418 ▲

USA

Washington

ATLANTIC OCEAN

Los Angeles

Ohio

30°

Gulf of California

Mississippi

New Orleans

Tropic of Cancer

SIERRA MADRE OCCIDENTAL

Rio Grande

SIERRA MADRE ORIENTAL

GULF OF MEXICO

Havana

BAHAMAS

MEXICO

CUBA

20°

Yucatán
Peninsula

Mexico City

**DOMINICAN
REPUBLIC**

JAMAICA

HAITI

BELIZE

Puerto
Rico (US)

Lesser
Antilles

HONDURAS

Guatemala City

*CARIBBEAN
SEA*

Tegucigalpa

NICARAGUA

GUATEMALA

**TRINIDAD
AND TOBAGO**

10°

PACIFIC OCEAN

EL SALVADOR

Managua

San José

Caracas

Orinoco

COSTA RICA

Panama

VENEZUELA

GUYANA

PANAMA

Bogotá

GUIANA HIGHLANDS

SURINAME

**FR
GUIANA**

COLOMBIA

height of land in meters

Galápagos Is
(Ecuador)

Quito

Equator   0°

4000

ECUADOR

Japurá

Belém

1000

Ucayali

Manaus

Amazon

200

S e l v a s

Recife

0

ANDES

Madera

0

PERU

BRAZIL

10°

2000 } sea depth

Lima

international boundary

L Titicaca

Ancohuma

▲ 6560

□ capital city

La Paz

BRAZILIAN HIGHLANDS

Brasília

● other important city

BOLIVIA

▲ mountain summit (height in meters)

Rio de Janeiro

Equatorial scale 1:54 000 000

20°

PARAGUAY

Paraguay

Asunción

São Paulo

Tropic of Capricorn

Gran
Chaco

CHILE

Paraná

URUGUAY

30°

Aconcagua

Santiago

▲ 6960

Buenos Aires

Montevideo

ARGENTINA

Colorado

40°

Patagonia

50°

**Falkland Islands
(UK)**

Tierra del Fuego

Cape
Horn

60°

110°   100°   90°   80°   70°   60°   50°   40°

NATIVE CULTURES AND THE ENVIRONMENT

While all of the native peoples of the New World had a common origin in Asia, there is no such thing as a "typical" American Indian (or Eskimo, for that matter). Since their initial migration (or migrations) into the Western Hemisphere, natural selection pressures—especially climate—in widely varying environments have produced phenotypic variations in native populations. All, however, have brown skins, dark eyes and straight, black hair.

Below left Jívaro of the Upano River, upper Amazon drainage, Ecuador. Native people of the American tropics tend to be smaller and less robust in physique than those in higher latitudes.

Below center Medicine Crow, a member of the Crow tribe, Montana. The mounted hunters of the Plains are the tallest and most rugged of New World populations.

Below right Nostak Eskimo men in summer clothing. As an adaptation to conditions of extreme cold, Eskimos (or Inuit) have chunky body proportions and relatively short extremities, with deposits of fat to protect the eyes.

On the eve of the Spanish "discovery" of the New World there were about 40 million native Americans living in the Western Hemisphere, from the Eskimos and Aleut of the high latitudes of North America, to the Ona and Yahgan of the Straits of Magellan and Cape Horn. Between the tropics of Cancer and Capricorn there had arisen and flourished some of the greatest and most brilliant civilizations the world has ever seen, although totally unknown to pre-Columbian Europe and Asia. Every type of culture known to the Old World was also present in the New, from primitive hunters and gatherers, to simple farming societies, to mighty empires.

Today, much of this ancient magnificence is little more than a memory, if even that, and centuries of European military, cultural and religious onslaught, along with the ravages of European diseases, have reduced the native populations to a fraction of what they once were. With the exception of Paraguay, where Guaraní is one of the national tongues, no native American language has any official status among the modern nation-states of the New World, nor has any American Indian representative been accredited to the United Nations. Treated as much-despised but necessary labor by Catholic Latin Americans, and as much-feared devils by Protestant Anglo-Americans, there was never much chance that American Indians in the areas most favorable for European

settlement would have much of a future, given the advanced nature of European technology as compared with that of even the most evolved native American cultures.

Language and race

Of the world's approximately 3000 languages, that is tongues that are mutually unintelligible, about 400 were spoken in the Western Hemisphere, although, as with population estimates, it is difficult to be exact about this. The problem in both areas of investigation is that the first censuses, and the first vocabularies or dictionaries, were recorded decades or even centuries after the initial European contact, when the turmoil caused by disease, repression, extermination and expulsion had taken its toll. Linguists, beginning with Major John Wesley Powell in the 19th century, have classified these languages into about 100 "families" of genetically related tongues, similar in scope to the Indo-European family (which includes most of the languages of Europe, Persia and India).

Such linguistic diversity argues for a very long period of cultural isolation of the New World from the Old. With the exception of Eskimo, speakers of which are found on both sides of the Bering Straits, no native American language has been found to have positive connections with any in the Old World, although some arguments have been advanced for the affinity of Athapascan (spoken in

Left Chaco Canyon, New Mexico, looking southeast. Isolated from modern American civilization, the Canyon has preserved the ruins of 12 pueblos (large villages consisting of numerous apartments) and over 300 smaller sites—in all, the components of an erstwhile large-scale trading network which was part of the larger Chaco "phenomenon" (see page 78). In the foreground lies the most famous and most excavated pueblo, Pueblo Bonito. The canyon dwellings were built by the Anasazi Indians, and flourished between the mid-10th and the mid-12th centuries AD. The seeming permanence of these constructions should not divert attention from the basic dependence of the Anasazi on agricultural conditions: their network probably suffered great contractions with recurrent droughts in the late 12th century.

northwestern North America and by the Navajo and Apache of the American Southwest) and certain languages of eastern Asia.

Even though one cannot point out Asiatic origins for New World languages, there is no doubt among physical anthropologists that native Americans are all of Mongoloid racial stock. Since they have been so long in the Western Hemisphere, with its extremes of environment, natural selection has operated on the initial populations to produce differences in physique and other phenotypical characters. Eskimos or Inuit, for example, who live in conditions of extreme cold, tend to have chunky torsos and short extremities, apparently an adaptation for lowering loss of body heat; and in general, American Indians in higher latitudes (other than the Eskimos) are taller and heavier than those in tropical regions. But there is no reason to think that there was an influx of peoples into pre-Columbian America from anywhere else but Asia.

The New World environment

While the land mass of North and South America is only a fraction of that of Eurasia and Africa combined, which may account for the New World's smaller indigenous population and fewer languages, the environment is far more varied, for pre-Columbian peoples were spread all the way from the Polar Eskimos of northern Greenland to the Fuegians of southernmost South America, at about 45 degrees South. It is thus impossible to generalize about the environment in which the native Americans were found.

The most striking geophysical feature of the Western Hemisphere is the great cordillera extending from Alaska, down through the Rocky Mountains, and continuing through the Andean mountain chain of western South America. East of this "backbone of the Americas" the land is largely low-lying, with broad river plains such as the Mississippian drainage of North America and the Orinoco and Amazon Basins of South America. Exceptions to this topography are the Appalachian Mountains of the eastern United States, and the Brazilian uplands.

Far more important than altitude, however, in setting the limits to New World cultural development and population, was the tolerance of major food plants to frost. Since these were largely tropical in origin—especially maize, beans, chili peppers and squashes—human population densities were highest in lower latitudes, where food was most abundant. In eastern North America, for example, maize cultivation barely extended north of the Great Lakes region, beyond which Indian populations were very sparse. Certainly the great native civilizations, such as the Aztec, Maya and Inca, depended entirely upon effective farming of indigenous food plants; it is therefore no accident that these complex cultures were found within the Tropics.

Environment and culture

Millennia of cultural development and environmental diversity have resulted in diverse cultural adaptations. The most complex cultures were those of Mesoamerica (those parts of Mexico and Central America that were civilized at the time of the Spanish conquest) and the Andean area, basically the territory of the Inca empire and its predecessors. These were the "nuclear" areas of the ancient New World, with large, highly organized political states, cities, monumental architecture and sculpture, and, most importantly, organized state religions.

Between the two "nuclear" areas lay Lower Central America, Colombia, western Venezuela and northern Ecuador, lumped by archaeologists, for want of a better term, as the "Intermediate Area." Here populations were high since maize agriculture was the rule, but the societal level never exceeded that of the chiefdom. The same was true of the Caribbean Islands, the first of the New World lands to be "discovered" by the expeditions of Columbus, and which he steadfastly believed to be outliers of Asia.

To the north and south of Mesoamerica and the Andean area existed cultures that were less complex, but nevertheless also dependent upon agriculture, such as the Mississippian culture of the eastern and southeastern United States, which produced such enormous towns as Cahokia, boasting the largest pyramidal structure in the entire New World.

East of the Andean chain, in the tropical forest of the Orinoco and Amazon Basins, were (and still are) societies on the tribal and chiefdom level with an economic base of manioc—rather than maize—agriculture. While these may seem "primitive" to western eyes, the key to settled life and even to some aspects of religion in pre-Columbian South America may be found here.

Those native Americans living beyond the range of effective farming, to the north or south of the area with sufficient frost-free days necessary to mature crops of tropical origin, perforce had to follow a hunting-and-gathering way of life. In some respects this showed similarity to the nomadic economy of the Late Pleistocene hunters who first colonized the Western Hemisphere. However it would be misleading to put all of the nonfarming peoples of ancient America into the same pigeonhole, for certain of them had highly specialized and often highly productive economies, such as the salmon fishermen of the Pacific Northwest, who lived in large settled villages, and the Eskimo-Aleut of northernmost North America, with their exploitation of sea mammals such as seals and whales.

Another *caveat* should be raised when dealing with native American cultures beyond the "nuclear" areas: that of the "ethnographic present." As Europeans and Euro-Americans exerted demographic, political and cultural pressure on the indigenous populations, they also introduced new elements which forever altered native life, while at the same time they were the same ones who described these cultures. A case in point is the traditional life-style of the Plains Indians of the American West, still considered the most "typical" of native Americans. Once heavily oriented toward the hunting of buffalo, this culture became completely dependent upon the domestic horse, introduced to North America by the Spaniards. The "ethnographic present"—the textbook recording of Plains culture—is nonetheless the post-contact period of horse nomadism.

ARCTIC OCEAN

Greenland

ARCTIC

Arctic Circle

Yukon

Baffin Island

Vestribygod

Iceland

WESTERN/SUBARCTIC

HUDSON
BAY

Davis Strait

Eystribygod

70°

60°

NORTH
WEST
COAST

NORTHERN
PLAINS

SOUTHERN
CANADIAN

EASTERN SUBARCTIC

L'Anse aux
Meadows

50°

PLATEAU

SOUTHERN
CANADIAN

Newfoundland

GREAT
BASIN

PRAIRIE

EASTERN
WOODLANDS

ATLANTIC OCEAN

40°

Missouri

Ohio

CALIFORNIA

San Juan

SOUTHERN
PLAINS

Mississippi

30°

voyages and *entradas* of
European explorers to 1600

North America

——— Norse explorers 1000-13
– – – John Cabot 1497
– · – Ponce de León 1513
–··– Verrazano 1524
– – – Narvaez- and Cabeza de Vaca 1529-36
——— Cartier 1535-36
——— De Soto 1539-43
——— Coronado 1540-42
— — — Cabrillo and Ferrelo 1542-43
——— Drake 1579
– – – Oñate 1598-1604

Mesoamerica

– – – Cortés 1519, 1524-25

South America and Antilles

——— Columbus 1492
——— Magellan 1519-22
——— Francisco Pizarro 1524-33
– – – Almagro 1535-37
–·–· Gonzalo Pizarro 1539-42

SOUTHWEST

Santa Barbara

NE MEXICO

Santiago

Tenochtitlan

Vera Cruz

Gulf of Mexico

Hispaniola

ANTILLES

Tropic of Cancer

20°

MESOAMERICA

Caribbean Sea

density of population
per 100 square kilometers c.1500

high (more than 100)

medium (1-100)

low (less than 1)

Equatorial scale 1:54 000 000

CIRCUM-CARIBBEAN

10°

PACIFIC OCEAN

Panama

Orinoco

Quito

AMAZONIA

Equator

Tumbes

Amazon

Cajamarca

NORTHERN
AND CENTRAL
ANDES

Lima

Cuzco

EASTERN
HIGHLANDS

20°

GRAN
CHACO

Tropic of Capricorn

SOUTHERN
ANDES

Parana

Coquimbo

PAMPAS

30°

TIERRA
DEL
FUEGO

Magellan
Strait

40°

50°

60°

GREENLAND

Alaska

CANADA

USA

MEXICO

BELIZE
HONDURAS

GUATEMALA
EL SALVADOR
NICARAGUA
COSTA RICA

PANAMA

VENEZUELA

COLOMBIA

ECUADOR

BRAZIL

PERU

BOLIVIA

PARAGUAY

present-day density of
American Indian population
per 100 square kilometers

more than 100

10-100

1-10

less than 1

mestizo population as a
percentage of total population

● more than 50%

◐ 10-50%

○ less than 10%

CHILE

ARGENTINA

URUGUAY

EUROPEAN DISCOVERY
AND CONQUEST

Native populations and European discovery in the 16th century
A picture of New World demography on the eve of Columbus's discovery is necessarily highly conjectural. Population estimates for the native Indians at the turn of the 16th century vary wildly from one source to another. A map which adopts wide-band density classes blurs the truth, but is perhaps the only way to arrive at something like a consensus representation. There is no doubt, however, as to the immediate and devastating consequences visited upon the native population in the wake of the arrival of the first European explorers. Throughout the Americas native communities were devastated, usually by the rapid spread of European diseases, but in places this was compounded by fierce wars of extermination waged against them. Against these scourges the Indians had little power of resistance; only in regions remote from European settlement did the native population stand a chance of survival.

The numbers of natives never recovered, but the late 15th-century pattern of distribution has persisted (*inset*). Peoples of pure Indian blood are, today, still most numerous in the Andean and Middle American nations and are also populous in those states of the USA where Indian reservations have been established. Many millions more can claim partial descent from the indigenous population: known as *mestizos*, the mixed Indian-European peoples account for a large proportion of inhabitants in Latin American countries today.

The notion, or delusion, that Europeans "discovered" a New World in 1492 AD, or more realistically around 1000, is peculiar to Europeans and their descendants. Native Americans familiar with their own past know that their Asiatic ancestors "discovered" this hemisphere as far back as the Ice Age, and many American Indians in the United States, for example, find European claims ludicrous.

Nevertheless there is a continued fascination on the part of Europeans and Euro-Americans with the earliest contacts between their ancestors and the American Indians, and it is of undeniable importance that this contact was to be of lasting benefit to the white populations of the Eastern Hemisphere, and an unmitigated disaster to the brown-skinned peoples of the Western.

Claims of pre-Viking Age interaction between Europe and North America are clouded by much wishful thinking and by ethnic patriotism. This is particularly true of the supposed voyages by Irish monks to the New World, although, as the English historian Geoffrey Ashe reminds us, there may be a grain of truth to be discerned in the various legends surrounding the voyage of Brendan, the 6th-century Irish monk, in search of an earthly paradise called the "Land promised to the Saints." That the Irish ascetic monks were quite capable of reaching very distant shores in fairly primitive craft to establish their far-flung communities is evidenced by their colonization of the Orkneys, Shetland, the Faroes and quite probably Iceland. The story of Brendan's oceanic pilgrimage to the north and west is recounted in several sources of much later date, and was known over much of western Europe; Columbus was well acquainted with it before his first expedition. Brendan and his monk companions may have reached Greenland and, on another trip, have actually touched upon the more temperate lands of the continental New World. These would have been identified with the earthly paradise of his quest.

However, there is absolutely no archaeological evidence for any early Irish voyages to the Western Hemisphere, and the Brendan legend itself is so full of marvels that most of it must have been fable. This is not, however, the case with the great Viking explorations around the year 1000. The Norse colonization of Iceland and Greenland is a fact; land-hungry younger sons and their families from coastal Norway conquered the North Atlantic and established far-flung colonies in these distant lands. Norse artifacts have even been found on Ellesmere Island, in the high Arctic of North America. All of this was made possible by their advanced knowledge of shipbuilding and seacraft: the Norse ships were light years beyond the Irish curraghs in their technical refinement.

Greenland had first been sighted by a man called Gunnbjörn early in the 10th century; in 982 the famous Eirik the Red set sail to find the land

Gunnbjörn had seen, did so, and thoroughly explored its coasts. He found no living souls, although Eskimos had existed there in earlier times and disappeared. On his return to Iceland, Eirik outfitted a colonizing expedition, with 400 persons, along with cattle, sheep and goats. Two colonies were founded, a western and an eastern, although both were on what we could call the southwestern coast of this polar land. After 1000 Greenland was part of the world of Christian Europe, with churches and eventually a bishop, and with regular commerce with Norway, but by some time after 1400 all of the inhabitants had mysteriously died out.

Since the Davis Strait which separates Greenland from Baffin Island represented no barrier to Norse seafarers, it was not long before the Greenland Vikings were acquiring knowledge of the coastal regions of northeasternmost North America. The Norse sagas describe three lands: first, Helluland, a barren, cold place generally identified with the east coast of Baffin Island (which lies athwart the Arctic Circle); second, Markland, lying to the south of Helluland, heavily forested and almost certainly the coast of modern Labrador; and third Vinland. Early European maps and the sagas themselves suggest that the last-named was a long, narrow peninsula or island extending northward in the direction of Markland. This place, unlike the first two, was said to be habitable, with wild grapes and "self-sown wheat."

The Greenlanders' Saga tells us that Vinland was first seen in 986 by a voyager accidentally blown off course, but was first actually visited and settled by Leif Eiriksson. Subsequent expeditions to Vinland made possible a more-or-less permanent colony there, although there were bitter clashes with a native people whom they called Skraelings, almost certainly the Eskimos.

Where and what was Vinland? Wild claims and rampant speculation have placed it all the way south to Cape Cod and Rhode Island, but years of search and research by the Norwegian scholar Helge Ingstad have conclusively demonstrated that it was the northern tip of Newfoundland, where he discovered and excavated a Norse settlement at a place called L'Anse aux Meadows. This is the only indisputably Norse site or settlement in North America, and must be the place described by the sagas; a series of radiocarbon dates fixes its occupation at about 1000. The house foundations, simple Norse artifacts and evidence for the smelting of bog iron are typical of medieval Norse settlements in Norway, Iceland and Greenland.

How much effect did this contact have upon the peoples of the New World? Probably very little. The Dorset culture Eskimos who occupied northernmost Newfoundland probably appreciated the forged iron which the Vikings brought or made on the spot, and certain Viking artifacts must have circulated through Eskimo trade networks into the

Arctic, but European influence on native American cultures was minimal until the arrival of the Spaniards and Portuguese centuries later.

The voyages of Columbus

In talking of "discovery" one must distinguish between actual and effective discovery. As an example of the distinction to be made, the famed Inca site of Machu Picchu was discovered long before Hiram Bingham's expedition of 1911 (certainly the local inhabitants of the neighboring valleys had always known about it), but it was Bingham who brought it into world cognizance. Thus it was with Columbus: the Vikings had really discovered the New World, but it was Columbus who put it on the map and whose explorations led to wholesale European colonization and to the continuing holocaust that has engulfed the native Americans over the past five centuries.

Christopher Columbus was a poor Genoese eventually elevated by Their Catholic Majesties Ferdinand and Isabella to the title of "Admiral of the Ocean and Governor-General of the Indies." Following a rebuff to Columbus from King John II of Portugal, the Spanish sovereigns agreed to support an expedition to cross the Atlantic and reach the East Indies. Now Columbus knew, as did every educated person in Europe, that the earth was round; he knew of the supposed voyages of Brendan to reach the "promised land" in the west; and he had visited Iceland, where he must have learned of the Viking discoveries and settlement of Greenland and Vinland. But, relying on the theoretical geography of Paolo Toscanelli, he seriously underestimated the width of the Atlantic and thought that the eastern coasts and island systems of Asia were not very far from Europe. In spite of his four great voyages of discovery, he remained convinced that he had merely reached the East Indies by an Atlantic route, and not an entirely "new" world.

It was shortly after midnight on Friday 12 October 1492 that the New World was first sighted from the caravel *Niña*; the next morning they saw naked people, and the admiral went ashore to unfurl the royal pennant and claim the new land for the Spanish crown. This was a small isle known to the natives as Guanahaní, but which they named San Salvador—one of the many islands of the Bahamas. The natives were guileless and friendly, and Columbus, in hopes that they would be more easily converted to Christianity if they were treated with kindness, gave them red caps and worthless necklaces of glass beads. Thus began the first interaction between Europeans and American Indians.

On his first voyage the admiral touched upon Cuba and left a small colony on Hispaniola; on the subsequent three he explored the West Indies, landed on the South American mainland at the mouth of the Orinoco, and sailed along the coast of Honduras (where he encountered a large Maya trading canoe).

The Portuguese explorations and colonizations had generally extended south and east, around Africa and to India. A continuing diplomatic dispute between the two nations led Pope Alexander VI to draw a north–south line dividing the world up between two powers; in 1494 this was settled by common consent (in the Treaty of Tordesillas) as

being about 45 degrees West, with Spain getting everything west of the line, and Portugal everything east. Since the line passed through the South American mainland Portugal was able to claim what is now eastern Brazil (which they subsequently discovered in 1500) from the mouth of the Amazon south.

It is thought by some scholars that Basque fishermen and perhaps people from Bristol had been working the banks off northeastern North America for their rich cod harvests even before Columbus's first voyage, and may have touched on the New World. At any rate, in 1497 Bristol merchants fitted out a ship which sailed west under the Genoese captain John Cabot and probably discovered Newfoundland and the mainland. It would be another century, however, before the English and their rivals, the French, began thinking about colonizing North America.

NORTH AMERICA IN THE 16th CENTURY

The 16th century was a twilight period in the history of European exploration in North America. The warm climatic episode that had allowed the Norse to colonize Greenland in the first place waned over the following centuries, and the Greenland colonies also died out by the early part of the 15th century. The experiences of the Norse reached later European explorers as little more than rumor, if at all. Portuguese or other fishermen may have kept the knowledge of North America alive through the 15th century, but we have no certain evidence.

At the beginning of the 16th century, Europeans at first thought that they had indeed found Asia, or at least a series of islands lying off the coast of Asia. Initial exploration was often more concerned with

Above The voyages of Columbus gravitated around Hispaniola, which became a center for early Spanish operations. Columbus, of course, thought that he had reached offshore islands of Asia. His arrival on Hispaniola was depicted in an engraving by the Belgian artist Théodore de Bry a century after the event. De Bry, who never visited the New World, illustrated the 14-volume *Historia Americae* — scenes from travel in America. His point of view was always European, however. Here he shows a crowd of Indians bringing to the newly arrived Spanish expedition gifts that resemble objects European jewelers were to make from melted New World gold, rather than objects made by Indians. In fact the Indians presented Columbus with parrots, spears and balls of cotton thread. De Bry depicts these Taíno Indians wearing loincloths. Actually they wore no clothes except feathers and gold ornaments, and they painted their bodies red and black.

The pattern of European conquest in the 16th century The speed and success with which the Spaniards carved a vast empire for themselves in the Americas attest to the highly effective organization of the last great Mesoamerican and Andean civilizations. By supplanting the Aztec and Inca rulers, the *conquistadores* immediately took over the reins that controlled millions of people. In time their lands passed to the Spanish crown, whose claim over Portugal to the lion's share of the newly discovered continent had been established since 1494.

how to get around these obstacles than with how to exploit them, and hope for a passage through to the Pacific remained alive through the century. Many explorers did little more than sail along the coast. Most penetrated inland only short distances when they did land. Major *entradas* (inland explorations) were carried out mainly by a handful of Spanish explorers, most notably Hernando de Soto, Francisco Vásquez de Coronado, and Alvar Núñez Cabeza de Vaca.

Many explorers, particularly those that penetrated the interior, hoped to duplicate the profitable conquests of Cortés and Pizarro. Initial coastal settlements by the English and French during this century were established in large part to provide bases from which to raid Spanish treasure ships, and Spanish coastal settlements were established mainly to protect them. Some coastal enclaves were established by Spanish missionaries hoping to convert Indians. Attempts to establish viable, self-sufficient agricultural colonies in North America were not seriously launched until the 17th century.

Skilled but illiterate and secretive fishermen may have found Newfoundland fisheries in the 15th century. Certainly by the 16th century Basque, Breton, Portuguese, English and French

fishing boats were exploiting the fisheries of the Grand Bank annually. By the middle of the century there were at least 50 boats in the area each season. This rose to over 100 by 1580 and reached 200–300 by the end of the century. Southern European fishermen carried salt to cure fish and would have needed to land only occasionally to take on water, firewood and food.

Northern Europeans did not have access to cheap salt, and therefore established temporary land stations to dry their catch before taking it home. By the middle of the 16th century beaver felt hats were becoming the fashion rage in Europe. It did not take long for this new industry to deplete the supply of European beavers and thereby create a demand for pelts from other sources. It is likely that fishermen discovered that they could make some money on the side by trading at their coastal fishing stations with Indians. Thus, decades before they met Hudson, Champlain and the other explorers of the early 17th century, coastal Indian communities had already had experience of European traders. They already knew what the Europeans were looking for, and what they themselves most wanted in return.

Coastal exploration

The records of 16th-century European exploration in America north of Mexico are incomplete and uncertain. Nevertheless it is clear that in at least half of the years of that century there were significant contacts between Europeans and Indians at one or more points on the continent, more often than not along the coast. Gaspar Côrte-Real sighted Cape Farewell, Greenland, in 1500 and returned to sail along the northeast coast of Labrador and Newfoundland before being lost at sea the following year. A surviving ship returned to Portugal and inspired Miguel Côrte-Real to follow his brother's route in 1502. He too was lost at sea.

Sebastian Cabot followed his father's route to America around 1508, but left little information about the voyage. Juan Ponce de León explored the coast of Florida in 1513. Antonio de Alaminos, who later served as pilot for Hernan Cortés in the conquest of Mexico, touched the same coast in 1517. João Fagundes explored the Newfoundland coast around 1520. Ponce de León attempted to establish a colony in Florida in 1521, but was mortally wounded in an attack by Indians. Giovanni da Verrazano, an Italian working for the French, explored the coast from Carolina northward, making contact with Indians at several points, through the summer of 1524. Estavão Gomes, a Portuguese working for the Spanish, followed him within the next few months, but the details of the voyage are not known. In 1526 Lucas Vasquez de Ayllón founded, then abandoned, the settlement of San Miguel de Gualdape, on what is now the coast of South Carolina. The following year John Rut took an English ship along the coast from north to south, reversing the route of Verrazano.

In 1528, as Rut was returning to England, Panfilo de Narvaez attempted to explore Florida. In 1520 Narvaez had tried and failed to bring Cortés back under the control of Diego Velázquez on Mexican soil; his efforts now, eight years later, fared no better. He went ashore with a landing party around Tampa Bay and lost contact with his

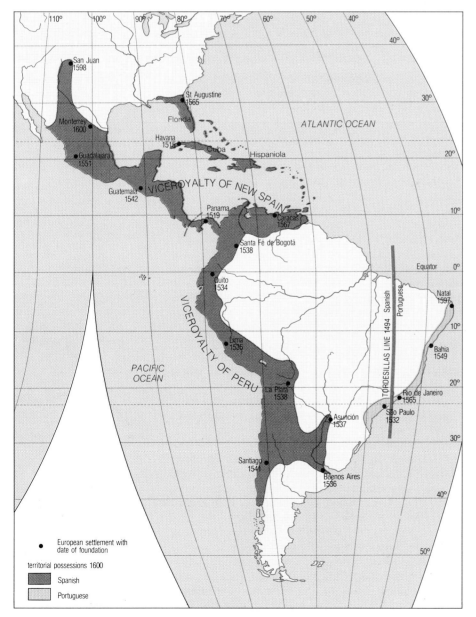

European settlement with date of foundation

territorial possessions 1600

Spanish

Portuguese

San Juan 1598
St Augustine 1565
Florida
Monterrey 1600
Havana 1515
Guadalajara 1551
Cuba
Hispaniola
ATLANTIC OCEAN
Guatemala 1542
VICEROYALTY OF NEW SPAIN
Panama 1519
Caracas 1567
Santa Fé de Bogotá 1538
Equator
Quito 1534
Natal 1597
VICEROYALTY OF PERU
TORDESILLAS LINE 1494
Spanish
Portuguese
Lima 1535
Bahia 1549
PACIFIC OCEAN
La Plata 1538
Rio de Janeiro 1565
Asunción 1537
São Paulo 1532
Santiago 1544
Buenos Aires 1536

ships. The party explored overland along the coastal plain into northwestern Florida, and there took to the sea again in boats built on the spot. After following the Gulf Coast to the vicinity of modern Galveston, Texas, the boats were dispersed by a storm. Narvaez and most of his men were lost. However one boat carrying Alvar Núñez Cabeza de Vaca, an African man named Estevan, and a few others made it to shore, and thus began a seven-year involuntary *entrada* across the deserts of Texas and northern Mexico. Cabeza de Vaca limped into a Spanish outpost in western Mexico in 1536, and later wrote a journal of his travels among the Indians.

Jacques Cartier made his first voyage to Canada in 1534. His second voyage stretched over the following two years, but his attempt to establish a colony at Standacone (modern Québec) did not succeed. Richard Hore also explored (less successfully) the same region for the English at about the same time.

Inland exploration

Hernando de Soto began his *entrada* into the Southeast in 1539. Marcos de Niza, accompanied by Cabeza de Vaca's companion Estevan, explored northward into the Southwest from Mexico in the same year. The later *entrada* set up the Coronado expedition of the following year. In 1541 there were two major Spanish *entradas* underway at the same time as Cartier launched his third voyage to the Northeast.

In the following year Cartier returned to France after his tasks and his new settlement of Charlesbourge-Royal were taken over by a new expedition under Roberval, and the Coronado expedition returned to Mexico after having come within a few hundred kilometers of the de Soto expedition. De Soto's men needed another year to complete their return to Mexico. Roberval also returned home in 1543.

Meanwhile in 1542 Juan Rodríguez Cabrillo explored the coast of California. He missed the Golden Gate, as Drake would 37 years later, but spent some time in Drakes Bay. Cabrillo died early the next year, leaving Bartolomé Ferrelo to complete the voyage.

Fray Luis de Cancer tried to establish a mission on Tampa Bay in 1549, but was killed by Indians who remembered de Soto's visit ten years earlier. Ten years later, however, Tristan de Luna y Arellano was able to establish a base at Ochuse on Pensacola Bay. After two years, in 1561, Angel de Villafane relieved de Luna and later attempted but failed to settle Santa Elena on the east coast. Nevertheless, Pedro Menéndez de Avilés was able to use the occasion to explore the coast as far north as Chesapeake Bay. The French Protestant Jean Ribault founded the settlement of Charlesfort on Parris Island in 1562. René Goulaine de Laudonnière founded the more substantial Fort Caroline on the St Johns River two years later. In 1565 de Laudonnière accepted supplies from John Hawkins, now on his second voyage against the Spanish. Menéndez de Avilés, however, took the French settlements, executed the French he captured, and established the Spanish settlements of St Augustine, San Mateo and Santa Elena. In the following year Pedro de Coronas tried but failed to

extend Spanish influence by establishing a post on Chesapeake Bay.

John Hawkins made his third voyage in 1567, his second-in-command being a man in his middle twenties named Francis Drake. David Ingram may have been one of his crew and may have been put ashore on the Gulf Coast. Ingram later claimed to have walked from there to New Brunswick over the course of the following two years, visiting Indian villages along the way, but the story is doubted by many historians. The French took revenge on the Spanish in 1568, when Dominique de Gourges destroyed the Spanish settlement at San Mateo. Spanish Jesuits were able to establish a mission on the York River in 1570, but St Augustine was raided by the English and the Jesuits were wiped out by Indians the following year.

While the Spanish gathered up the pieces of their southern settlements, other European explorers turned to the task of seeking an alternative northwest passage to Asia. Eannes Côrte-Real looked for it, followed by the English explorer Martin Frobisher in 1576. Frobisher conducted his second and third voyages in the two years following that, during which time the French briefly tried to reestablish themselves north of Santa Elena. In 1579 Francis Drake explored the California coast, missing San Francisco Bay as Cabrillo had before him, but sailing north as far as Vancouver Island before returning to the bay that now bears his name, and then striking westward across the Pacific.

The reports and impressions of American Indians that reached Europe in the 16th century largely created a favorable response. Accounts of their suffering at the hands of the Spanish, as illustrated by de Bry (*above*), evoked sympathy, and the attractive drawings of the English explorer John White (*right*) fostered a sense of the Indians' gentility, which even appeared in Shakespeare's *The Tempest*.

Spanish interest in the Southwest revived in 1581. Francisco Sánchez Chamuscado led a small party of soldiers and priests northward into Pueblo country, leaving one of the priests dead and two others to their fates when he returned the next year. Antonio de Espejo went looking for the surviving priests in 1582, but turned the *entrada* into a prospecting expedition upon hearing of their deaths.

Humphrey Gilbert explored the Newfoundland coast and Etienne Bellenger explored the Bay of Fundy in 1583. Philip Amadas and Arthur Barlowe explored the coast for Walter Raleigh in 1584 in preparation for Raleigh's settlement of Roanoke the following year. That year also saw John Davis's first voyage in search of a northwest passage. In 1586 Francis Drake wiped out Spanish St Augustine, Roanoke was abandoned, and Davis tried a second time. In 1587 there was a third try by Davis and a second by the Roanoke settlers. Vincente Gonzáles detected the Roanoke colony after his exploration of Chesapeake Bay in 1588, but John White found no trace of the settlers when he went there to relieve them in 1590.

The southern Atlantic coast was left to the Spanish during the last decade of the century while French, Basque, Portuguese and English fishermen contested the northern coast. George Drake raided the Magdalen Islands in 1593, and a year later Stevan de Bocall, a Basque working for the English, explored the Newfoundland coast. In 1597 the English tried to colonize the Magdalen Islands, but were driven off. It would be a new century before the English were able to establish permanent colonies in North America.

At the same time the Spanish were becoming more serious about exploration in the Southwest. Juan de Oñate took a large colonizing party north into New Mexico in 1598, and established a colony at San Juan in the upper Rio Grande Valley. There he began an oppressive Spanish rule of Indian pueblos which lasted for 80 years.

Although 16th-century contacts between Europeans and Indians were tentative, sporadic and usually confined to the margin of the continent, they set the tone for later more intense contact. Trade goods began to flow in both directions, and the cultures of the two continents began to alter each other in ways that would be much less subtle in the next century.

Population and devastation

The Indian populations found by the Europeans are still being reconstructed. Epidemics often preceded descriptive accounts, making population size estimates difficult for modern scholars. The best estimates currently available indicate low densities of 0·1–1 person per 100 square kilometers in the Arctic, Subarctic, Plains and Great Basin areas. Medium densities of 1–100 people per 100 square kilometers were probably encountered in the Southern Canadian, Plateau and Northeastern Mexico areas. High densities, of more than 100 people per 100 square kilometers, probably characterized the rest of the continent.

Epidemics of European origin were already devastating Mesoamerica in the early 16th century, and isolated outbreaks of disease in North America are reported here and there in a few of the surviving documents. After 1600 European exploration became more frequent, involved larger expeditions, and led to permanent colonies. At the same time epidemics of smallpox, measles, influenza and other lethal pathogens became commonplace, and Indian populations in North America began to decline drastically. By this time the Indian populations of Mexico had already reached a nadir, which was only 5 percent of the number alive in 1492.

Even without the one-way spread of lethal epidemics, the Indian cultures of North America were at an adaptive disadvantage in the face of European expansion. Europe was at the core of a growing world economic system, and its spread was promoted by territorially based nation states of an advanced type which had not yet evolved in America north of Mexico. The nations of North America still lacked many of the features of state organization, including well-defined territorial boundaries. Population collapse after 1600 AD may have only speeded an inevitable process.

LATIN AMERICA IN THE 16th CENTURY

The debate over the true nature of the subjugation of the native American Indians of Latin America (Mexico, Central America, South America and the Spanish-speaking Caribbean) by Spaniards and Portuguese in the century after 1492 began almost a decade before the process of colonization was extended to the mainland territories of Mexico and Peru. It was conducted, moreover, not by foreign critics of Iberian expansion but by jurists and churchmen of influence and authority within the courts of Madrid and Lisbon.

In Spanish America the Dominican friar Antonio de Montesinos told the settlers of Hispaniola (the modern Haiti and Dominican Republic) as early as 1511 in a well-publicized sermon that they were in mortal sin because of the "cruel and horrible" servitude which they imposed upon that island's native inhabitants, the Taínos. Estimates of the size of the native population of Hispaniola in 1492 vary widely, but it was probably less than 3 million: by 1539 the Taínos had been virtually wiped out by a combination of extensive cruelty and overwork, and the scourge of European diseases.

By 1539 the urgency of framing effective legislation to curb the excesses of the *conquistadores* had ceased to reflect simply a social and moral necessity; it had also become of fundamental political importance, as the Spanish crown received from Peru reports of the bitter civil wars being fought by rival bands of Spaniards competing for the spoils of conquest, and sought means of imposing its own authority. Whereas in the Caribbean the Spaniards had encountered native inhabitants in an intermediate state of development, with settled societies and some degree of political organization, but resistant to enslavement and other forms of conscription, the conquests of Mexico in 1519–21 and of Peru in 1533 had brought them face-to-face with complex societies, with high degrees of administrative and social organization. The immediate rewards were the accumulated treasure stocks of not only the Aztec and the Inca but also of the many civilizations which had preceded them. Behind the booty, however, lay the far richer prize of access to the labor and tribute of millions of Indians already accustomed before the arrival of the Spaniards to socio-economic exploration by empire builders.

The conquerors of Peru had divided by 1536 into two rather fluid groups, the Pizarrists (followers of Francisco de Pizarro and his four half-brothers), and the Almagrists (followers of Diego de Almagro, Pizarro's partner in the expedition from Panama to Peru, who had returned from Chile disappointed at his failure to find there a city to rival Cuzco, the Inca capital). The leaders of the warring factions were motivated by the lust for power, their followers by the quest for grants (encomiendas) of Indians from whom they could demand either tribute or labor service. In theory the encomienda system, which had originated in Hispaniola (although its peninsular origins lay in the reconquest of Spain from the Moors), represented a compromise between the crown's recognition of the conquerors' rights to enjoy access to Indian labor and its rejection of the idea that Indians might be enslaved indiscriminately: its advantages included the preservation of the communal nature of Indian society, for the holders of grants of Indians (encomenderos) tended to live apart from their charges, leaving their own hereditary leaders (caciques or curacas) to collect and deliver tribute.

In practice, however, as Las Casas tirelessly pointed out, Spaniards tended to ignore the duties imposed upon them by the system—the preservation and protection of the Indians, the provision of priests and schools—while imposing tribute and labor demands of such intensity that they distorted and destroyed native communities.

The crown responded to Las Casas's appeals with a comprehensive code of New Laws in 1542, which immediately deprived of their encomiendas crown officials, ecclesiastics, and all who had been involved in the Peruvian disturbances, declared that remaining encomiendas would revert to the crown on the death of their holders, and made it quite clear that no further grants would be made. In effect the system was being abolished. The spontaneous reaction of the Spaniards in Peru, virtually all of whom had fought in the civil wars and thus faced immediate loss of their grants, was to settle their internal differences, and under the command of Gonzalo Pizarro (Francisco, like Diego de Almagro, had already died in the disturbances) to take up arms against the first viceroy of Peru, Blasco Nuñez Vela, who arrived in Lima in 1544 to enforce the New Laws. The crown's decision in 1545 to revoke the most extreme clauses of the legislation—primarily on the basis of representations from Mexico that, without encomenderos, the viceroyalty of New Spain could not be protected from Indian revolts such as that of the Mixtons which had occurred in northern Mexico in 1540–41—came too late to save Nuñez, who died in battle against Pizarro early in 1546. It proved adequate, however, to persuade a sufficient number of influential settlers to support a new crown representative, Pedro de la Gasca, who arrived in Peru in 1547, against Gonzalo Pizarro. After a bloody battle near Cuzco in May 1548

Pizarro was executed, and the encomiendas of his supporters who had failed to cross in time to the royalist lines were redistributed to the leaders of La Gasca's army. Almost simultaneously, preparations were under way in Valladolid for a formal debate before a panel of judges between the "Apostle of the Indians," Las Casas, and the principal apologist for the conquest, Juan Ginés de Sepúlveda, who believed that the atrocities denounced by Las Casas, although distasteful, were less important than the responsibility of Spaniards to impose Christian culture upon American natives "who require . . . to be placed under the authority of civilized and virtuous princes and nations, so that they might learn from the might, wisdom and law of their conquerors to practice better morals, worthier customs and a more civilized way of life." Although a formal result was not announced, the crown refused the latter permission to publish his works. Las Casas, by contrast, was allowed to bring out the first edition of the famous *Very Brief Account of the Destruction of the Indies* in 1552.

The "black legend" of European rule in Latin America, although not named as such until centuries later, was created by Las Casas and other friars who witnessed the casual cruelty of get-rich-quick conquerors in the Caribbean islands and coasts during the first few decades after 1492, when crown authority was relatively ineffective and when the longer-term economic advantages to the settlers themselves of attempting to preserve the native population were not fully appreciated. The worst excesses were curbed in the centers of advanced native civilization—Mexico, Central America and Peru—in the second half of the 16th century, to be replaced by more systematic, controlled forms of exploitation, intended to provide Spanish society with access to Indian labor and Indian production by means of a variety of devices which, like the encomienda system, were designed to reconcile the theoretical liberty of the natives with the demands of the settlers. Although the encomienda survived in both New Spain and Peru until the early 17th century, the majority of grants reverted to the crown after two generations, and the territories thus released were placed under the control of provincial governors—corregidores—whose responsibilities included the control of the tribute system. This involved the collection for the crown in biannual installments of a head-tax payable by adult male Indians in recognition of their subservience.

The other principal institution employed to make Indians work for Spaniards was the conscription of workers by the viceregal authorities on a quota basis to work either for private individuals or for municipal corporations.

The varied fates of native populations

In Peru as a whole the native population is estimated to have fallen from 9 million in 1533 to little more than 500 000 by the early 17th century; it remained at this low point until the early 18th century, rising to 700 000 in 1800. On the coast the collapse was almost total, primarily because of the impact of epidemic diseases—the first smallpox epidemic, which killed the Inca emperor Huayna Capac, actually preceded the physical arrival of Pizarro—although Spanish cruelty, extensive war-

Inca bewail the fate of a captive of the Spanish, who execute him "without guilt."

fare (which also antedated the conquest) and the psychological impact of the destruction of their world upon the Indians' ability to reproduce were powerful contributory factors. The pattern of decline was similar in New Spain (Mexico and Central America), where a native population variously estimated to have numbered between 11 and 25 million on the eve of conquest (the lower figure commands more support among recent commentators) had fallen to 1·25 million by 1625 (rising to 2·5 million in 1800). Again disease was the major factor.

Research on the more decentralized native populations of the vast regions to the east of the Andes and in southern South America is much less advanced, partly because these areas were never fully assimilated into the empires of Spain and Portugal and thus did not yield the colonial tribute counts which provide the basis for the reconstruction of the preconquest populations. The Araucanian population of modern Chile and Patagonia is thought to have numbered about 1 million in the early 16th century. It was never properly assimilated into the Spanish empire, partly because its seminomadic, decentralized structure made it impossible for small groups of conquerors to subdue simply by striking, as in the cases of Mexico and Peru, at the center of elaborate imperial systems and inserting themselves in the places of former Aztec and Inca overlords. The conquest of Chile, consequently, was a long process of frontier warfare, relieved by occasional treaties, which gradually drove the Araucanians to the south, where perhaps 100 000 preserved their independence from white rule until subdued in the 19th century.

Subjugation by brutality: a spurred Spaniard kicks a kneeling Indian.

The population of what became Portuguese Brazil when the first Europeans arrived in 1500 is also very difficult to estimate, partly because it comprised so many different tribes, partly because the Portuguese crown showed far less interest than its Spanish counterpart in either counting or protecting the native inhabitants. Estimates range from about 2·5 million to 5 million, with recent commentators favoring the higher figure. What is certain is that when systematic Portuguese colonization began in 1533 the whole littoral was inhabited by scattered tribes belonging to the Tupi-Guaraní family, but that by 1600 major depopulation had occurred. Although epidemic disease was a significant factor in this process—an epidemic of smallpox in Bahia killed 30 000 in 1562–65, for example—wars of extermination and enslavement were of relatively greater importance than in many areas of Spanish America. The Tupinamba Indians of the Bahian coast, for example, were deliberately dispersed, enslaved and killed by the third governor-general of Brazil, Mem de Sá (1557–72), who destroyed more than 300 villages around Salvador, the capital of Brazil in the 16th century. The labor shortage on the coast provoked by this policy, although satisfied ultimately by the import of Negro slaves, led in the early 17th century to slave raids along the Amazon in the north and into Paraguay in the south. In each case they took Portuguese pioneers—and the eventual frontiers of Brazil—into vast tracts of territory nominally allocated to Spain, but which most Spaniards shunned because of the absence of easily exploited precious metals and easily assimilated native inhabitants. The Jesuit missionaries who entered Paraguay in 1610 themselves organized the Guaraní to resist Portuguese penetration, thereby preserving an estimated 100 000 of them from acculturation or worse until the Society was expelled by the Spanish crown in 1767. In western Paraguay a smaller number of Chaco Indians, like many scattered Amazonian tribes, were preserved only by their remoteness from European settlement. In the Amazon Basin as a whole the total number of survivors perhaps reached 1 million.

The Jesuit missions in Paraguay, based upon the segregation of the Indian from all Europeans other than missionaries, represented in one sense a logical extension of a number of experiments undertaken by Las Casas in the first half of the 16th century to demonstrate to the crown that the native inhabitants of the Americas were capable of living harmonious, Christian lives in isolation from settler society. Although the Dominican's attempts to prove this point did not succeed, the notion that society might be constructed around separate "republics" of Spaniards and Indians, each with its own hierarchy of social and political control, was one which remained strong in Spanish colonial legislation well into the 17th century. To a certain extent it reflected the necessity of preserving and even extending the privileges of native nobles as a means of enabling handfuls of Spaniards to control the millions of common Indians who survived the immediate conquest. In Peru puppet Inca emperors were preserved by Spain in Cuzco until 1549, and many females from the native aristocracy married encomenderos. Sayri Túpac, grandson of the last undisputed Inca emperor, Huayna Capac, lived in great style in Yucay in the late 1550s. In 1616 Sayri's grandaughter, whose father had been captain-general of Chile, was granted the title Marquesa of Oropesa. In Mexico, where two of the daughters of Motechuhzoma were granted perpetual encomiendas over Indian towns, a similar policy was implemented. In each area the crown recognized the status and privileges of Indian nobles until the 18th century.

The preservation of a native élite theoretically permitted the physical isolation of Indian communities from Spanish towns, one benefit of which would be the prevention of some of the abuses reported by the critics of Indian policy in the first half of the 16th century. However, even as the crown was formulating legislation to this end, irresistible social and economic pressures—including the lack of Spanish women, personal servitude, the migration of Indians to towns, and the establishment of Spanish estates adjacent to Indian communities—were undermining it by creating a large segment of population which was neither Indian nor Spanish but mixed or mestizo. Superficially European culture and values dominated Latin American society in the 16th and subsequent centuries. However, in contrast to the North American experience, the native people of at least those parts of Latin America with the most advanced preconquest societies succeeded in surviving the ravages of the first century of colonialism, merging eventually their blood and their culture with those of their European rulers to form the foundations of the mestizo societies of the 20th century.

SPECULATION AND STUDY

Speculation about who the New World's inhabitants were, and whence they had come, began with the earliest contacts. Columbus thought them natives of the East Indies, perhaps subject to the Great Khan described by Marco Polo. Spaniards eager to utilize them as forced labor wondered whether they were human at all, and whether they had souls; if the answer was negative, then they could be enslaved for work in mines and on plantations.

Once the Church decided that natives had souls which could be saved, the work of conversion began, and missionaries arrived in the Spanish possessions. During the 16th century there were friars and priests with a considerable degree of learning. Several native traditions which they found in Mexico spoke of the arrival of the ancestral Indians in boats from across the sea to the east, and many missionaries were convinced that they were dealing with descendants of the Ten Lost Tribes of Israel described in the Old Testament. The fact that no native tribe or nation spoke Hebrew failed to discourage this theory, which persisted into later centuries, and which still has adherents.

In 1590 the Jesuit priest José de Acosta brought out his *Natural and Moral History of the Indies,* in which he presented a rival theory: that the New World natives most closely resembled not the Jews but the peoples of Tartary, and that they had thus crossed from northeastern Asia into this hemisphere. It is the Acosta theory, needless to say, that has survived the test of time. He had no way of knowing, however, the when, where and why of the migration from Asia to the New World, since in his time western Europeans knew nothing of Siberia, Alaska or the Bering Straits.

Following the American Revolution, as white Americans poured west across the Appalachians into Indian territory, a new set of speculations about the Indians began to appear, especially in the first decades of the 19th century. As they moved into the Ohio and Mississippi river drainages they found ancient mounds which the contemporary Indian tribes could not explain. In some of them were burials with copper objects, pearls, mica and other exotic and wonderful offerings. The mysterious people who had built them became known as the "Moundbuilders." In the racist and generally anti-Indian thought of the day it was felt that these could not have been the dark-skinned Indians but a white race which had disappeared long ago.

The idea that white people had been in America long before Columbus also took off from the late and largely spurious legend of Madoc, the Welsh chieftain who had supposedly journeyed west to the New World. It was long believed, and still is by some, that there were "white" Indians among Plains tribes like the Mandan, descended from Madoc's Welsh immigrants.

Such notions surely influenced Joseph Smith, Jr (1805–44), the founder of the Mormon religion. As a young man in upstate New York he claimed to have been visited by an angel who showed him plates of gold inscribed with characters later said to be "reformed Egyptian" and who loaned him magic spectacles to read and translate them. He dictated the text from memory, and this became known as the Book of Mormon.

The Book of Mormon contains an account of two transatlantic migrations from the Holy Land to the New World. The first to arrive were the Jaredites (whom Mormon authorities now hold to be the Olmec of ancient Mexico). The second consisted of one Lehi, his family and friends. Following Lehi's death in the new land, leadership passed to the younger son, Nephi, and the people became known as Nephites. The Nephites were builders of cities and temples, and had brought with them wheat, cattle, horses and other Old World items. Nephi's elder brothers, however, became resentful at being cut out of their inheritance, for which God cursed them with dark skins; these and their descendants became known as the Lamanites, and were the ancestors of the American Indians we see today. The Book of Mormon story ends with the total annihilation of the Nephites by the Lamanites.

When Joseph Smith first read about the great discoveries of Stephens and Catherwood among the ruined Maya cities of Mexico and Central America, he immediately declared these to be "Nephite," that is, built by white men instead of by dark-skinned Indians, whose general degradation rendered them incapable of such cultural feats.

Smith was not alone in receiving inspiration from the Ten Lost Tribes story. Edward King, Viscount Kingsborough (born in 1795), died bankrupt in a debtors' prison, ruined by the enormous expense of publishing all known manuscripts from preconquest Mexico in a vain effort to prove that the civilized peoples of that land were descended from those peripatetic Hebrews. His quixotic enterprise nevertheless led to the first complete and scholarly dissemination of some of the most important manuscripts which we have, such as the Maya Dresden Codex.

Even wilder theories about the native Americans and their cultures have been proposed and defended, some of them involving sunken continents like Atlantis and Mu, or even visitors from outer space, as in the very popular books by Erich von Däniken. This reflects a general unwillingness on the part of Europeans and Euro-Americans to allow the American Indians their great achievements.

Nonetheless, and in contrast to all of the above, it must be admitted that there has been some recent scholarship on the possible transmission of certain cultural traits from Asia across the Pacific Ocean that must be considered seriously. In particular, there are features of the Mesoamerican calendrical system which argue for transpacific diffusion; for

Above The existence of Maya centers in Mexico and Guatemala reached public awareness in North America and Europe in the mid-19th century, thanks to the interests and talents of two remarkable men: John Lloyd Stephens (1805–52), a U.S. citizen, and Frederick Catherwood (1799–1854), an Englishman. Together they explored Maya sites—many previously unknown—in two arduous journeys (1839–40, 1841–42). Stephens published vivid accounts of their experiences, and Catherwood produced sketches and lithographs that were both accurate and evocative. Here, in this lithograph of a temple at Tulum, Catherwood can be seen to the right of the entrance.

Right Thomas Jefferson (1743–1826), author, statesman, landowner and precocious archaeologist. His excavation of an Indian mound anticipated scientific archaeology: the excavation was intended to test hypotheses; it exposed the mound's stratification; and was recorded meticulously.

example, it is probably no accident that the Maya eclipse calendar in the Dresden Codex operates on exactly the same principles as the one previously developed in Han-dynasty China.

How and when such diffusion from East or Southeast Asia took place is not known. Some features suggesting Asiatic origin could have been brought via Siberia into Alaska. It is highly unlikely that these early hunters carried no mental baggage at all: certain features of the animal-oriented, shamanistic religions of the New World might be part of a very ancient, Asiatic substratum. Some culture traits, however, cannot be this old: as a good example, Paul Tolstoy has convincingly demonstrated that the complex technology used to produce bark paper in the New World tropics (for instance, the bark paper books of the Maya) must have originated in Southeast Asia and Indonesia, specifically the Celebes and Moluccas. So diffusionist theories in the hands of reputable scholars can be respectable, but unfortunately the lunatic fringe will not go away.

The age of archaeology
It was that gifted polymath Thomas Jefferson who initiated the science of archaeology. At some time before 1782, prior to his election as President of the United States, Jefferson directed the trenching of a

mound on his estate in Virginia, and kept a careful record of his observations. In the report he published in 1784 he noted that there were four superimposed layers to the mound, each with multiple burials, and drew well-reasoned conclusions from his data on the practice of group burial by the Indians. (He never supposed the mounds to have been built by any other than the native Americans.)

Sadly it was another century before stratigraphic excavation would again be practiced anywhere in the world. But the 19th century was the age of archaeological exploration on a grand scale, and it was in this time span that most of the ancient civilizations of the New World were discovered, their ruins mapped, and traditions about them analyzed. With a few exceptions (such as Caleb Atwater, who in his 1820 publication was the first to treat the Ohio mounds adequately, but thought them the product of Hindus who had migrated through Mexico), these ancient civilizations were considered American Indian products.

Although Antonio del Río had explored the Classic Maya site of Palenque at the beginning of the 19th century, it was the monumental discoveries of the American lawyer John L. Stephens and the English topographical artist Frederick Catherwood, published in 1841 and 1844, that fired the public imagination with the great magnificence of the early Maya civilization of the Mexican and Central American jungles. In their books they established a standard of written and graphic recording that has hardly been surpassed.

Other early explorers of New World prehistory included Ephraim Squier and George Davis among the Hopewell and Mississippian mounds of the Mississippi Valley (published 1848), William H. Holmes of the Smithsonian Institution among ancient cities of Mexico and Central America, and again Squier along with Johann Tschudi and others among the ruins of Peru and Bolivia. Alexander von Humboldt has been much touted for his researches and travels in Latin America, but his contributions to the development of New World archaeology were relatively slight.

The 19th century also saw the rise of the great American research institutions devoted to anthropology and archaeology, such as the Peabody Museum of Harvard, the Bureau of American Ethnology and the University of California. For all of that century, however, American and New World archaeology remained prestratigraphic, and there was little knowledge of cultural sequences or the time depth of American Indian cultures. But one should not belittle the enormous contribution that was made in those days. A striking example of this consists of the explorations and photographic record made of Maya cities and inscribed monuments by the Austrian Teobert Maler (for the Peabody Museum), and by the Englishman Alfred P. Maudslay; their magnificent publications still form the basis for Maya epigraphic studies.

The next step was what Gordon Willey and Jeremy Sabloff have called the "stratigraphic revolution." The use of stratigraphy (i.e. the establishment of layers of deposition on a site) as a research tactic in archaeology had its origin in the Scotsman Charles Lyell's geological studies, and was refined by the work and publication of General Pitt-Rivers in England. Its arrival in the New World was amazingly tardy. It was only in a publication of 1903 that the German archaeologist Max Uhle (later to be known as the "father of Peruvian archaeology") published his stratigraphic excavations of a shell mound at Emeryville, in the San Francisco Bay area. The first such dig in Mesoamerica only took place in 1911, when the Mexican Manuel Gamio, under the direction of the great anthropologist Franz Boas, sunk a stratigraphic pit at Atzcapotzalco, near Mexico City, and revealed an archaeological sequence of Formative (then called "Archaic") to Teotihuacan to Aztec culture. For North America Nels C. Nelson was the pioneer, with his stratigraphic excavations of 1913 and 1915 in the Pueblo ruins of the Galisteo Basin in New Mexico; he was certainly influenced by the examples of Uhle and the Europeans in this most basic of all archaeological techniques.

The first half of the 20th century was the great age of scientific archaeology, often on a very grand scale, in Canada, the United States and Latin America. Research organizations with enormous resources, such as the Carnegie Institution of Washington which led the field in Maya research, or the University of California which concentrated upon Peru, or Harvard University in the American Southwest, were the rule of the day. Relative cultural chronologies were developed for every nook and cranny of the New World, from the Arctic to Tierra del Fuego, and cultures were classified by area and developmental level. This was the period which saw the rise of local, non-U.S. institutions, such as Mexico's National Institute of Anthropology and History, as major forces in gathering knowledge about the native peoples of the New World.

Modern revolutions in archaeology

But how old was it all? It was one thing to work out a *relative* chronology—Culture A is older than Culture B, which in turn is older than Culture C—but what did this mean in terms of calendar years? By 1940 geologists and archaeologists had established that the American Indians had been in the Western Hemisphere by at least 11 000 years ago by using geologic dating methods, for example varve analysis. In the American Southwest the astronomer A.E. Douglass had discovered the tree-ring or dendrochronological method of dating beams from ancient Pueblo apartment dwellings, which produced an accurate method of dating prehistoric ruins and cultures in that area absolutely. And in the Maya region the refinement of a correlation between the Maya and Christian calendars, first worked out by the newspaper editor Joseph T. Goodman in the 19th century, gave an absolute chronology for the 600-year span of Classic Maya civilization and its multitude of dated stone monuments.

The real revolution in New World archaeology came about in the late 1940s, when the University of Chicago chemist Willard F. Libby perfected the carbon 14 or radiocarbon technique of dating ancient organic materials, such as charcoal from old hearths. Prior to this epoch-making discovery, few were the archaeologists who were willing to grant any great antiquity to most New World cultures, and published chronologies for most culture areas were wildly off the mark. The radiocarbon method usually gave far greater time depth to most cultures outside the American Southwest and the Maya area, although in some cases, such as the Basketmaker sequence of the pre-Pueblo period in the Southwest, chronologies were drastically revised upward in the time scale. Radiocarbon analysis did more than change ideas about dating: it also dramatically revised concepts of cultural process, as with the role of the Olmec civilization with its now far greater antiquity than had previously been conceived of.

A second revolution has consisted of advances in techniques of physical and chemical analysis of artifacts, which have permitted the detection of ancient trading networks and methods of procurement, from ceramics to stones and metals.

And finally, there has been a strong intellectual current in recent years deriving on the one hand from biology and ecology—the analysis of how ancient human groups have adapted culturally to changing environments—and on the other from social anthropology—determining the substructures and processes of ancient American Indian societies from their archaeological remains. These are both aspects of the much-celebrated "New Archaeology"; how "new" it is and how important it is to the understanding of New World prehistory will be judged by history.

PART TWO
THE FIRST AMERICANS

THE ORIGINAL SETTLEMENT

The biological evolution of our species took place largely in the context of the Pleistocene or Ice Age, a geological epoch which began about 2·5 million years ago. There is not the slightest doubt that this evolution from apelike ancestors to modern forms of mankind took place in the Old World, not in the New, and that the earliest human migrations into the New World occurred very late in the Pleistocene. The most telling argument for this view is that no archaic forms of the genus *Homo* have ever been discovered in the Western Hemisphere, not even the relatively late Neanderthals. All American Indian skeletal remains found in ancient deposits are morphologically modern.

Within the Ice Age there were a number of successive, long periods of intensive glaciation and a worldwide lowering of temperature. These episodes were separated by interglacials, during which temperatures returned to those of today. The latest glaciation, called the Wisconsin in North America, was the most severe of all, and lasted from approximately 80 000 years ago until about 7000 BC, when the world's glaciers began their final retreat.

At the Wisconsin maximum, tremendous ice sheets covered northern North America and northernmost Eurasia, while solid pack ice lay on the ocean between the two great glaciers. It is estimated that during this time about 30 percent of the earth's land area bore the icy burden of the Wisconsin glaciers and their equivalent in Eurasia, the Würm glaciers. So much water was drawn into this cover that the sea level fell by at least 85 meters, exposing much of what is now continental shelf and, most importantly, exposing a land bridge between Siberia and Alaska. North America itself

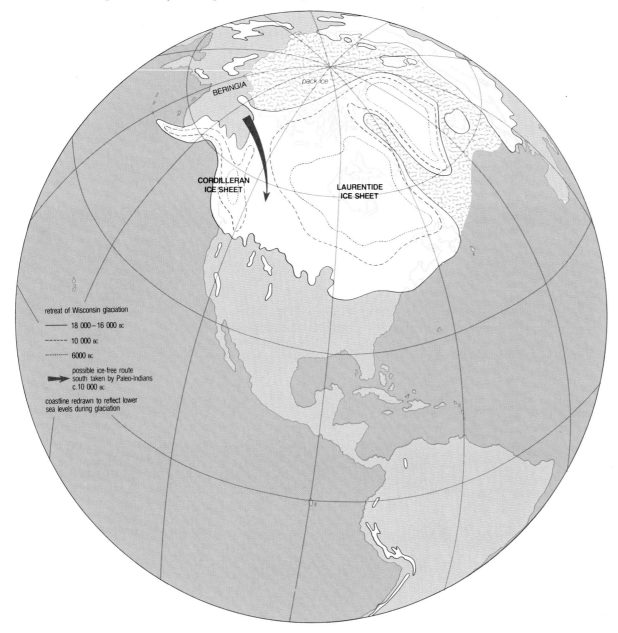

BERINGIA

pack ice

CORDILLERAN
ICE SHEET

LAURENTIDE
ICE SHEET

retreat of Wisconsin glaciation

—— 18 000 – 16 000 BC

----- 10 000 BC

········· 6000 BC

➤ possible ice-free route
south taken by Paleo-Indians
c.10 000 BC

coastline redrawn to reflect lower
sea levels during glaciation

Extent of the Wisconsin glaciation
Large areas of the Northern Hemisphere were covered by massive ice sheets during the Late Pleistocene, when humans first entered the New World. So much water was taken up in ice that the sea level was drastically lowered, exposing a broad, ice-free land bridge between Siberia and Alaska. According to some archaeologists the earliest Paleo-Indian hunters were confined to the Alaskan portion of Beringia until an ice-free corridor leading to the south opened up around 10 000 BC, resulting in widespread over-hunting and extinction of game by carriers of the Clovis culture. Others state that there is no definite proof that such a corridor existed at that time, and that the ancestors of the American Indians had already moved to lower latitudes *prior* to the coalescence of the Cordilleran and Laurentide ice sheets c. 18 000 BC.

Above The Bering Strait as seen from Little Diomede Island (USA). In the center of the picture is Big Diomede Island (USSR), while in the far background is the coast of Siberia (East Cape or Mys Dezhneva). This was all dry land during the Late Pleistocene, allowing easy access to the New World by bands of hunters and gatherers, but even in its present state the Strait has never been a barrier to movements of people and goods. In fact, until the Soviet government put an end to the practice, Eskimos regularly moved back and forth across the Strait.

was covered by an ice sheet up to 3 kilometers thick, as far south as the confluence of the Ohio and Mississippi Rivers, while in the higher elevations in Mexico and in the Andean chain there were major glaciers.

For most of the Wisconsin it is clear that the New World was unpeopled. When the first immigrants managed to penetrate the unglaciated part of the continent they would have entered an environment very different from today's. For instance, just to the south of the ice sheet's edge was tundra, cutting across what is now the Great Plains, the Midwest, and Pennsylvania and New Jersey. Further south was a broad band of boreal forest covering much of the middle part of the United States. In other words the state of Virginia then looked much like southern Labrador today. Grasslands probably covered much of the lower-altitude lands in the western United States and in Mexico.

The first immigrants would have found this new land a hunter's paradise. Large herds of very large herbivorous mammals roamed the late Pleistocene landscape—in North America these would have included horses, mammoths, mastodons, giant bison and camelids. Added to the population of browsers were formidable animals like the Dire wolf, an enormous and now extinct species, and the giant ground sloth. This remarkable fauna was to perish with the advent of humans and the retreat of the glaciers.

When did man arrive in North America?

The exact date of arrival of *Homo sapiens* in the Western Hemisphere remains one of archaeology's thorniest problems: there is little agreement among scholars about when and how this took place. Agreeing *where* presents fewer difficulties. Most of Alaska was unglaciated, along with the Yukon Valley, as was much of eastern Siberia. During the

Wisconsin both areas were connected by an enormous land bridge, since worldwide lowering of the sea level exposed a 1600-kilometer-wide platform (now under the Chukchi and Bering Seas and the Bering Strait). Human groups could then have walked dry-shod from Siberia to Alaska across what was a tundra-covered, ice-free land bridge. But even today the Bering Strait is a gateway rather than a barrier between the two hemispheres, especially for people like the Eskimo who have boats. There is no compelling reason why the first Asiatic migrants could not have traveled by sea, for radiocarbon evidence shows that the ancestors of the modern aborigines had crossed to Australia, which was never attached to any continental land mass during the Ice Age, by at least 20 000 years ago, and must perforce have possessed boats.

On the subject of the early peopling of the Americas archaeologists are divided into two camps. On the one hand there are those who point to radiocarbon dates for sites and crude lithic cultures going back to 20 000 years ago and even beyond. On the other there are those who find the evidence for any occupation of the New World older than 10 000 BC extremely shaky on many grounds. C. Vance Haynes Jr and Paul C. Martin, for instance, argue that the first fully accepted Paleo-Indian culture, Clovis, appears shortly after that date in the western United States and that its origins lie in Alaska. They hypothesize that the ancestral American Indians were able to migrate from the north by an ice-free corridor that appeared at the time between the western, Cordilleran, ice sheet, and the eastern, Laurentide, ice sheet. The Clovis people had remarkably efficient, bifacially flaked projectile points, and it was this innovation, according to Martin, which resulted in the rapid extinction, through human "overkill," of the Pleistocene large animals (megafauna).

Proponents of earlier, pre-Clovis occupations in the Americas point out three main flaws in these hypotheses. First, the evidence for such an ice-free corridor at that time down the eastern side of the Rocky Mountains is weak. Second, the Pleistocene megafauna could have been killed off by climatic change rather than by humans. Third, the earliest known industries in Alaska are characterized by microblades of Asiatic type and are no older than the oldest Clovis sites. Thus they argue that Clovis and similar industries could never have evolved from Alaskan antecedents but must be a native North American invention developed out of a far older and simpler cultural base in the New World.

Professor Irving Rouse has proposed a scheme for early man in the Americas which is adopted here in modified form, based on the typology of stone tools. Three "stone ages" are identified for the Western Hemisphere: Lower, Middle and Upper Lithic.

The earliest cultures of the Stone Age: the Lower Lithic

Although harsh and often justified criticism has been leveled at many claims for man's antiquity in the New World preceding 10 000 BC, there is convincing evidence for the arrival of man far earlier than this date. Rouse's Lower Lithic period is characterized by the manufacture of irregular stone flakes, trimmed only on their edges. It may have begun earlier than 20 000 years ago. Oddly enough our best data on the Lower Lithic come not from Alaska, where they are nonexistent, nor even from Canada or the United States, but from Mesoamerica and South America.

In dealing with reputed remains from this very early era, one has to be extremely careful. Nevertheless there are some Lower Lithic sites which can survive the accusations of the skeptics. The Old Crow Basin of the northern Yukon territory in Canada lies in easternmost Beringia which was, in the words of Dr William Irving, "the Pleistocene subcontinent that subsumes the unglaciated westernmost parts of northern North America and eastern Siberia." It lay, then, north of the ice which separated this land from the richer area to the south, which was presumably unreachable for at least part of late Wisconsin times. The Old Crow complex as defined by its discoverers consists largely of cracked and worked bone from Pleistocene mammals, rather than stone tools. Dates of 29 100, 27 000 and 25 750 years ago have been obtained on a skin flesher of caribou bone and on two worked mammoth bones from the basin, and these seem to have been altered while the bone was still fresh.

Old Crow has no real stratigraphy, but the Meadowcroft Rockshelter, a multicomponent site located 48 kilometers southwest of Pittsburgh, Pennsylvania, on the Ohio border, does. Meadowcroft lies on a small tributary of the Ohio River, in what was an unglaciated part of the Appalachian Plateau. It presents what its excavators, Dr James Adovasio and his collaborators, rightly claim as "the best evidence to date of the pre-Clovis occupation of the hemisphere." Stratum I, the lowest in the rockshelter, has no stone artifacts, but produced two carbon 14 dates in excess of 17 000 years ago on a charcoal concentration (which must be the result of human activity) and on a carbon-

ized fragment of cut, bark-like material. Just above it lies Lower Stratum IIa; charcoal from fire-pits in the lower third of the layer dated to 10 850 –14 225 years before present (c. 8900–12 275 BC). The artifacts, all of stone, consisted of rhomboidal flake "knives," blades, unifaces (flakes worked on only one side), bifaces, gravers and microengravers, denticulates and waste chips, along with one bifacial lanceolate point. No extinct fauna have turned up in the early Meadowcroft layers, which has given ammunition to the critics, but this seems to be an excellent candidate for Lower Lithic status.

Meadowcroft is not the only site in Anglo-America to produce data on the Lower Lithic. Wilson Butte Cave in south-central Idaho has two radiocarbon dates of 14 500 and 15 000 years on bones associated with three stone artifacts of Lower Lithic type. Even more convincing are the data from the Levi Rockshelter in Texas, excavated in 1959–60 and in 1974 by Dr Herbert Alexander. Here a well-stratified series of Paleo-Indian strata turned up definite proof of a Lower Lithic horizon.

Very early, pre-Clovis remains have also been discovered in what is now Latin America. In the Mexican state of Puebla, about 125 kilometers east-southeast from Mexico City, Dr Cynthia Irwin-Williams located and excavated several temporary camps of early hunters on the edge of the modern reservoir created by the Valsequillo dam. Here there are two well-stratified occupations, each with a broad range of extinct mammals which had been brought in for local butchering: mammoths, mastodons, horses, antelope, Dire wolves and smaller creatures. Rouse notes that the artifact assemblage consists of only flakes, with trimming limited to the edges; two of them are unifacial projectile points. The entire inventory of tools resembles that of other Lower Lithic sites in the Americas.

In South America proper the excavations of Dr Richard S. MacNeish at Pikimachay Cave in the Ayacucho Basin of highland Peru have produced tantalizing, if still controversial, data on the Lower Lithic. From the lowest layer, attributed by MacNeish to the Paccaisasa phase, come several large, retouched flakes and bones of extinct animals including sloths and horses or camels. There are also radiocarbon dates ranging from 14 700 to 20 000 before present.

Monte Verde, in south-central Chile, is another South American candidate for Lower Lithic status. Radiocarbon-dated between 3500 and 12 500 years ago, this was an extremely ancient village (the oldest found in the New World), with rows of wooden houses, other wooden structures, wood and stone tools, plant remains and mastodon bones. So far it is unique.

In summary, no one knows when the ancestors of the American Indians entered the Americas. Our present knowledge suggests it might have been over 20 000 years ago. The Bering land bridge probably played a major role, but if, as seems likely, the early Asiatic immigrants and explorers had boats they could have colonized the Pacific coast to the south of the Cordilleran ice sheets. The origins of the well-established, Stone Age cultures of the Middle Lithic, such as Clovis and Folsom, lie in the still poorly known Lower Lithic.

Folsom point

Major point traditions of the Middle Lithic

After 10 000 BC, to the south of the Laurentide ice sheet, Lower Lithic industries began to be replaced by Middle Lithic ones, which are characterized by bifacially worked projectile points. Professor Rouse believes that these might have evolved from the simpler unifacial points made on flakes found in such localities as Ayacucho and Valsequillo, but the process probably took place independently in a number of New World regions. Unlike the case for the Lower Lithic, the validity of the early dates on Middle Lithic sites is unquestioned.

Before 1926 all claims of ancient American remains, that is, traces of early American Indians who might have lived in the late Ice Age and hunted animals now extinct, were received with well-based skepticism. In the summer of that year a group of scientists from the Denver Museum of Natural History made a remarkable discovery near Folsom, New Mexico: stone tools in definite association with the bones of an extinct species of bison (*Bison antiquus*). Lodged between the ribs of the animal was a finely made, bifacially chipped spear point which had been finished by removing a blade from the base up, leaving a fluting-like channel on each surface. The search for the first Americans suddenly became respectable, but until the advent of carbon 14 dating there was no real way to date sites of the Folsom culture.

It soon became apparent that there were hunting cultures even more ancient than Folsom in the western United States, associated with another type of projectile point called Clovis, which was certainly ancestral to Folsom. Clovis points tend to be larger than Folsom, and are generally fluted by having more than one channel flake removed from each side. The final flake was the longest, leaving a flute which covers only the bottom third or half of the total length of the point. Fluting, which has no precedent in any Old World stone industry, was a highly advanced technological process, and must have had a function. One suggestion is that it made hafting onto a wooden shaft easier and more secure. In favor of this is the fact that the side edges of the point are usually ground down the length of the fluting, as if to protect the bindings from abrasion.

Clovis is one of the best-dated and most widespread Paleo-Indian cultures. It began shortly after 10 000 BC and lasted until about 9200 BC. Clovis was the culture of small bands of hunting-and-gathering peoples (though we know very little about the gathering) whose main targets were the great herds of Woolly and Imperial mammoths that roamed the western plains before the close of the Pleistocene. Most of the "classic" Clovis sites of the west are killing-and-butchering stations. At the Lehner Ranch site in southern Arizona, for instance, Emil Haury excavated the remains of nine mammoths along with bones from horses, *Bison antiquus* and tapirs. During the slaughter and subsequent processing the Clovis people had lost 13 Clovis points (one of rock crystal) and eight butchering tools in the carcasses of their victims. The animals were apparently attacked while watering along a stream.

The "type site" for the Clovis culture is Blackwater Draw, near Clovis, New Mexico. Here Clovis remains were found stratified beneath Folsom artifacts, which in turn were overlaid by materials from the late Paleo-Indian Plano culture. During the Pleistocene, this region, now relatively arid, was covered with lakes and ponds. Blackwater Draw was then a large, spring-fed lake attracting large game animals such as camels, horses and bison which were driven into the boggy margins and killed.

Western Clovis culture was matched by similar and probably contemporary developments in the rest of North America, where many camp sites of general Clovis affiliation have been found—in particular Clovis and Clovis-like points are probably more common in the east than in the west. The northeasternmost Clovis-period site is Debert, in central Nova Scotia in Canada, a hunting-and-gathering camp which was occupied when the glacial ice was less than 100 kilometers to the north. Although no faunal remains survive, it is believed that the Debert people would have hunted caribou and other tundra game in a region which is now heavily wooded. Debert is dated by radiocarbon to 8600 BC and the similar Bull Brook location in Massachusetts to about 7000 BC, suggesting to some that eastern Clovis sites are later than western ones, and in culture derivative from them. However most observers feel that they were approximately contemporary, but may have endured through the time when Folsom succeeded Clovis on the western plains.

The Clovis Fluted point tradition is, in fact, found over a very extensive area of the New World, although most of the Clovis finds are from the surface rather than from stratified sites. A few Clovis-like points have been found in Alaska (the tradition perhaps reaching there via the Mackenzie Corridor when this had opened up between the Cordilleran and Laurentide ice sheets), and fluted points are known from scattered locations in Mexico, Guatemala and as far south as Turrialba and Guanacaste Province in Costa Rica and Madden Lake in Panama.

As one moves south from North America toward South America, the Fluted point tradition merges with the Fishtail point tradition, fishtail-shaped projectile points with fluted bases.

The Clovis mammoth-hunters reigned supreme in the western United States all the way from Montana to the Mexican border for about a millennium. Then, about 9000 BC, the smaller, more delicate Folsom fluted points evolved from Clovis points; this was concurrent with the near extinction of the great elephants and their replacement as the principal quarry of hunting bands by the smaller bison (*Bison antiquus*). Whether these two developments were related is uncertain, but they probably were. The original Folsom site in New Mexico has already been mentioned. This was a kill site, where 23 bison had been trapped, slaughtered and butchered, and where several seasons of fieldwork recovered 19 Folsom points.

The best-studied Folsom site is Lindenmeier, near Fort Collins, Colorado. In late Wisconsin times this was located on the marshy banks of a lake, with a base camp and a nearby kill site; one carbon 14 determination is about 8800 BC. Elephants must have still survived but in reduced numbers, for there were some mammoth remains. On the other hand there is abundant evidence for the killing and butchering of many bison. In addition to the usual

The archaeological world remained unconvinced of the antiquity of man in the New World until the find of a fluted point (shown here) and other artifacts associated with the skeleton of the extinct Long-horned bison, during 1926 excavations near Folsom, New Mexico.

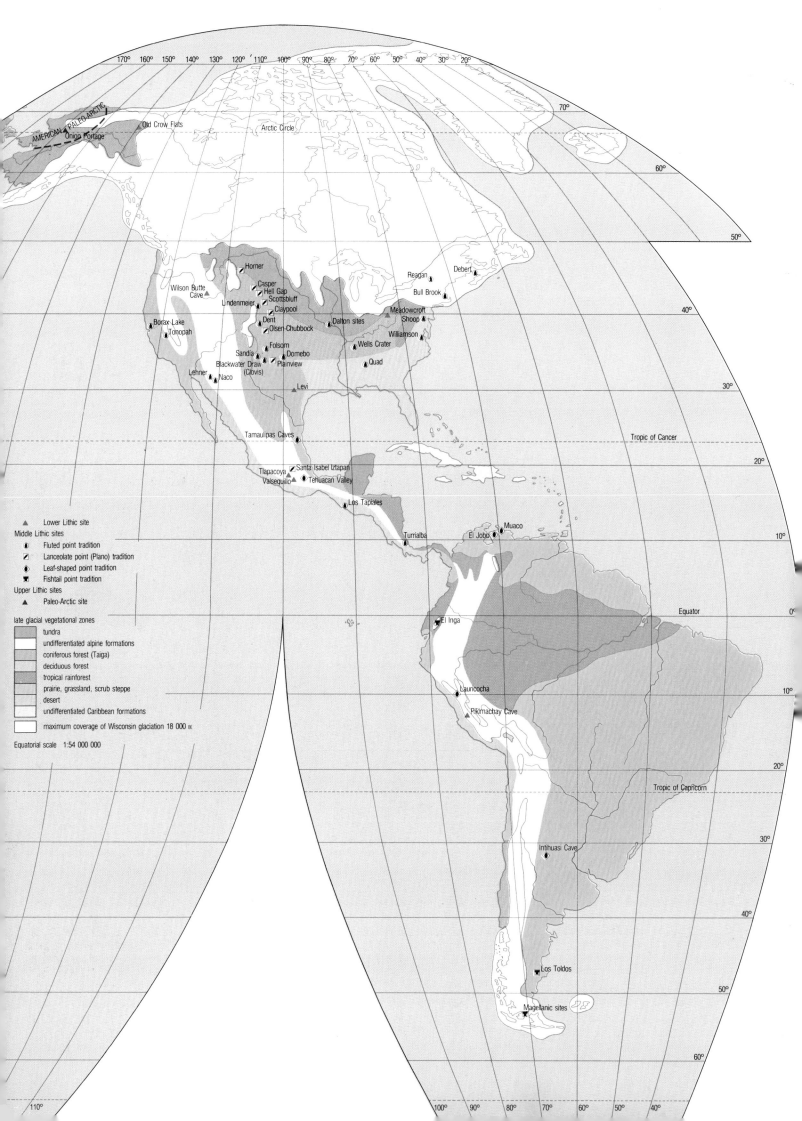

Lower Lithic site ▲

Middle Lithic sites
   ◖ Fluted point tradition
   ◪ Lanceolate point (Plano) tradition
   ◈ Leaf-shaped point tradition
   ▼ Fishtail point tradition

Upper Lithic sites
   ▲ Paleo-Arctic site

late glacial vegetational zones
   tundra
   undifferentiated alpine formations
   coniferous forest (Taiga)
   deciduous forest
   tropical rainforest
   prairie, grassland, scrub steppe
   desert
   undifferentiated Caribbean formations
   maximum coverage of Wisconsin glaciation 18 000 BC

Equatorial scale 1:54 000 000

Clovis point

Folsom projectile points there were several kinds of scrapers used in dressing hides, crescent-shaped spokeshaves used for straightening and smoothing dart or spear shafts, graving and cutting tools, prismatic flakes and drills. Although preservation was poor, some bone tools did survive, including awls and eyed needles, perhaps indicating the production of baskets and tailored skin clothing.

A problem is posed in the archaeology of the western United States by what are called Plainview points. These are like an unfluted Folsom, and are earlier than Folsom in the north (that is at the long-occupied site of Hell Gap, in eastern Wyoming), but later than Folsom in the south, as in Texas sites. Jesse Jennings suggests that they therefore began in the north and diffused to the south.

The Fluted point tradition was a phenomenon associated with the hunting of very large game animals which occurred in abundance in the Late Pleistocene. As these became extinct, either through "overkill," as Martin suggests, or through climatic change (or a combination of both), the tradition abruptly disappeared over much of its range in the 8th millennium BC, as the glacial ice sheets began their retreat. It was displaced by other traditions, particularly by the Lanceolate point tradition of southern origin.

Other point traditions of the Middle Lithic

As the Ice Age waned in North America, bifacial points, principally employed in the dispatching of bison, flourished and diversified on the Great Plains. Each type is named for the site where it was first recognized by archaeologists: e.g. Agate Basin, Midland, Scottsbluff, Hell Gap, Eden, Claypool and Milnesand. These varied industries have been grouped under the name Plano. Plano points are beautifully pressure-flaked, and many of them are almost works of art, made from fine materials like jasper and honey-colored flint. The flake scars on them meet along the center ridge of the blade to give the impression that a single transverse flake has extended across the entire blade, in a ripple effect.

Some of early America's best-documented kill sites belong to the Lanceolate point tradition. At the Olsen-Chubbock site in east-central Colorado, dated to about 6500 BC, the remains of nearly 200 *Bison occidentalis* (a species beginning to be replaced by the modern *Bison bison*) were found at the bottom of a long arroyo; they had been stampeded down a slope into the ravine, where they were killed, then butchered. The excavator, Dr Joe Ben Wheat, has estimated that the herd would have provided over 22 700 kilograms of meat, along with edible internal organs and fat, enough food to sustain about 150 people for 23 days. The victims included calves only a few days old, which places the drive in late May or early June.

The Lanceolate point tradition seems to persist until about 5000 BC, when the Pleistocene had long been over. The fossil fauna had all become extinct, and far drier and warmer conditions had ushered in the North American Archaic, with a very different life-style.

The two other lithic traditions of Paleo-Indian America have American affiliations and probably origins, arising independently from a Lower Lithic base. These are the Leaf-shaped point and Fishtail

point traditions. There is some reason to believe that the Leaf-shaped point tradition has an antiquity equal to at least that of Clovis, and may be of even earlier roots.

The Leaf-shaped point tradition most likely originated in northern South America, and is widely distributed over that continent, for instance in the Ayacucho rockshelters in the Peruvian highlands excavated by Richard MacNeish. In Mesoamerica it is manifest in the lenticular, percussion-chipped Lerma points, which turn up in the earliest occupation of the Tehuacan Valley, in the state of Puebla, a region which was the object of a long-term archaeological-ecological project directed by MacNeish. During this Ajuereado phase, which according to carbon 14 dates was earlier than 7000 BC, the inhabitants of the valley (who may never have numbered more than three nomadic families of four to eight people each) hunted extinct horse and pronghorn antelope with spears tipped with Lerma points, and seasonally migrated through a series of microenvironments which would have afforded them different plant and animal foods (including such humble creatures as jackrabbits, gophers and rats) at different times of the year.

In the Valley of Mexico itself there is excellent evidence for the meeting of the Leaf-shaped point tradition (from the north) and the Lanceolate point tradition (from the south). The valley was once filled by a great lake which endured from the Pleistocene until it was drained and desiccated by the Spanish colonial and republican regimes following the conquest of the Aztecs. During the Late Pleistocene the lake seems to have reached its greatest extent, and the entire basin then comprised prime hunting grounds for the American Indian bands occupying it.

The Leaf-shaped point tradition, although predominantly a South American cultural phenomenon, penetrated far north into North America proper, being found in very ancient layers in Wilson Butte Cave in Idaho, but its real roots lie in the southern continent.

That human groups had reached the southernmost part of the New World before 9000 BC was conclusively demonstrated by the late Junius Bird. In 1937 he excavated two caves, Fell's and Palliaike, near Magellan Strait. At that time radiocarbon dating had not yet been invented, and the age of the first occupation of the caves was unknown, but subsequently charcoal from two hearths was dated at 9370 and 9082 BC. This would make the earliest human culture in the "uttermost part of the Earth" at least in part contemporary with Clovis of North America: all unglaciated parts of the hemisphere had been occupied by this time.

The Period I levels of the Magellanic sequence produced 16 whole and fragmentary Fishtail points of basalt, chert and quartzite, in association with the bones of an extinct horse (*Parahipparion saldasi*), a giant ground sloth (*Mylodon listai*) and a guanaco (the wild camelid ancestral to both llamas and alpacas). The stems of the points resemble the tail of a minnow, and are often thinned by fluting, while the sides of the stems have been dulled by grinding, both being techniques they share with Clovis points. Also present were leaf-shaped points, bone flakes and awls and crude chopping tools. In the overlying Period II horse and sloth were apparently extinct, and there were only bone projectile points. There is a fairly wide distribution of the Fishtail point tradition in southernmost South America.

Blade traditions of the Upper Lithic

Professor Rouse's Upper Lithic age describes industries and complexes of Asian Upper Paleolithic origin which were confined in late Wisconsin times to the north of the Laurentide and Cordilleran ice sheets, specifically to the Beringian subcontinent of northeastern Siberia, the Bering land bridge and Alaska. He assigns these cultures to a separate, Upper Lithic age because of the presence of large blades and/or microblades, trimmed only along the edges. Some of these were struck off bifacially prepared cores, but most of them were removed from large flakes, at least in North America. There is a general, but not complete, absence of bifacial projectile points. Jayson Smith calls this the Northeast Asian-Northwest American Microblade Tradition (NAMANT). Its recognition is critical to understanding the earliest Americans, since the carriers of this tradition arrived in the New World at a relatively late date (about 14 000 years ago), and they only spread south along the Mackenzie Corridor after the recession of the last Wisconsin advance, about 7000 BC. Many students therefore conclude: first, that NAMANT carriers could have had nothing to do with the origin of the Middle Lithic traditions such as Clovis, which were already established in the hemisphere by the time of their arrival; secondly, that bifacial Middle Lithic traditions must have arisen independently in North and South America to the south of the Wisconsin ice, from an early, primitive Lower Lithic tradition which had spread from Asia into the New World before the coalescence of the two North American ice sheets, and before the entrance of NAMANT.

There are three NAMANT subtraditions which can be detected. One is Diuktoid, named from the type site on the Aldan River, a tributary of Siberia's Lena River. Diuktai is a cave which produced mammoth and Musk ox bones in association with microblades from bifacially chipped cores. There are some leaf-shaped points, but they are atypical, since Diuktoid projectiles were typical of the Upper Lithic age by normally being tipped with bone points having microblades set in grooves along their sides. Radiocarbon dates are 11 120 and 10 140 BC.

The second subtradition is Asian inland-coastal, which extended from Japan north to the Kamchatka Peninsula, with many microblades. The carbon 14 dates of 12 340-8410 BC make the bifacially worked points in the subtradition's deposits too late to be ancestral to the Middle Lithic of the New World.

The American Paleo-Arctic is the third subtradition. Here archaeologists have found that microblades were typically struck-off flakes rather than prepared cores. There are no bifacially worked projectile points, only bone points in typical NAMANT style, with microblades set in grooves on the sides of the points. The best-known site of this subtradition is Onion Portage, on the Kobuk River in northwestern Alaska, which enters the Chukchi Sea not far north of the Bering Strait. Dis-

covered by the late Louis Giddings, there are two successive microlithic complexes at this deeply stratified site: first, Akmak, which Giddings estimated at 13 000–6650 BC (only the latter part of the phase is radiocarbon-dated); second Kobuk, dated to 6250–6050 BC. This station, the setting for many successive campsites over the millennia, was undoubtedly important for fishing (Arctic char, shee and other species) as it was for the hunting of large game such as caribou.

The Upper Lithic is 100 percent Asiatic in its content, and clearly an offshoot of the blade traditions and highly specialized hunting-and-gathering economies of the Eurasian continent during the Upper Paleolithic. It probably has little to do with the origins or the cultural evolution of the American Indian, and is more likely the forerunner of the very rich, but relatively late, fishing, seal-and-whale-hunting, caribou-hunting life of the Eskimo (Inuit) and of the even more maritime-oriented life adaptations of their relatives, the Aleut.

Retrospect: the ecology of Paleo-Indian life

There are still many gaps in our knowledge of the Paleo-Indians of the New World. While it is highly probable that the first human beings came into North America south of the Wisconsin ice sheet before 10 000 BC, with a very simple tool kit, the evidence for this is not entirely satisfactory. There is much that we do not know (and may never know) about Beringia, from which these migrants must have been derived, simply because much of it now lies under the Chukchi and Bering Seas. Because of heavy vegetation cover and difficulties of travel the Paleo-Indian occupations of the tropical lowlands of Mesoamerica and South America are poorly known. And, finally, because of generally poor preservation in Paleo-Indian sites, while we understand a great deal about their stone-tool kits and the game they pursued, the role that plants played in their diets is very easy to underestimate.

This last point is an important one, since the procurement and processing of plant foods led to the earliest stage of plant domestication in Mesoamerica and the Andean area not long after the Wisconsin ice had begun its final retreat. The Paleo-Indians are often characterized as "big game hunters," but they may have been even more dependent on wild grass seeds, fruits, nuts and berries, and on small animals, than upon the spectacular megafauna such as elephants and horses. Data from sites like the Levi Rockshelter in Texas show that even the smallest and most humble animals entered into their diet.

The Paleo-Indian way of life, so similar in many respects to that of the Upper Paleolithic people of Eurasia, could have supported only a few people over very wide areas. The biologist Edward Deevey has calculated that on this level of cultural development it takes about 65 square kilometers to support one person. The present population of Mexico, for instance, is more than 70 million people; using the Deevey figures, in preagricultural, Paleo-Indian times it could never have surpassed 30 000 souls. Small wonder that Paleo-Indian remains, and particularly sites of pre-Clovis peoples, are so difficult to find.

PART THREE
NORTH AMERICA

THE ARCHAIC PERIOD

The Paleo-Indians of North America lived in environments that were very different from those of the last few millennia. They were free-wandering hunters and foragers. Many of the game animals they exploited became extinct as the Pleistocene ended (about 10 000 BC). The habitats that had supported Pleistocene plant and animal populations changed as the ice sheets melted faster than new ice could push southward. Those species that did not shift northward with the retreating ice died out and were replaced by others that expanded out of refuge areas. The role of human hunters in the extinction of major Pleistocene game species such as mastodons, mammoths, and Ice Age bison remains uncertain, the focus of continuing archaeological debate. What is certain is that later Indian communities had to cope with a mosaic of new and changing environments. After 8000 BC soils in newly deglaciated regions were young, and would evolve as they supported a succession of plant and animal species. Forest species expanded into new territories at varying rates, depending upon their propagation mechanisms. Climates changed rapidly as weather systems altered their movements around shrinking ice sheets.

Overall the current view of the continent after 8000 BC is one that stresses an initially rapid environmental readjustment, which slowed gradually over time as conditions settled toward their modern states. For Indian bands the initial part of this readjustment must have entailed considerable uncertainty, and archaeological remains reflect a series of broad unspecialized adaptations. As the environments became more stable Indian communities could risk more specialized adaptations to more predictable subsistence activities. Free-wandering patterns of movement settled into restricted wandering patterns, in

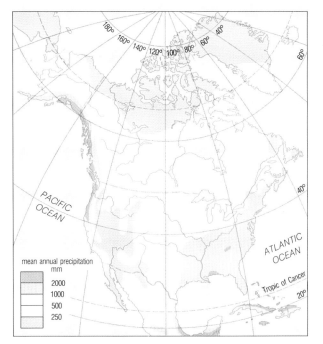

mean annual precipitation
mm

2000
1000
500
250

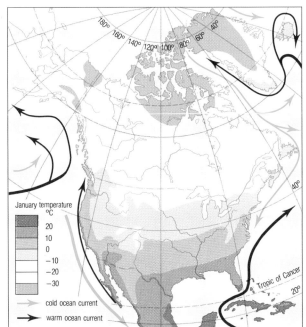

January temperature
°C

20
10
0
−10
−20
−30

cold ocean current

warm ocean current

The geography of North America varies from desert valleys that lie below sea level to some of the world's highest peaks. The geologically hot Yellowstone region lies on the continental divide. The Yellowstone River is shown (*below right*) near its source on the edge of the high plains. From here it flows northward before looping to the northeast to join the Missouri.

Canyon de Chelly cuts through the plateau of northeastern Arizona (*below left*). Here Chinle Wash flows past White House ruins. The canyon, once home to a series of flourishing Anasazi communities, now supports scattered Navajo farmsteads (see page 74).

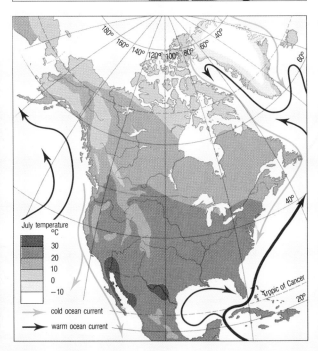

July temperature
°C

30
20
10
0
−10

cold ocean current

warm ocean current

Climate and vegetation of North America

Topography, soils and climate have combined to produce the mosaic of environmental zones seen in North America today. This map shows modern North American habitats as they would be without the alterations made first by prehistoric Indians and later more drastically by Euro-Americans. They evolved from a very different Ice Age landscape over the course of 10 000 years. Both the compositions and the boundaries of the environmental zones changed during that time, in some cases significantly. Indian communities necessarily adapted to conditions that gradually changed with time, and modern archaeologists concentrate on the exploration of the processes that facilitated human adaptation. Because in many cases neither the ancient environments nor prehistoric cultural adaptations have survived into recorded history, archaeology offers our only means to understand the cultural evolution of our species from hunting and gathering to settled farming. Because of the almost complete isolation of the peoples of the Western and Eastern Hemispheres from each other over this long period, the Americas offer an independent archaeological laboratory in which to explore the rise of civilization. Comparisons with developments in Europe, Asia and Africa allow archaeologists to discover both what is common to all of mankind, and what is unique to the cultures of ancient America.

tundra and ice
coniferous forest
deciduous forest
southeast and Atlantic coniferous forest
swamp forest
grassland
chaparral
semiarid scrub
desert
Central American pine and oak forest

scale 1:40 000 000

0   800km

0   600mi

which bands moved about according to regular habits within restricted territories. This long period, which archaeologists have named the Archaic, follows the specialized big-game hunting of the Paleo-Indians, but precedes the emergence of full-scale plant cultivation. By definition Archaic Indians made optimal use of an increasingly wide range of plant and animal species.

The principal weapon of the Archaic hunter was the atlatl, or spear thrower. In its simplest form this tool is a stick with a handle at one end and a stout hook at the other. The butt of a spear is fitted to the hook, and the hunter propels the spear by means of the spear thrower rather than by the hand directly. The spear thrower in effect lengthens the forearm by 50 centimeters (more or less), and permits the snap of the hand at the wrist to come into greater play. The additional speed imparted by both the lengthened arm and the increased effect of wrist motion made atlatl darts much more effective than larger hand-thrown spears.

Later in the Archaic period stone weights came to be used on atlatls. These would provide no effective advantage at all unless the atlatls were by this time being made of flexible material. Assuming that this was the case, Late Archaic hunters discovered the advantage of loading energy into their weapons by means of weighted flexible shafts, much as modern fishermen and golfers have discovered the advantage of flexible shafts.

The timing of the end of the Archaic varies greatly from one region to another. In some areas very early plant cultivation began to replace it as early as the 3rd millennium BC. In other areas Archaic systems of hunting and foraging persisted until after European colonization. Consequently a termination date of 700 BC for this long period has been chosen somewhat arbitrarily, with the understanding that the ecosystem type that characterized it was a variable over time and space as the environment that supported it.

The general problems of adaptation facing the Archaic Indians were similar in type to those faced by people throughout the world at this time. At a very general level the solutions were also similar. With the disappearance of Pleistocene game, the principal game animals became deer, moose and caribou. As the trend toward smaller game continued, the Indians gradually replaced a relatively extensive exploitation of large species with an intensive exploitation of many small species. On the foraging side they intensified the exploitation of nuts, fish and shellfish.

Increasing population density made it impossible for people to seek new resources by moving to unoccupied regions, for even marginal areas were filling up. As a consequence their patterns of movement settled into restricted wandering within defined territories, patterns that often took them to the same sites year after year in scheduled seasonal

Right Mount McKinley, now known as often by its Indian name "Denali," rises 6194 m. above central Alaska. This part of the Arctic was the homeland of Na-Dene Indians for thousands of years. In the earliest centuries of Indian expansion into the Americas this region was perhaps their primary corridor. The process, however, was not necessarily a dramatic migration. There has been enough time in the known archaeological sequence for a few small communities to expand and spread to their maximum extents without concerted long-distance migration.

Right Danger Cave, Utah—type site of the Desert Archaic—lies 34 m. above the modern level of the Great Salt Lake. Materials began accumulating in the cave around 9000 BC, eventually reaching a depth of 4 m. When excavated, the cave yielded thousands of artifacts, many of them of wood, fiber, bone, hide and other materials that would have perished in a wet environment. Because of this and thanks to finds from other similar sites archaeologists have a detailed understanding of Archaic Indian adaptation to a harsh desert environment.

rounds. The archaeological consequences of this shift include evidence of repeated occupations at carefully chosen sites, and the accumulation of midden debris at those sites. Simple portable tool kits were gradually replaced by larger more complex kits, and eventually heavy ground stone tools made their appearance. Heavy seed-grinding implements were made and used regularly, the transportation problem solved by the storage of separate implements at the sites visited during the course of a year. Food storage also increased, as did the keeping of material wealth.

Earlier social organizations appear to have been relatively egalitarian. High mobility, large band ranges and impermanent habitations had facilitated the acquisition and exchange of exotic lithic materials.

Archaic Indians had comparatively small band ranges, reduced mobility and less egalitarian organizations. Probably as a consequence of greater interband competition and reduced ranges,

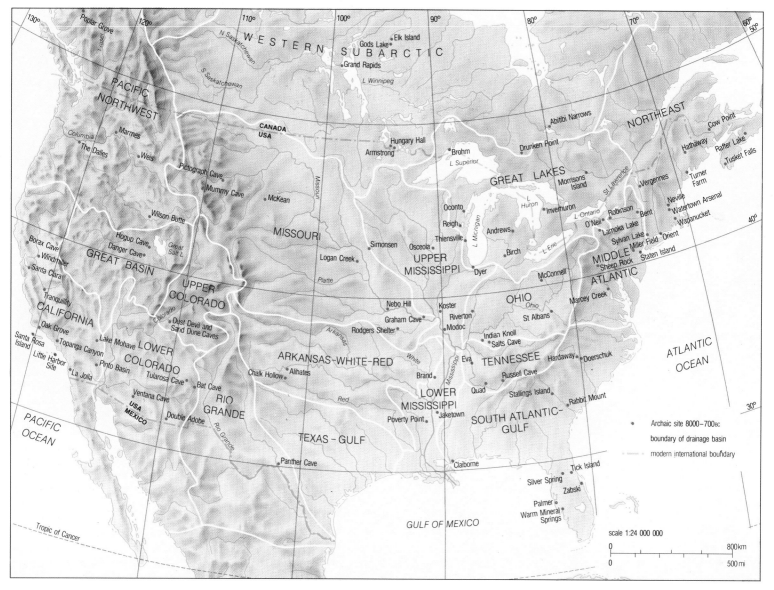

scale 1:24 000 000

Archaic site 8000–700 BC

boundary of drainage basin

modern international boundary

Poverty Point

Perhaps the most impressive Archaic site in North America is the complex of great earthworks at Poverty Point, Louisiana. The main complex, or village, is a set of six nested octagons, the outer one of which is about 1300 meters in diameter. Each octagon is a series of earthen ridges. Part of this complex of octagons was later eroded away by a nearby river, if it was ever built at all. A large mound west of the village and away from the river site stands over 20 meters high and is over 200 meters long at its base. That length includes a long ramp that descends toward the octagon complex. A somewhat small mound stands to the north. Although it is tempting to look southward for early Mexican inspiration, Poverty Point may have been neither more nor less than the outgrowth of long-term developmental trends in the North American Archaic.

The center of Poverty Point, 1500 – 700 BC (below right), now protected and open to the public, is its set of concentric octagons. The main mound to the west is positioned to provide a clear view of the sun rising over the center point of the octagons at the spring and fall equinoxes (below, far right). Whether this was deliberate or not is unknown. The plummet (below), made of hematite, was probably an item of fishing equipment.

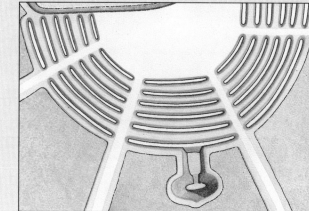

Among the artifacts recovered at Poverty Point are thousands of fired clay balls. These were apparently used for stone boiling in place of pebbles, which are difficult to find in the alluvial soils of the Mississippi Valley. The heating of food by dropping hot balls into it spared fragile or combustible vessels from direct exposure to fire. In a few cases, clay lumps take the shapes of bird effigies or human figurines. The figurine seen here (below) is less than 5 cm. tall.

Left: Archaic cultures of North America

Human ecosystems can be described in simplified form as involving environment, subsistence, technology, social organization and demography. Archaeologists have attempted to measure all of these variables for Archaic North America, with varying success. Because ecological boundaries are difficult to define even for modern conditions, and because conditions were so different during the Archaic, the continent has to be divided into regions on the basis of more permanent boundaries. These boundaries are major watershed divides, which have been stable for at least the last 10 000 years. These are river-drainage areas.

older patterns of extensive exchange of exotic raw materials were replaced by a resort to local materials. Archaic sites often contain tools made of relatively low-grade but locally available raw materials. Better materials remained in the hands of bands lucky enough to have inherited them within their own reduced territories.

By the end of the Archaic, many Indian bands were manipulating their environment. This involved the burning of tracts of forest to encourage deer grazing. It also included the occasional tending and perhaps unintentional propagation of plant species that were particularly desired. Also by the end of the Archaic new patterns of trade and exchange began to emerge. Superficially these appear similar to the pre-Archaic systems through which exotic lithic materials made their way from one egalitarian band to another. However the new systems appear to have been quite different in kind, judging by the use to which the exotic materials were put when they reached their archaeological destinations. Many exotic goods have been found associated with burials, used in contexts that suggest that they were designed to mark differential social rank in increasingly competitive societies. For example, exotic Ramah chert flowed southward through sites in the Maritime Provinces and Maine, ending up as prized possessions and eventually as grave goods. In contrast Paleo-Indian exotics ended up as broken and discarded tools in campsite debris. The Late Archaic pattern set the stage for the elaboration of long-distance exchange and social ranking that would flourish in the thousand years following 700 BC.

In at least the interior western portions of the continent climatic shifts toward warmer and drier conditions after the Pleistocene went beyond modern levels. Great Basin archaeologists have made more use of hypothesized long-term fluctuations in temperature than have archaeologists in most other regions of North America. The Anathermal, characterized by cool and moist conditions, is supposed to have dominated the period 7000–5000 BC. The Altithermal maximum (5000–2500 BC) is recorded at many sites, and dates of around 4400 BC for the peak are known. The Medithermal (after 2500 BC) saw a reversal toward modern conditions. This seeming climatic overcorrection created strong adaptive pressure for Archaic populations. However the subsequent relaxation of heat and arid conditions toward modern norms left them well positioned to move from food collection to food production.

CULTURE AREAS

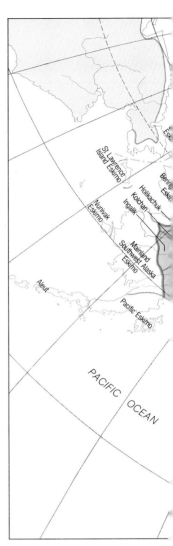

Anthropologists have traditionally divided the multitude of North American Indian cultures into geographically defined culture areas. This device has the advantage of grouping hundreds of local cultures into a smaller number of more manageable units. There are, however, some disadvantages that must be borne in mind if culture areas are not to be misused. First, the hard boundaries of cultural groups are for the most part an anthropological fiction. Nations were more often than not separated by buffer zones rather than European-style territorial boundaries. Second, the very definition of a culture area implies that there was once some sort of ideal culture type at its core, which more marginal cultures somehow sought to achieve. This too is a false impression, for all cultures sought to adapt as best they could to local conditions, and our groupings of them are a matter of convenience for the sake of generalization. Third, because of the previous two problems, culture areas can often gloss over important small-scale variations. They are used here with the understanding that they be used only for the convenience of initial generalization.

Although vast and interrupted by vacant areas, the Arctic is treated as a single culture area. The Subarctic is divided into Western and Eastern areas, a division that separates Na-Dene from Algonquian speakers. The Southern Canadian area has been set off between the Eastern Subarctic and the Eastern Woodlands. The Great Plains have been divided into northern and southern areas and the distinctive Prairie between these, and the Eastern Woodlands has also been given separate status. The Southwest has always been treated separately, but the portion of it lying in Mexico has too often been silently omitted. Similarly Northeast Mexico has not always been considered as a separate area. Finally the far west has been separated first into coastal and intermontane regions. These have been further subdivided into the Northwest Coast and California areas on the one hand, and into the Plateau and Great Basin on the other. In all cases boundaries and local names have followed standards established in the volumes of the *Handbook of North American Indians*. (Some volumes are still in the planning stages, and for the areas covered by these we have depended upon older sources. The unpublished volumes will cover the Northwest Coast, the Great Basin, the Plateau, the Plains and the Southeast.)

Several scholarly attempts have been made to group American Indian languages into a small set of families or phyla. These have been superficially successful, in the sense that the results have been published and used by other scholars. However,

Indigenous languages of North America I
Although immense, northern North America can be divided into four large culture areas dominated by three major language families. The Arctic is the domain of the speakers of Eskimo-Aleut languages. The Eastern Subarctic is dominated by speakers of Algonquian-Ritwan languages, while the Western Subarctic is the home of Na-Dene languages. Northwest Coast cultures speak languages belonging to Na-Dene and some smaller language families whose ancient derivations are still incompletely understood.

Left The area around Juneau is typical of the rugged Northwest Coast. Valleys often hold mountain glaciers rather than rivers, remnants of the Cordilleran ice sheet that once covered the entire region.

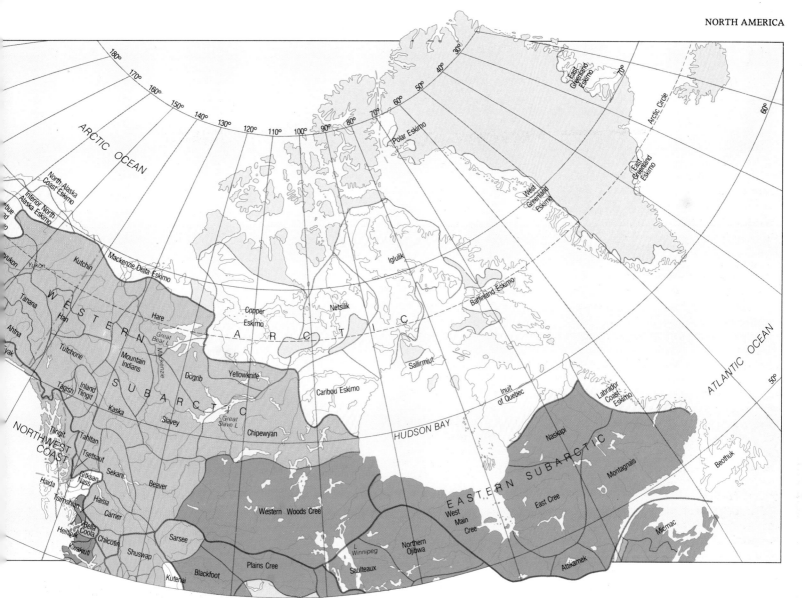

boundary of culture area
boundary of tribal territory

language families
Eskimo-Aleut
Na-Dene
Algonquian-Ritwan
Siouan
Salishan
Wakashan
Iroquoian
area of unknown or complex classification

scale 1:27 000 000

0   800km

0   600mi

specific analyses of these classification systems have repeatedly indicated that such efforts have been flawed by error, lack of evidence and misplaced optimism. The classification adopted here is consequently the most conservative one in current use. There are 21 families and 32 language isolates, that is, languages that are either so poorly known that we cannot classify them, or so bewildering that they defy classification. Of the 21 language families, 3 are groups of languages that are only tenuously related, and future linguistic research may require that they be broken into a large number of less inclusive families. Hokan may be 6 separate families and 5 isolates. Penutian may be 3 families and 2 isolates. Oregon Penutian may be only 4 language isolates. Although this conservative approach to language may imply as many as 30 families and 43 isolates, it also implies a high level of certainty as regards the constituents of those families. Future research will undoubtedly lead to a combination of families listed here as separate ones, but is is unlikely to lead to the dismantling of these classificatory units.

THE ARCTIC

Authorities agree that bands of early hunters first entered the Western Hemisphere by way of what is now Alaska. Much of the earliest movement must have been across broad areas of continental shelf that were once exposed by lower Ice Age sea levels, but are now submerged and inaccessible to archaeologists. Biologically modern man (*Homo sapiens sapiens*) evolved as a population in the Eastern Hemisphere, but entered the Americas as a relatively small trickle only after that evolution was completed around 40 000 years ago. Consequently the archaeological evidence for the first inhabitants of the Americas is necessarily meager, widely scattered, and difficult to recognize when compared with the large amount of evidence for even much earlier periods in the Eastern Hemisphere.

Arctic archaeology has developed in three national contexts, from Alaska across Canada to Greenland. There are differing traditions of scholarship between and within these contexts. However, varying taxonomies and interpretations can be synthesized through the use of five broad developmental stages having loosely defined beginning and ending dates to accommodate developmental lags in this vast region.

Stage I

Stage I began around 25 000 BC and ended around 5000 BC. The earliest putative evidence from this stage comes in the form of bone artifacts found at Old Crow, Yukon Territory, and some related sites

NORTHWEST COAST

1 Pentlatch
2 Sechelt
3 Squamish
4 Halkomelem
5 Nooksack
6 Straits
7 Nitinat
8 Makah
9 Quileute
10 Chemakum
11 Luchootseed
12 Twana
13 Quinault
14 Lower Chehalis
15 Upper Chehalis
16 Cowlitz
17 Kwalhiokwa
18 Klatskanie
19 Lower Chinook
20 Upper Chinook
21 Tillamook
22 Kalapuya
23 Alsea
24 Siuslaw
25 Coos
26 SW Oregon Athapaskan
27 Takelma

1 Pentlatch
2 Sechelt
3 Squamish
4 Halkomelem
5 Nooksack
6 Straits
7 Nitinat
8 Makah
9 Quileute
10 Chemakum
11 Luchootseed
12 Twana
13 Quinault
14 Lower Chehalis
15 Upper Chehalis
16 Cowlitz
17 Kwalhiokwa
18 Klatskanie
19 Lower Chinook
20 Upper Chinook
21 Tillamook
22 Kalapuya
23 Alsea
24 Siuslaw
25 Coos
26 SW Oregon Athapaskan
27 Takelma

CALIFORNIA

28 Tolowa
29 Karok
30 Shasta
31 Yurok
32 Chilula
33 Hupa
34 Wiyot
35 Whilkut
36 Chimariko
37 Mattole
38 Nongatl
39 Wintu
40 Yana
41 Nomlaki
42 Lassik
43 Sinkyone
44 Wailaki
45 Cahto
46 Yuki
47 Konkow
48 Patwin
49 Lake Miwok
50 Wappo
51 Coast Miwok
52 Foothill Yokuts
53 Monache
54 Tubatulabal
55 Kitanemuk
56 Tataviam

CALIFORNIA

28 Tolowa
29 Karok
30 Shasta
31 Yurok
32 Chilula
33 Hupa
34 Wiyot
35 Whilkut
36 Chimariko
37 Mattole
38 Nongatl
39 Wintu
40 Yana
41 Nomlaki
42 Lassik
43 Sinkyone
44 Wailaki
45 Cahto
46 Yuki
47 Konkow
48 Patwin
49 Lake Miwok
50 Wappo
51 Coast Miwok
52 Foothill Yokuts
53 Monache
54 Tubatulabal
55 Kitanemuk
56 Tataviam

PACIFIC OCEAN

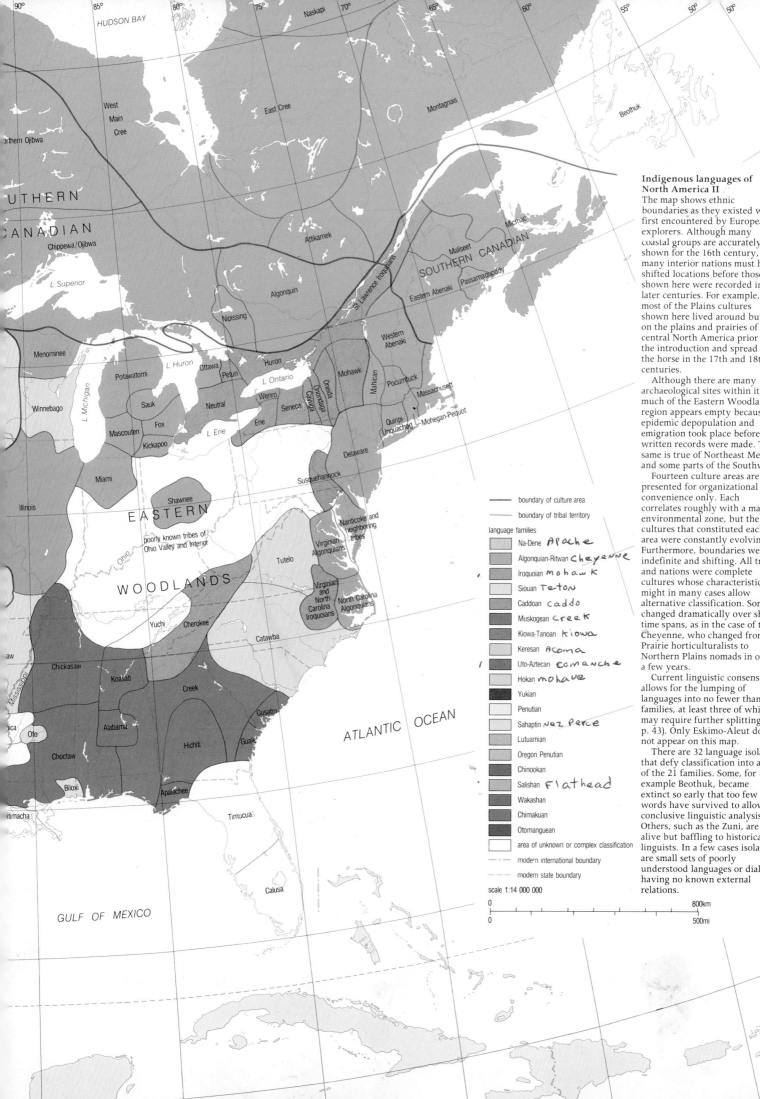

Indigenous languages of North America II

The map shows ethnic boundaries as they existed when first encountered by European explorers. Although many coastal groups are accurately shown for the 16th century, many interior nations must have shifted locations before those shown here were recorded in later centuries. For example, most of the Plains cultures shown here lived around but not on the plains and prairies of central North America prior to the introduction and spread of the horse in the 17th and 18th centuries.

Although there are many archaeological sites within it, much of the Eastern Woodlands region appears empty because epidemic depopulation and emigration took place before any written records were made. The same is true of Northeast Mexico and some parts of the Southwest.

Fourteen culture areas are presented for organizational convenience only. Each correlates roughly with a major environmental zone, but the cultures that constituted each area were constantly evolving. Furthermore, boundaries were indefinite and shifting. All tribes and nations were complete cultures whose characteristics might in many cases allow alternative classification. Some changed dramatically over short time spans, as in the case of the Cheyenne, who changed from Prairie horticulturalists to Northern Plains nomads in only a few years.

Current linguistic consensus allows for the lumping of languages into no fewer than 21 families, at least three of which may require further splitting (see p. 43). Only Eskimo-Aleut does not appear on this map.

There are 32 language isolates that defy classification into any of the 21 families. Some, for example Beothuk, became extinct so early that too few words have survived to allow conclusive linguistic analysis. Others, such as the Zuni, are alive but baffling to historical linguists. In a few cases isolates are small sets of poorly understood languages or dialects having no known external relations.

Legend:

- boundary of culture area
- boundary of tribal territory

language families

- Na-Dene — Apache
- Algonquian-Ritwan — Cheyenne
- Iroquoian — mohawk
- Siouan — Teton
- Caddoan — caddo
- Muskogean — Creek
- Kiowa-Tanoan — Kiowa
- Keresan — Acoma
- Uto-Aztecan — Comanche
- Hokan — mohave
- Yukian
- Penutian
- Sahaptin — Nez Perce
- Lutuamian
- Oregon Penutian
- Chinookan
- Salishan — Flathead
- Wakashan
- Chimakuan
- Otomanguean
- area of unknown or complex classification
- modern international boundary
- modern state boundary

scale 1:14 000 000

0   800km
0   500mi

nearby. This may mark the advent of human pre-history in the Americas. A few authorities accept earlier dates for remains elsewhere in the hemisphere, and some reject all claims for evidence dating much before 14 000 years ago. The earliest indisputable evidence from the Arctic comes in the form of several stone-tool assemblages dating to 9000–6000 BC, which are generally referred to as the American Paleo-Arctic tradition. The assemblages contain cores, blades and microblades, and are associated with modern faunal species along with some specimens of bison and possibly horse and elk.

The related Anangula tradition, which is named for its Aleutian Island type site, may have already been adapted to maritime resources. While most American Paleo-Arctic sites contain bifacial tools, the Anangula assemblage is dominated by unifacial tools, as is the very similar assemblage at the Gallagher Flint station.

The materials in all sites from the later millennia of Stage I are fundamentally similar to evidence from interior Siberia. This similarity has led some archaeologists to refer to all early materials from both sides of the Bering Strait as belonging to an inclusive "Beringian" tradition.

Stage II

Although hunting and foraging could never be replaced by more advanced food production in the Arctic, regional variations in resource availability led to early differences in tool kits. Stage II began around 5000 BC, and by 4000 BC the evidence from both Anangula and Ocean Bay indicates that coastal hunters were adapted to marine resources not available to interior hunters. Evidence from Onion Portage and contemporary interior sites in both tundra and forested environments suggests a variable adaptation to interior resources, but one having enough consistency over the region to justify its identification as the Northern Archaic tradition. Some archaeologists interpret this tradition as one having southern origins in earlier Paleo-Indian developments, while others interpret it as an in-place development out of the previous stage. It may be that the people responsible for the Northern Archaic tradition were ancestral to historic Athapaskan-speaking peoples of western North America, but there is as yet little agreement with regard to this hypothesis.

Stage III

Stage II evolved into Stage III between 2500 BC and 1900 BC, the earliest transitions occurring in northern Alaska and in the Aleutian Islands. With the advent of this stage Arctic prehistory became an Eskimo rather than an American Indian phenomenon. Modern Eskimo languages are distantly but clearly related to Aleut. Their separation appears to have begun at least as early as Stage III, because from this time on the Aleutian tradition develops as a separate archaeological tradition in isolation from the later stages of Arctic archaeology.

In northern Alaska Stage III is marked by the emergence of a distinctive tool assemblage known as the Arctic Small Tool tradition. This early Eskimo tradition developed and dispersed rapidly through the maritime Arctic zone extending from the Alaska Peninsula to Greenland. The Aleuts did

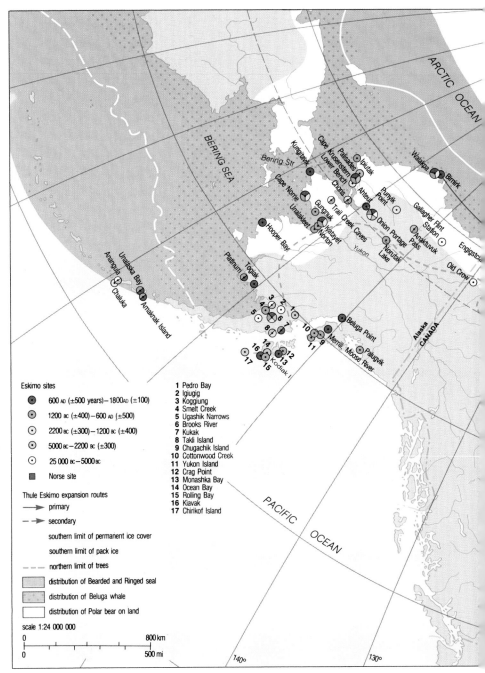

Eskimo sites

- 600 AD (±500 years)–1800 AD (±100)
- 1200 BC (±400)–600 AD (±500)
- 2200 BC (±300)–1200 BC (±400)
- 5000 BC–2200 BC (±300)
- 25 000 BC–5000 BC

■ Norse site

Thule Eskimo expansion routes
→ primary
⇢ secondary

southern limit of permanent ice cover
southern limit of pack ice
northern limit of trees
distribution of Bearded and Ringed seal
distribution of Beluga whale
distribution of Polar bear on land

scale 1:24 000 000

0   800 km
0   500 mi

1 Pedro Bay
2 Igiugig
3 Koggiung
4 Smelt Creek
5 Ugashik Narrows
6 Brooks River
7 Kukak
8 Takli Island
9 Chugachik Island
10 Cottonwood Creek
11 Yukon Island
12 Crag Point
13 Monashka Bay
14 Ocean Bay
15 Rolling Bay
16 Kiavak
17 Chirikof Island

not participate in this development, which may well have developed in eastern Siberia before dispersing eastward through the American Arctic. The tradition generally lacked the oil lamps that would characterize historical Eskimo cultures, so these early Eskimos necessarily still depended upon wood for light and heat. They exploited a balanced range of marine and terrestrial game, and in some regions lived in substantial semi-subterranean houses. Their tool kit included sophisticated microblades, designed as cutting edges for larger composite tools made of bone, ivory and wood.

The Arctic Small Tool tradition underwent diversification as it spread eastward. Sites containing components of "Independence I" culture in Canada and Greenland may contrast significantly with those labeled Pre-Dorset (Canada) or Sarqaq (Greenland). Developments were in place by 1900 BC; the adaptation persisted in some parts to 800 BC.

Stage IV

The beginning of Stage IV is marked by the evolu-

Archaeology of the Arctic
The Eskimo and Aleut adapted to harsh Arctic environments. Throughout prehistory they stayed generally beyond the treeline, in a bleak maritime zone lying between permanent ice and the southern limit of drifting floes. Their domain was shared by polar bears on land. Seals, Beluga whales and other sea mammal species off the coast supplied critical protein and oil for heat and light. Prehistoric Arctic chronologies have their greatest depth and complexities in the west. The Aleut broke away from their Eskimo relatives early on, taking up a specialized maritime tradition on their islands off southwestern Alaska. Coastal western and northern Alaska became staging grounds for later Eskimo developments. Canadian and Greenland Arctic prehistory was dominated first by an eastward expansion of Dorset Eskimos, later by a similar expansion of Thule Eskimos, who completely replaced their predecessors.

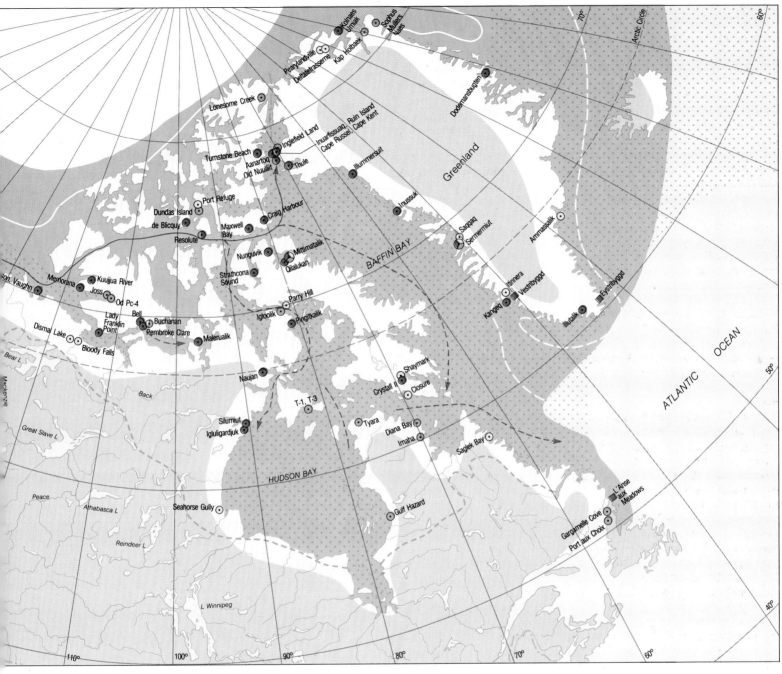

tionary disappearance of the Arctic Small Tool tradition as Eskimo adaptation shifted increasingly toward the exploitation of marine resources, especially sea mammals. The shift began earliest, possibly around 1600 BC, in northern Alaska. Here Stage IV involved a succession of phases, Choris, Norton and Ipiutak. A puzzling development known as Old Whaling culture appears abruptly and then disappears a century later at Cape Krusenstern during this period. There was less diversity south of Bering Strait, where the stage is defined by Norton culture alone. The Aleutian Islanders continued to develop in isolation. Although there is similar continuity in the Kodiak Island region, there is enough known in this stage to define the Kachemak tradition. Some archaeologists see an Independence II development out of earlier Independence I culture in Greenland at this time. More general in the eastern Arctic, however, is the emergence of Dorset culture from Pre-Dorset in both Canada and Greenland. Harpoons, coastal site locations and refuse bones all indicate a Dorset dependence upon marine mammals, especially seals

and walrus. The bow and arrow and small stone lamps are occasionally found in Dorset sites, but the crude pottery found in Alaskan Norton culture sites is absent in Dorset culture.

Some of the hallmarks of historical Eskimo culture, such as snow knives for the construction of snow igloos, ice creepers and small sled runners, make their first appearance in Dorset. Curiously, however, dogs, bows and arrows and drills drop out of inventories in many later Dorset sites. These changes occur as stone lamps, and presumably the exploitation of oil-producing sea mammals, increase in importance. The changes may indicate a shift away from both terrestrial and marine hunting to an economy focused on the latter alone. Fragments from Dorset sites indicate that their kayaks, important in marine hunting, were technically as advanced as later ones.

Stage V
Stage V begins as early as 100 AD in the Bering Strait region as Old Bering Sea culture developed from a Norton-like ancestor, and then gave rise to

Birnirk culture around 900 AD in northern Alaska. In this cultural and physical setting Birnirk culture evolved in turn into Thule culture. Thule Eskimo culture was adopted by the other Eskimo communities of Alaska, but its most dramatic effect on the Arctic was its rapid spread eastward. Thule Eskimos submerged Dorset Eskimos in what was probably a complex process involving some actual replacement of Dorset by Thule Eskimos as well as enculturation of remnant Dorset communities. By the time of first historical contact, Eskimo speech was composed of dialects of a single language from Greenland to northern Alaska, presumed earlier Dorset language(s) having been entirely replaced.

Thule expansion was fueled by technological supremacy that included use of both large umiaks and fleets of kayaks, the bow and arrow, built-up dog sleds, advanced harpoons, whale-oil lamps, snow igloos and dozens of specialized gadgets. The favorable climatic conditions that drew the Norse westward allowed the Thule Eskimo and the whales they hunted to spread eastward, where the two cultures eventually competed for resources in Greenland. The widespread Thule culture, and its somewhat more diverse analogues in Alaska, persisted into historical times as the rich and complex series of cultures customarily lumped as Eskimo.

THE EASTERN WOODLANDS: BURIAL MOUND BUILDERS
700 BC – 400 AD

By the end of the Archaic, Indian cultures in several parts of North America had moved from intensive foraging to the actual cultivation of some indigenous plants. These plants by no means had the importance that true domesticates have for agriculturalists, and their manipulation may not have even looked much like modern cultivation. Nonetheless the importance of sunflower, goosefoot, pigweed, knotweed, maygrass, marsh elder, gourd, squash and perhaps some early strains of maize was increasing, and the beginnings of horticulture were being practiced alongside traditional intensive hunting and gathering. The resulting new subsistence pattern has been called the "cultivating ecosystem type" by some archaeologists.

Seeds were important, but not all of the plants tended at this time were exploited for their seeds. Sunflowers included at least one species cultivated for its tubers, a species later named rather inappropriately the "Jerusalem artichoke." Tropical cucurbits (gourd and squash) came to North America through Mexico, and were used for their flesh as well as their seeds. Beginning around 2500 BC in a few places in the Mississippi drainage, and lasting to at least 400 AD in some, Indians exerted much more control over the propagation and production of these plants than earlier foragers could have imagined, if somewhat less than true horticulturalists can achieve. The low yield of the early cultigens relative to later domesticates suggests that they served mainly to buffer temporary shortages in hunted and gathered wild foods. They were less than true staples, but they were storable and made a critical difference for people threatened mainly by the rare but lethal episode of starvation. This threat would have been sharpened by the gradual restriction of Indian communities to small,

Ohio's Serpent Mound winds along a prominent hilltop, its tail a tight coil in the distance. Its uncoiled length is approximately 400 m. (see *below*). The serpent's head, in the foreground in this old southward-looking view, is difficult to interpret. The oval ring mound appears to be clasped in the serpent's mouth. The specific inspiration for this unique earthwork can only be guessed; bird and serpent imagery dominated 2000 years of Eastern Woodlands prehistory. The lack of archaeological clues from within the mound has made archaeological dating and attribution almost as difficult. Serpent Mound might be either Adena or Hopewell; there are known Adena mounds nearby, but the scale and complexity of the monument seem more consistent with Hopewell culture to many archaeologists. Modern visitors are able to view the serpent from a tower standing to the east of the house (now torn down) seen near the coiled tail. The site was saved from destruction in an early example of archaeological conservation, and is now owned and protected by the state of Ohio.

well-defined territories in which unpredictable failures in natural harvests could only be buffered by deliberate surplus production and careful storage.

Adena culture

The new cultivating ecosystem type became the base upon which the Adena and later Hopewell cultural phenomena were built. Adena culture developed in the Ohio River Valley by at least 700 BC, perhaps as early as 1100 BC. Late Archaic developments such as the Glacial Kame and Red Ocher complexes appear to have influenced the

development of Adena, and one can see the Archaic themes of rudimentary cultivation and the renewal of long-distance exchange in it. Over 200 Adena sites are known for its heartland in southern Ohio and the adjacent portions of West Virginia, Pennsylvania, Kentucky and Indiana. Earthworks are typical of Ohio Adena sites. Ridges of earth were thrown up in large circles, squares, pentagons or occasionally along the irregular edges of natural elevations. Many are 100 meters in diameter, but seem to be meant more as sacred enclosures than as true defensive works. Sometimes removal of earth from the interior of the works to provide material

for their construction left an interior ditch, which looked like an internal moat to the Europeans that discovered them 2000 years later.

Adena people also built burial mounds, the largest of which is probably that of Miamisburg, Ohio. The burials under these monuments were placed sometimes in simple clay-lined basins, at other times in large log tombs big enough to contain up to three people. The dead found in simpler graves had often first been cremated. The more elaborate graves contain evidence that the dead were smeared with red ocher or graphite, and often contain more high-quality grave goods as well. Some smaller mounds, constructed either inside or outside the larger earthworks, appear to have been built in one operation for a single individual. Others, especially those with log tombs, appear to have been left open for long periods so that new burials could be added from time to time. Eventually the tombs were closed, and still later they collapsed under the weight of the earthen mounds. Mounds sometimes appear to have been built over the burned remains of structures, whose post molds can still be traced in the subsoil.

Adena women made pottery, which had been added to some Late Archaic household inventories, but it was not particularly well made and played no important role in burial ceremonialism. Adena grave goods usually included reel-shaped gorgets, carved tablets and tubular pipes. All of these were typically made of banded slate or some other fine-grained stone that would take a high polish. The tablets bear carved curvilinear designs, or abstract zoomorphic designs, usually a bird of prey. They may have been used to apply designs to fabrics, or perhaps to lay down designs on skin, either temporarily or in preparation for tattooing.

Tubular pipes are an important artifact class because they reveal the presence of native tobacco long before the tiny tobacco seeds first appear as direct botanical evidence. Smoking apparently spread from South American origins, and the presence of tubular pipes indicates that the tobacco plant, complex smoking equipment and by inference smoking ritual were all present in Adena society.

The hardy tobacco that was smoked by American Indians in the 16th century was much more potent than the milder species that Europeans found to replace it after 1600. The plant virtually reproduces itself once established, and would have fitted well within the complex of plants tended and used by the Adena Indians. The potent plant could produce almost narcotic effects, and undoubtedly served ancient shamanistic purposes as well as the social and political ones for which it is so well known in the historical period.

Adena craftsmen imported native copper from northern Michigan to hammer into bracelets, beads, rings, gorgets and axes. These and the other luxury goods were often included as grave goods, marks of rank that taken together indicate that Adena society was in the early stages of social stratification. The society was probably still firmly rooted in the principles of kinship, but the practice of long-distance trade and the unequal treatment of the dead combine to suggest that clan heads were high-ranking individuals and the conduits for exchange between kin groups. This is a pattern that is well known for some historical American Indian societies.

Hopewell craftsmen

Hopewell craftsmen took all of the traits of Adena culture and elaborated them to new levels of size and complexity. Much of the excavation of Hopewell sites was carried out in the 19th century, when neither modern technical capabilities nor excavation standards were well developed. As a consequence we have few well-dated Hopewell sites. Many sites have been destroyed by looting or farming, and many of the artifacts taken from them

have disappeared. Mounds were often excavated while village sites were ignored; we still know too little of Hopewell domestic life.

We do know that Hopewell burial mounds were often built in two stages, not unlike Adena mounds. Log tombs were constructed, then covered over with mounds of earth. A typical Hopewell mound might be 12 meters high and 30 meters across at the base. Around the mounds were often earthwork enclosures much more elaborate than any attempted by Adena architects. Circular, rectangular, square and octagonal earthworks can exceed 500 meters in diameter or length. Two or more are sometimes linked by causeways. Burial mounds are sometimes scattered around within an area of large earthworks, as at Mound City, Ohio. At other times immense complexes of earthworks appear to have been constructed for their own sake, as at Newark, Ohio. The great Serpent Mound in Ohio appears to have functioned as a sacred effigy rather than as a burial place.

The contents of Ohio Hopewell mounds surpassed anything seen in Adena mounds. Native copper was beaten into ear spools, cutouts, artificial noses (probably for the dead), gorgets, beads, pendants and even panpipes. Thin sheets of copper were embossed with designs and heavier ones were used as breastplates. Heavy nuggets were beaten into axes, adzes, celts and awls. One elaborate copper headdress imitates a pair of deer antlers. Meteoric iron and nuggets of gold and silver were also used to make foil. This in turn was used to jacket ear spools, adzes and other objects made of less impressive materials. Cubes of galena, crystals of quartz and chlorite were kept as charms.

Mica was imported from the Appalachian Mountains and used for the production of cutouts similar in form to the copper ones. Serpents, human hands, heads, swastikas and bird talons were all popular forms. Conch and other shells, the jaws and teeth of alligators, sharks and barracudas were all imported. Turtle shells and Grizzly bear canines were also collected.

Chipped stone tools were manufactured from a wide variety of exotic cherts, chalcedony and obsidian. From mundane prototypes Hopewell craftsmen fashioned beautiful implements that may have been only for show. In a similar elevation of everyday pottery, Hopewell artisans created a series of fine ceramic types that were used only as grave goods. Some of these bear zones of decoration arranged as panels around the vessel. Hopewell potters also made human effigy figurines, exquisite but unlike those found in Mexico or the Southwest. From these archaeologists have been able to reconstruct what may have been ideal forms of Hopewell dress and hair styling.

Stone carving took several forms, the most notable of which may be the Hopewell platform pipe. These pipes often feature an animal effigy perched atop an arched rectangular tablet. The pipe bowl is in the animal's head or back, and the smoke was drawn through a hole exiting at the end of the rectangular tablet. Human heads, frogs, toads, waterfowl, owls, hawks, ravens, bears and other animal effigies all appear on these pipes. Two unique artifacts—one a large thumb, 18 centimeters long, the other a beetle monster—are among those made from a hard dense form of coal. Other

Adena-Hopewell and related cultures
The Adena cult had its center in Ohio, but its influences can be found at sites as far away as Vermont, eastern New York, New Jersey and Maryland. These outliers were once thought to have originated as the result of a migration of Adena colonists out of Ohio. It now seems more likely that the outlier sites were built by local people influenced as the result of being drawn into the Adena trading network. It is possible that finished Adena goods were traded to these outlying areas in exchange for raw materials.

Adena culture peaked in Ohio by 100 BC and was waning by 400 AD. It may have persisted until 700 AD in West Virginia, but in southern Ohio it was being replaced by Hopewell culture 900 years earlier. It may be that the inspiration for Ohio Hopewell came from Illinois, but there can be no doubt that Ohio was the center for the widespread development of what has been called the Hopewell Interaction Sphere.

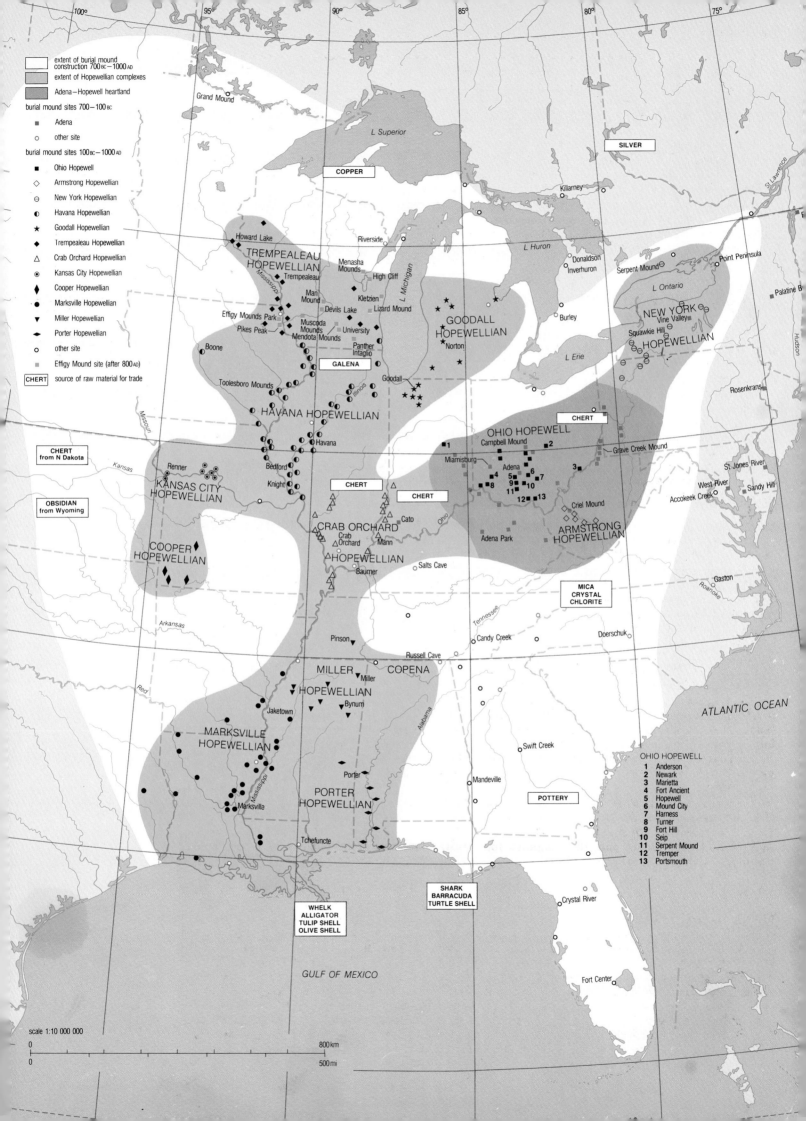

extent of burial mound
construction 700 BC–1000 AD

extent of Hopewellian complexes

Adena–Hopewell heartland

burial mound sites 700–100 BC

■ Adena
○ other site

burial mound sites 100 BC–1000 AD

■ Ohio Hopewell
◇ Armstrong Hopewellian
⊖ New York Hopewellian
◑ Havana Hopewellian
★ Goodall Hopewellian
◆ Trempealeau Hopewellian
△ Crab Orchard Hopewellian
⊙ Kansas City Hopewellian
⧫ Cooper Hopewellian
● Marksville Hopewellian
▼ Miller Hopewellian
◆ Porter Hopewellian
○ other site
■ Effigy Mound site (after 800 AD)

CHERT   source of raw material for trade

Grand Mound

L Superior

SILVER

COPPER

Killarney

St Lawrence

Riverside   L Huron   Donaldson   Point Peninsula

Howard Lake   Inverhuron   Palatine B

TREMPEALEAU   Menasha   Serpent Mound
HOPEWELLIAN   Mounds   High Cliff   NEW YORK

Trempealeau   Vine Valley   HOPEWELLIAN
Man   Kletzien   L Michigan   Burley   Squawkie Hill
Mound   Devils Lake   Lizard Mound   GOODALL
Effigy Mounds Park   Muscoda   HOPEWELLIAN   L Ontario
Pikes Peak   Mounds   University   Norton   L Erie   Rosenkrans
Mendota Mounds   Panther
Boone   Intaglio   Goodall   CHERT   Grave Creek Mound
GALENA   OHIO HOPEWELL   St Jones River
Toolesboro Mounds   Campbell Mound   2
Illinois   1   West River   Sandy Hill
HAVANA HOPEWELLIAN   Miamisburg   3   Accokeek Creek
CHERT   Adena   4 5 6 7
from N Dakota   Havana   8 9 10   Gaston
Renner   Bedford   CHERT   11
KANSAS CITY   12 13   Criel Mound
OBSIDIAN   HOPEWELLIAN   Knight   CHERT   ARMSTRONG
from Wyoming   HOPEWELLIAN
CRAB ORCHARD   Cato   Adena Park
COOPER   Crab   Ohio
HOPEWELLIAN   Orchard   Mann   MICA
HOPEWELLIAN   Salts Cave   CRYSTAL
Baumer   CHLORITE
Tennessee   Doerschuk
Arkansas   Roanoke
Candy Creek   Gaston
Pinson   ATLANTIC OCEAN
Russell Cave
MILLER   COPENA
Miller   Alabama
Jaketown   HOPEWELLIAN   Bynum
MARKSVILLE   Swift Creek
HOPEWELLIAN   Porter
Mandeville
Marksville   POTTERY
PORTER
HOPEWELLIAN
Tchefuncte   Crystal River
SHARK
BARRACUDA
TURTLE SHELL
WHELK
ALLIGATOR
TULIP SHELL
OLIVE SHELL
GULF OF MEXICO   Fort Center

OHIO HOPEWELL
1 Anderson
2 Newark
3 Marietta
4 Fort Ancient
5 Hopewell
6 Mound City
7 Harness
8 Turner
9 Fort Hill
10 Seip
11 Serpent Mound
12 Tremper
13 Portsmouth

scale 1:10 000 000

0 ————————————— 800 km
0 ————————————— 500 mi

objects are sometimes made from red pipestone.

To support the acquisition of goods of such variety and quality the Hopewell created a trade network of almost continental proportions. Obsidian and Grizzly bear teeth were imported from Yellowstone Park, Wyoming. Catlinite came from Minnesota, chalcedony from North Dakota. Mica, quartz crystal and chlorite came from the Appalachians. Galena came from Illinois, copper from upper Michigan. Shells, turtle shell, shark teeth and barracuda jaws came from the Gulf Coast. Silver nuggets were imported from Ontario. Local raw materials included Ohio pipestone, banded slate, Flint Ridge chert and the clays for their figurines and funerary pottery.

As a reflex to the Ohio Hopewell demand for raw materials, Indian communities at their sources adopted the trappings and presumably the practices of the Hopewell cult. Hopewellian variants were grafted to local cultures and flourished for as long as the trade network survived. Beyond these centers other cultures took on the basic idea of burial mound construction until tens of thousands of mounds dotted the landscape from the Plains eastward through most of the woodlands of the East. Hopewellian developments occurred in 13 specific areas. It is not clear what, if anything, some of these Hopewellian centers were supplying to the Ohio Hopewell in exchange for the finished goods and implied ritual information they received.

Conspicuous consumption is a continuing theme in Hopewell sites. The trading system was maintained over time at least in part because there was a steady consumption of luxury goods in burial programs. Most of the Yellowstone obsidian found in Ohio turned up in a single grave; the individual who had acquired this large stock of raw material took it with him when he died. A smaller percentage of obsidian by weight has turned up as finished products in contemporary Ohio sites. Thus burial programs created a steady demand for the goods that moved in the Hopewell trading system, a demand that could not have been equaled if goods had been hoarded as wealth and passed on to heirs.

Hopewell culture was also waning by 400 AD. Although it may have continued for a time in a few core localities, the trade network that had sustained it was breaking down, though the reasons for this are not yet fully known. Perhaps new strains of domesticated plants were being introduced from Mexico and the cultivating ecosystem that sustained Hopewell communities was under pressure from a more adaptive ecosystem. Competition for the rich river bottomlands that supported the new intensive horticultural system could have been incompatible with maintenance of the aging Hopewell trading network. Another possibility is that subtle climatic shifts, perhaps to drier conditions, depressed food production overall and weakened their ability to sustain the trading system and the burial programs that depended upon it.

While collapsing at the center, mound-building traditions in Wisconsin and the adjacent parts of Iowa and Minnesota spun off a development that would last a few centuries longer. Mound construction was turned to the production of effigy mound sites after 700 AD. Mounds were con-

Hopewell Burial Goods

The focus of Hopewell culture was in the Scioto River Valley of southern Ohio, where monumental mounds and other earthworks were constructed between 100 BC and 600 AD. Geometric earthworks were ceremonial enclosures, and many of the larger ones contained arrays of burial mounds. The often beautiful artifacts for which Hopewell artisans are famous were designed as grave offerings. Mortuary ceremonies created a steady demand for exotic grave goods, the raw materials for which were drawn from distant sources.

Unfortunately many mounds were looted for their grave goods before the emergence of modern archaeological techniques and ethical standards. Few artifacts are adequately documented or dated. The map on page 51 shows the locations of major Hopewell sites as well as the raw material sources that were linked to them by the far-flung Hopewell trading network. Finished goods sometimes appear at sites near the sources of raw materials, suggesting that Hopewell was not so much a single culture as an international system linking groups that were socially and linguistically distinct.

Below left This sheet mica cutout is a hand from mound 25 at the Hopewell type site in Ross County, Ohio. Twenty-nine cm. long, it is larger than life.

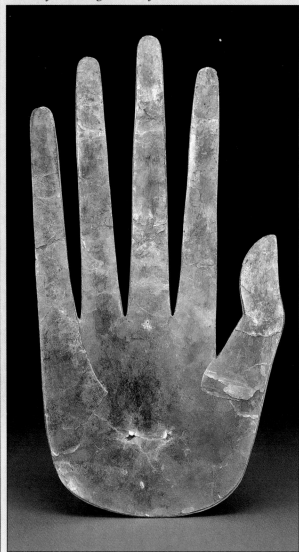

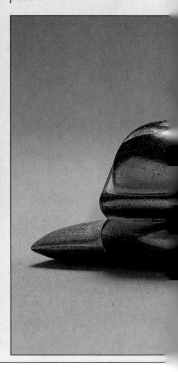

Below The steatite (soapstone) panther effigy pipe is from the Mann site, Indiana. The pipe, which is 16 cm. long, was found in 1916, but its right foreleg was missing. It was recovered in a careful reexcavation of the site over 20 years later. The stylized figure is not standard Ohio Hopewell, but is related instead to contemporary Allison/Copena culture. Unusually in this case the effigy faces away from the smoker and smoke was drawn through the small platform on which the animal's rear legs are perched.

Left This embossed copper falcon comes from mound 7 at Mound City, Ohio, a site now protected as a National Monument. Native copper was mined from glacial deposits in northern Michigan, and shipped to Ohio where it was typically pounded and annealed into sheets. Birds of prey were a popular Hopewell theme. This one is just over 30 cm. long.

Below This beaver effigy platform pipe was discovered in Bedford Mound, Illinois, in 1955. It was carved from pipestone, stands only 4·5 cm. high, and is decorated with freshwater pearl and bone inlays. Tobacco was loaded into a bowl in the beaver's back, and smoke was drawn through the hole at the near end of the platform. Effigies usually faced the smoker.

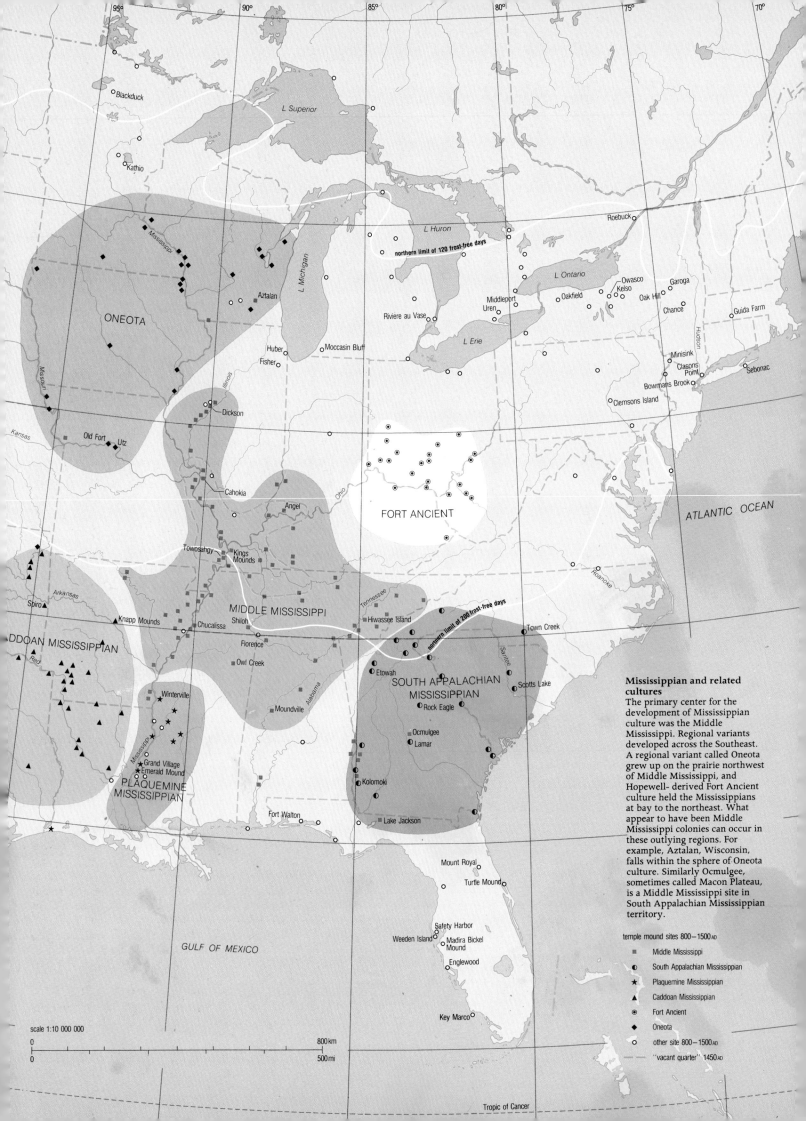

95° 90° 85° 80° 75° 70°

○ Blackduck

L Superior

○ Kathio

Roebuck ○

L Huron

northern limit of 120 frost-free days

○ Owasco
Kelso ○ Garoga ○
Oak Hill ○

L Ontario

ONEOTA

Oakfield ○
Chance ○

Aztalan

Middleport ○
Uren ○

Riviere au Vase ○

L Erie

Guida Farm ○

Hudson

Huber ○
Moccasin Bluff ○

Fisher ○

Minisink ○
Clasons Point ○
Sebonac ○

Bowmans Brook ○

Clemsons Island ○

Illinois

Dickson ○

Old Fort Utz
○   ■

Kansas

Cahokia

Angel

Ohio

FORT ANCIENT

ATLANTIC OCEAN

Towosahgy ○
Kings Mounds

Tennessee

Spiro ▲

Arkansas

MIDDLE MISSISSIPPI

Hiwassee Island ○

Roanoke

northern limit of 200 frost-free days

Town Creek ◑

Knapp Mounds ▲
Chucalissa ■
Shiloh ○

Red

DDOAN MISSISSIPPIAN

Florence ○

Owl Creek ○

Etowah ◑

Santee

Scotts Lake ◑

SOUTH APPALACHIAN
MISSISSIPPIAN

Rock Eagle ◑

Winterville ★

Moundville ■

Alabama

Ocmulgee ○
Lamar ○

Grand Village ★
Emerald Mound ★

Kolomoki ◑

PLAQUEMINE
MISSISSIPPIAN

Mississippi

Fort Walton ○

Lake Jackson ○

Mount Royal ○

Turtle Mound ○

GULF OF MEXICO

Safety Harbor ○
Weeden Island ○ Madira Bickel Mound ○

Englewood ○

Mississippian and related cultures

The primary center for the development of Mississippian culture was the Middle Mississippi. Regional variants developed across the Southeast. A regional variant called Oneota grew up on the prairie northwest of Middle Mississippi, and Hopewell-derived Fort Ancient culture held the Mississippians at bay to the northeast. What appear to have been Middle Mississippi colonies can occur in these outlying regions. For example, Aztalan, Wisconsin, falls within the sphere of Oneota culture. Similarly Ocmulgee, sometimes called Macon Plateau, is a Middle Mississippi site in South Appalachian Mississippian territory.

temple mound sites 800–1500 AD

■ Middle Mississippi
◑ South Appalachian Mississippian
★ Plaquemine Mississippian
▲ Caddoan Mississippian
◉ Fort Ancient
◆ Oneota
○ other site 800–1500 AD
--- "vacant quarter" 1450 AD

Key Marco ○

scale 1:10 000 000

0 _____ 800 km
0 _____ 500 mi

Tropic of Cancer

structed in the forms of panthers, bears, humans and birds. Bird effigies around Madison, Wisconsin, have huge wingspans, one measuring 190 meters. Man Mound was a human effigy 65 meters from head to toe (before its feet were cut off by road construction). One panther figure is actually a negative mound, an intaglio dug into what is now a residential lawn. Effigy mound sites contain flexed and bundled secondary burials, but few grave goods. Were it not for the interesting forms of the mounds themselves, this phenomenon would be just another secondary development on the margin of Hopewellian influence.

In the Ohio heartland the successors of the Hopewell turned their earthwork construction skills to the building of earthen fortifications. The resulting Fort Ancient culture was contemporaneous with Mississippian developments that followed Hopewell as the next widespread development in Eastern Woodlands prehistory.

Right This kneeling feline figure, which stands just over 15 cm. tall, is smaller than it may appear to be. It is one of many rare wooden artifacts that were preserved in the wet Key Marco site in Collier County, Florida. It belongs to late prehistoric Calusa culture, which thrived beyond the reach of Mississippian expansion just before the European discovery of America.

Moundville

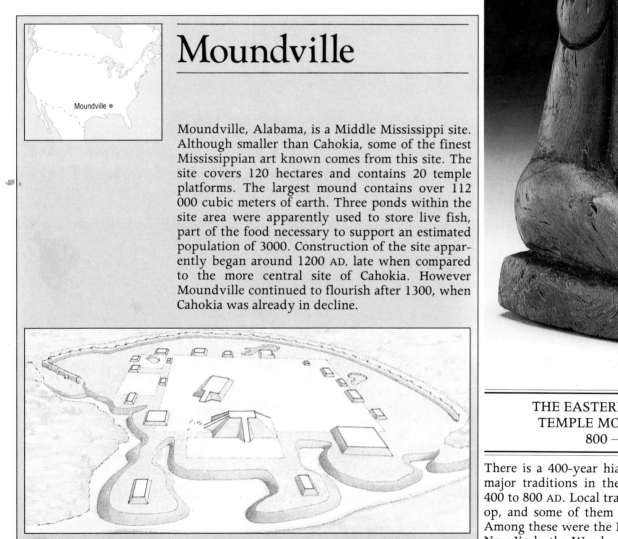

Moundville, Alabama, is a Middle Mississippi site. Although smaller than Cahokia, some of the finest Mississippian art known comes from this site. The site covers 120 hectares and contains 20 temple platforms. The largest mound contains over 112 000 cubic meters of earth. Three ponds within the site area were apparently used to store live fish, part of the food necessary to support an estimated population of 3000. Construction of the site apparently began around 1200 AD, late when compared to the more central site of Cahokia. However Moundville continued to flourish after 1300, when Cahokia was already in decline.

Above Looking southward over a reconstruction of Moundville, Alabama, one can see the principal structures and palisade of this Middle Mississippian city. Borrow pits that supplied material for mound construction were apparently used as artificial ponds in which fish were stored.

Left The hand-eye motif is one of many that comprise the symbolism of the Southern Cult. This one is a detail from a stone palette found at Moundville (see p.58). The meanings of this symbol and of others of the Southern Cult are still being debated by archaeologists.

THE EASTERN WOODLANDS: TEMPLE MOUND BUILDERS 800 – 1500 AD

There is a 400-year hiatus in the development of major traditions in the Eastern Woodlands from 400 to 800 AD. Local traditions continued to develop, and some of them throve during this period. Among these were the Point Peninsula tradition of New York, the Weeden Island tradition of Florida, the Gulf tradition of Louisiana and the Effigy Mound tradition of Wisconsin. However, the interregional Hopewell trading system that had tied many of these together and had even led to their participation in Hopewell cult activities was gone. By 800 AD a new transcendent cultural development had taken hold in the Eastern Woodlands and was expanding by means of a new set of mechanisms. The new tradition is generally known as the Mississippian.

The Mississippian tradition was based on the

Cahokia

The site of Cahokia lies in East St Louis, Illinois. It is the largest prehistoric city north of Mexico. It was founded around 600 AD, and contains over 100 mounds in an area of about 13 square kilometers. At its peak, between 1050 and 1250, as many as 10 000 people lived there. At the center of Cahokia lies an immense earthen mound, 316 meters long and 241 meters wide at the base, rising to over 30 meters in height, called Monks Mound. It contains over 600 000 cubic meters of earth and was constructed in stages by Middle Mississippi Indians carrying baskets filled with 18 kilogram loads.

The center of the city is composed of Monks Mound and 16 smaller mounds surrounded by a palisade on three sides, Cahokia Creek defining the fourth side. The majority of mounds lie outside the palisaded inner core. A smaller mound elsewhere in the city yielded the burial of a high-ranking individual. Around him were caches of arrowheads, polished stone, mica, six sacrificed male retainers and a separate mass grave containing 53 women.

Cahokia began to decline after 1250, but its colonies at Angel, Aztalan and other sites flourished even as the original center of Middle Mississippi culture shrank. In the end Cahokia was at the center of the population collapse that preceded European contact.

The oblique view of the prehistoric city of Cahokia (*right*) is from the west. It is approximately the perspective that would be obtainable with a telescope from the top of the modern arch in St Louis, Missouri. The palisade, its position confirmed through excavation, contained about 120 hectares and 17 major structures around 1200 AD. The community within and surrounding the palisaded core probably numbered well over 10 000. The city (*above right*) contained over 100 mounds, but the largest was Monks Mound, which still rises to a height of over 30 m. Its base is larger than that of the Great Pyramid of Egypt, and approaches the size of the immense Mexican pyramid at Cholula, Puebla.

An effigy bottle of a nursing mother and child (*above*) comes from the Cahokia area and is attributed to an artisan of that Middle Mississippian center. The vessel stands 15 cm. high.

Cahokia was at the center of at least 50 communities in the rich American Bottom region of the Mississippi Valley. There were other centers along the Mississippi and its tributaries, and colonial outposts as well. The political and economic bases of this seeming empire remain uncertain.

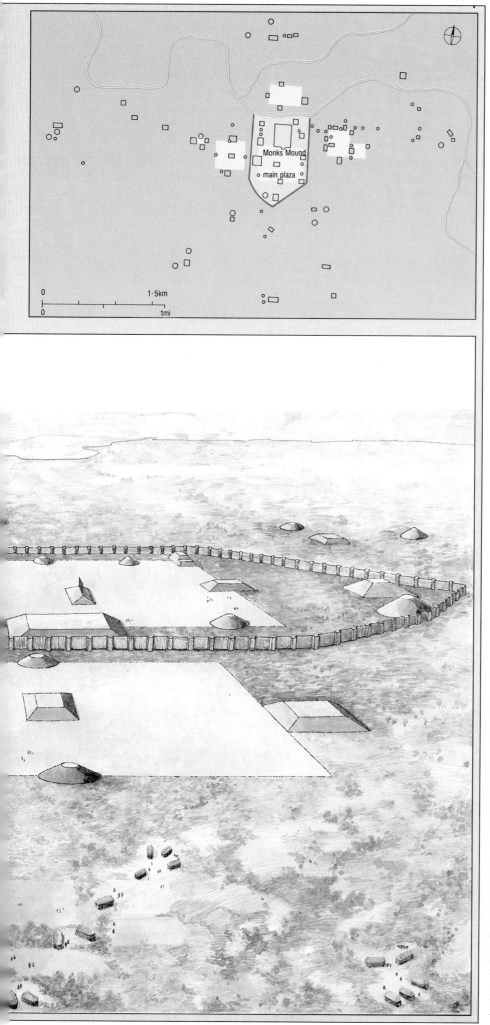

introduction of new strains of maize from Mexico. Earlier strains of true plant domesticates may well have been limited to parts of the Eastern Woodlands that experienced growing seasons of 200 days or more. These included 12- and 14-row varieties of corn. The newer strains appear to have included some that could be adapted to growing seasons as short as 120 frost-free days. These included a hardy 8-row variety of corn. Furthermore, Mexican beans were added to the inventory of plant domesticates by at least 1000 AD. This addition provided an important protein supplement, releasing populations from density constraints based on the availability of wild animal protein sources. Meat was still a necessary part of the diet, but not the critical resource it had been previously. With beans the "three sisters" trio of maize, beans and squash—the dominant domesticates of late prehistoric horticultural systems —was in place. Beans and corn complement one another almost perfectly. Corn lacks two critical amino acids, but in combination with beans, which are rich in both of them, corn provides enough protein for all but the most demanding members of a human population.

The populations of Hopewell times might have had densities as high as 40 people per 100 square kilometers, according to research conducted in Illinois. The ecosystem that supported Mississippian expansion eventually allowed densities of over five times as many. Further, the Mississippian ecosystem focused on the rich and productive bottomlands of the major rivers of interior North America, prime land that was in relatively short supply. The population densities that the new ecosystem made possible when coupled with the scarcity of desirable land led to an aggressive expansion of the new system at the expense of the old. While Hopewellian expansion appears to have been an ideological one that used the trading system as its conduit, Mississippian expansion appears often to have involved colonization and the takeover of prime land by societies having clear adaptive advantages over earlier residents.

In another area of technology, the bow and arrow probably appeared during the hiatus between 400 and 800 AD. The atlatl (spear thrower), which had been the principal hunting weapon since Paleo-Indian times, was not immediately replaced. However the bow and arrow became the dominant weapon through the course of late prehistory in the Eastern Woodlands, and the atlatl was gone by the end of prehistory. A second technological addition was that of true hoes, an indication that the new horticultural ecosystem emphasized plant domesticates much more than the earlier cultivating ecosystem had.

Mississippian settlements were larger than any seen previously. They qualified as true towns, sometimes as preindustrial cities, and often contained temple mounds and other urban features showing Mexican influence. Intensive riverine horticulture supported these centers, principally in the rich alluvial valleys of the Mississippi, Ohio, Tennessee, Arkansas and Red rivers and their larger tributaries.

Mississippian society and economy
Mississippian towns typically contain from 1 to 20

The Southern Cult

Shell carving was an important medium to the Mississippians. Whole conches or shell disks were incised with characteristic designs. A series of very specific motifs is found on engraved shell in sites across the southern Mississippian variants. This complex of motifs, strangely rare in Middle Mississippian sites, has come to be known as the Southern Cult. Common motifs are a sunburst, an elaborate cross, a human eye in the palm of an open hand, an arrow with attached lobes, the forked eye, the weeping eye and several abstract designs. Although common on engraved shell, these motifs also occur on wood, carved stone, chipped stone, painted textiles and embossed native copper sheets. The whole of the Southern Cult shows some Mexican influence, but it also reflects Hopewell and other elements of Eastern Woodlands heritage. Objects bearing the motifs of the Southern Cult appear most frequently at large sites, and are clearly related to ceremonies conducted on and around the large earthen temple mounds. The cult did not become fully elaborated until after 1000 AD, and it lasted until the arrival of De Soto. However the southeastern Mississippians were among the first North Americans to be devastated by epidemics, and much of what we might otherwise know about the Southern Cult died out with its practitioners before it could be recorded. A notable partial exception to this is the Natchez case. French explorers visited Grand Village and Emerald Mound while the Plaquemine Mississippian was still functioning, and the descriptions they provided have often been used by archaeologists to illuminate their discoveries.

The Southern Cult was strongest from the Caddoan area eastward across the South to Georgia, but elements of it can also be found farther north.

Bared teeth suggest that the shell effigy (*bottom left*) represents a trophy head. The forked eye is a familiar Southern Cult motif, and with other incised designs this might represent either tattooed or painted facial decoration. The topknot hairstyle dates further back, to at least Hopewell times. This work is only 6 cm. high.

The shell disk (*below left*) has two holes near the top which probably allowed it to be suspended as a gorget. It bears another male profile, with designs that might represent painting or tattooing.

The repoussé copper profile of a man (*below*) is from Craig Mound at the Spiro site in Oklahoma. The piece is 24 cm. high and bears familiar Southern Cult elements, most notably the forked symbol around the eye.

Right This engraved stone palette measures over 30 cm. in diameter and bears several Southern Cult motifs. Two horned rattlesnakes, twice knotted, surround a hand-eye symbol. The piece comes from the Moundville site in Alabama.

Above right Death is a familiar theme in the Southern Cult. This effigy vessel, which stands about 16 cm. high, was found in the vicinity of Paducah, Kentucky. It represents a trophy head, its eyes lashed shut and its lips shrunken back to reveal its teeth. Multiple perforations in the ears and the central tab on the hairline are common on such vessels, but the purpose of the latter is uncertain.
Right A portion of an incised conch shell depicts a man paddling a dugout equipped with cult trappings.

flat-topped temple mounds that served as platforms for temples or other public structures. In some cases these structures were residences for the elite. The sites were often stockaded, with residences both inside and outside the stockade lines.

Horticulture in the surrounding fields was intensive. In some cases corn fields were planted twice in a single season, each crop being harvested while the corn was still soft and green, to be eaten immediately. Other fields were planted only once, the corn allowed to ripen and dry for storage. Beans were planted with the corn and the vines allowed to use the corn stalks for support, while squash, gourd, sunflowers and other local domesticates were either planted or encouraged around the margins of the fields. Intensive cultivation of this type was possible because deeply rooted grasses could not establish themselves on the frequently flooded bottomlands. Digging sticks and hoes were sufficient for the production of large yields. This was not the case for the surrounding uplands, where the ground remained largely uncultivated until the plow and draft animals necessary to pull it were introduced from Europe.

Unlike Mexico and the Southwest, Mississippian farmers did not manage water, either through irrigation or field drainage. Instead of expanding into areas where water control would have been necessary, Mississippian farmers competed for the best alluvial land. The evidence of warfare is strong for an area that might appear to modern farmers to have been rich in productive land. The stringent land requirements of the Mississippians led to competition for the best fields even in areas where slightly less productive or slightly more risky alternatives were available.

Mississippian societies were apparently ranked societies with permanent offices. Leadership in these chiefdoms was probably permanent and in some way hereditary. Smaller communities were politically satellites of larger ones, and politically dominant central communities contain disproportionately numerous and elaborate public structures. At Cahokia and Moundville, two well-studied Mississippian centers, chiefdoms appear to have achieved considerable complexity, such that some scholars believe that state organization had emerged there. There were probably two or more levels of superordinate political offices at these centers, but state organization remains a hypothesis open to future research.

Portable Mississippian artifacts include polished stone axes, bowls and pipes. In the case of axes, the pieces often include both the handle and the bit, all carved from a single piece of dense stone. Pottery continues the plastic decorative techniques of earlier periods, but new ideas appear in the form of trophy-head vessels, long-necked water jugs, round-bottomed pots and other forms suggesting Mexican influences. Later Mississippian sites sometimes contain painted vessels, rare in the Eastern Woodlands. Many carry two colors and some involved the use of negative painting, in which a wax coating is applied over the first color before the vessel is dipped in the second color. Firing carries away the wax and all of the second color applied over it. The design color is actually the first color showing through where the wax design was applied.

Emerald Mound

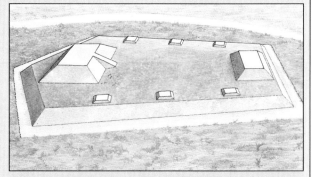

Emerald Mound was at the center of one of the principal villages of the historical Natchez, carriers of the Plaquemine variant of the Mississippian along with some other nations of the lower Mississippi Valley. The site lies near the modern city of Natchez, Mississippi, the southern terminus of the Natchez Trace, originally an Indian trail linking this area with that of Nashville, Tennessee.

French explorers from Louisiana visited the Natchez prior to their destruction by disease and warfare. Their records describe a functioning Mississippian culture; it has sometimes been used as a model for understanding the prehistoric cultures responsible for Mississippian remains here and elsewhere in the Eastern Woodlands.

The Natchez were ruled by a chieftain known as the Great Sun. In this matrilineal chiefdom, leadership was passed to a ruler's sister's son, and all of society was divided into four well-defined classes. There was some upward social mobility according to strict rules. There were at least nine Natchez towns in the 16th century, each of them equipped with public architecture like that seen at Emerald Mound.

Above right Emerald Mound is a natural hill that was flattened and modified to an overall size of 133 by 235 m. The resulting platform was used as a base for two truncated pyramids, the larger of which is almost 10 m. high, nearly 20 m. above the surrounding countryside. With the smaller pyramid at the other end of the platform, and smaller structures on the sides, the structures formed a large plaza on which games and public rituals were conducted.

Right This stone pipe, 17 cm. long, from the Emerald Mound site, represents a kneeling prisoner.

Middle Mississippi and Oneota sites were apparently constructed by the ancestors of Siouan-speaking Indians that in some cases still live in the region. Curiously there may have been an expanding "vacant quarter" in the heartland of Middle Mississippi by 1450 AD. This is much too early for it to have been the consequence of introduced European diseases. Instead it must have been a population collapse or at least serious decline brought about by indigenous factors. New evidence suggests that most preindustrial cities in the New World were population sinks. As such they were large and socially attractive urban centers, but fundamentally unhealthy. Tuberculosis was a native ailment. It depended upon dense and long-term human habitations for its survival. There were other ailments related to crowding and the absence of efficient waste-disposal systems, not the least of which involved endemic intestinal parasites. It now appears that preindustrial cities may well have depended upon a steady flow of immigrants, and that without them fertility could not keep up with increased mortality. If that was the case, the collapse of Middle Mississippi cities at the core of the region can be seen as the natural result of the depletion of the pool of potential immigrants in the hinterlands.

THE EASTERN WOODLANDS: THE NORTHERN IROQUOIANS

Indian bands, tribes and nations peripheral to the Mississippian florescence in many cases continued

to practice mixed-hunting, gathering, fishing and cultivating subsistence patterns. The older and simpler cultivating ecosystem continued to work well in the centuries following 800 AD. However most communities that practiced any cultivation at all gradually adopted the more hardy strains of maize and beans. These could be cultivated as far north as the limit of 120 frost-free days. Beyond that limit even rudimentary cultivation was rarely practiced. Consequently the old cultivation pattern involving squash, gourds and an array of local plants such as goosefoot and sunflower was completely replaced by maize-beans-squash horticulture over the course of the last centuries of prehistory.

However outside the limits of Mississippian expansion the new horticultural ecosystem did not involve intensive cultivation on alluvial floodplains. Instead, an extensive upland pattern emerged. The farmers of the Northeast, for example, practiced shifting cultivation, sometimes known as slash-and-burn or swidden agriculture. A single crop of corn was planted each year, intercropped with beans and squash. Old fields were abandoned when they became depleted or infested with pests, and new fields were cut from the forest every few years. Villages were moved to locations near new fields, often every 20 years or so. Wild foods, particularly deer, supplemented the crops. The large permanent cities of the more intensive Mississippian horticulturalists were never possible in the context of this upland adaptation, but it was nonetheless successful until the arrival of European colonists.

Right Late prehistoric Iroquois villages were typically palisaded. This one is the historical Mohawk village of Caughnawaga, occupied around 1690. But this time epidemics had caused village sizes to shrink, and shorter longhouses having three main hearths as a standard were common. This site is a rare completely preserved Iroquois village and can be easily reached by visitors. Despite their position peripheral to the Mississippian expansion, the Iroquoians were at the center of colonial conflicts between European powers.

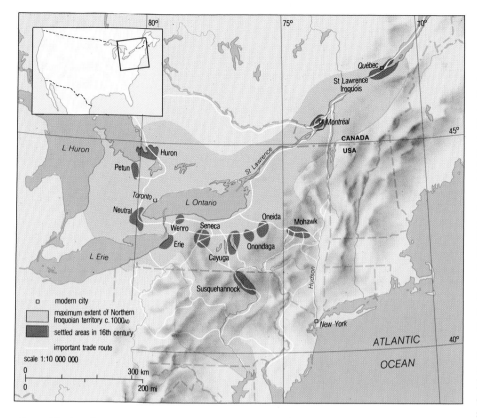

Above: The Northern Iroquoians
The ancestors of the nations that would be known as the Northern Iroquoians probably entered the Northeast between 1700 and 700 BC. Linguistic evidence indicates that they broke from their Cherokee relatives and disrupted neighboring Algonquian languages sometime in that period. Archaeological evidence shows mainly continuity after that time, but by about 1000 AD they were distributed over the shaded region shown here. By 1600 advanced horticulture had allowed, and conflict had required, a contraction into small national territories.

Oneota sites northwest of Middle Mississippi exemplify the upland ecosystem in that region, as do Northern Iroquoian sites in the Northeast. A major difference between the two is that Oneota culture was so altered by European influences by the time explorers pushed that far west that we cannot observe their ecosystem through historical documents. The Iroquoians, on the other hand, are well documented for the decades before their upland ecosystem type had been drastically altered, and they serve as a useful example.

The Iroquoians

The Iroquoians adopted an upland horticultural system based on improved strains of the three sisters (maize, beans and squash) by 1000 AD. The shift toward more dependence upon cultivation soon produced trends toward population nucleation on three levels. First, individual family households began joining together and living in multifamily dwellings. Women were almost certainly the traditional cultivators, and the new importance of horticulture reinforced their importance in subsistence and domestic affairs. The new multifamily houses were probably occupied by families connected by kinship through related women.

The second level at which nucleation progressed was at the village level. Multifamily houses began to be built next to others of the same type in growing villages. To the extent that archaeologists can be sure of such things, it is likely that each house came to hold a clan segment (lineage), and that villages developed councils of lineage heads to manage local affairs. Kinship relations, whether real or fictive, were extended to facilitate cooperative effort and the maintenance of order.

At a third level the villages of Northern Iroquoians began to move toward each other in the course of regular relocations. By the time early European explorers encountered them they had contracted from a very dispersed series of small scattered communities to 13 tribal areas. The 12 Northern Iroquoian nations that resulted from this process of tribalization were the St Lawrence Iroquois, Mohawk, Oneida, Onondaga, Cayuga, Seneca, Susquehannock, Wenro, Erie, Neutral, Petun and Huron.

The violent competition that characterized Mississippian expansion spread to the Iroquoians as well. Many later Iroquoian villages were palisaded, and warfare could account for some of the tendency for villages to grow as households nucleated and for villages to move closer together in the formation of discrete tribes.

Despite the competition a network of trade routes linked Iroquoian villages and tribal village clusters. These included both canoe routes and overland trails. When European goods appeared at coastal contact points in the 16th century, they spread rapidly inland along these preexisting routes. The fur trade that grew out of these early contacts drew the Iroquoian nations into the world economic system, and set up new dynamics of exchange, competition and warfare that would profoundly influence colonial history in the Northeast.

The League of the Iroquois was initially a formal truce between the nations of the Iroquois proper— the Mohawk, Oneida, Onondaga, Cayuga and Seneca. It may be that the League was formed as a means to control worsening intertribal violence, perhaps for the five Iroquois nations to gain an advantage against other Northern Iroquoians and non-Iroquoian neighbors in the continuing cycles of warfare. It is not yet clear whether the League emerged before or after first contact with Europeans, and it is possible that the contact played little or no causative role. Later, however, the League became the vehicle for the formation of the Iroquois Confederacy, a political alliance that was made both possible and necessary by European trade and the competition between contending European powers in North America. At no

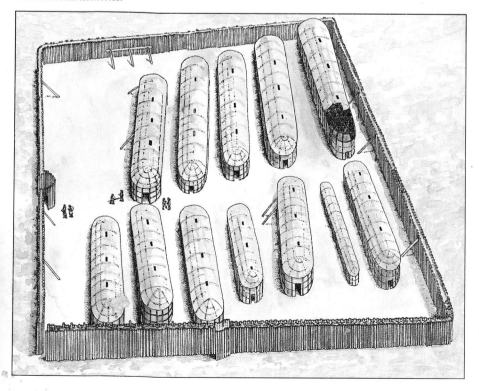

time, however, did either the League or the Confederacy constitute true chiefdom political organization, let alone state organization. It is probably the case that none of the upland horticulturalists that flourished at the margins of Mississippian developments moved beyond kinship-based, ranked tribal organizations. Hereditary positions developed only to the extent that leaders were traditionally chosen from high-ranking lineages. Political organization of villages and ties between villages remained consensual despite the appearance of formality.

The Iroquoian case illustrates what went on beyond the limits of the chiefdoms and near-states that formed the core of the Mississippian phenomenon. Their upland ecosystem and tribal organization were sufficient in the face of the somewhat lower horticultural potential their regions offered. However, the Iroquois case also illustrates that this adaptive system was insufficient when faced with the competition of transplanted European agriculturalists. European colonists practiced all three components of true agriculture: horticulture, husbandry and forestry. Eurasian draft animals, unmatched by any potential domesticates of the American continents, allowed their owners both to produce and to haul fertilizer and plow soils not available to farmers working only with hoes and digging sticks. These advantages also allowed Europeans to practice intensive cultivation in the Northeast, where Indian farmers had been forced to rely on extensive techniques. Europeans enclosed their fields and lived in permanent settlements, while the Indians lived in semipermanent settlements and depended upon shifting cultivation. With these advantages, and backed as well by territorially based nation-state organizations, the Europeans had an adaptive advantage that would have been irresistible even had European epidemics not paved the way for colonization. As it was, smallpox and other Eurasian infections reduced American Indian populations by as much

as 95 percent locally in some instances, clearing the land of competitors sometimes before the first European colonists even saw it.

THE GREAT PLAINS
250 BC – 1500 AD

The center of the North American continent is dominated by northern temperate grasslands. Mammals there tend to be grazing and burrowing species. This was once the heartland of the bison, but pronghorn antelope, Mule deer, White-tailed deer, elk, American black bear and Grizzly bear

Left Before the introduction of the horse, the nomads of the Great Plains were pedestrians. Exploitation of herds of American bison required ingenuity in the absence of machines and powerful weapons. Buffalo jumps such as this one were commonly used. Long converging lines of rock cairns and hunters funneled charging herds to a cliff where the pressure of the stampede insured that at least some of the animals would fall to their deaths. Analysis of butchering techniques indicates that much of the meat was left to rot.

Above The advent of mounted nomadism on the Great Plains completely altered Indian cultures of the region. Former horticulturalists were drawn into horse nomadism, and the cultural and linguistic mix of the Prairies and the Plains areas took on new complexity. Curiously, this very recent variation on the theme of American Indian cultures has come to symbolize the whole in the minds of many. In truth, the development was ephemeral, lasting little more than a century in most areas, usually less.

were all once present as well. In the west the grasslands are higher and drier, and the vegetation is primarily of short-grass species. Climatic differences between the northern and southern portions of the short-grass plains have led researchers to distinguish this variation as well in defining culture areas. The lower and wetter eastern portion of the grasslands is dominated by tall-grass species, and is here called prairie to distinguish it from the drier western plains. A prairie peninsula extends eastward across southern Wisconsin and most of Illinois to northeastern Indiana.

The Great Plains hold plants that produced a variety of seeds, fruits and tubers for Archaic gatherers. A few of these were among the potential cultigens tended by early cultivators in the Eastern Woodlands. However, the Great Plains were so marginal for farming that systems of cultivation had to be developed first elsewhere and then carried up the river valleys of the prairie by communities already adept at horticulture. Consequently the post-Archaic prehistory of the Great Plains primarily involved the spread of eastern cultures or at least eastern influences westward into the region. In a few cases groups having their origins in the Southwest appear to have moved onto the Plains as well.

Although the popular image of the North Ameri-

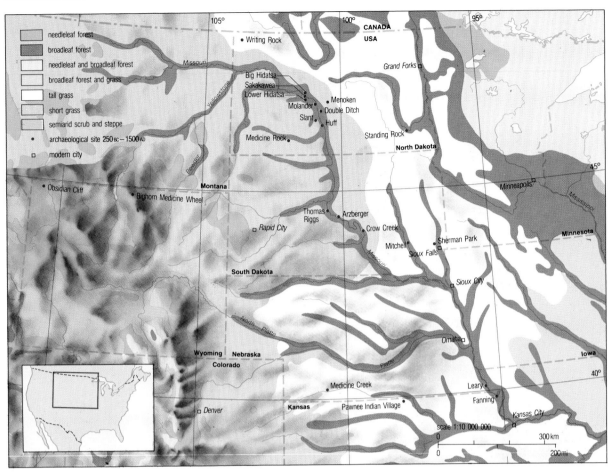

Farmers and hunters of the Great Plains
The Missouri River Valley was a major focus of Plains Village development. Sites of the Initial Middle Missouri tradition number over 35 and are scattered mostly along the South Dakota portion of the Missouri Valley. Sites of what is called the Extended Middle Missouri lie mostly along the North Dakota course of the Missouri. Villages were compact clusters of elongated rectangular multifamily houses. Late in prehistory, drought and population movements resulting from it led to the compression of Terminal Middle Missouri villages into a smaller stretch of Missouri River Valley, where they eventually came to be known as the historical Hidatsa and Mandan. Middle Missouri village sites include Arzberger, Huff, Thomas Riggs, Crow Creek, Medicine Creek, Big Hidatsa, Sakakawea, Lower Hidatsa, Molander, Menoken, Double Ditch and Slant.

Plains Village phases in the Central Plains include the Upper Republican, Nebraska, Smoky Hill and Pomona in Kansas and Nebraska. They date to 1000–1400 AD, and are known collectively as the Central Plains tradition.

can Indian is usually that of the Plains warrior on horseback, that image is of recent origin. The native American horse died out with other Pleistocene game 10 000 years ago, and American Indians did not have access to the horse until the Spanish reintroduced it in the 16th century. The horse made huge bison herds more accessible than they had been to unmounted nomads, and the new adaptive strategy drew many horticulturalists away from their villages and into a nomadic hunting way of life. Just as pastoralism was not possible in Eurasia until after agriculturalists had domesticated herd animals, mounted nomadic Plains Indian cultures were not possible until the introduction of the horse.

Archaic hunter-gatherers on the Great Plains were not numerous. Their population density was low, and eastern cultivators moving westward up the valleys of Mississippi tributaries met little resistance. The first wave of eastern farmers to penetrate the prairie moved in during the Plains Woodland period, between 250 BC and 950 AD. These communities were at least inspired by and perhaps derived from Hopewellian cultures. The Kansas City Hopewellian was established near the modern city, and evidence from these sites indicates that maize was one of the crops grown by these prairie participants in the Hopewell trade network. The Cooper Hopewellian further south is less well known, but appears to have been similar to the Kansas City variant. Prairie Hopewellian communities were up to 3–4 hectares in size. Pottery from these sites shows Hopewell influences. Finished products of native copper, obsidian and stone indicate that they were participating in Hopewell trade, but just what these prairie communities were contributing to the

system remains unclear. The raw materials most sought after on the Great Plains by the Ohio Hopewell included obsidian from Yellowstone Park and high-grade chalcedony from western North Dakota. It may be that the route for these materials was down the Missouri River, and the trade controlled by the Kansas City Hopewellians.

Other Plains Woodland complexes further upstream to the west had simpler inventories. Several have been identified in Kansas and Nebraska, and recent work has turned up evidence that they had penetrated as far westward as eastern Colorado. Evidence from the Southern Plains is comparatively scanty. Although Woodland pottery is sometimes found, the impression is one of a continuing Archaic way of life. Similarly, in the northwestern Plains, Archaic hunting and gathering, particularly communal bison hunting, continued through and after the Plains Woodland period.

Burial mound construction occurred in the eastern Dakotas and southern Manitoba, the northwestern limits of this phenomenon. Some are linear earthworks, others conical mounds. Log-covered pits were often dug to contain burials under the mounds. A Plains flavor was added to this basically eastern tradition in the northeast Plains by the inclusion in many mounds of bison skeletons or skulls. Burial mound construction appears to have spread into this area through Minnesota, a successor of Hopewell similar to the Effigy Mound tradition in Wisconsin. The bearers of the northeastern Plains mound-building tradition were probably ancestral to the historical Dakota, Assiniboin and Cheyenne Indians.

Late in the Plains Woodland period, the bow and arrow was introduced as a new hunting weapon on the Plains. The source was probably among the Athapascan (Na-Dene) hunters of western Canada, who in turn had received the innovative weapon from the Eskimo. Acquisition of the bow and arrow may even have something to do with the successful expansion of Northern Athapascans southward through the western Plains and eventually into the Southwest.

The Plains Village period

The Plains Woodland period was followed by the Plains Village period, which lasted from 900 to 1850 AD. This new wave of eastern influence and eastern colonies had its origins in Mississippian developments. The new Plains Village communities were more substantial than those of the Plains Woodland period in several ways. First, their settlements were comparatively large, permanent, sometimes fortified by dry moats and stockades, and usually equipped with numerous underground storage pits. Second, their houses were multifamily lodges—larger, more permanent and more substantial than those seen earlier on the Plains. Third, they carried a larger and more complex inventory of tools, including more varied pottery, hoes and other tools made from a variety of materials.

The horticultural system implied by Plains Village sites clearly involved the use of advanced strains of maize and beans along with other domesticates. Farming was restricted to the alluvial bottomlands of larger rivers, and in that sense the system copied the intensive techniques of Middle Mississippi horticulture. However, in some other respects the Plains Village adaptation was more similar to the shifting upland horticultural systems found elsewhere around the margins of Mississippian expansion. Plains Village communities probably never achieved chiefdom status, much less the near-state organization of some Mississippian centers.

Their houses were square or rectangular permanent structures, dispersed in small unfortified clusters along river bluffs. Drought appears to have forced the abandonment of many villages during the 13th century, particularly those furthest west in the drier High Plains. The Central Plains village populations fell back downstream in a consolidation process that led to the Coalescent tradition. This in turn spread up the Missouri, taking with it innovations such as the circular four-post earth lodge during the period 1450–1680. The Pawnee remained behind as one of the historical descendants of the Coalescent tradition, while their close relatives, the Arikara, joined the Mandan and Hidatsa in the Middle Missouri area.

At the end of prehistory many horticultural communities abandoned their settled way of life and became equestrian nomads. The cultural map of the Great Plains changed quickly and drastically. Oneota communities became the Siouan-speaking tribes known historically as the Oto, Missouri and Iowa. Similarly the Wichita split off from the Caddoan Mississippian, and the Crow split off from the Hidatsa. Pawnee, Quapaw, Kansa, Osage, Ponca and Omaha communities all left the fringes of the Eastern Woodlands to take up at least part-time bison-hunting on horseback. In the north various Dakota groups moved with the Assiniboin and Cheyenne from settled communities into portable tipi villages on the plains. The Arapaho, Blackfeet, Nez Perce, Comanche and some Shoshone and Apache shifted from an Archaic pattern of hunting and gathering on foot to more productive and interesting mounted nomadism. The Kiowa, whose ancestors had probably been Archaic-style hunter-gatherers on the Plains all along, joined the others on horseback. In the end the Mandan, Hidatsa and Arikara were rare survivals of the late prehistoric horticultural way of life, remaining in their permanent villages and trading for the bison meat that the new mounted nomads brought in from the surrounding Plains.

Archaeological sites attributable to the Plains nomads are often visible only as tipi rings. Notable exceptions are the medicine wheels scattered from Wyoming to Alberta. The largest of these is a circle of boulders with 28 spokes and a boulder cairn at its hub located in the Bighorn Mountains of Wyoming.

These structures may relate somehow to historical Sun Dance lodges, open ceremonial structures used by several historical Plains Indian cultures. The Sun Dance was often performed around the summer solstice, and alignments with the sun's rising point on the horizon on that day have been found in the medicine wheels.

Below Sun symbols occur throughout North America. They are particularly prevalent on later sites, where the decorative arts are usually more developed and the chances for preservation are good. However, earlier examples also survive as petroglyphs (pecked designs) or pictographs (painted designs) on rock outcrops. A Plains hand drum bears a cross symbol similar to that seen earlier on a trophy head effigy.

The medicine wheels of the High Plains (*below*) are apparently giant sun symbols as well as precincts in which sun-oriented ceremonies could take place. The principal spoke on these large wheels is often directed at the point of sunrise on the summer solstice. Historical ceremonial lodges (*below right*) perpetuate the same circular form, often with entrances facing the rising sun.

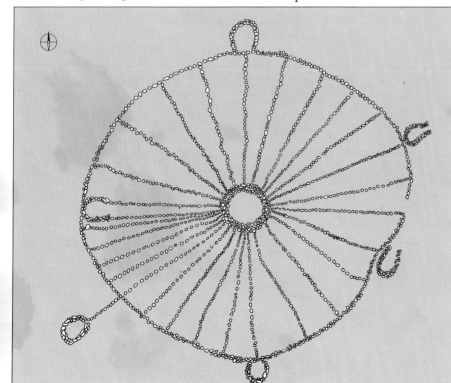

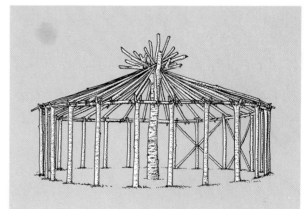

THE DESERT WEST
1000 BC – 1800 AD

The Desert West is composed of two distinct sub-regions, the Great Basin and the Plateau. The rivers of the Great Basin flow inward from the rim of mountains marking its border to brackish lakes, where water stagnates and evaporates. The largest such lake is the Great Salt Lake of Utah. No river drains the Great Basin externally, and scanty rainfall leaves many shallow lakes and streams dry for most of the year. Before the advent of modern irrigation and transportation systems there was too little food in the Great Basin to support more than a thin population and a hunting-and-foraging way of life.

An exception to this severe restriction can be found in the development of Fremont culture in Utah. The Fremont tradition was established as an offshoot of Anasazi, perhaps as early as 400 AD. However it disappeared during the general contraction of Southwest traditions around 1300, leaving no clear modern descendants. (The Fremont tradition is also discussed in the section dealing with the Southwest.)

Elsewhere the Great Basin extends to south-eastern Oregon, southernmost Idaho, the eastern

Left The Bryce Canyon region of the Desert West features the stunning Pink Cliffs as well as scenery more common to the Great Basin. Groves of juniper, piñon and an occasional yellow pine compete with desert shrubs on the ridges. Willows, birches, maples and cottonwoods grow in the cooler and moister canyons. The snow piles deeply during the winter, and prehistoric Indians had to take refuge in substantial winter dwellings.

Below: The Desert West
The Great Basin extends over Nevada, Utah and parts of both Oregon and California. From the mountains rivers flow inward, but evaporation and percolation overtake them; none escapes to the sea. Variation in altitude is the primary determinant of plant and animal life. Prehistoric Indians found greatest success in moving up and down slopes with the cycles of days and seasons.

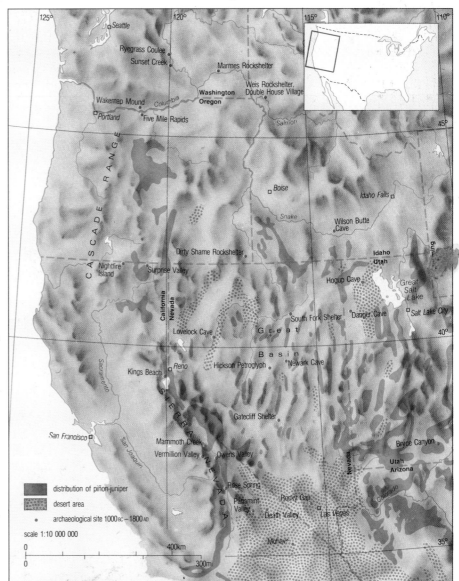

fringe of California and to all but the southernmost corner of Nevada. Nothing equivalent to Fremont culture was ever established prehistorically in this vast area, and cultures there remained essentially Archaic in type until the end of prehistory.

The Plateau is the intermontane province just north of the Great Basin. It is drained principally by two great river systems, the Columbia and the Fraser. The Plateau occupies most of Idaho, northeastern Oregon, eastern Washington, and extends into British Columbia. The principal difference between developments in the Great Basin and those on the Plateau has been that Plateau cultures had access to major riverine resources that the Great Basin lacked.

The Great Basin

Long prehistoric sequences have been established by careful excavation at sites such as Danger Cave and Hogup Cave. The dry caves have yielded not only durable evidence such as projectile points, milling stones and bone tools, but also net fragments, coiled and twined basketry, and other fiber artifacts. Diets have been reconstructed from both the seed and other contents of human coprolites, as well as from the direct analysis of faunal remains in the deposits. Bison, antelope, sheep and deer are present, but are not numerous when compared with small rodents, hares and rabbits. Clearly the Archaic tendency toward maximization of small game in large numbers had progressed further than in most regions by the end of prehistory. Waterfowl and shore birds were taken in earlier millennia, but these are not common in deposits after 1200 BC, evidence that the marshlands were continuing to dry up and that human communities were even more stressed by this rigorous environment.

Nineteenth-century documents indicate that Great Basin cultures often migrated annually between stream-bank camps on the valley floor and piñon groves on the mountain slopes. Piñon nuts were gathered in the fall, stored and used up through the course of the winter. Research in central Nevada indicates that this pattern dates back to at least 2500 BC.

The Fremont tradition displaced Archaic bands in Utah for 900 years. Some may have survived as ecologically marginal hunter-gatherers among the Fremont villages, but most must have been either displaced or absorbed. The Fremont culture collapsed in the course of 14th-century droughts and Utah was taken over by ancestral Shoshone, Ute, Paiute and other speakers of languages belonging to the Numic branch of Uto-Aztecan languages. They expanded northeastward out of a core area in the desert of southeastern California and southern Nevada. Some kept moving, and eventually after the introduction of the horse spread a new practice of mounted nomadism on the Great Plains.

The Numic expansion may be the most intriguing problem currently before Great Basin archaeologists. In cultural-ecological terms they were clearly less advanced than many of the communities they replaced. In one example already cited they replace Fremont horticulturalists, in another semisedentary ancestors of the Klamath. It may be that environmental stress forced out the more advanced adaptations and created new harsher conditions to which ancestral Numic peoples were particularly well adapted. In this case the Numic bands would have been preadapted in the California-Nevada desert to fill the void left when Fremont and other communities departed.

The Plateau

Long-term cultural development on the Plateau differed from that of the Great Basin in large part because of the presence of more moisture and major river systems to carry it to the sea. The Columbian and Fraser systems consequently provided tributaries that served as spawning grounds for large runs of Pacific salmon species. Salmon and other riverine resources provided early Plateau cultures with food supplies that supplemented those also found in the Great Basin. By the 1st millennium BC many Plateau bands had settled into semipermanent villages of semisubterranean earth lodges—substantial structures that were not suitable for the more nomadic bands of the Great Basin. This settlement pattern survived until the historical period.

The exploitation of salmon may have been less well developed, or at least not as ancient, on the Columbia as on the Fraser river system. A steep drop where the Columbia passes through the Cascade Mountains might have kept out migrating salmon for long periods, forcing early Sahaptin-speaking communities to adopt foraging techniques more like those of the Great Basin than those of the Fraser drainage. Meanwhile the Salishan-speakers of the Fraser drainage maintained a strong riverine orientation and relatively close contacts with their linguistic relatives downstream on the Northwest Coast. The Cascade Landslide around 1265 AD restored the salmon runs to the upper Columbia tributaries.

The historical Klamath-Modoc lived in an extension of the Plateau wedged between California, Great Basin and Northwest Coast environments. Their territory centered on Klamath Lake, Oregon, in historical times. They typically lived in large semisubterranean earth lodges, which they abandoned and partially dismantled every summer, living in brush shelters while the earth lodges aired and dried out. This pattern is found archaeologically in the sites of Surprise Valley, California, dating to 4000–3000 BC. Its subsequent disappearance there may relate to a withdrawal by the cultural ancestors of the Klamath and an expansion by early Numic people. Evidence from Nightfire Island indicates that earth lodges were in use there by at least 2100 BC and continued until historical times.

THE PREHISTORIC SOUTHWEST

Archaeologists have defined three major and two minor prehistoric cultural traditions for the Southwest. At their maximum extents these traditions spread over most of Arizona, New Mexico and Utah. They also extended over portions of Colorado, California and Nevada in the United States, as well as Sonora and Chihuahua, Mexico. The major traditions are known by the names Hohokam, Mogollon and Anasazi. The other two are the Patayan and the Fremont traditions, both generally

Below Neither the origins nor the ultimate fate of Fremont culture are clearly understood. However, figurines like this example (10 cm. high) clearly indicate the links this temporary and marginal cultural development had with the Anasazi and Hohokam traditions to the south.

Right: The Prehistoric Southwest
Five traditions cover the later prehistory of the Southwest. Three of them, Anasazi, Hohokam and Mogollon, are regarded as the major Southwest traditions. Two more, Patayan and Fremont, are generally regarded as peripheral to the major developments. The geographical extents of these traditions appear to overlap. In some instances this overlap was real, and communities sometimes found themselves participating simultaneously in two very different cultural traditions. In other cases the overlap is more apparent than real, the consequence of the contraction of one tradition and the subsequent expansion of another into the abandoned area. An archaeological map such as this one, which compresses the product of centuries onto a single sheet, inevitably produces such overlap.

The map shows the maximum extent of each tradition. Clearly, they could not have reached those maxima simultaneously. Perhaps less clearly, each tradition expanded first in one direction, then in another, so that it is probable that in no case did any extend to the maximum shown at any particular point in time. All had shrunk by the time the Spanish arrived.

The major sites of the Southwest are shown against the backdrop of the five traditions. In all cases they are either sites currently open to the public, or sites that although closed are so important in the archaeological literature that they should be noted.

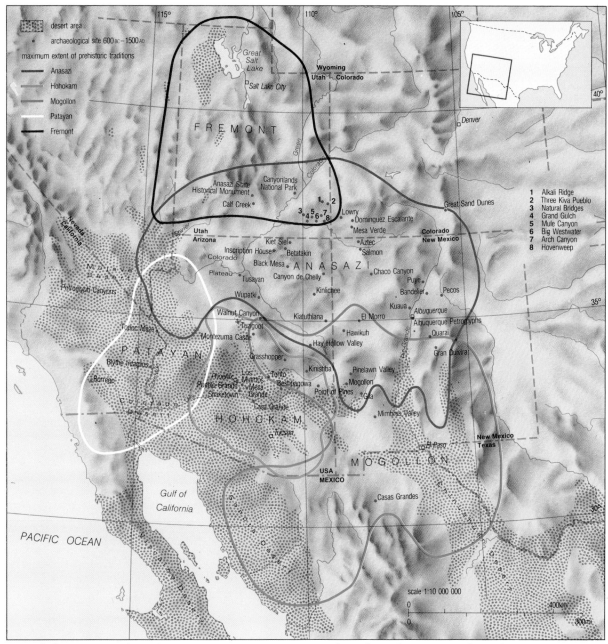

Overleaf Montezuma's Castle is not a castle; nor has it anything to do with the Mexican emperor killed by Cortés. This imaginatively named cliff dwelling is located in the Verde Valley of central Arizona, and is one of many Southwestern sites open to the public. Indians of what is known as Sinagua culture built this and nearby sites, largely influenced by Anasazi culture. Environmental deterioration later forced their abandonment of the Verde Valley.

regarded as marginal to the primary traditions of the Southwest.

Tree-ring dating (dendrochronology) has been used for several decades to date Southwest sites very precisely, often to particular years. The technique has been particularly productive for Anasazi and to a lesser degree Mogollon sites. This has been mainly due to arid conditions that simultaneously made tree rings very sensitive to widespread but minor climatic fluctuations, and allowed their preservation in archaeological sites. Hohokam chronology is least adequately developed because appropriate wood remains have not been preserved in many Hohokam sites. In such cases archaeologists have had to depend upon radiocarbon, archaeomagnetic and obsidian hydration dating techniques.

The prehistoric traditions of the Southwest began to emerge from Archaic beginnings sometime before 2000 years ago. Pottery and horticulture became available from Mexican sources, and the settled way of life that they imply began to emerge perhaps as early as 300 BC. Eventually each expanded to particular limits but the maximum extent of one tradition did not necessarily border on that of another. Areas of overlap were occasionally real, in the sense that villages of two traditions coexisted in an area marginal to both of two traditions. More often, however, areas of overlap were produced as one tradition abandoned an area and another moved into it.

Hohokam
Problems related to dating techniques have made the dating of the origins of Hohokam difficult and controversial. There is little agreement with regard to events prior to 600 AD, although Hohokam chronology following that date is relatively clear. Excavations at Snaketown led some researchers to conclude that the tradition was founded as early as 300 BC. Others have criticized this very early date, and propose a beginning date as late as 300 AD or even 500.

Hohokam culture was centered in the southern Arizona desert, later the home of the Pima Alto and Papago Indians. These groups are widely believed to be the living descendants of the Hohokam tradition. It is possible that the Hohokam tradition intruded into the Southwest from Mexico, its bearers bringing Mexican traits to the prehistoric

Southwest. This possibility is increasingly discounted by archaeologists who prefer a more complex interpretation involving in-place evolution, trade and ceremonial interaction with cultures further to the south.

Hohokam farmers used irrigation to extract crops from the desert. This technique is twice as costly as terracing and four times as costly as field contouring, but productive enough to justify the high cost. Two annual crops were possible, the first in March and April when snow melted in distant mountains, the second in August when mountain rains fell.

Hohokam sites are often marked by red-on-buff pottery types. Vessels often have broad shoulders and low centers of gravity, designed at least in part for maximum display of painted decorations. Other typical artifacts include long-bitted stone axes with deep grooves for hafting, stone palates, deeply serrated projectile points, copper bells and shell ornaments. The palates may have been coated with a thin film of water and used as mirrors, or used more simply for the grinding of pigments. The copper bells were made by the lost-wax method and may constitute additional evidence of continuing trade relations with Mexico, their presumed source. The shell ornaments, most made from material imported from the Gulf of California, were cut into bracelets and beads.

More noticeable on Hohokam sites after 600 AD are their ball courts and low platform mounds, both indicators of Mexican influence. Both Snaketown and Pueblo Grande have impressive ball courts. Rubber balls, the latex for which must have originated in Mexico, have been found in Hohokam sites. Platform mounds are usually only 1 meter high (rarely more than 3 meters), rectangular, and as long as 30 meters. Such structures were concentrated in central communities such as Mesa Grande, suggesting that larger communities controlled both nearby smaller communities and the networks of irrigation canals that served them all. This in turn suggests that Hohokam communities were organized into chiefdoms, as opposed to independent villages.

People living in the Verde Valley of central Arizona, on the northern fringe of Hohokam territory, developed a hybrid culture that drew upon the three major traditions. This culture, called Sinagua, flourished after 1100 AD as a consequence of the deposition of fertile ash mulch by a local volcanic eruption. The florescence caused by the eruption at Sunset Crater is recorded at the sites of Tuzigoot and Montezuma Castle (the latter an inappropriate allusion). The Sinagua people apparently found themselves overextended when normal conditions returned, and the area was generally abandoned after 1300. Many Sinagua groups moved to Hohokam villages where they attached themselves to form dual communities. This might explain Salado culture when it appears in Hohokam territory. The site of Casa Grande, Arizona, is an example of this cultural fusion. While Hohokam people continued to cremate their dead and bury the ashes in traditional red-on-buff vessels, the Salado immigrants made red, black and white polychrome vessels for burial with uncremated remains.

Traditional Hohokam residences were shallow pit houses—actually houses built of wattle and daub in shallow depressions dug down to the hard caliche floor that underlies much of the desert sand in this region. Under Salado influence Hohokam villages became rectangular adobe enclosures after 1300. The outer walls of these villages enclose caliche-adobe (dried mud) structures built entirely above ground. The Great House at Casa Grande was built of successive layers of puddled adobe, the walls massive at the base but tapered toward the top. The Great House was four stories high at its core, although the central room at ground level was filled with solid adobe for strength. Archaeologists speculate that Salado immigrants had been accustomed to working with stone masonry such as that seen at Tuzigoot, that Hohokam country was lacking in the necessary stone material, and that their mistrust of adopted Hohokam adobe technology shows in the massiveness of their constructions.

Crop failures and perhaps Apache raids forced a collapse of the Hohokam political system by 1450. By the time of the first Spanish *entradas* chiefdom political organizations were gone and the irrigation systems they had created and maintained were abandoned. The descendants of the Hohokam had retreated to small scattered villages.

Mogollon

The earliest date for the Mogollon tradition depends on the dating of the first evidence of Mogollon ceramics. Although still uncertain, this dating is less controversial than that of Hohokam. Many archaeologists accept a beginning date sometime in the 3rd century AD. Later, after the first appearance of a diagnostic red-on-brown pottery type, Mogollon settlements expanded along secondary drainages. These settlements were characterized by houses in larger numbers but smaller sizes, suggesting a shift in residential patterns. The dating of these events in the Mimbres Valley indicates that they were advancing in the latter part of the 9th century AD.

The detailed study of the large site of Casas Grandes in Chihuahua indicates that this site was within the sphere of the Mogollon tradition. Archaeologists there believe that major building began around 1060, declined after 1261 and ended by 1350. Furthermore, the location of the site has led some investigators to propose that it was a conduit for intervention by Mexican *pochteca* (a class of long-distance traders known to have been the vanguard for Aztec imperial expansion in the 16th century). Although resolution of the controversy is essential for the understanding of broad trends in the Southwest, more work will have to be completed before the regional picture is clear.

Before 1000 AD Mogollon residences were usually pit houses. After that date there was increasing preference for above-ground multiroom structures. This trend began first in the northern part of Mogollon territory, where Anasazi influences were strong. The shift might relate to the disappearance of male-oriented residence and the emergence of the female-oriented residential patterns known for historical Pueblo communities. The evolution of ceremonial kivas supports this interpretation. Kivas are survivals of the older pit house that served as ceremonial rooms for male kinsmen, who do not live together in female-

oriented residential systems. Some are called great kivas because of their large sizes. These occasionally measure 10 meters in diameter, but occur one to a village, suggesting that they functioned as ceremonial centers for the entire community rather than for a single set of male clansmen. Smaller kivas apparently each served the male members of a particular clan.

During the same period a distinctive black-on-white pottery style developed in the Mimbres Valley. This pottery is characterized by geometric designs as well as stylized human and animal forms. The vessels were often used as grave offerings, and as such were ritually killed by being broken or punctured. The designs have proved to be particularly attractive to the modern artistic eye, and the demand for specimens has led to looting and irreparable damage to many Mimbres sites.

The Mogollon tradition underwent a decline beginning around 1100 AD. This may have been briefly reversed around 1250, but accelerated again through the 14th century. The tradition collapsed in upon itself, as did the other major Southwest traditions as climatic changes disrupted what had always been a precarious system of food production. Drought, crop failure and perhaps marauding Apaches forced the remaining Mogollon communities into a few enclaves. Some remnants may have taken up residence with Anasazi or Hohokam survivors. Zuni Pueblo appears to be composed at least in part of Mogollon descendants.

Anasazi

Although many archaeologists have accepted a date of 3000 BC for the introduction of maize to the Southwest, recent reanalysis has indicated that a date as late as 750 BC may be more appropriate. Villages of pit houses began to appear in the Four Corners area of Arizona, New Mexico, Utah and Colorado by 185 BC. At this time the carriers of the Anasazi tradition did not manufacture pottery, and the early periods of the tradition are consequently called first Basketmaker, then Modified Basketmaker before 700 AD. The first "Pueblo" period begins at this date, and the subsequent periods of the Anasazi tradition are well defined by tree-ring dates.

The initial pit houses of the Anasazi were shallow and simple compared with later examples. As newer houses were dug deeper and deeper, what was once a smoke hole came to be the entrance to an entirely underground residence. Deeper later houses required ventilator shafts to provide a draft to carry smoke out through the ceiling entrance. Small deflector walls regulated the draft in what became an increasingly formal house style. The house floor even came to require a precisely placed *sipapu*—a small hole symbolizing the hole through which humanity originally emerged from the underworld.

The Anasazi developed their own ceramic styles after 500 AD, but with considerable influence from the Hohokam and Mogollon traditions. Distinctive black-on-white types proliferated. Somewhat later the Anasazi began to shift from pit-house residences to above-ground apartments built of stone or adobe. As was the case for the Mogollon, pit houses were retained as kivas, which were used by male clansmen for ceremonial and social purposes.

Mimbres Pottery

Mimbres culture was a branch of the great Mogollon tradition of the Southwest. It centered on the Mimbres River in southwestern New Mexico, and was a relatively small and isolated chapter in Southwest prehistory. The Mimbres River flows only about 100 kilometers before evaporation overtakes it and it disappears in the hot playas around the Mexican border.

The course of Mimbres culture was similar, though played out over time rather than space, for it disappeared before history and the Spanish *entradas* reached the region. What makes Mimbres culture special, despite its small size and the absence of definite modern descendants, is its pottery, which after centuries still delights the eye.

Below The creature depicted in this bowl combines the attributes of man, bat and deer, perhaps indicators of shamanistic transformation. The Style III bowl carries both red and orange paint on a white background, and is consequently classified as Mimbres polychrome.

Below Two highly stylized mountain sheep illustrate why Mimbres bowls appeal to the abstract preferences of modern art connoisseurs. Unfortunately the demand for such pieces has led to the looting of many sites. This average-sized Style III specimen measures about 24 cm. in diameter.

Below A Style III bowl carries the image of a bat, this time uncomplicated by human or other animal attributes. Instead the bat is decorated with rather typical Southwestern geometric embellishments. The piece, which has been only lightly restored, appears to lack a killing hole.

Mesa Verde and Canyon de Chelly

Although Mesa Verde is a national park located in Colorado and Canyon de Chelly is a national monument in Arizona, both are settings for important Anasazi sites on the portion of the Southwest plateau known as Four Corners. In both cases, streams have cut deeply into the plateau, creating steep cliffs that often have protective overhangs. During and after the 12th century, Anasazi masons concentrated new villages in these protected locations, building the cliff dwellings for which the region is famous.

As small square apartments accumulated in cliff dwellings, those built first near the back became storage rooms. Open space at the front was typically excavated and filled to produce a courtyard with circular subterranean kivas. These served as meeting places for the male members of matrilineal clans, who otherwise resided scattered through the village in the homes of their wives.

The cliff dwellings were largely abandoned by early in the 14th century. Following abandonment, most of the Southwest was given up by horticulturalists to the nomadic Navajo and Apache.

Access to Mesa Verde is by automobile. Canyon de Chelly has a tour road only along the rim. Access to the cliff dwellings is usually by way of conducted truck tours.

Below The core of Mesa Verde National Park lies 32 km. south of the park entrance. Tour roads allow visitors to view ruins both on top of and within the walls of the canyons that dissect the mesa. Visitors usually begin with a guided tour of Spruce Tree House, a major cliff dwelling near the museum and park headquarters.

Traces of farming terraces and field lines can still be discerned on the flat top of the mesa. Pithouse villages began to appear in this part of the Southwest by the 2nd century BC. There were apartment dwellings on the mesa top by 700 AD, but after another 450 years they were relocated almost entirely to large niches in the canyon cliffs.

Overleaf Cliff Palace, seen during winter from the cliff above, holds over 200 rooms and 23 kivas. Some of the round kivas, now roofless, can be distinguished in this picture. When roofed they contributed to the flat open space in front of the apartments. The roofs of lower rooms provided balconies for higher rearward rooms, but many of the forward rooms are now gone, and the doorways of upper rooms open on to thin air.

Below A close-up shows a mix of trapezoidal and keyhole doorways, with the pilasters of an unroofed kiva in the foreground. Older interior rooms, buried and darkened by later construction, were used for storage. Cliff Palace had more than the usual number of kivas per residential apartment, leading archaeologists to speculate that this village may have served as a central place for all of the residents of Mesa Verde.

About 150 km. away in Arizona, White House ruin (*right*) lies tucked in its own niche, still protected by the ominous cliffs of Canyon de Chelly.

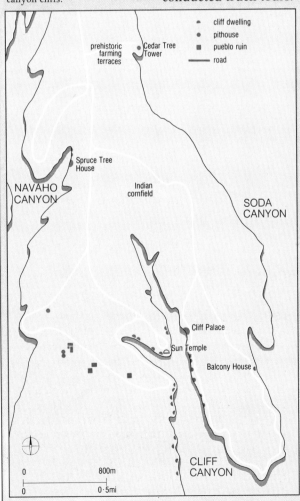

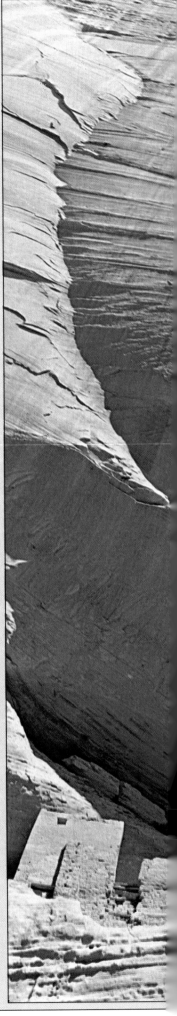

The tradition also expanded widely during this period. New villages appeared further and further from the original Anasazi core area, reaching a maximum extent around 1100.

Surface rooms appeared at Mesa Verde by 700 AD. Up to 950 most Mesa Verde villages were compact apartment complexes perched above the cliffs. By 1150, however, virtually all Mesa Verde villages had moved to protected locations within the cliffs. Large natural rockshelters allowed the construction of complexes such as Cliff Palace, which contains over 200 rooms and 23 kivas. Access was difficult and well protected. Nevertheless the relatively high ratio of kivas to rooms suggests that Cliff Palace served as a ceremonial center for many of the cliff-dwelling villages of Mesa Verde.

The Southwest abandonments have for decades been attributed to a disastrous drought from 1276 to 1299. Acceptance of this hypothesis is no longer universal, but it is clearly the case that the Anasazi and other traditions shrank drastically beginning around 1300. Anasazi retrenchment was followed by invasion. There is little strong evidence for Navajo and Apache invaders until around 1500. Within decades, however, they were joined by the Spanish, and the Indian villages of the Southwest came under both native and foreign domination. Nevertheless the descendants of the major Southwest traditions persist today as vigorous communities.

Fremont

The Fremont tradition was a peripheral culture that developed in Utah as a consequence of Anasazi influence. This development may have begun as early as 400 AD but whether it originated in the migration of Anasazi people into Utah or was a local development based only on Anasazi influence is still being debated. The bearers of Fremont culture could have been the local Uto-Aztecan ancestors of modern groups such as the Shoshone. One investigator has even suggested that they were Na-Dene speakers and connected to the Navajo/Apache and the expansion of their language family southward from Canada. Most archaeologists appear to accept an evolution of Fremont in place—the consequence of Archaic origins and Anasazi influence. Fremont sites began to be abandoned as early as 950 AD. The culture was contracting by 1150 and few sites survived beyond 1300. The ultimate fate of the Fremont people remains unknown.

Patayan

The Patayan tradition is sometimes called Hakataya, but in either case it is considered a peripheral tradition in Southwest prehistory. The tradition appears to have been borne by the Hokan-speaking (specifically Yuman) Indians of the Colorado River region. Modern descendants include the Yumans of western Arizona and southeastern California. The earliest ceramics date to around 500 AD, but the tradition never developed in the large villages of the major Southwest traditions. Several regional variants have been defined, one of which led to Sinagua culture in the Verde Valley of central Arizona. This culture has already been noted in connection with its florescence and eventual fusion with the Hohokam tradition.

Chaco Canyon

Although archaeologists still disagree about the specific nature of the Chaco phenomenon, there is no doubt that it existed. The Chaco system, however it is defined, eventually spread over 53 000 square kilometers of the San Juan drainage and surrounding uplands. Large planned towns concentrate in Chaco Canyon (now protected as a national monument), but there were also major outliers such as Aztec and Salmon ruins. There are 125 known planned towns with public architecture in this network, many connected by prehistoric roads, of which over 400 kilometers have been identified thus far. The most impressive towns in Chaco Canyon are large D-shaped communities, for example Pueblo Bonito and Chetro Ketl.

Chaco sites flourished from 950 to 1300 AD. They remained central to a widespread system of trade even as the boundaries of the Anasazi tradition shifted. Chaco Canyon was on the northern edge of the system in the 10th and 11th centuries, but on its southern edge in the 12th century. Some archaeologists argue that Chaco Canyon was both a ceremonial center and the center of trade in food and luxury goods, particularly turquoise. Others see the expansion of the Chaco phenomenon as less a systemic expansion designed to bring in more goods than a population expansion designed to accommodate a growing Chaco population. Points of disagreement focus on whether outliers were previously independent towns drawn into the system or colonies sent out by it. Related to this is the debate over whether the road network and the trading system it supported were primarily designed to redistribute subsistence goods or luxury items. It may be that all of these explanations apply.

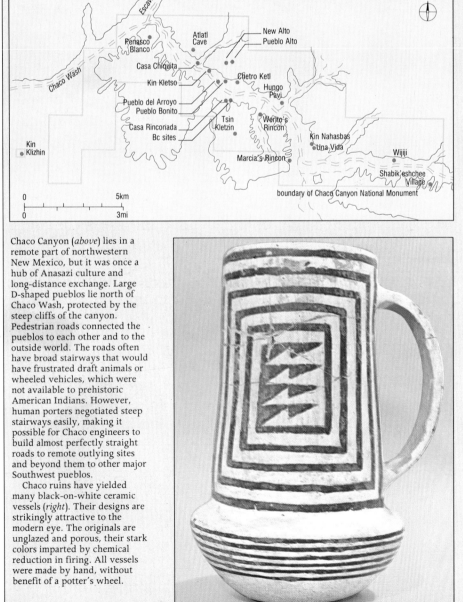

Chaco Canyon (*above*) lies in a remote part of northwestern New Mexico, but it was once a hub of Anasazi culture and long-distance exchange. Large D-shaped pueblos lie north of Chaco Wash, protected by the steep cliffs of the canyon. Pedestrian roads connected the pueblos to each other and to the outside world. The roads often have broad stairways that would have frustrated draft animals or wheeled vehicles, which were not available to prehistoric American Indians. However, human porters negotiated steep stairways easily, making it possible for Chaco engineers to build almost perfectly straight roads to remote outlying sites and beyond them to other major Southwest pueblos.

Chaco ruins have yielded many black-on-white ceramic vessels (*right*). Their designs are strikingly attractive to the modern eye. The originals are unglazed and porous, their stark colors imparted by chemical reduction in firing. All vessels were made by hand, without benefit of a potter's wheel.

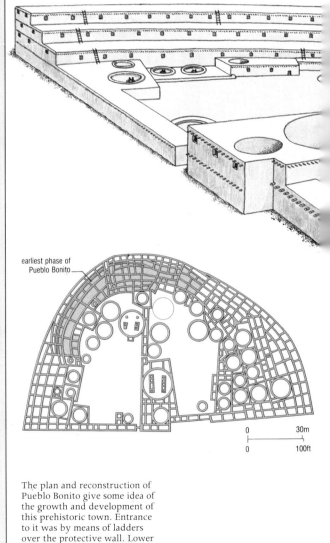

earliest phase of Pueblo Bonito

The plan and reconstruction of Pueblo Bonito give some idea of the growth and development of this prehistoric town. Entrance to it was by means of ladders over the protective wall. Lower interior rooms were probably used mainly for storage. The step-like design allowed residents to use the roofs of lower rooms as open balconies.

Pueblo Bonito (*below*), the most impressive of the D-shaped pueblo ruins in Chaco Canyon, is here seen from the top of the canyon cliff to its rear. Interior details of the great kiva near the flat side of the village are visible. Other kivas, some nearly as large, can be seen arrayed nearer the residential rooms built around the curving real wall of the pueblo. Steel beams now brace the rear wall, which once rose four stories. The site covers over a hectare and once held at least 800 rooms (*center*). The population was probably over 1200. It was the largest apartment building in North America until a larger one was constructed in 19th-century New York City. Chaco Canyon was the hub of a network of ancient roads that linked it to several outlier villages. The villages were consequently linked to the center of a major prehistoric system of trade and interchange.

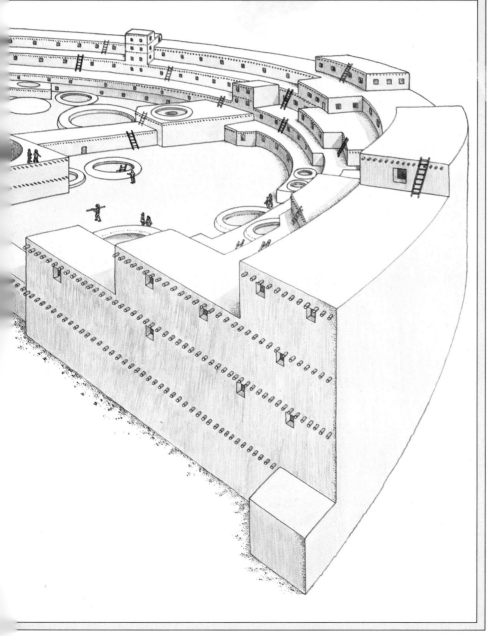

CALIFORNIA
500 – 1800 AD

The California culture area falls almost entirely within the borders of the modern state. Although the culture area is not unusually large, it contains an unusual amount of environmental diversity. Some of it results from variation in latitude—ten degrees or over 1100 kilometers from north to south. Some results from variation in altitude—from sea level to 4400 meters. Some results from topography, which forces heavy rainfall on some western slopes while shielding more interior valleys from moisture. Thus there are deep redwood forests, oak parkland, near desert and tracts of chaparral scrub. Sharp environmental variation from one locale to another has produced a multitude of microenvironments in California, many of them rich in natural food resources. These conditions both discouraged the adoption of even rudimentary cultivation, and promoted the tendency for communities to restrict themselves to small territories.

As is still the case today, California attracted and accommodated immigrants of many backgrounds. There was an unusual number of separate language families. Indians from diverse backgrounds adapted in small groups to an equally diverse environmental mosaic. The result by the end of prehistory was a complex series of about 500 small tribal organizations which varied widely in speech, subsistence, technology, religion and social organization. Yet all of them continued to practice an essentially Archaic way of life until European colonization of the region.

Ironically the hunting and foraging way of life was so successful in this rich series of environments that California had a relatively dense aboriginal population. The contrast of this with other regional population densities in North America was probably not as great as was once thought, but it was nonetheless high.

The complexity of California prehistory compels archaeologists to discuss it either at great length and in considerable detail, or alternatively at uncomfortably high levels of generalization. Space considerations necessitate the latter approach in this section.

Beginning in the Archaic, by perhaps 2000 BC, California Indians moved steadily away from highly diffuse adaptations and toward exploitation of specific resources that were locally abundant. In one locale the primary resource might be acorns, in another sea mammals, in yet another fish. This specialization paralleled the rudimentary cultivation practices of Late Archaic Indians elsewhere in temperate North America. By 500 AD this particular process had produced about 500 specialized small tribes.

Patterns of deliberate surplus food production, storage, trade and redistribution were all well developed. These mechanisms allowed them to buffer both predicted seasonal shortages and unpredictable sporadic shortages in food supplies. Surplus food could be stored for one's own use or for trade with nearby groups facing an unexpected shortfall. Shell money emerged as a mechanism to

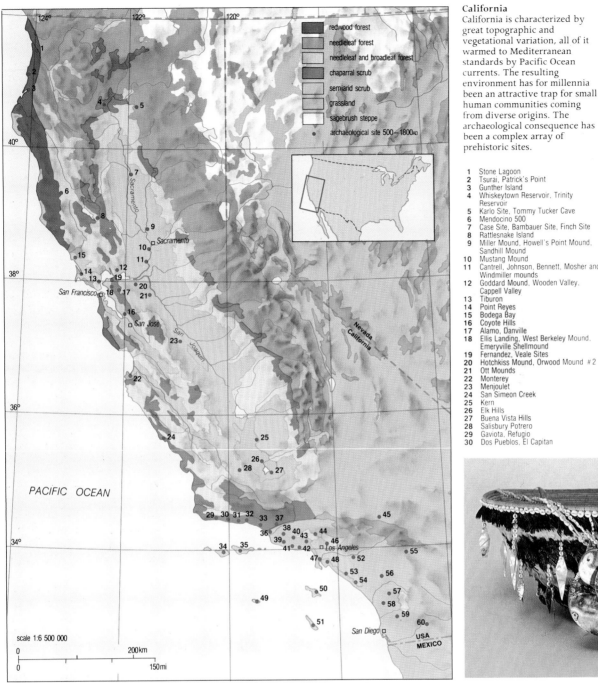

redwood forest
needleleaf forest
needleleaf and broadleaf forest
chaparral scrub
semiarid scrub
grassland
sagebrush steppe
● archaeological site 500–1800AD

PACIFIC OCEAN

scale 1:6 500 000

0 ———— 200km
0 ———— 150mi

California

California is characterized by great topographic and vegetational variation, all of it warmed to Mediterranean standards by Pacific Ocean currents. The resulting environment has for millennia been an attractive trap for small human communities coming from diverse origins. The archaeological consequence has been a complex array of prehistoric sites.

1 Stone Lagoon
2 Tsurai, Patrick's Point
3 Gunther Island
4 Whiskeytown Reservoir, Trinity Reservoir
5 Karlo Site, Tommy Tucker Cave
6 Mendocino 500
7 Case Site, Bambauer Site, Finch Site
8 Rattlesnake Island
9 Miller Mound, Howell's Point Mound, Sandhill Mound
10 Mustang Mound
11 Cantrell, Johnson, Bennett, Mosher and Windmiller mounds
12 Goddard Mound, Wooden Valley, Cappell Valley
13 Tiburon
14 Point Reyes
15 Bodega Bay
16 Coyote Hills
17 Alamo, Danville
18 Ellis Landing, West Berkeley Mound, Emeryville Shellmound
19 Fernandez, Veale Sites
20 Hotchkiss Mound, Orwood Mound #2
21 Ott Mounds
22 Monterey
23 Menjoulet
24 San Simeon Creek
25 Kern
26 Elk Hills
27 Buena Vista Hills
28 Salisbury Potrero
29 Gaviota, Refugio
30 Dos Pueblos, El Capitan

31 Goleta Slough
32 Burton Mound
33 Rincon Point
34 Santa Rosa Island
35 Santa Cruz Island
36 Shishilop, Pitas Point
37 Soule Park, Mutah Flat
38 Conejo Rock Shelter, Ventura 70
39 Big Sycamore, Little Sycamore and Deer Canyons
40 Century Ranch, Medea Village, Medea Creek
41 Zuma Creek, Arroyo Sequit, Lechuza Canyon
42 Malibu Canyon, Paradise Cove, Corral Canyon, Point Dume, Trancas Canyon
43 Topanga Canyon, Mulholland
44 Chatsworth, Encino, Big Tujunga
45 Las Flores Ranch
46 Yang-na
47 Malaga Cove
48 Bixby Slough
49 San Nicolas Island
50 Santa Catalina Island
51 San Clemente Island
52 Santiago Canyon, Black Star Canyon
53 Newport Bay, Big Canyon
54 Goff's Island, Cotton Point
55 Snow Creek
56 Temecula Creek, Vail Ranch
57 Pauma
58 Rancho San Luis Rey
59 San Vicente
60 Pine Valley, Dripping Springs

make the system work more efficiently. Like modern money it stored value with which food or other items could be acquired at a later date.

Local production teams were organized to harvest acorns, catch fish or trap rabbits in large numbers, and the high degree of environmental diversity made it possible to redistribute surplus production to neighboring groups even though the only means of transportation were canoe and human porters. Such patterns of food redistribution are impossible in regions where the lack of significant environmental diversity prevents the overproduction of goods for redistribution to nearby areas where they are either unavailable or in short supply.

In other parts of the world where extreme environmental diversity allowed such patterns of surplus production and redistribution to emerge, the development has often brought regional political control with it. Such was the case in highland South America, where environmental diversity due mainly to altitude variation allowed local

specialization in food production. Chiefdoms and true state organizations emerged to control trade and redistribution there, and "empire" is not too strong a word to describe the evolutionary endpoint of that process. Curiously, nothing similar emerged in California. The reason may have something to do with the lack of horticulture in California, and the consequent absence of field ownership or water-control systems.

Political leadership in California was usually in the hands of a local big man. Such an individual often rose to high rank through the force of his own personality. In many cases he organized and led the local production teams. He was often a wealthy individual who held the loyalty of his community by redistributing that wealth through the kin-based society he led, whether as bribes, charity or the sponsorship of feasts and religious celebrations. Trade with nearby communities was conducted through such men, none of whom seems ever to have significantly extended his political powers much beyond his own locale. How and

Above The Pomo Indians of California are famous for their exquisite gift baskets. Although fine ceramics had been made for centuries in the nearby Southwest, the craftswomen of aboriginal California preferred to turn their talents to the elaboration of coiled basketry. Fine coils were stitched together with very thin wrapping fibers, and the feathers of hummingbirds, woodpeckers, quail and other small birds were worked into the design on the exterior surface. Layers of feathers were added to form the final feather mosaic.

why California cultures developed dense populations, stable food supplies and great wealth without developing more complex forms of political organization is a subject of continuing interest to anthropologists.

The diversity of 500 specialized cultures in California has produced a bewildering array of very specific artifact types. Coastal cultures, lacking seeds and nuts, depended instead on mussels, abalone and marine mammals. In their sites are found beads, pendants, fishhooks and amulets of shell. Interior cultures dependent upon seeds, especially acorns in some areas, developed elaborate mortars, pestles and milling stones. Pottery, available in the nearby Southwest, was ignored in preference for basketry, which in turn came in as many styles as there were local cultures to produce it. Perhaps the most famous are the fine Pomo baskets with their surface decorations of hummingbird, woodpecker and other bird feather mosaics. The Canaliño people, hunters of sea mammals and ancestors of the historical Chumash, carved stone bowls, perhaps for use as oil lamps, and built large

plank canoes. The Chumash are also known for their large colorful pictographs, many of which are still preserved on rock outcrops in coastal southern California. Steatite became a popular raw material for the manufacture of both stone bowls and smoking pipes in southern California. The bow and arrow was introduced to California before this final period of prehistory, and each local culture appears to have made its own series of distinctive projectile point types. These few examples indicate the complexity of local specifics in California archaeology.

THE NORTHWEST COAST
3000 BC – 1800 AD

Compared with California there is little vegetational diversity on the Northwest Coast. Mountain ranges that parallel the coast have produced a temperate rain forest along the entire strip of coastal land from the Alaska panhandle to the northern border of California. Ocean currents and relatively warm air masses drench the Northwest Coast in misty rainfall from fall until spring, encouraging natural food production and swelling streams. The major Columbia and Fraser Rivers that pierce the mountains from interior sources as well as the smaller rivers that rise in the mountains are all filled with migratory fish during the spring and summer months. Although the Northwest Coast lacked the complex local environmental diversity of California, it had nearly the same level of environmental richness spread uniformly over the culture area. The consequence for the cultures found here in historical times was an adaptive pattern well known for its unexpectedly dense populations, elaborate ceremonialism, and emphasis on both material wealth and the social rank it represented.

Archaic cultures had moved into the Northwest Coast by at least 7700 BC. It may be that the region was too cut up by glacial ice or otherwise too hostile to attract people before that date. It is also possible that older sites have been lost due to post-Pleistocene rise in sea level.

After 3000 BC all parts of the Northwest Coast began to participate in a general development toward cultural patterns seen at the end of prehistory. Exploitation of marine shellfish led to the gradual accumulation of large shell middens. Bone and ground-slate implements diagnostic of Northwest Coast cultures begin to appear in sites around Prince Rupert by 3500 BC. By about the time of Christ stone labrets, stone clubs and ground-slate points are common. These are later replaced by composite tools making greater use of bone and shell. A similar sequence of events is found around the Strait of Georgia and in the Fraser Canyon.

Subsistence patterns over the last 2000 years have emphasized the exploitation of fish runs, sea-mammal hunting and shellfishing, as well as more traditional fishing, fowling and land-mammal hunting activities. The intensive foraging pattern allowed the emergence of large nearly permanent settlements. The giant cedar trees of the region provided straight-grained trunks which Indians learned to split into planks using only wedges and mauls. The planks in turn became the principal

Below: The Northwest Coast
There is less regional vegetational diversity on the Northwest Coast than in the California area south of it. The region is tightly constrained by high mountains that rise just east of the coastline. Most rivers are relatively short mountain streams: only two, the Fraser and the Columbia, penetrate the mountains to drain the interior plateau.

Although archaeology has disproved the notion that the Northwest Coast came to be inhabited only in recent millennia, it is still the case that travel overland is difficult. The topography promoted travel by boat, and encouraged the development of linguistically distinct cultural enclaves in pockets along the coast. Once established, the Northwest Coast Indians throve amid rich and varied natural resources, producing distinctive artwork that still lives.

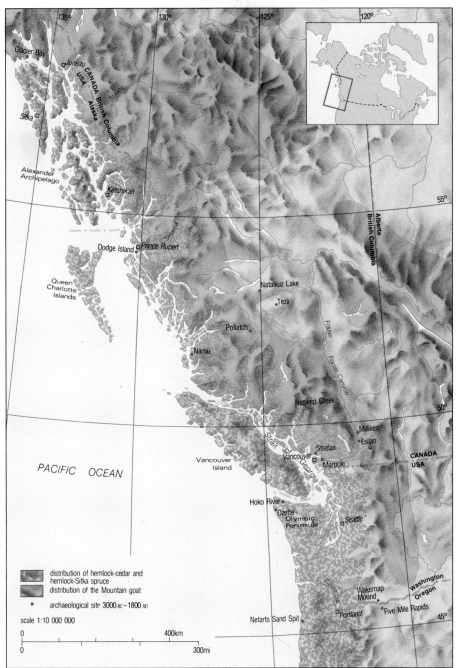

distribution of hemlock-cedar and hemlock-Sitka spruce
distribution of the Mountain goat
• archaeological site 3000 BC–1800 AD
scale 1:10 000 000
0 _____ 400km
0 _____ 300mi

building materials for Northwest Coast houses. Dugout boats were also developed, and by the end of prehistory local craftsmen were building large war canoes of dugout logs.

The Northwest Coast emphasis on wealth and social stratification was well established by 500 AD. The natural wealth of the environment produced huge food surpluses, but the environment was so uniform and the range of foods available in virtually every locale so great that trade and redistribution of subsistence goods were never much developed between communities. The exception may be a tendency for upstream and downstream relatives on individual river systems to exchange goods, but even here the exchange was not critical enough to lead to the emergence of higher-level political systems.

However, natural wealth led to the production of surplus goods and elaborate material items. Mountain goat hair was used to produce fancy Chilkat blankets. Shell, copper and bone were used to decorate pipes, spoons and other artifacts, or to make elaborate ceremonial goods. Curiously, work in ground slate and other stone material was gradually abandoned. Late in prehistory iron began to appear in flotsam from the western Pacific. The cutting tools that could be made from iron helped spur the development of decorative wood carving, for which Northwest Coast cultures may be best known. Their elaborately decorated totem poles, carved boxes, house poles, planks, boats and masks appear to have been a rather late development, perhaps replacing waning interest in stone carving.

Carved wooden goods joined copper, basketry and textile goods as indicators of wealth and rank. These became both the symbols and currency of rank and social mobility. The eventual end product was the historical potlatch ceremony, which featured extravagant gift-giving or even the deliberate destruction of hoarded surpluses for the sake of rank validation. Piles of trade blankets, boxes of refined candlefish oil, copper plates and even human slaves were sometimes ritually destroyed when giving them away failed to be a sufficiently strong statement.

Many known sites on the Northwest Coast are late. This is particularly the case in the southern portion of the region. The site of Ozette on the Olympic Peninsula is especially spectacular. The nearby Hoko River sites are also impressive. Despite the lateness of many known sites, the mix of seemingly unrelated language families on the Northwest Coast suggests long traditions of separate development. The Tlingit of southern Alaska may have broken away from early Na-Dene in interior Canada and moved across the mountains to the coast. The Coast Salish speakers of coastal Washington and British Columbia have obvious common roots with the Salish of the interior Fraser drainage. However, the small Wakashan, Chimakuan, Oregon Penutian and Chinookan language families, as well as the isolated Haida and Tsimshian, all seem to belong to peoples without roots in the rest of North American prehistory. Linguistics and archaeology will gradually clarify their circumstances, but at present there is a wide gap between incomplete archaeological sequences and the deep splits implied by linguistic contrasts.

Left Northwest Coast totem poles were carved for a variety of reasons. Some were heraldic in character, depicting in colorful blendings of myth and history the origins of the family or clan that owned it. Some told of important historical events. Others were mortuary poles, erected to commemorate the dead. Some were simple house posts turned into works of art by architects that were not satisfied with mere utility. Still others were potlatch poles, erected to commemorate the status-giving extravaganzas for which the Northwest Coast is famous. A few served more specialized purposes, such as to ridicule and shame a scoundrel.

PART FOUR
MESOAMERICA

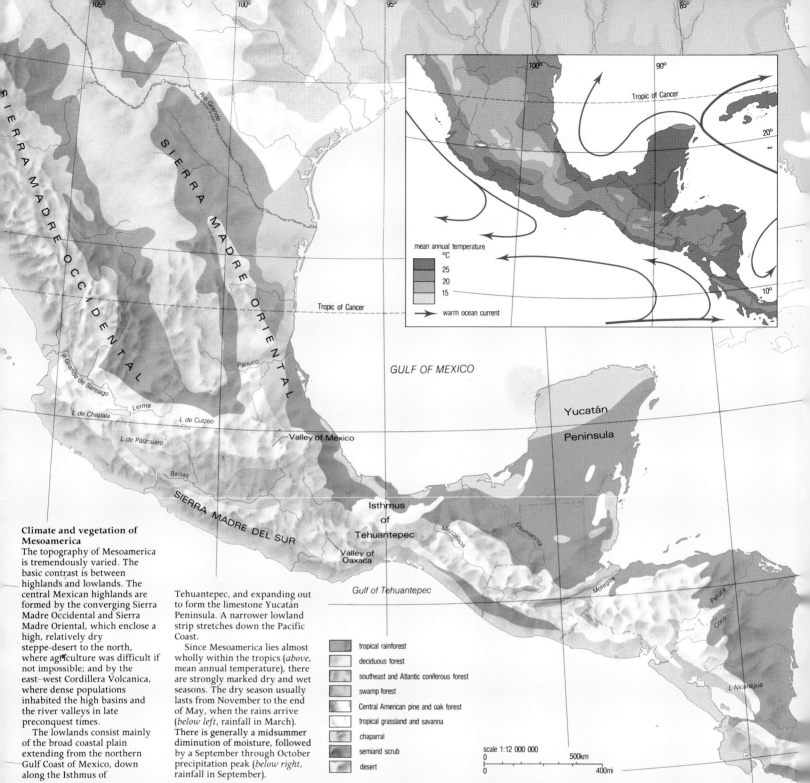

GULF OF MEXICO

Yucatán

Peninsula

SIERRA MADRE OCCIDENTAL

SIERRA MADRE ORIENTAL

SIERRA MADRE DEL SUR

Río Grande

Pánuco

Río Grande de Santiago

Lerma

L de Chapala

L de Cutzeo

L de Pátzcuaro

Valley of Mexico

Balsas

Isthmus
of
Tehuantepec

Valley of
Oaxaca

Gulf of Tehuantepec

Mezcalapa

Usumacinta

Motagua

Patuca

Coco

L. Nicaragua

Tropic of Cancer

mean annual temperature
°C
25
20
15
→ warm ocean current

Tropic of Cancer

Climate and vegetation of Mesoamerica

The topography of Mesoamerica is tremendously varied. The basic contrast is between highlands and lowlands. The central Mexican highlands are formed by the converging Sierra Madre Occidental and Sierra Madre Oriental, which enclose a high, relatively dry steppe-desert to the north, where agriculture was difficult if not impossible; and by the east–west Cordillera Volcanica, where dense populations inhabited the high basins and the river valleys in late preconquest times.

The lowlands consist mainly of the broad coastal plain extending from the northern Gulf Coast of Mexico, down along the Isthmus of Tehuantepec, and expanding out to form the limestone Yucatán Peninsula. A narrower lowland strip stretches down the Pacific Coast.

Since Mesoamerica lies almost wholly within the tropics (*above*, mean annual temperature), there are strongly marked dry and wet seasons. The dry season usually lasts from November to the end of May, when the rains arrive (*below left*, rainfall in March). There is generally a midsummer diminution of moisture, followed by a September through October precipitation peak (*below right*, rainfall in September).

tropical rainforest
deciduous forest
southeast and Atlantic coniferous forest
swamp forest
Central American pine and oak forest
tropical grassland and savanna
chaparral
semiarid scrub
desert

scale 1:12 000 000
0   500km
0   400mi

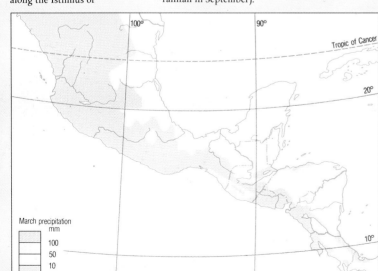

March precipitation
mm
100
50
10

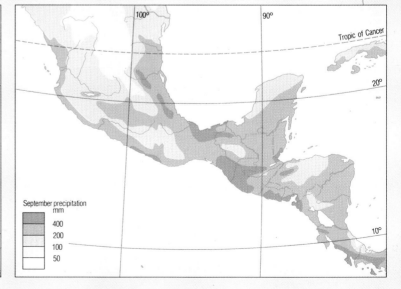

September precipitation
mm
400
200
100
50

84

CULTURES AND THE NATURAL SETTING

One of the most populous areas of preconquest Mesoamerica was the region of river valleys and basins within and around the Cordillera Volcanica—the mass of mountains that lies across central Mexico. Rich volcanic soils and reliable seasonal rainfall permitted successful agriculture, on which rose the state of Teotihuacan and the empire of the Aztec. Xochicalco (*below*) lies south of the Cordillera, which is seen in the background. It flourished in the 8th century, as Teotihuacan to the north was in decline. It may have been under Maya governance, providing a link between the Maya heartlands and central Mexico.

"Mesoamerica" is the term first proposed by the anthropologist Paul Kirchhoff to describe that part of Mexico and neighboring Central America which was civilized at the time of the Spanish conquest. What do we mean by civilized? Certainly a level of sociopolitical complexity that implies urbanism—Mesoamericans lived in cities and towns, although there was always a large rural population—and public art and architecture on an impressive scale. Kirchhoff drew up a list of culture traits, the totality of which he said characterized Mesoamerica in contrast to other large culture areas in the New World, such as the Greater Southwest, the Intermediate Area and the Andean Area. These included pyramids and temples, widespread human sacrifice, ritual penitence by bloodletting, a very complex sacred calendar based on the permutation of a 260-day cycle with an approximate year of 365 days, hieroglyphic writing (unique to Mesoamerica), a complex pantheon of gods, a game played with a rubber ball in a specially made court, and large and well-organized markets.

As elsewhere in the hemisphere such elaborate culture traits rested on a highly developed agricultural base which was of considerable antiquity: Mesoamericans had been farming maize, beans, squashes, chili peppers and other cultigens for over six millennia before the Spanish arrived. Cultivation took many forms in Mesoamerica's diverse environments, but one of the most developed (and one cited by Kirchhoff) was raised-field, or *chinampa*, agriculture, once thought to have been restricted to the Aztec but now known to have been widespread in aboriginal Latin America, including the Maya area.

There are many differences in general character and in detail between cultures as widely separated in time and space as Aztec and Classic Maya, but also increasing evidence for the basic similarity shared by all Mesoamerican civilizations. The universal possession of the 260-day sacred almanac, with its 20 day-signs and 13 coefficients, would argue for interaction between these cultures

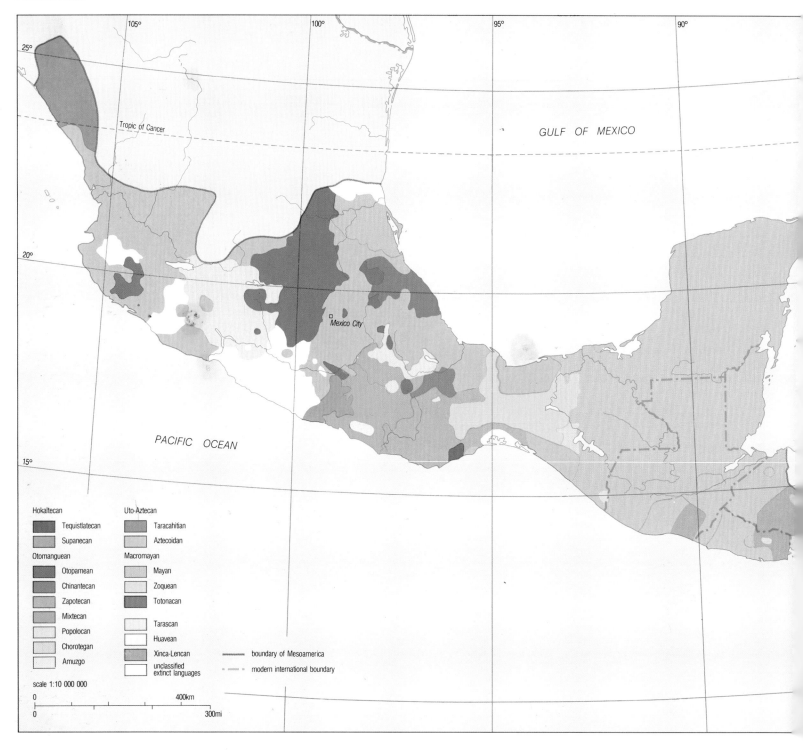

Hokaltecan
- Tequistlatecan
- Supanecan

Otomanguean
- Otopamean
- Chinantecan
- Zapotecan
- Mixtecan
- Popolocan
- Chorotegan
- Amuzgo

Uto-Aztecan
- Taracahitian
- Aztecoidan

Macromayan
- Mayan
- Zoquean
- Totonacan

- Tarascan
- Huavean
- Xinca-Lencan
- unclassified extinct languages

boundary of Mesoamerica
modern international boundary

scale 1:10 000 000

0   400km
0   300mi

over a very long period of time, as well as for a degree of genetic unity. There are abundant data, for instance, which establish the presence of central Mexican peoples like the Teotihuacanos and the Toltec in the Maya lowlands, and recent scholarship has shown a strong Maya presence in several highland areas of central Mexico. Reliefs depict Teotihuacan delegations at Monte Albán in Oaxaca, and there was a ward of traders from Oaxaca in the great city of Teotihuacan itself.

It is now generally agreed among Mesoamericanists that at least part of this fundamental unity goes back to a common cultural origin in the first high culture of Mesoamerica: the Olmec, which flourished from about 1200 to 400 BC and which originated on the Gulf Coast of southern Veracruz and Tabasco. The Olmec were the first to build large temple-pyramids, to carve and move stone monu-

ments on a grand scale, and to develop an involved religion and art focusing on a deity complex. They were the great civilizing force, and played a role in Mesoamerica similar to that of the Sumerians in Mesopotamia or the Chinese in East Asia. Wherever they or their influence (or heritage) went, that became a core region of Mesoamerica.

The natural setting

While Mesoamerica lies wholly within the tropics, there is an enormous environmental diversity within it. Differences in topography and climate, from well-watered, jungle-covered lowland plains to icy mountain peaks over 5000 meters in height, have produced great regional diversity in kinds of crops grown and in times of harvest, and in the natural products available for local use and to trade. The result has been that preconquest

Indigenous languages of Mesoamerica

More than 200 distinct languages were once spoken in Mexico and Central America. Linguistic analysis has grouped most of these into 22 language families, 19 of which can be formed into four phyla (large groupings of related language families which share a common origin). Three families have no apparent relation with any others: Tarascan (the tongue of a powerful kingdom in western Mexico); Huavean, on the southern coast of the Isthmus of Tehuatepec; Xinca-Lencan of Guatemala and Honduras.

The most widely distributed family within Mesoamerica is Aztecoidan, known from northern Mexico to Costa Rica. Its most important language was Nahuatl, the *lingua franca* of the Aztec empire; the closely related Nahuat was spoken in Veracruz and by the Pipil of Guatemala and Honduras.

The most cohesive language family is Mayan, with an almost unbroken distribution. Huastec is the only exception, lying far up the Gulf Coast of Mexico; how it came to be separated from the rest of the Mayan languages is unclear.

Right The Temple of the Jaguar at Tikal (see p. 116). Maya civilization of the Yucatán Peninsula flourished amid tropical rain forest.

Mesoamerica saw a large amount of interregional economic symbiosis and the early growth of markets and trading networks. There are even suggestions from the Tehuacan Valley of Puebla that such symbiotic interdependence may go far back into the preceramic era.

There is a basic contrast in the environments of Mesoamerica: highlands versus lowlands. The Mexican highlands are shaped by the Sierra Madre Occidental and the Sierra Madre Oriental, sweeping down from the north; between them they enclose a broad altiplano which is basically desert. This inland desert or dry grassland has such plants as mesquite, Joshua trees and various cactuses and agaves. There agriculture was difficult if not impossible, so that the desert-dwellers, known to the Aztec as the Chichimeca, were barbarian, nomadic hunters-and-collectors outside the northern frontier of Mesoamerica. The western Sierra Madre is relatively well watered and so allowed for an extension of Mesoamerican culture quite far to the north; it was this corridor through which Mesoamerican influence and perhaps trade passed to southwestern settlements, for example that at Casas Grandes in Chihuahua.

Where the two Sierra Madres coalesce is an east–west volcanic cordillera, with dozens of extinct, dormant and active volcanoes. These mighty uplands, originally clothed with pine and oak forests (and with Alpine flora on the higher peaks), are the dominant feature of central Mexico. While there are some large river valleys, such as the Lerma, far more important for the evolution of ancient cultures were the inland basins which are to be found across this highland landscape. Most impressive of these was the Valley of Mexico, almost 8000 square kilometers in area, which once contained a great lake—the Lake of the Moon—now almost completely obliterated by post-conquest drainage and by the urban sprawl of modern Mexico City. The people who lived in the basin often dominated Mesoamerican culture and politics, from the Early Classic Teotihuacan state to the mighty Aztec empire.

Other basins to the west were also of great significance, particularly the one surrounding Lake Pátzcuaro, seat of the Tarascan state and homeland of Tarascan culture.

As one moves southwest from the volcanic cordillera one enters more ancient highlands which are extremely dissected, forming many more, relatively isolated valleys. This is particularly true of Oaxaca in southeast Mexico, where a great diversity of cultures and tongues evolved in preconquest times. The Valley of Oaxaca is actually a coalescence of three river valleys, and was the locus of the Zapotec civilization of Monte Albán.

The Isthmus of Tehuantepec is a kind of constriction in the waist of Mesoamerica. With an altitude varying from sea level to less than 250 meters it provides an easy route between the lowlands bordering the Gulf of Mexico and those facing the Gulf of Tehuantepec. It also provides the connecting link between the Maya area and the rest of Mesoamerica to the west.

The rugged highlands of Chiapas and Guatemala are partly metamorphic, partly volcanic in origin. The picture-postcard beauty of the string of volcanoes of southern Guatemala is justly famed.

Because of the rich, volcanic soils and because of the fertility of basins and valleys in the Maya highlands, population densities were and still are very high. Instead of the shifting cultivation practiced by so many Maya in the lowlands to the north, highland fields tend to be fixed, with short fallow periods, so that agricultural production is high.

From the Texas border south and southeast to the Isthmus of Tehuantepec, and then east to the base of the Yucatán Peninsula is an almost unbroken coastal plain bordering the Gulf of Mexico. Many of the largest (but not the longest) rivers in Mexico undulate across this plain, and the soils are generally rich and alluvial in origin. Several major prehispanic civilizations were found from the Rio Pánuco south, most notably the precocious Olmec culture on the northern side of the Isthmus of Tehuantepec.

Jutting up into the Gulf of Mexico is "the great green thumb," as someone once put it, of the Yucatán Peninsula—a vast limestone shelf that has gradually emerged from the sea over several million years. Hillier and wetter in the south (as in the Petén of northern Guatemala), and flatter and drier in the north, this was where the great lowland Maya civilization rose and fell in the Classic era. Yucatán topography is of the limestone karst type, so that while rivers and streams are rare (the Usumacinta and Belize river systems are exceptions), there are numerous caves and sinkholes where water may be obtained. Best known are the circular sinkholes called *cenotes* in northern Yucatán, long used by the Maya for drinking water—and sometimes the final destination of victims sacrificed to the Rain God.

Because Mesoamerica lies to the south of the Tropic of Cancer, the annual rainfall regimen is of tropical type, and agricultural practices have had to adapt to this fact. There is a strongly marked dry season (although less so in Olmec country) which lasts from the end of November to the end of May. During this season it rains only infrequently in the lowlands, and hardly at all in the highlands. The rains come in late May or early June, and farmers in the lowlands must already have cleared their fields by felling the forest and burning the brush, and have planted their seeds (unless they have had recourse to raised-field methods, in which case cultivation could have been a year-round business). By late July or early August there is a temporary drop in rainfall—when the afternoon thunder showers fail to materialize—but then precipitation picks up again in earnest, and very heavy rains fall again in September, October and early November.

Some of the environmental diversity of Mesoamerica is caused by differential rainfall, and this may have a lot to do with why certain regions produced early and influential civilizations, and why others remained internally marginal. The Olmec area of southern Veracruz and the southern Maya lowlands receive a high amount of rainfall annually, especially in September; these regions were the focuses of very early civilizational activity. Guerrero (a southern Mexican state) is extremely desiccated and would only have interested such peoples as the Olmec when irrigation agriculture became a viable and known technique of raising food crops. It was always internally marginal, from the cultural point of view.

CULTURE ERAS

The Tehuacan Valley
The best evidence for the beginnings of Mesoamerican agriculture and for the transition from hunting-and-gathering to sedentary villages comes from the Tehuacan Valley. It is extremely dry, allowing for perfect preservation of ancient plant remains in caves and rockshelters. By 5000 BC a primitive form of domestic maize appears, but other foods were also being planted.

While the Tehuacan Valley is, broadly speaking, a desert, it is also divided into ecological sub-areas, each of which was exploited at different seasons of the year. During the Archaic period, when only bands and macrobands inhabited the valley, these would have moved in patterned seasonal migrations through these microenvironments. Planting of early domesticated crops was probably carried out on the humid river bottoms, since elsewhere agriculture was largely precluded before the adoption of irrigation in the Formative period.

The end of the Pleistocene in Mesoamerica resulted in drastically altered conditions for its inhabitants, at least in the highlands of central and southern Mexico. As the ice receded in the higher latitudes of North America, temperatures rose to today's norms or perhaps even higher. Much of what is now the Republic of Mexico became more desiccated, and deserts appeared in what had previously been lush grasslands. In the humid lowlands, of course, we do not really know what these changes meant. But in much of Mesoamerica the great herds of grazing animals such as mammoths, mastodons, horses and giant bison disappeared, leaving the more humble fauna such as deer, rabbits and jackrabbits as prey for bands of hunters.

It should be remembered that these ancient Mesoamericans had almost certainly been more dependent upon their abilities as collectors of plant foods than upon their hunting prowess. The Mesoamerican landscape, whether highland or lowland, has always been rich in wild plant foods, and these must have been heavily exploited. The harvesting of larger fruits, more abundant grains,

heavier root crops and superior mutations in general would have unwittingly favored selection of plant populations amenable for domestication.

The question might be asked, what differentiates a domestic species from a wild one? The great Russian plant biologist N.I. Vavilov once defined domestication as evolution directed by the hand of man. The most productive species of domesticated grain, on which the very existence of our planet depends, are total captives of mankind, in the sense that they now cannot disperse their seeds without human intervention. Maize or Indian corn is a case in point: the cob and its seeds are completely enclosed in the mature ear with husks, which must be stripped off before the kernels can become viable progenitors of future generations. Manioc or cassava is another: at the low altitudes at which it is commonly grown it produces no seeds and must be propagated by cuttings.

The new stage on which Mesoamerican populations embarked after about 7000 BC is called the Archaic or Incipient Agricultural. It lasted until the initiation of the Formative period, after 2000 BC, when settled life became the norm and villages were established throughout the area. While the soundest archaeological evidence for this stage comes from the highlands, it should always be kept in mind that preservation of organic materials is very poor in the tropical lowlands, and that some of the most significant interaction between man and plants may have taken place there, but not left any trace.

The Tehuacan sequence

The search for the origins of agriculture in Mesoamerica has mainly been the work of one man: Richard S. MacNeish. His early work in caves and rockshelters in Tamaulipas, Mexico, took place beyond the northern frontier of Mesoamerica, but it showed that in the centuries between the close of the Ice Age and the beginnings of the Formative period small bands of Indians were beginning to tamper with the evolution of important food plants, such as maize, beans, pumpkin, squash and chili peppers. The earliest domesticated plant of all proved to be the bottle gourd, not suitable for the table but used as a container and probably a fishnet float.

The origins of maize (*Zea mays*) are still clouded in controversy. At one time archaeologists and botanists thought that it had arisen under human selection from another closely related grass, *teosinte*, which grows wild and as an unwanted weed in Indian cornfields in southern and western Mexico, and in Guatemala. A later school of botanists led by Paul C. Mangelsdorf decided that teosinte was not the ancestor of corn but an offspring, the result of hybridization between early domestic maize and another grass belonging to the genus *Tripsacum*; and that the progenitor of maize ought to be a now extinct wild maize which had at

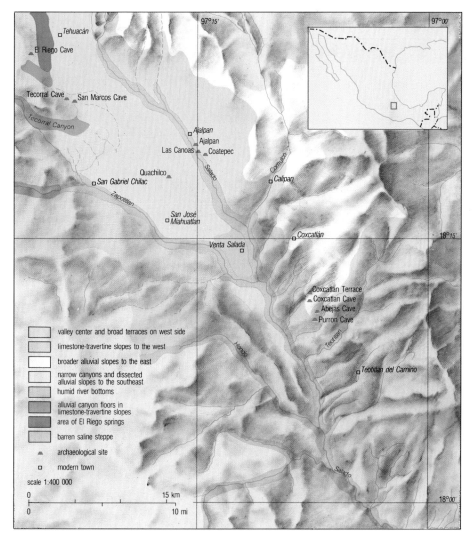

that time the ability to disperse its seeds without the intervention of man.

In an attempt to find further evidence bearing on this problem, and to cast further light on this previously unknown era in Mesoamerican prehistory—by now called the Archaic stage—MacNeish began exploring the Tehuacan Valley in Puebla, an arid region with bone-dry caves and rockshelters in which otherwise perishable food remains would have survived. A long sequence of stratified occupations of these caves was established, and the human ecology of these early bands worked out. During the El Riego phase (c. 7000–5000 BC), camps and caves were occupied by seminomadic microbands who moved seasonally through a series of microenvironments (much like the Desert Culture people of North America), to harvest seeds and other plant foods as they ripened. They were also planting avocado, chili peppers, grain amaranth, walnut squash and cotton.

By about 5000 BC, during the subsequent Coxcatlan phase, domestic maize—of an extremely primitive and probably unproductive sort—appears in the Tehuacan sequence. Exactly where the initial domestication took place, whether in southern Mexico or Central America, remains unknown. Along with the cobs of domestic corn were tiny cobs of what was at first thought to be wild corn—the long-sought-for ancestor. However some botanists, for example Walton Galinat, believe this to be teosinte, and this is in line with the most recent botanic thinking: that corn arose as a monstrous mutation of teosinte, and that these sports were selected for by the Mesoamerican Indians. Needless to say, the dust has not yet settled on the controversy.

The ever-increasing reliance on domestic crops had clearcut consequences. Ground stone querns (or *metates*) and handstones began to be manufactured to process these foods, especially corn, and there was decreasing reliance on the hunting of game. By the Abejas phase (c. 3400–2300 BC) very fine bowls and neckless jars were being manufactured from stone, and these foreshadow in their forms the pottery that was soon to be made. Increasing ability to harvest and store domestic plants allowed these people to become more sedentary, and one Abejas village of circular pithouses was discovered on the valley floor. Nomadism was gradually replaced by sedentism. The true mark of settled life is pottery, which is too fragile to be taken from one camp to another throughout the year. The first appears in the poorly known Purrón phase (c. 2300–1500 BC), the final Archaic occupation of the Tehuacan area.

The Archaic period elsewhere

Because the Tehuacan Archaic sequence is so complete and so abundantly documented there is a tendency to think of that valley as the *actual* place where maize and other Mesoamerican cultigens were first brought under domestication. However, these might have been domesticated at different times and different places: corn, for example, might have been "tamed" by man anywhere from central Mexico to Panama. It should also be cautioned that the role of the lowlands in this process is not at all well known because of poor preservation of plant remains.

In Oaxaca, Kent Flannery and his associates from the University of Michigan have discovered caves and open-air sites belonging to the Archaic period. Remains of bottle gourds and pumpkins were recovered, along with pollen of what seems to be teosinte (the latter associated with levels dated to 7400–6700 BC).

It may be that in the coastal lowlands, particularly that part bordering the Gulf of Mexico, manioc or cassava played a role comparable to that of maize in the highlands. It is significant that at the preceramic village site of Santa Luisa, in northern Veracruz, the archaeologist Jeffrey Wilkerson failed to find *metates* and *manos*—manioc preparation does not require such tools. In Belize, Richard MacNeish has recently found a major occupation of the northern part of that country during the time interval from the Paleo-Indians to the earliest Formative villagers. However no plant remains are available for these Belize Archaic sites, but there is an increasing number of grinding tools used in the preparation of plant foods as one moves up in the sequence. Certainly those Mesoamericans living along the littoral area of both Atlantic and Pacific coasts would have placed great reliance upon fish, shellfish, and other marine and estuary food resources.

Preserved remains of cob, husks and spikelets from the San Marcos Cave in the Tehuacan Valley permit the reconstruction of wild maize. Husks enclosed the kernels until maturity, when they were released.

Left Five thousand years are represented in the evolution of maize from the tiny wild corn cob to a modern example from about 1500 AD. Modern corn is much larger and more productive than wild species; otherwise, botanical properties have changed only slightly.

Center left Organ cactus and thorn scrub seen from the Coxcatlan Cave. Radiocarbon dating of organic remains disclosed more than 10 000 years of occupation in 28 levels of excavation.

Below: The Archaic and Formative periods
Any attempt to correlate early settlement patterns with favorable environmental circumstances is fraught with danger, not least because of the random nature of archaeological discovery. Nevertheless, evidence of cultivation found at sites in Tamaulipas and Tehuacan attests to the adaptability of early Mesoamerican peoples when an arid climate began to set in around 7000 BC. The settled village life based on farming that subsequently emerged in the Formative tended to flourish in the more humid areas — the Pacific and Gulf Coasts, the Maya Lowlands and the fertile highland valleys of Oaxaca and Mexico.

The Archaic period: forerunner of the Formative

The greatest change in the lives of the preconquest Indians of the New World was the development of agriculture: it made possible villages, then towns, and finally cities and civilization. In Mesoamerica this twin process of domestication and sedentism took place throughout the Archaic. Continued selection of more productive varieties of corn, beans, squashes, pumpkins and other plants meant a steady improvement in productivity and greatly expanded populations. On the eve of the Formative, around 2000 BC, almost all of the arts and living conditions of the Formative had been established, with such items as a wide variety of ground stone tools for food processing, pottery, occasional clay figurines, cordage, basketry, special treatment of the dead and open-air villages. More complex traits, such as established art styles, complex religions, temples and temple-pyramids, were yet to come.

FORMATIVE VILLAGES

To an earlier generation of archaeologists the oldest-known cultural remains from Mesoamerica consisted of simple pottery bowl and jar fragments, along with handmade clay figurines of nude females. While they had no way of accurately dating these materials they knew that they characterized village cultures which underlay ruins of the great Classic cities of Mexico and the Maya area, and they called them "Archaic" or "Preclassic" in tribute to their antiquity. It was known that the peoples who produced them were farmers, and the idea took hold that this "Preclassic" era was the New World equivalent to the Old World Neolithic.

Today it is increasingly clear that this epoch, which is now generally called the Formative, was far more varied in complexity than this simple picture suggests. In fact we now know that simple villagers coexisted with the rulers and priests of some very developed civilizations during this period. The radiocarbon technique has enabled us to fix dates to the Formative, but it should be remembered that these are in terms of radiocarbon years: the calendar-year dates for remains that have been dated by the Carbon 14 method to 1200 BC, for instance, should be lengthened by about 300 years. Olmec civilization thus begins about 1500 BC in true years, but about 1200 BC in radiocarbon years.

It is not easy to find Paleo-Indian and Archaic (or preceramic) sites in Mesoamerica; Formative sites, on the other hand, are ubiquitous, although in the Maya area they are often obscured by later constructions of the Classic period which have been built on top of them. There must have been a real population explosion of a Malthusian sort to produce such an abundance of remains. A vast improvement in maize varieties had taken place, principally through hybrid introgression and the introduction of teosinte genes into stocks of domestic corn. This resulted in far larger ears and therefore greater yields. Settled villages now became the rule rather than the exception. Hamlets, villages and even small towns of thatch-roofed huts were found everywhere in Meso-

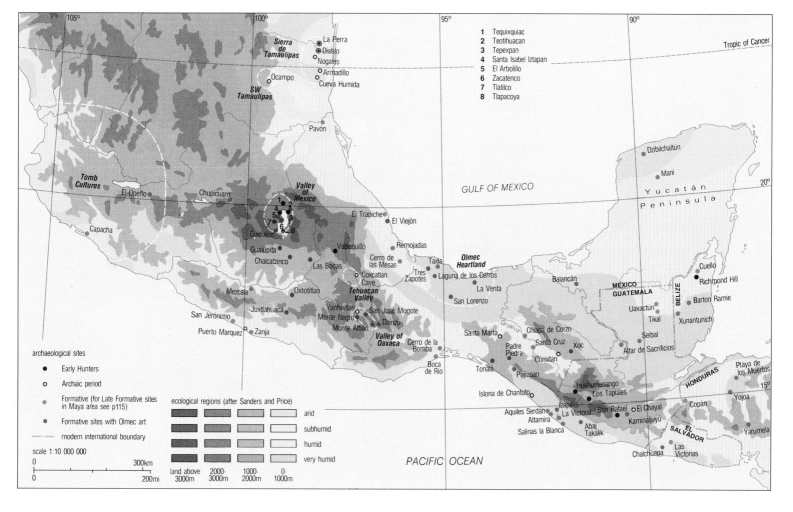

1 Tequixquiac
2 Teotihuacan
3 Tepexpan
4 Santa Isabel Iztapan
5 El Arbolillo
6 Zacatenco
7 Tlatilco
8 Tlapacoya

archaeological sites
● Early Hunters
○ Archaic period
● Formative (for Late Formative sites in Maya area see p115)
● Formative sites with Olmec art
--- modern international boundary

scale 1:10 000 000
0   300km
0   200mi

ecological regions (after Sanders and Price)
arid
subhumid
humid
very humid

land above 3000m | 2000-3000m | 1000-2000m | 0-1000m

america, and the manufacture of pottery, clay figurines, and loom-woven cotton textiles was universal.

The question of exactly where the transition from the Archaic to the Formative pattern took place is still controversial. Those archaeologists who have mainly worked in the highlands have looked to central Mexico, especially the Valley of Mexico, as the *fons et origo* of the Formative, while others with more lowland experience favor the humid, hot coastal plains, expecially along the Pacific coast of Chiapas and Guatemala; most recently one archaeologist has advanced a claim for northern Belize, but few colleagues are yet ready to follow him.

It is generally accepted that the Early Formative lasts, in terms of radiocarbon years, from about 2000 or 1600 BC to about 900 BC; that the Middle Formative extends from 900 BC to about 300 BC; and that the Late Formative continues from 300 BC until the opening of the Classic period—the time of Christ in central Mexico and 290 AD in the Maya lowlands.

The Pacific coast

The Pacific coast of much of Mexico is rocky and precipitous, with a few favored bay areas like Acapulco, but as one moves southeast along it past the Isthmus of Tehuantepec it expands into a broad plain which continues through the state of Chiapas into Guatemala. This extremely hot but fertile plain is one of the richest archaeological areas in the world, being dotted with countless groups of earthen mounds which are sometimes faced with river cobbles. Largely neglected by archaeologists, perhaps because of the pervasive heat, this plain was nonetheless a very early locus of fully sedentary village life and a corridor for the movement of peoples and ideas throughout the Formative and even later. During the first part of the Early Formative, until the rise of the Olmec on the Gulf Coast, southeastern Chiapas and neighboring Guatemala comprised what was probably the most innovative region of Mesoamerica.

The earliest ceramics of this region (known as Xoconochco to the far later Aztec) are quite complex and sophisticated. The Formative sequence begins with the Barra culture, in which very thin-walled redware neckless jars, or *tecomates*, decorated in various plastic techniques, predominate. Barra is believed to date to about 1600 BC, and is followed by the better-known Ocós culture of 1500 BC. Ocós sites are favorably placed so as to enjoy the benefits of both the littoral and the inland environments; thus, they could fish, gather shellfish and hunt turtles in the lagoon-estuary system, as well as plant their corn and other crops on the rich soils further in from the shore. La Victoria, a small village of about 10 or 12 houses sitting on low earthen platforms, is an example of such a settlement: it was sited right next to a now-extinct tidal estuary.

Ocós ceramics, consisting largely of *tecomates* and flat-bottomed bowls with outslanting sides, are decorated in a bewildering variety of techniques, including rocker-stamping (produced by making curved zigzags across the wet clay with the crinkly edge of a shell) and iridescent, pinkish slip—a technique only known elsewhere in Ecuador, and

believed by many to have diffused from there through sea trade. Ocós figurines are equally sophisticated and comprise an extraordinary gallery of grotesque human and animal forms. Known best from the large Ocós site of Aquiles Serdán on the Chiapas coast, they may well represent the earliest body of art in Mesoamerica.

Ocós is followed by several other village cultures, curiously enough with far simpler ceramics and figurines. Cuadros, a contemporary of the earliest Olmec culture on the Gulf Coast, is most notable for the find of fossilized corncobs, in which the organic material had been replaced over time by carbonates leached from layers of discarded shells. Mangelsdorf was able to identify these as belonging to the primitive Nal-Tel variety, still grown in Yucatán. Cuadros and Cuadros-like pottery are spread over much of the Pacific coast and Guatemala, and have even been found at the site of Las Victorias in western El Salvador; here the impetus of diffusion was certainly the spread of Olmec culture and perhaps peoples. Conchas follows Cuadros, and continues the littoral/farming tradition into the Middle Formative, with strong ties to the Las Charcas culture of highland Guatemala and with the Mexican Gulf Coast.

Highland Guatemala

Guatemala City sits in a broad, fertile valley near the continental divide, and is surrounded by hills and mountains of volcanic origin. The western side of the city used to be one of the richest archaeological zones of the country, but has been largely destroyed through real-estate development. Given the name Kaminaljuyú by a pioneer Guatemalan archaeologist, the zone has a long cultural sequence which includes a Middle Formative village occupation called Las Charcas. It is best known from a series of bottle-shaped storage pits cut down into the underlying volcanic tufa; these contained some fine white and red-on-white ceramics, clay figurines and food remains such as corncobs and avocado pits. We know little about the cultural complexity reached by the Las Charcas people, but there is some admittedly tenuous evidence that they might have constructed earthen mounds to support perishable temples. However, since they were coeval with the great Olmec civilization typified by the Middle Formative site of La Venta, this is hardly surprising.

The Maya lowlands

We now know, mainly from MacNeish's investigations, that people were present in some numbers in the Maya lowlands prior to the inception of the Formative, so that it is no surprise to find abundant evidence for Formative peoples in the Petén-Yucatán Peninsula. However the claim by Norman Hammond that in the Swasey culture of the Cuello site, in northern Belize, he has found an Early Formative occupation of the Maya lowlands far older than anything on the Pacific coast and predating the Olmec of the Gulf Coast has not gone unchallenged. Not only do the radiocarbon dates span a millennium—something unusual for an archaeological phase—but the ceramics look Middle or even Late Formative. Nevertheless Swasey does cast light on the early Maya diet in the lowlands, for there were preserved cobs of popcorn and yam, cocoyam and possibly manioc.

We are on far better ground with the sequence in the Petén, which begins with the Middle Formative Xe phase, perhaps about 800 BC; this is immediately followed by the Mamóm phase, in which the Petén and Yucatán first see the buildup of quite heavy populations, and the establishment of villages on every bit of dry ground. Characterized by the orangy-red ceramics which were to be typical of the lowland Maya throughout the Formative, this culture probably saw the rise of plaster-covered temple platforms, but these are very difficult to uncover because of the towering overburdens of Late Formative and Classic constructions.

The Grijalva Basin of Chiapas

Before it cuts through a mighty gorge on its way to the Gulf Coast plain, the Grijalva River of Chiapas flows through a hot, relatively dry depression that in spite of its desiccated appearance was the locus of many ancient settlements throughout the Formative period. The most intensely excavated site in the Grijalva Basin is Chiapa de Corzo, which has a long series of successive occupations extending through the Spanish conquest into the colonial period. From 1500 to about 800 BC the Early Formative people of the area ground their maize on milling stones, produced pottery which largely consisted of globular, neckless jars or *tecomates*, and produced handmade clay figurines. The entire pottery complex is closely allied with the Ocós and Conchas phases of the Pacific coast, with the same emphasis on rocker-stamping. But central Chiapas at this date was also tied culturally to the sophisticated Olmec of the Gulf Coast. One clay figurine from Chiapa de Corzo is definitely Olmec, and one downstream site, now flooded by waters backed up by the Malpaso Dam, had a ceramic complex closely related to the San Lorenzo phase of Olmec civilization, but without the stone monuments which characterize that culture.

Oaxaca

A now discredited notion about the Valley of Oaxaca, homeland of the Zapotec civilization, was that prior to Monte Albán I (a Middle Formative manifestation) the valley had been filled by a great lake which precluded early settlement. Thus until the University of Michigan project there had been no search for really ancient sites on the valley bottomlands. In fact a long Formative sequence for the valley has now been determined, culminating in the establishment of the hilltop citadel of Monte Albán as the dominating force over much of central Oaxaca.

During the Early Formative San José phase (1150–850 BC), which shows clearcut signs of contact with the Olmec of Veracruz, the village site of San José Mogote, located to the northwest of Monte Albán, consisted of 80–100 houses with thatched roofs and daubed, whitewashed walls. Household activities included spinning, weaving, sewing and food preparation on the part of the women, while men manufactured iron-ore mirrors (a widely traded prestige item in the Early Formative), and shell and mica ornaments. The subsistence base of the village was the raising of crops such as maize, chili peppers and squashes, with avocados possibly being brought in from the lowlands.

Some of the pottery at San José Mogote is definitely of Olmec inspiration, with designs drawn from the repertoire of Olmec religious iconography carved or incised on the exteriors of bowls. The exact nature of the Olmec impact on the Valley of Oaxaca has yet to be determined, but Flannery and his associates look less to an actual Olmec presence than to the model of a tribal, village-living people emulating the prestigious high culture of Veracruz.

The Valley of Mexico

The great lake (the Lake of the Moon) that once filled much of the Valley of Mexico, along with the swampy, reed-covered margins, must have been a major resource to the Formative villagers who lived near it, providing them with abundant fish and waterfowl, and perhaps also the protein-rich algae that were so prized by the later Aztec. This situ-

Above Highland scrub landscape in southern Mexico between the Valley of Oaxaca and the Tehuacan Valley. It was this kind of terrain that had to be brought into cultivation when a nomadic existence was replaced by a sedentary way of life.

ation, and the richness of the valley soils, allowed the establishment of fairly large farming populations, even in the Early Formative.

The largest and most spectacular of the settlements that sprang up in the valley was Tlatilco (which is described in the section on the Olmec, since the Olmec cultural presence is exceptionally strong there). Olmec peoples from southern Veracruz may very well have been among its inhabitants. Its chronological position was long misunderstood, since a past archaeological generation could not conceive that a culture so complex and sophisticated could have preceded the simple village sites which were then taken to be the earliest farming settlements in the valley.

Zacatenco and El Arbolillo, the sites in question, are in fact largely of the Middle Formative period and later than Tlatilco. They were once villages of modest size situated above the northwestern shore of Lake Texcoco, the largest of the bodies of water making up the great lake. Known principally from trenching carried out in the 1920s and 1930s, their earliest occupations are typified by ceramics far simpler than those of Tlatilco, along with thousands of nude or partly clothed female figurines whose function is still in dispute. (Was this a fertility cult?) Vast quantities of household refuse were strewn about the daubed pole-and-thatch huts in which they lived, including the bones of deer which they hunted in the adjacent hills with lances fitted with obsidian points. There is no trace whatsoever of the Olmec. After 900 BC this influence disappeared, and the valley became a cultural backwater, not to recover its former importance until the rise of Teotihuacan civilization about the time of Christ.

During the Late Formative, after 400 or 300 BC, there was a brief moment of glory in the southwestern side of the valley, with the construction of a great stone-faced, circular "pyramid" at the site of Cuicuilco; this 27-meter-high temple platform, which was once crowned with a conical construction, may have been the focus of a cult to the Old Fire God, for clay incense burners in the form of this important deity were found there. Cuicuilco, however, was fated to be short-lived, for a mighty eruption of Xictli volcano covered it with a thick layer of lava and forced the residents of the village or town around it to flee.

OLMEC CIVILIZATION

The emergence of Mesoamerican civilization, and perhaps even the earliest move toward the Mesoamerican state, took place in the swampy lowland of southern Veracruz and neighboring Tabasco, fronting the Gulf of Mexico. This is the Olmec heartland, for within this area are located most major Olmec sites and virtually all known Olmec stone monuments. The region is basically a coastal plain, with occasional low hills; the only significant relief consists of the Tuxtla Mountains, an active volcanic formation from which the Olmec obtained the basalt for their sculptures. This is among the wettest parts of Mesoamerica, with most precipitation falling from late May through November, but there is no strongly marked dry season, for winter northers bring in cold rain and drizzle at frequent intervals in the wintertime. The result is that maize and other crops can be grown here the year round.

Perhaps the most significant factor in the Olmec landscape is the extensive flooding which takes place during the rainy season, when water from the swollen rivers covers all lowlying places; as the waters recede, a layer of rich mud remains along the natural river levees. These levees are the most productive land in Mexico, and it is probably this Nile-like situation, combined with rapidly increasing population, that gave rise to the complex culture of the Olmec.

The exact number of Olmec sites in the heartland is unknown (survey is difficult here because of dense vegetation), but most seem to be placed on low hills or plateaus near the river levees and above the flood-prone savannas. Since all stone had to be imported and was used only for monuments, drains and grinding implements, stone architecture is nonexistent; perishable structures of pole and thatch stood atop mounds of earthen fill and brightly colored clays.

The chronology of Olmec civilization was long a subject of controversy, as most Mayanists refused to believe that its strange and highly complex style of art, with its enormous basalt monuments and beautifully carved jades, could predate the Classic Maya. In the last three decades, however, extensive excavations and a long series of radiocarbon determinations have conclusively proved that the Olmec phenomenon, whether within the heartland or beyond its confines, is surely Formative in date. In fact, we can now distinguish two "horizons": one confined to the latter part of the Early Formative period (i.e. 1200–900 BC), followed by a Middle Formative horizon at 900–400 BC. By the Late Formative, Olmec culture had in effect disappeared.

Below Olmec civilization is recognized principally from its distinctive sculptural style, which combines simplicity of line with powerful, massive form. The resulting monumental effect is evident in works at all scales, from the colossal head opposite to this tiny jade bust.

The Olmec heartland
The Olmec heartland is singularly deficient in many raw materials which were paradoxically prized by the San Lorenzo elite. Obsidian, for example, which played a role in Mesoamerica similar to steel in western civilization, is found only in volcanic regions of Mexico and Guatemala far from the heartland. Iron ore was another much prized substance that had to be imported.

El Mes

Cerro El Vigia
source of basalt for Tres Zapotes monuments

Nestepe

Tres Zapotes
probably the last major Olmec site, after the destruction of La Venta

Punta Roca Partida
source of prismatic basalt columns at La Venta
site

GULF OF MEXICO

Right Monument 17, San
Lorenzo, one of eight colossal
heads discovered at the site. It
was fashioned from a basalt
boulder brought from the slopes
of the Cerro Cintepec, in the
Tuxtla Mountains, and is a
portrait of an Olmec ruler. The
headgear of each colossal head is
marked with its own distinctive
device. In this case it is a net-like
covering of cords joining drilled
iron ore beads, a cache of which
was found next to the head
during excavation.

□ *San Andrés Tuxtla*

T U X T L A   M O U N T A I N S

Isla de
Tenaspi

San Martín
Pajapan

Los Mangos

Cerro Cintepec
major source of basalt used for
Olmec monuments at San Lorenzo
Tenochtitlán, La Venta

□ Llano del Jicaro

■ La Venta
major Olmec site,
after the destruction
of San Lorenzo

Laguna de los Cerros
probably contemporary with
San Lorenzo, but unexcavated

Coatzacoalcos

Los Soldados

Acayucan □   *Jáltipan* □

Cruz del Milagro

Antonio Plaza

Coatzacoalcos

Arroyo Sonso
Olmec "wrestler" found here

San Lorenzo
earliest of the Olmec ceremonial centers,
flourishing between 1200 and 900 BC

Tenochtitlán ■

Chiquito

Potrero
Nuevo

Usumacinta

Estero Rabón   Los Idolos

Medias
Aguas

Coatzacoalcos

Las Limas
large greenstone figure, key to Olmec
iconography, found here

Legend (main map)

▢	land above 200m
▨	levées and flood-prone savannah
	marsh
– – –	Olmec heartland
■	major Olmec center
▨	isolated find of Olmec sculpture
□	modern town or city

scale 1:750 000

0 ————————— 30km

0 ————————— 20mi

Inset map

— Olmec heartland

— trade route

■ Olmec or Olmec-
   influenced site

GULF OF MEXICO

scale 1:14 000 000

0 ——————— 300km

0 ——————— 200mi

YUCATÁN

20°

Tampico □

Ⓞ

Ⓞ

Tlatilco   Ⓞ

Mexico City   ■ El Viejón

Tlapacoya   Ⓞ Ⓞ   *Veracruz*

Gualupita   Ⓞ Ⓞ

Chalcatzinco

Las Bocas   Ⓑ Ⓑ

Ⓢ   Tres Zapotes   Ⓑ

Oxtotitlán Cave

Juxtlahuaca Cave   Laguna de
                         los Cerros

Acapulco □   Ⓘ *Oaxaca*   ■ San Lorenzo   Ⓑ

                                    La Venta ■

                                    Balancán ■

                    Isthmus of
                    Tehuantepec

mineral deposits   Ⓢ Ⓘ

Ⓑ   basalt, used in Olmec   Padre Piedra ■
    monuments   Xoc ■

Ⓞ   obsidian, for San Lorenzo   Pijijiapan ■

Ⓘ   iron ore, for mirrors

Ⓢ   serpentine   Izapa ■   Ⓙ

Ⓙ   apple-green jade   La Blanca ■ *Guatemala*
                                  Abaj Takalik *City*   Ⓞ

□   modern city   Chalchuapa ■   Ⓞ   15°

PACIFIC OCEAN   to Costa Rica
                                         for jade?

scale 1:750 000

The Supernatural World of the Olmec

Bottom left Deities incised on the shoulders and knees of the Las Limas figure. All have the cleft heads typical of Olmec gods. Upper left, a deity known elsewhere only on incised bowls from the Mexican highlands, perhaps Xipe Totec, the patron of springtime among later cultures. Upper right, the Harpy Eagle God, with the bird's feather crest appearing as eyebrows. Lower right, the Shark God, with crescent-shaped eye and prominent tooth. Lower left, possibly the head of the Feathered Serpent, marked by crossed bands in its eye.

The first art to appear in Mesoamerica was that of the Olmec. Except for portraits of rulers (such as the colossal heads), this was basically religious in content, being focused upon a wide variety of supernaturals which combined features of the animal world with those of humans, blending into each other in bewildering complexity. Only in recent years have we come to realize that the Olmec had an extensive pantheon, for it used to be thought that their only god was the characteristic "were-jaguar," which combined the features of a snarling jaguar with those of a bawling infant.

Thanks to the chance discovery in 1965 of a large greenstone figure at Las Limas, Veracruz, we can now appreciate that there were many Olmec gods, each with its own attributes, although these were freely exchanged with those of other supernaturals. The Las Limas figure depicts a young man or adolescent seated tailor-fashion, holding the familiar were-jaguar infant in his arms; four other deities, all with the mysterious cleft heads typical of Olmec gods, are incised on his shoulder and knees. These gave the first clues to the structure of Maya iconography, but not necessarily to its meaning.

The formidable, dangerous animals that predominate in Olmec iconography may perhaps have been totemic, and by their natural distribution show that the cult must have originated in a tropical forest not far from a seacoast. These are the harpy eagle, which feeds on monkeys in the jungle canopy, the jaguar (the largest of the world's spotted cats), the alligator-like cayman, the serpent and the shark.

Right A jade Olmec Dragon. This protean monster, probably an earth deity, shows the combinatory tendency of Olmec iconography: here the basic animal is a cayman, but it has the down-turned mouth of the were-jaguar, a humanoid nose, and harpy eagle crests for eyebrows. The Dragon may have been the most important of the Olmec gods, for it appears in monumental art, in small-scale jade carvings, and, in a kind of shorthand form, carved upon household and funerary ceramics in both lowlands and highlands.

Left Greenstone figure from Las Limas, Veracruz, probably dating to the period 800–400 BC. Most likely this is a portrait celebrating the accession to power of a young man or boy. The floppy were-jaguar figure in his arms may symbolize his royal descent, as identical infantile deities are carried by rulers in the frontal niches of Olmec thrones. Height: 55 cm.

Right Harpy Eagle God in jade. Height 5·8 cm. The Olmec were Mesoamerica's greatest jade carvers, as this masterpiece, dating to the 800–400 BC period, attests. The anthropomorphic element in all Olmec animal deities can be seen here; only the beak, above the were-jaguarlike mouth, and the stylized crest give away its raptorial nature.

Right Monument 52, San Lorenzo. Height: 90 cm. This is the infantile Were-Jaguar God, identical to the figure carried by the Las Limas figure down to the smallest details. The monument was found at the head of a deeply buried stone drain system, so the creature may be connected with water, perhaps as a rain deity.

Below Shark God in Olmec blue-green jade, from the Pacific coast of Guatemala. Middle Formative, 800–400 BC.

Above Pottery bowl from Tlapacoya, Valley of Mexico. Height 13 cm. Early Formative period, 1200–900 BC. Incised and carved upon the surface is the same deity head that can be seen on the Las Limas figure's right shoulder, with curving bands through the eye, and snarling, jaguar-like mouth.

Left Kneeling stone figure of a shaman undergoing transformation into a jaguar.

La Venta

At the center of La Venta, now largely destroyed by oil operations, is Complex A, an imperfectly known cluster of great mounds and ritual offerings with Middle Formative radiocarbon dates (c. 900–400 BC). The complex, which has the usual linear layout (but this time orientated to 8 degrees west of true north), is dominated by the so-called "Great Pyramid," actually a 30-meter-high mound in the shape of a fluted cone; it has been estimated to contain more than 100 000 cubic meters of fill. Whether it might also contain a great Olmec tomb is anyone's guess, as it has never been probed.

The Pyramid is the largest of its time in Mexico. It has been estimated that its construction required 800 000 man-days, and that the elite of the complex required the support of a hinterland population of 18 000 people.

Right La Venta's 30-m.-high Great Pyramid and series of low platforms — architecture of modest size by Mesoamerican standards — belie Olmec artistic ingenuity and the sheer physical effort that produced the carved stone monuments and finely worked jade recovered at the site. Because of the threat of destruction from the development of a petro-chemical complex on the island of La Venta, the monuments were removed to a public park in Villahermosa, Tabasco.

Below Altar 4 at La Venta. "Altar" is almost certainly a misnomer as the function of such structures is unknown. The figure holds a rope which runs around the corner to a bound captive.

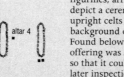

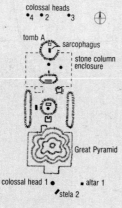

colossal heads
•4 •2   •3

tomb A
sarcophagus
stone column enclosure

Great Pyramid

colossal head 1   ▪ altar 1
stela 2

altar 5   altar 4

0   80m
0   300ft

Right Offering 4, La Venta. This is a group of jade and serpentine figurines, arranged so as to depict a ceremony; the narrow, upright celts may represent a background of basalt columns. Found below the surface, this offering was apparently marked so that it could be uncovered for later inspection by the Olmec.

San Lorenzo

Very few heartland Olmec sites have been properly investigated. The only one which has been mapped in detail and for which we have a good archaeological sequence is San Lorenzo Tenochtitlán—actually a complex of three sites near a side branch of the Río Coatzacoalcos, which drains much of the northern part of the Isthmus of Tehuantepec. Although San Lorenzo itself had been occupied by Formative people as early as 1500 BC, it took its present shape and reached the apogee of its existence between 1200 and 900 BC, during the San Lorenzo phase. San Lorenzo covers the top of a 50-meter-high plateau or mesa which is about 1·25 kilometers long from north to south; it is known from the Yale University excavations that the mesa is partly artificial down to a depth in some places of 7 meters. Manmade ridges jut out from the mesa on the northwest, west and south sides. It is estimated that this gigantic construction contains tens of thousands of cubic meters of fill, clay and sand, all of which had to be carried in by human labor.

The most striking feature about San Lorenzo, along with other Gulf Coast Olmec centers, is the number, size and beauty of its monuments. The first artists in Mesoamerica were the Olmec sculptors, and they produced a distinctive style which ranks with any in the world. The monuments, all of which were fashioned from basalt brought laboriously from a source in the Tuxtla Mountains, some 80 kilometers north-northwest from San Lorenzo, include eight colossal heads, the largest of which is 2·3 meters high and probably weighs over 20 tonnes. It is virtually certain that these heads are portraits of Olmec rulers; their faces, with thickened, everted lip and flat noses, are reminiscent of the physiognomies to be seen in some southeastern Asiatic populations, but each is distinctive, as is the emblematic device on their protective helmets. In fact, these may have been worn in the sacred ballgame which we know from clay figurines to have been played by the Olmec.

Other monuments include "altars," great table-top oblongs, the fronts of which show cross-legged rulers seated in niches, each either holding a were-jaguar baby in his arms, or else grasping a cord binding captives taken in war, most likely symbols glorifying the ruling elite by the celebration of royal succession and martial prowess. A host of other sculptures suggests the identification of the San Lorenzo rulers with the divine pantheon, an exceedingly complex series of grotesque supernaturals combining human and animal features, mostly marked by the Olmec canon of downturned, snarling mouth and infantile anthropomorphism.

Another clearly nonpractical aspect to San Lorenzo, which was surely a ceremonial center in the strictest sense, is the presence of an extraordinary system of stone drains—U-shaped pieces of basalt laid end-to-end and fitted with stone covers. These are believed to have drawn off water from artificial ponds on the surface of the site which were probably used for ritual bathing. Since the Olmec were without metal tools to work stone, the amount of labor involved in producing such a system is staggering.

San Lorenzo might have been a center revered all over Early Formative Mesoamerica for its sanctity; here must have lived the mightiest of Olmec rulers and priests. It is impossible to estimate the population of the entire region, but the presence of about 200 earthen house mounds suggests a figure of about 1000 supporters and retainers within the ceremonial center. Abundant *manos* and *metates* indicate that maize agriculture, carried out on the river levees and in the more upland areas, was the base of the economy, but preserved faunal remains show that they relied heavily upon the fishing of snook, and the killing of turtles and domestic dogs for their meat supply. They were almost surely cannibals, for the remains of what seem to be slaughtered captives occur in kitchen middens.

The Olmec heartland is singularly deficient in many raw materials which were paradoxically prized by the San Lorenzo elite. Obsidian, for instance, which played a role in Mesoamerica similar to steel in western civilization, is found only in volcanic regions of Mexico and Guatemala far from the heartland. Yet probably several tonnes of this volcanic glass, so useful for cutting instruments, were imported by San Lorenzo from a wide variety of natural sources, as is proved by trace-element analysis. Another much-prized and imported substance was iron ore capable of taking a high polish, for this was turned into parabolic, concave mirrors which must have played a great ritual role. One finely tooled, lodestone sliver may well have acted as the world's first known compass, dedicated to geomantic purposes.

While the vast bulk of San Lorenzo-phase ceramics consists of neckless jars used to cook maize (probably as *tamales*), many vessels are carved with designs symbolic of Olmec deities. Significantly, these household vessels, when found outside the heartland such as in highland Mexico, occur in very high-status burials. The same can be said of the large, hollow, white-ware ceramic figures of babies. These nude, sexless and altogether mystifying creatures were apparently the focus of some sort of cult, temporally confined to the 1200–900 BC period, but we have no idea of their significance.

For unknown reasons, a vast destruction was visited upon San Lorenzo around 900 BC. A probably coeval cataclysm happened at its twin site of Laguna de los Cerros, but due to lack of excavation there we know very little about it. At San Lorenzo all of the available monuments on the surface at the time were deliberately mutilated— by smashing, pitting and grinding, slotting and so forth—and the remains dragged into long lines on the ridges, where they were carefully covered up. Invasion, revolution, periodic ritual destruction? All of these have been championed as destructive causes, but because the Olmec had no written records, we shall probably never know. At any rate, San Lorenzo never fully recovered, and while occupied sporadically until the Spanish conquest, was never the same place again.

La Venta

Its political successor seems to have been La Venta, located on an island in a swamp by the Río Tonalá, near the eastern edge of the Olmec heartland.

Middle Formative La Venta has some unique features not found in the earlier San Lorenzo. For one thing, the Olmec had by this time located

Olmec sites beyond the heartland

That the Olmec art style and influence had extended far beyond the borders of the heartland has long been known from excavations—legal and illegal—in the Mexican highlands. Some of the more striking of these finds belong to the San Lorenzo horizon, and have come from rich burials below house floors in large villages or towns. Best known of such sites is Tlatilco, on the north-western periphery of Mexico City, where hundreds of lavishly stocked sub-floor burials have been excavated: side by side with obviously local ceramic products are white-ware Olmec figurines and hollow "babies," and carved ceramic vessels which might well have been produced at San Lorenzo and exported to client rulers whom the San Lorenzo elite might have considered barbarians. Other such Olmec-influenced sites are known for the states of Puebla (particularly Las Bocas) and Morelos (Gualupita).

Chalcatzingo, situated about 120 kilometers southeast of Mexico City, is one of the most impressive sites in all Mesoamerica. Here, in the eastern part of the state of Morelos, three great peaks rise from the nearly flat valley floor. At the base of the cliff of the central peak, along the top edge of the talus slope, a Mexican investigator discovered in 1934 a series of bas reliefs on enormous boulders which she immediately identified as Olmec, similar to the carvings then known for La Venta. Excavations conducted by the University of Illinois have shown that, while the earliest occupation of Chalcatzingo dates to the Early Formative, and has ceramics and figurines similar to those of Tlatilco, the major period of activity at the site, including the rock carvings, belongs to the Middle Formative and is thus contemporary with La Venta rather than with San Lorenzo.

The greatest of the carvings, Relief 1, depicts a skirted woman with towering headdress seated upon a throne, within a cave-like opening formed by the open maw of the Olmec Dragon, the civilization's principal deity. From its mouth emanates steam or smoke, while above the scene, which surely represents a female ruler of Chalcatzingo, three stylized rain clouds give off phallic drops. The nearby Relief 2 shows an ithyphallic, prone and bound captive being threatened by two Olmec warriors wearing were-jaguar masks, perhaps a scene of conquest, while another relief depicts two rampant jaguar deities attacking nude men.

Sporadic finds of objects in Olmec style have been made for many years in the state of Guerrero, which fronts on the Pacific in southern Mexico, and in fact such a large quantity of magnificent, blue-green Olmec jades has come from that region that the late artist-archaeologist Miguel Covarrubias proposed Guerrero as the *fons et origo* of Olmec civilization. However, this is highly unlikely as the region is one of desert valleys and rugged, desiccated mountains. That the Olmec *were* in Guerrero is certain, but they surely would have settled there only after they had learned the art of irrigation.

Until 1966 no truly Olmec site was known for Guerrero. In July of that year Gillett Griffin, of Princeton University, and Carlo Gay, a retired Italian industrialist, discovered the remarkable cave paintings of Juxtlahuaca, known for decades previously, but not recognized for what they are:

Olmec cave paintings in the state of Guerrero combine human-animal motifs with rain-fertility and origin myth iconography. This scene of a ruler and a captive from a cave at Juxtlahuaca must have contained a message, but the exact personages or groups remain unknown. Similar Olmec ruler and animal themes are seen in the Oxtotitlan cave paintings, 125 km. north of Juxtlahuaca. Gulf Coast contact with the highlands began by about 1000 BC; Guerrero cave paintings are believed to date to between 900 and 700 BC.

several major sources of jade, which was to remain until the conquest the major symbol of Meso-american wealth. Serpentine had been known in the San Lorenzo phase, but the three great buried mosaic pavements of complex A, in the form of stylized were-jaguar masks, each containing about 485 serpentine blocks, are special to La Venta. Along the north–south center line of Complex A, excavators have found a number of buried votive offerings, including cruciform deposits of jade celts and concave iron-ore mirrors, along with the spectacular Offering No. 4, a group of celts and figurines of jade and serpentine arranged in a kind of conversation piece.

Like San Lorenzo, La Venta also had its paroxysm of destruction, when its colossal heads, "altars" (more likely thrones), and other sculptures were mutilated in almost identical fashion. Olmec civilization in the heartland was largely extinguished, although the site of Tres Zapotes, on the western flanks of the Tuxtlas, carried on an epi-Olmec culture, which shares many elements with the proto-Maya Izapan civilization developing in the Late Formative in Chiapas and Guatemala, including the genesis of writing and the calendar.

genitals from which blood flows in flowery patterns. Long called *Danzantes* ("dancers"), there is little doubt that they are actually portraits of rulers slain in Monte Albán's wars of conquest. Associated with them are hieroglyphs which must indicate their names, along with more elaborate inscriptions including notations in the 52-year Calendar Round system. This is the earliest body of writing in Mesoamerica, since the Olmec used only a very rudimentary script at the end of their span; it may be that it was the Zapotec who invented writing and the Mesoamerican calendar in the first place.

Monte Albán II is a Late Formative occupation of the site that develops out of Monte Albán I. The most notable structure of the period at the capital site is building J, a stone monument with a ground plan like a great arrowhead, with gloomy interior passages built on the principle of the corbel vault, or "false" arch. Monte Albán II was marked by even more widespread conquests than I, including the Cuicatec country. These triumphs are celebrated by slabs fixed into the walls of the building, bearing long hieroglyphic inscriptions giving the place-name of the conquered town and the date on which it transpired. "Art of conquest" would be an apt term for the sculpture of pre-Classic Monte Albán, as the Zapotec consolidated one of the largest states in early Mesoamerica.

Dainzú, to the southeast of Oaxaca City, has a very similar sculptural style during Monte Albán II times, but here the emphasis is not upon captives but upon ballplayers clad in protective uniforms (the large rubber ball used in the game was solid and extremely dangerous) which include headgear similar to the jousting helmets of medieval Europe. Some of the figures, nonetheless, may very well be dead.

TOMB CULTURES OF WESTERN MEXICO

Some of the most common objects in museum collections of pre-Columbian art are large, hollow, pottery figures of people and animals from western Mexico. These are often executed in a lively, naturalistic style that immediately endears them to the viewer. All of them seem to come from tombs in the western states of Colima, Nayarit and Jalisco, but regrettably no professional archaeologist has ever been able to excavate and record an intact tomb, although looted ones have been described.

The tombs themselves were generally cut down from the surface into the underlying volcanic tufa, and are sometimes reached by deep shafts. Since the skeletons are of no interest to the plunderers, these are often left in place, giving clearcut evidence that each tomb, sometimes with multiple chambers, was used for family or lineage burials over a considerable period of time.

Because of the lack of archaeological information on these tombs and the clay figures, their exact dating is not known, but probably all of them belong to the latter part of the Formative period. The oldest figures are probably the so-called "Chinesco" ones from Nayarit. Like all of the more-or-less human figures from the area they seem to come in male-female pairs (perhaps representing

Left "Danzante," a Monte Albán stone slab carved in bas relief. To the Zapotecs a naked human figure in contorted pose symbolized a slain captive. More than 300 such slabs were set in rows at structure L, one of the earliest buildings at Monte Albán, commemorating conquest. In later Monte Albán times at least 100 were unceremoniously redeposited as the construction material of new buildings.

Right The elongated head, distinctly rimmed eyes, hatchet nose and static pose characterize hollow "Ameca Gray" terracotta figures from Jalisco. Typical of West Mexican mortuary offerings, vast quantities of quixotic human and animal representations are best known from museum and private collections, as, deplorably, looters virtually cleaned out the tombs before proper archaeological work could be carried out.

Olmec. Juxtlahuaca lies among the bone-dry hills of east-central Guerrero, and is a down-sloping cavern extending about 1·25 kilometers into one of these hills. The paintings occupy two chambers near the very end of the cavern, and must have been the focus of a rite connected with the cult of the dead and the Underworld. The principal painting, in black and various earth colors, shows what seems to be a captive cringing below an imposing Olmec ruler, with black beard and horizontally striped tunic, and jaguar leggings and arm coverings. In the final chambers a great red-painted snake appears on a slab jutting out from the cave wall. The crossed bands in its eye and the panache of green feathers on its head reveal this to be one of the most ancient and important Mesoamerican deities, the Feathered Serpent.

There is now no dispute over the primacy of the Olmec civilization of the "heartland": this was Mesoamerica's first complex society. Olmec objects and influence are found all the way from central Mexico down to Costa Rica. Whether by emulation or conquest or trade, or missionary enterprise (or combinations of any or all of these), the Olmec example of a society ruled by an elite class devoted to the worship of gods and ancestors became the rule in many areas outside the heartland. Some of these regions, such as the Valley of Oaxaca, seem almost to have been autochthonous developments, while others, such as the early Maya, seem to have been direct descendants of the Olmec.

Early Zapotec civilization

Monte Albán is a hilltop site strategically located at the place where the three arms of the Valley of Oaxaca join, and was the center of Zapotec military, cultural and political power from its inception about 500 BC until its decline after 800 AD. Its earliest rulers, during the Middle Formative Monte Albán I phase, had its summit leveled into a series of broad plazas. A temple platform bordering one of these was faced with an extraordinary series of stone slabs carved in low relief; these show nude male figures in low but bold relief, with closed eyes, open mouths, and often with mutilated

ancestors), but are wonderfully stylized with slanting eyes and greatly elongated, seated bodies.

In the later Nayarit style there are warriors; village groups complete with houses, people and even temples; and ballcourts complete with players and spectators.

Artistically speaking, the most impressive figures come from tombs in Colima, and include humans engaged in a wide variety of activities (such as carrying loads of pottery to market) and dogs. The latter are of the special breed that was fattened on corn and used as a source of meat in ancient Mexico.

It was long thought that West Mexican tomb sculpture was a genre art, depicting the here-and-now in a way calculated to amuse the honored dead in the hereafter. Recently, however, the anthropologist Peter Furst has called this interpretation into question, by suggesting that this basically funerary art has two important themes: shamanism and the world of the dead. The so-called warriors, for instance, are actually in a stance adopted by New World shamans when they are doing battle with evil spirits or other shamans, while the Nayarit two-story house groups apparently depict an upper world of the living and a lower world of the defunct. And one might also point out that dogs, in

Right: Tomb cultures of western Mexico
Many thousands of large pottery figures are known to have come from deeply buried tombs reached by shafts cut down through natural volcanic tuff in the western Mexican states of Colima, Jalisco and Nayarit. These tombs, which often have multiple chambers as though for the interment of whole families or lineages, have never been dated satisfactorily, but can probably be placed in the Late Formative period.

Colima tomb figures are exceptionally well made, and often depict warriors brandishing clubs and spears. It has been suggested that these might be shamans in the fighting stance taken to counter evil spirits or rivals shamans.

Jalisco is a very large state, the archaeology of which is poorly known. Its tomb figures are highly variable in style and may cover a long time period.

The oldest tomb figures are probably those in "Chinesco" style from Nayarit. Later Nayarit figures regularly occur in male-female pairs, probably indicating that most of this West Mexican tomb art is concerned with ancestral figures. The most renowned tomb sculpture from the state consists of individual two-story houses and even complete villages, sometimes with dozens of small figures engaged in a variety of activities. Ballcourt scenes carried out in clay are also known.

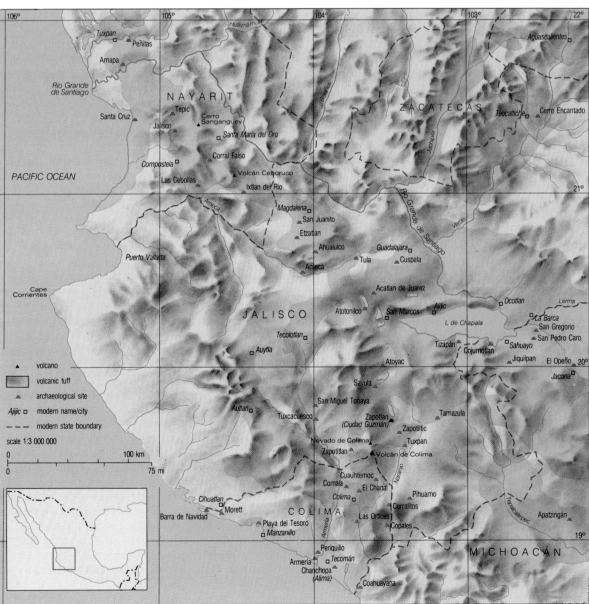

volcano
volcanic tuff
archaeological site
Ajijic   modern name/city
- - -   modern state boundary
scale 1:3 000 000
0   100 km
0   75 mi

Mesoamerican thought, were believed to conduct their masters' souls across their version of the River Styx on the dread voyage to the underworld.

Unsatisfactory as our knowledge now is, we nevertheless can gain an almost unique view into the world of early Mesoamerica through these figures.

CLASSIC TEOTIHUACAN AND ITS EMPIRE

The relative obscurity and cultural backwardness into which the Valley of Mexico had fallen after the decline of Olmec influence were dramatically reversed about the beginning of the Christian era with the rise of Teotihuacan. The establishment of this greatest of all preconquest American cities marks the beginning of the Classic era in Mesoamerica, at least as far as central Mexico is concerned. (The Classic period opens more than two centuries later in the Maya lowlands.) No city, no state, no culture exerted more influence over the rest of Mesoamerica than did Teotihuacan, not even the Olmec or the Toltec or the Aztec, so it is virtually certain that Teotihuacan was the capital of an empire even mightier than that of the Aztec. This is not to say that there were no independent entities within its territory (such, in fact, existed for the Aztec). The Zapotec of Classic Monte Albán, for instance, seem to have maintained their political integrity and dealt with the Teotihuacanos on a diplomatic footing, but even their culture bears the imprint of Teotihuacan.

The city of Teotihuacan

This great metropolis lies in the valley of Teotihuacan, a well-watered plain on the northeastern side of the Valley of Mexico, where the San Juan River and its tributaries drain into Lake Texcoco. Adding to the agricultural amenities of this favored region are some large, perennial springs which, along with the less dependable watercourses, offered the possibility of irrigation. William Sanders and his associates have long championed the idea that Teotihuacan was an irrigation, or "hydraulic," civilization, but unfortunately firm evidence for canals of this early date in the valley has been scant indeed.

The city is one of the best- and most extensively investigated archaeological sites in the New World: much of this work has been carried out by René Millon of the University of Rochester, who directed the Teotihuacan Mapping Project. It is now known that the urbanized zone of Teotihuacan covers over 20 square kilometers. While there is some Late Formative settlement in the northwestern part of the city, most of it seems to have been surveyed and laid out on a grid pattern in one massive operation. Exactly how large the population was can only be conjectured, but a reasonable guess might lie between 125 000 and 250 000—far greater than most Old World cities of its day. The basic modular unit of Teotihuacan city planning was a one-story, square apartment complex 50–60 meters on each side, surrounded by a high exterior wall. Within the more affluent compounds, usually located closer to the Avenue of the Dead than the others, roofed living and sleeping quarters gave onto open spaces like Roman atria, which were generally flanked by low entablature-batter platforms on which family or lineage rituals might have taken place. In these upper- or middle-class apartment complexes the interior walls were painted in stylized, highly repetitive patterns of mythological figures and scenes. The most renowned of these is the so-called Paradise of Tlaloc in the Tepantitla Palace, which is supposed to depict the heaven to which went those blessed by a watery death (such as drowning, lightning strikes or dropsy), but which is more likely to have been a realm presided over by a widespread Spider Goddess. Its multitude of dancing and playing figures, in a landscape of trees, flowers and butterflies, is justly famous.

Away from the elite residences of the center of the city were the far less impressive dwellings of the city's artisans and lesser merchants. Excavations have shown these to have been more like the rabbit warrens of the traditional city of medieval Europe or the Middle East, with tiny rooms, crowded conditions and mean alleys between dwellings.

Hundreds of obsidian workshops have been discovered within the city, for obsidian was a major local resource which was indispensable as a material for edged tools in ancient Mesoamerica and Teotihuacan controlled some of the most important obsidian quarries. The city also produced elite ceramics which were widely exported throughout Mesoamerica, especially to the Maya area. Typical of the kind of high-status Teotihuacan ceramics which were imitated, or even imported, by foreign elites within the Teotihuacan cultural orbit are slab-footed tripod cylinders fitted with lids. These are often stuccoed and painted in the Teotihuacan mural style with mythological scenes. Thin Orange ware, perhaps produced in the modern state of Puebla, is another hallmark of the city's influence over the rest of Mesoamerica, for it appears in offerings to the honored dead as far away as the Maya area.

The economy and culture of Teotihuacan

A prime question of Mesoamericanists is: what was the economic basis which gave rise to Teotihuacan and enabled it to establish its overwhelming preeminence? As far as agriculture is concerned, the Valley of Teotihuacan, even if irrigation *had* been practiced, could never have supported a population as large as the ancient city. However, on the Millon maps there are clear indications of *chinampas* in one section of Teotihuacan. In Aztec times *chinampas* (the misnamed "floating gardens") were rectangular plots of land left by canal-cutting in the swampy margins of the great lake, made fertile by periodic applications of pond weeds and mud. They were incredibly fertile and provided the "breadbasket" for the Aztec capital. *Chinampas* still survive in the Xochimilco zone to the south of Mexico City; significantly, the orientation of the Xochimilco canal grid is exactly the same as that of Teotihuacan, and it seems likely that the subsistence base of the ancient city comprised the entire Valley of Mexico, including its *chinampas*.

There can also be no doubt that Teotihuacan was heavily involved in trade with the rest of Mesoamerica. Thousands of artisans were engaged in

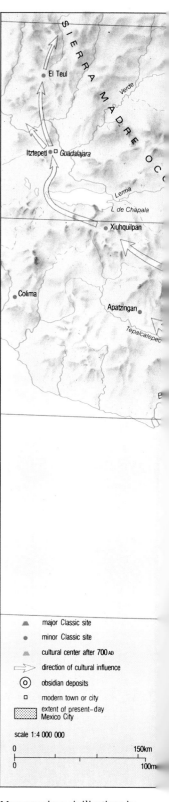

▲	major Classic site
●	minor Classic site
⧄	cultural center after 700 AD
⇨	direction of cultural influence
◎	obsidian deposits
□	modern town or city
▦	extent of present-day Mexico City

scale 1:4 000 000

0   150km

0   100m

Mesoamerican civilizations in the Classic period
The Classic florescence of Mesoamerican civilization, which began in the 2nd century AD, was a period in which the ruling classes had consolidated their power and began to exercise an influence—political and cultural—across surrounding territory. Beneath this intellectual elite the meager lot of the peasantry had, by contrast, hardly changed from Formative times. No center enjoyed a greater success than did Teotihuacan. It grew to extend a vast trade network across much of Mesoamerica, including the Maya lands. With

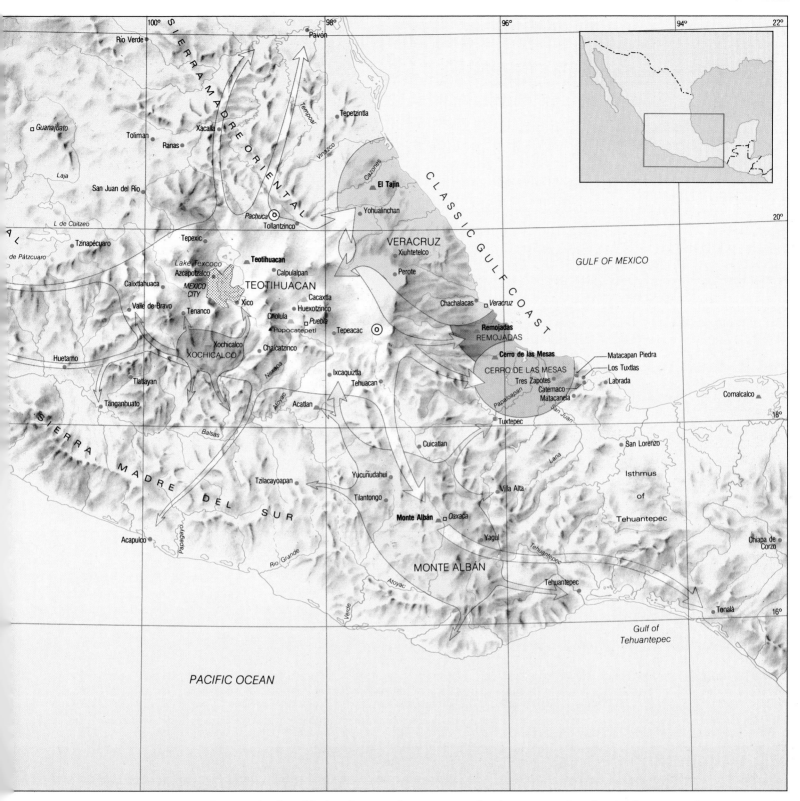

commercial transaction came cultural exchange: the art of the Teotihuacanos dominated the styles of the other rising civilizations of the day and, in return, Teotihuacan received the influence of the Gulf Coast and Monte Albán styles, at least in its germinal stages. When Teotihuacan fell in the 7th century the relationship of the highland Mexicans with the Maya, one hitherto dominated by the former, began to change. Evidence from such sites as Cacaxtla and Xochicalco—as well as from later Monte Albán—reveals a powerful Maya presence in the period following Teotihuacan's collapse.

producing obsidian blades, knives, dart points and other much-needed tools for the foreign market, particularly from the fine, greenish obsidian from the Pachuca mines which Teotihuacan controlled. Archaeological research has shown that foreign merchants and perhaps artisans had taken up residence in the great city. The Millon project disclosed an entire Oaxaca ward, complete with its own Zapotec gray-ware idols, and the Swedish excavations of the 1930s turned up, in another section of the city, Early Classic Maya polychrome pottery manufactured in the Petén lowlands.

It should be emphasized that, while scattered Teotihuacan hieroglyphs, probably mostly calendrical, have been identified, there are no written

documents for the civilization. Thus any reconstruction of the polity and society of Teotihuacan must remain a matter of conjecture. How one reconstructs these depends on the degree to which one is willing to project back into the distant past the Aztec model of empire, for which we have detailed documentation. Were the Aztec, through the Toltec, the cultural heirs of Teotihuacan? Did the Teotihuacanos speak an ancestral form of Nahua, or Nahuatl, the Aztec tongue? We know that the Aztec state was an empire of conquest, and that the mainstay of their economy was less the production of food and the other necessities of life than the heavy tribute enforced from subjugated and usually unwilling peoples. The evidence of the

Teotihuacan •

Teotihuacan

Right Plan of the ceremonial center of Teotihuacan. The Teotihuacan Mapping Project's aerial and surface survey identified more than 5000 structures including 2300 residences. Intense building activity began about 400 AD when the city took on the shape it was to retain until its collapse.

Below The Pyramid of the Sun faces west onto the great concourse. Mounds lining this north–south axis, largely unexcavated until the 1960s, were thought to contain burials; hence the misnomer, Street of the Dead. Archaeologists, however, uncovered platforms which are thought to be temple bases, and spaces in which priests carried out ritual activities. Structures in front of the pyramid may have housed the priests themselves. The dominant mountain, Cerro Gordo, serves as a dramatic background for the Pyramid of the Moon, and was undoubtedly the focal point for the alignment of the main avenue.

The main axis of Teotihuacan is the Avenue of the Dead, running approximately north–south (in fact, it is oriented to 15°03′ east of true north, apparently for astronomical reasons). Aerial photography has revealed that there is an east–west avenue lying at right angles to it. The center of the city as defined by these avenues would be just in front of the great square enclosure, probably the royal palace, known as the *Ciudadela*, or "Citadel." Teotihuacan was thus divided into quarters like those which we know existed in the much later Aztec capital of Tenochtitlan.

Teotihuacan's most imposing structure—one which can be seen from many kilometers away—is the Pyramid of the Sun. Tunneling carried out by archaeologists over the last six decades has shown that it was largely constructed at the end of the Late Formative by laborers bringing in millions of adobes and basketloads of rubble. In its final form it rose up in four great tiers to the 70-meter-high summit, on which probably stood a temple structure with a flat roof. Whether this temple was actually devoted to the worship of the sun, as Aztec tradition would have it, is unknown, but a recent discovery underneath the pyramid suggests why the pyramid was built there in the first place. This proved to be a natural cave, enlarged by the ancients into a clover-leaf-shaped chamber, and

reached by a tunnel, directly beneath the very center of the pyramid. It has been suggested on ethnohistorical grounds that the earliest Teotihuacanos might have viewed this as a supernatural "Place of Emergence," a kind of cave-womb from which the ancestors of the tribes came. Since the Pyramid of the Sun is not only the earliest but also the largest ritual structure in the city, it might also explain why the city was founded there, and not elsewhere, in the Valley of Mexico.

There are other important ritual buildings. The Pyramid of the Moon, less imposing than the Pyramid of the Sun, is situated at the northern end of the Avenue of the Dead. Like many of the important structures at Teotihuacan, its exterior exhibits a typically Teotihuacano architectural motif: a rectangular, framed entablature above a sloping batter. All such exteriors are covered with thick, white plaster, and were usually painted red or with polychrome mythological scenes. The *Ciudadela* has already been mentioned. This is basically a broad, sunken courtyard which contains near its center the imposing Temple of Quetzalcoatl, a four-sided entablature-batter pyramid on which austere relief figures of Feathered Serpents alternate with Fire Serpents, expressing the basic opposition between greenness and life on the one hand, and hot, fiery deserts on the other.

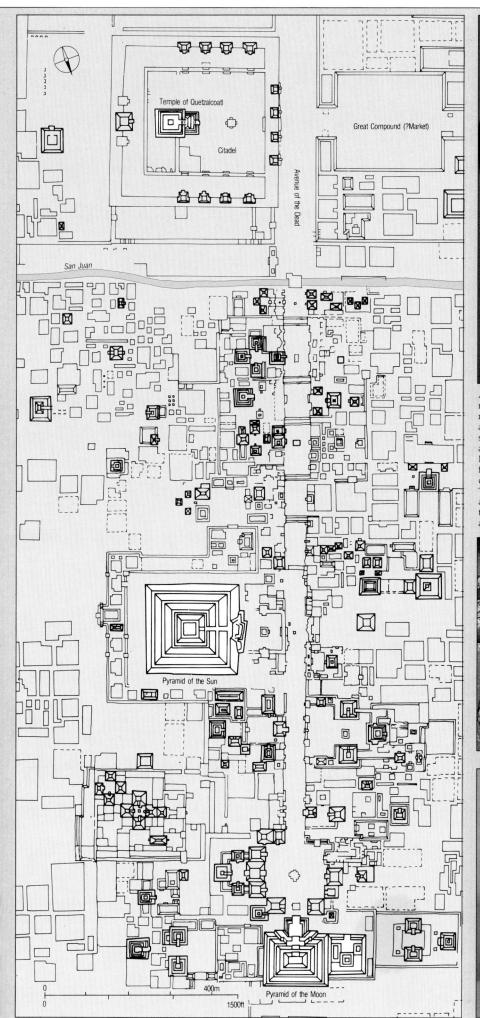

Above Stone and terracotta masks are diagnostic among the many kinds of Teotihuacan artifacts. Life-size, or slightly smaller, they may have been attached to mummy bundles. Perhaps intended as portraits, facial configuration and dimension are recognizably Teotihuacan. Similar proportions are repeated in mass-produced terracotta figurines and censers, and in this tiny jade masquette.

Below A more naturalistic rendering of an eagle, dated to the earliest period of mural painting, is repeated on the base of the platform in the Temple of the Feathered Shells.

Bottom This stuccoed and painted tripod vessel features the head of a feathered jaguar, a common theme in Teotihuacan art.

The Mesoamerican Ballgame

The ballgame was pan-Mesoamerican in scope. It was played with a large, solid rubber ball in a specially made court, between two opposing teams. The earliest courts date from Olmec times, and were simple, basinlike structures with earthen retaining walls. By the Classic period, masonry courts with sloping playing surfaces were found throughout Mesoamerica except for Teotihuacan, where sunken sections of the Avenue of the Dead may have played the same role. Although the ball could not be held in the hand during play, and the best shots were delivered from the hip, the rules of the game and how it was scored are poorly understood. Equipment to protect the players from injury included a wide, heavy belt of wood and leather, hippads, kneepads, gloves and in some areas even helmets. Nevertheless, because of the speed and weight of the ball the game was very dangerous.

The ballgame was not a mere athletic contest. The court itself was a cosmological diagram, with the ball symbolizing the sun. The game was deeply imbued with the imagery of death and sacrifice, and the post-game ceremonies seem to have included the sacrifice of the losers.

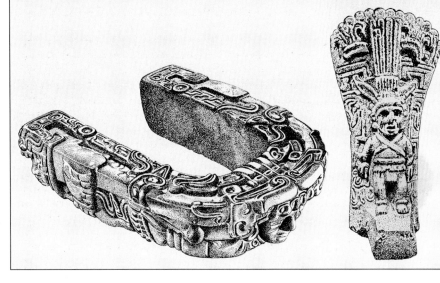

Above left Relief panel from ballcourt at El Tajín, Veracruz, Mexico. Late Classic. The captain of the losing team is stretched over a sacrificial stone while a victor drives his knife into his chest.
Far left Green stone "yoke," Classic Central Veracruz culture. Yokes are stone replicas of the protective belts of wood and leather, and were worn by ballplayers in post-game ceremonies.
Center left Basalt *palma* depicting a bound captive. Classic Central Veracruz culture. *Palmas* are spatulate stones which were placed on the front of yokes worn during post-game rites.
Left Basalt *hacha*, or thin stone head, depicting a vulture. *Hachas* were apparently worn like *palmas* on the front of yokes.

"Teotihuacan horizon" in Mesoamerica suggests very much the same state of affairs, but on a far grander scale.

The Teotihuacan state was not only moved by economic forces, it was also guided by ideology. While the Olmec had their gods and their pantheon, we can identify these with later Mesoamerican deities only in the most indirect way. However with Teotihuacan we now have gods who are quite recognizable in terms of later Mesoamerican religious systems, particularly Aztec. Present are Tlaloc, the Rain God; Chalchiuhtlicue, the Water Goddess and consort of Tlaloc; Mictlantecuhtli, Lord of the Underworld; Quetzalcoatl, the Feathered Serpent; and a host of others who formed part of the Teotihuacan state cult. As the Mexican scholar Ignacio Bernal has stressed, with Teotihuacan we are in the presence of the first fully Mesoamerican culture.

The downfall of Teotihuacan

As the dominating cultural force in Mesoamerica, Teotihuacan came to an end in the 7th century AD. For want of written records it is always difficult to be sure about the factors causing the demise of ancient states. The late George Vaillant once surmised that there might have been a degradation of the environment caused by massive deforestation of the Mexican highlands. All of the untold amounts of lime plaster that went into the construction of Teotihuacan would have to have been produced by the burning of staggering amounts of wood.

One thing is sure, though: much of the city was destroyed by flames, either the result of invasion or of internal insurrection. Evidence for this is particularly strong in the more elite zones flanking the Avenue of the Dead. The impressive Palace of the Quetzal-Butterfly, on the west side of the plaza in front of the Pyramid of the Moon, was completely burned and destroyed. People did continue to live in the city, however, at least in those parts spared destruction, right through the Aztec period.

When the Aztec emperors made their annual pilgrimage to Teotihuacan, the city was largely in ruins. Its glories were only remembered in mythological terms: this had been a city built by giants, so important that the gods created the world anew in that place.

CLASSIC VERACRUZ CIVILIZATION

During the last centuries before the birth of Christ, whatever was left of Olmec culture had been so transformed that it was scarcely recognizable as such. At great and long-occupied centers like Tres Zapotes, on the slopes of the Tuxtla Mountains, a few Olmec sculptural traditions remained, but links were far stronger with the Proto-Maya Izapan tradition in Chiapas and Guatemala than with the more ancient Olmec. Most significantly, the intellectuals and elite of southern Veracruz, toward the end of the final century BC, had begun to calculate dates in the calendar known as the Long Count; this great advance was shared with the Izapan tradition, and eventually led to the Classic Maya calendar. After the 6th century AD, however, the

Above Rollout of a Late Classic vase from the Central Maya area. Two contestants propel between them a rubber ball, exaggerated to huge dimensions, in front of a stepped playing surface. This may illustrate a scene in the *Popol Vuh* (the epic of the Quiché Maya) in which two sets of twins are challenged in turn to a ballgame with the Lords of the Underworld.

Left The I-shaped ballcourt at Xochicalco, Morelos, Mexico. End of the Late Classic. This is one of the earliest courts with rings on the vertical walls above the playing surfaces. According to late tradition, a player who drove the ball through a ring not only won the game but also the clothing and jewelry of the spectators.

use of the Long Count completely died out everywhere except the Maya lowlands.

Cerro de las Mesas

Occupied from the Middle Formative through the Post-Classic, Cerro de las Mesas is a very large mound site, only now being mapped by Barbara Stark of Arizona State University; the long archaeological sequence of the site is as yet poorly known. Excavations and explorations carried out by Matthew Stirling, however, suggested that its period of apogee was the Early Classic, roughly from 300 to 600 AD, contemporary with Teotihuacan's era of hegemony. Little is known about the site's architecture, which was mainly built in earth and clay, but Cerro de las Mesas has a large number of stone monuments, none of them Olmec. Two of these are stelae bearing Long Count dates which fall in the years 468 AD and 533 AD respectively; associated with them are relief figures of striding male individuals. The events recorded by the dates are probably historical.

That the rulers of Classic Cerro de las Mesas were collectors of a kind is demonstrated by the chance discovery of an enormous cache of jade and serpentine objects buried underneath a clay stairway; included in this virtual treasure trove were such items as a jade canoe incised with La Venta-style Olmec were-jaguar faces, jade celts of Costa Rican provenance, and Early Classic Maya jade plaques and earspools. Cerro de las Mesas is also noted, like other central Veracruz sites of the Early Classic period, for large, hollow pottery figures of their deities, including a particularly remarkable (and androgynous) idol of the Old Fire God.

El Tajín and Classic Veracruz civilization

If one trait may be said to characterize the Classic civilization of Veracruz, it is the ballgame—a highly ritual contest which has deep roots in Olmec culture. On the Gulf Coast this pan-Mesoamerican game was intimately associated with human sacrifice and the Underworld, perhaps including the immolation of the captain of the losing team.

Three kinds of stone objects are particularly frequent in collections from Classic Veracruz, and all three can be proved to be associated with the ballgame. The first of these is the stone "yoke," a U-shaped object representing the protective belt of wood and leather worn about the waist during the game. The second is the *hacha* or "thin stone head"; and the third is the *palma* or "palmate stone"; either of these could be stood on the front of the "yoke" during the post-game sacrificial ceremonies. These objects are richly carved with mythological, Underworld motifs against a background of interlaced, raised-edge scrolls which are the hallmark of central Veracruz art during the Classic period, wherever it is found. This style is often associated in the literature with the Totonac, and it may be significant that the Totonac claimed to have built Teotihuacan. Several stone reliefs in central Veracruz are known for Teotihuacan, as well as a temple platform near the Avenue of the Dead embellished with polychrome murals with Veracruz scrollwork motifs.

The "type site" of Classic Veracruz civilization is El Tajín, in the Totonac country of north-central Veracruz, a fertile region of low hills noted for its

El Tajín

Above The Death God emerges from an intricate scrollwork design, a monument on the steps of a structure at El Tajín.

Right The Pyramid of the Niches (18 m. high), probably the oldest building at El Tajín, is thought to date to 600 AD. Three hundred and sixty-five niches, 0·6 m. deep, cover all four sides of the pyramid, creating a sharp play of light and shadow under the tropical Veracruz sky.

Below View of El Tajín with the
Pyramid of the Niches in the
center, surrounded by pyramids
and ballcourts. Tajín Chico, a
section of later construction and
different orientation, lies to the
north. Largely composed of
unexcavated mounds, the
ceremonial center covers only 60
hectares of an archaeological
zone of 950 hectares. At least 12
mounds are known to be
ballcourts, the largest number
that has been identified at any
Mesoamerican site. The
chronology of El Tajín is poorly
understood, but the Veracruz
settlement is considered to have
been at its apogee in the Late
Classic period.

The most noteworthy structure at El Tajín is the
Pyramid of the Niches, a four-sided stepped pyramid with an east-facing stairway and 365 niches,
each reputed by legend to have contained an idol
for a day of the year. Other extant buildings at El
Tajín, perhaps palaces or administrative structures,
had flat roofs of poured concrete. The dominant
decorative motif in Tajín architecture was the
stepped fret, perhaps representing rain clouds.

There are at least three stone ballcourts known
at El Tajín. The greatest of these has three stone
reliefs on each facing wall, all carried out in the
typical Veracruz interlocking scrollwork, but the
subject matter is far from decorative: there are
scenes of human sacrifice in ballcourts, with the
participants wearing the regulation "yokes" and
palmas. Another relief shows a god drawing
blood from his penis in a typically Mesoamerican
act of autosacrifice. While Classic Veracroz iconography has barely been studied seriously, it is clear
that there are close relationships with the Underworld ideology of the Classic Maya elite.

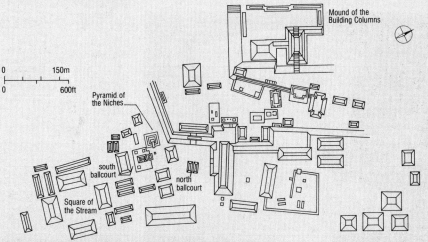

Above The Mound of the
Building Columns overlooks the
plaza of Tajín Chico. So named
for six columns made of stacked
stone disks 25 cm. thick, an
architectural device unique at
Tajín, the building is probably
of the latest phase.

Left The southwest panel (1·7 m.
high by 2 m. wide) of the south
ballcourt. The central bird-man
figure lifts his arms over a prone
sacrificial figure, flanked by
musicians holding respectively a
rattle and percussion instrument.
A skeletal figure floats amid
scroll designs above the sacrifice
scene. The ballgame and ritual
sacrifice, presented in narrative
style on carved stone panels,
decorate El Tajín's major
structures.

production of vanilla. This is a very large conglomeration of stone architecture, largely of the Late Classic period (600–900 AD), reminiscent of some of the great Classic centers of the Maya lowlands.

Veracruz and Teotihuacan

The Teotihuacan presence is not so obvious at Cerro de las Mesas and El Tajín, perhaps because of the lack of modern excavation at these sites. But at the mound site of Matacapan, in the Tuxtla Mountains, there is clearcut evidence that the Teotihuacanos had established a way-station, perhaps a post regulating long-distance trade. In the Early Classic they built several earth-and-clay platforms in the archetypical entablature-and-batter style that exactly presage the elite burial platforms of one of their more distant outposts: Kaminaljuyú, in highland Guatemala.

The Remojadas culture

Mound groups dot the central Veracruz lowlands. Although only a few of these have been investigated archaeologically, most of them can probably be ascribed to the Classic period. Many mounds have produced pottery burial figures, in what has been called the Remojadas style, often decorated with bitumen paint or *chapopote*, dating from the Late Formative until the Early Post-Classic (after 900 AD).

Most striking of these are huge, hollow figures of the gods and goddesses worshiped by the Classic

Above A grinning boy; one of the many "Remojadas" figurines from central Veracruz. The exuberant expression gives prominence to the style's realism yet the design incorporates geometric features. The meaning of such figures awaits explanation. Other Remojadas sculpture includes warriors, ballgame-players, lovers and animals.

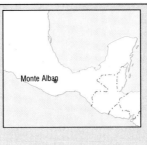

Monte Albán

Below Stela 6 depicts a bound man standing on a place glyph; a speech scroll issues from his mouth. It is one of 15 stelae, recovered in period III contexts (100 – 600 AD), showing captives or conquerors. Evidence for an earlier writing system and concerns with conquest appear as early as period I (500 BC – 200 AD).

In the Classic period Monte Albán was a major, stone-built ceremonial center, with plazas, terraces, temple platforms and one very large (and still unexcavated) pyramid. The platforms seem to have supported low temples with flat, beamed roofs, somewhat in the style of Teotihuacan, but differing from it in details of the entablatures. During the Mexican excavations of the 1930s, Alfonso Caso and his colleagues uncovered 170 underground tombs at Monte Albán, most of them Classic (Monte Albán IIIA and B) in date, and many of them very elaborate.

There are large numbers of stelae and other reliefs in Classic Monte Albán, many of them set architectonically into platforms. On these appears a script which, while definitely descended from Monte Albán I and II writing, is largely unread. Only the calendrical notations are even partially understood: they seem to have expressed days in terms of the 52-year Calendar Round (i.e. in terms of a day in the 260-day count, along with the year in a cycle of 52 years), as well as in a 13-day "week." The dates mainly appear to be associated with conquest events, a heritage from Formative Monte Albán. Bound captives often stand on a sign indicating the name of the town conquered by the lords of Monte Albán. One relief seems to have a more peaceful theme. According to Joyce Marcus, it represents a procession of envoys from Teotihuacan, bearing offerings or gifts to the Zapotec authorities. Apparently relations with the mighty empire were amicable.

Below Buildings in the main plaza of Monte Albán were laid out in period III. The population had reached its maximum, perhaps upward of 20 000. Residences, built on terraces cut into the sides of the mountain, housed the vast majority of Monte Albán inhabitants. Civic and ceremonial activities were

carried out in the main plaza. Buildings were added and enlarged; elaborately decorated tombs with rich offerings abounded. By period IV, Monte Albán's glory had faded. The population at Monte Albán dispersed as settlements in the valley grew into important centers.

Bottom Numerous terracotta urns were recovered in Monte Albán burials, as well as at other valley sites. Here a personage is identified by a buccal mask with bifid tongue. The conical hat (occasionally found with glyph C), pectoral, bead necklace and loincloth are usually combined on this kind of figure.

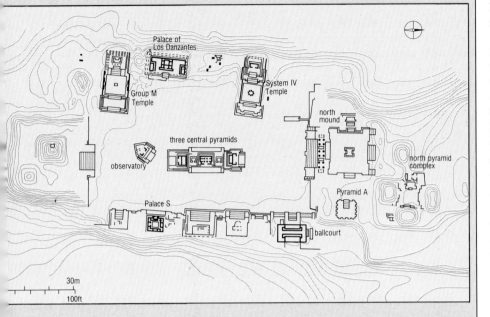

Below View of the southwestern side of Monte Albán. During Monte Albán period II (200 BC – 100 AD), a large part of the top of the 400-m.-high mountain was leveled and building activity commenced in earnest. Mound J (seen partially on the right; dated to period II), shaped like an arrowhead, may have been an observatory although 50 carved slabs with conquest glyphs line its sides.

peoples of Vcracruz, particularly the Cihuateteo—deified women who had died in childbirth and apotheosized as dread warrior goddesses. More pleasing to the modern eye are the "laughing figures" of idiotically grinning boys and girls with upraised hands. There is no convincing explanation of these, although it has been suggested that they represent the result of ingesting some kind of hallucinogenic plant, such as psychotropic mushrooms.

Further work on the Remojadas culture is much needed. In part its Late Classic manifestation is under strong Maya influence. The Teotihuacan element may also be present, for the geographer Alfred Siemens has discovered widespread relic *chinampas* in the area, with the same orientation (about 15° east of true north) as Teotihuacan itself. However, they remain to be dated.

The Zapotec of Classic Monte Albán

The three-armed Valley of Oaxaca saw complete continuity between the Formative and Classic splendors of the Zapotec state, which had been established at the hilltop site of Monte Albán by at least 400 BC. During the Formative there were only a few ritual-political centers in the valley; by the Classic several hundred. Not only was the prominent hill on which Monte Albán is placed completely terraced to support residential units, but all adjacent hills were also altered. This was a truly urban civilization, not quite the equal of Teotihuacan, but it was considerably more urbanized than the contemporary Classic Maya civilization.

Recent archaeological investigations have shown that the Zapotecs of the Classic period had extensively irrigated the somewhat dry valley bottomlands, allowing a considerable population build-up.

The study of the religious iconography of Monte Albán is still in its infancy. One of the problems is that a large number of Monte Albán urns in public collections are modern forgeries (according to thermoluminescence tests). An early colonial Spanish dictionary gives the names of a few Zapotec deities, but this must be only a partial list; prominent among them is Cocijo, the Rain God, but a Maize God is also named. The gods of the urns and the tomb murals are not easy to identify, but surely present is the Old Fire God, the Maize God and the Rain God. Also represented in their pantheon are several deities known for the Classic Maya, such as the Jaguar God of the Underworld and also an aged chthonic deity who is called Pauahtun by the Maya.

The Classic Monte Albán civilization began to collapse soon after 700 AD, as did Teotihuacan—the lowland Maya were soon to follow. In the final centuries of the Classic, Monte Albán IIIB was succeeded by Monte Albán IV, known mainly from the large and important site of Lambityeco, where a very elaborate tomb fronted with clay sculptures of a pair of aged deities has been found. Interestingly enough, two wares known to have been made in the Maya lowlands in the final centuries of the Classic were found in Monte Albán IV deposits, a case of Maya intrusion, which is also known from contemporaneous sites in the central Mexican highlands.

THE EMERGENCE OF MAYA CIVILIZATION

There can be little doubt that Classic Maya culture stood head and shoulders above other civilizations of the pre-Spanish New World. The Maya would certainly be the only aboriginal American people to claim the attention of historians of science. Their achievements have been long appreciated by European and American scholars, largely through their art, which is deceptively "realistic" according to Western standards, but it is now understood that the very premises upon which this art was based are totally alien to the Euroamerican mindset.

The critical area for the formation of proto-Maya civilization was the Pacific coastal plain of Chiapas and Guatemala, and the Guatemalan highlands around modern-day Guatemala City. Here there are a number of sites that have monumental reliefs in a style definitely ancestral to the earliest art in the Maya lowlands, and sometimes Long Count calendrical inscriptions far earlier than those known for the Classic Maya.

The Izapan civilization

Izapa is a key site in the early development of Maya civilization, located on the Pacific plain of Chiapas, very near the Guatemalan border. It consists of a large number of earthen mounds faced with river cobbles, and was occupied over a long period of time, from the Early Formative on. Its apogee was during the Late Formative, when many stone monuments were carved. They include the first example of the stela-"altar" complex that was to become typical of the Classic Maya in the lowlands.

The style of monumental relief carving at Izapa and related sites is cluttered and thoroughly baroque, quite different from the earlier and more "classic" Olmec style, but surely derived from it. There are complex scenes of gods performing actions. Other scenes are clearly related to the great Hero Twins myth of the *Popol Vuh* (the sacred book of one of the highland Maya nations).

While Izapa has no calendrical notations nor anything approaching writing on its monuments, it was certainly the major civilizational center in an area noted in Post-Classic and colonial times for its immense production of high-quality cacao beans, the source for the chocolate that was so prized by pre-Spanish peoples in Mesoamerica. (So highly regarded was the cacao tree that its beans were utilized as money in Aztec times.) It was cacao that probably accounts for the civilizational precocity of the Pacific coastal plain.

Kaminaljuyú

Probably the area most crucial to the transmission of this Izapan civilization to the Maya of the Petén was the region around Kaminaljuyú, on the western outskirts of modern Guatemala City. Before its destruction by unbridled real estate development, there were several hundred great platform mounds at the site, most of them Late Formative in date, but some of Early Classic age, along with associated plazas.

The sheer vastness of some of these centers staggers the imagination. During the Late Formative Chicanel phase of Maya culture, El Mirador saw the construction of the largest of all pyramidal constructions in the Western Hemisphere; it and its underlying substructure reach a combined height of 70 meters. These enormous, stucco-covered platform temples have a common feature wherever they are found: gigantic deity masks flanking the stairways.

There is also some evidence that lowland Maya agricultural practices, probably mostly dependent on the shifting, slash-and-burn method, were beginning to intensify at this time, for at least some of the raised fields known for the swampier areas of the southern lowlands seem to be of this date. This may account for the undoubted population explosion for which there is increasing evidence in the Late Formative. At any rate, population pressure and the leavening effect of Izapan and Kaminaljuyú culture soon resulted in Classic Maya civilization as we know it.

CLASSIC MAYA CIVILIZATION

The Classic Maya civilization is the only fully literate culture in the aboriginal New World. On its many stone monuments is carved a history which can now be read, thanks to remarkable advances made in hieroglyphic decipherment over the past quarter century.

The "typical" Maya civilization is that which flourished in the lowlands of the Petén-Yucatán Peninsula in the six centuries from about 300 AD to 900. It was characterized by towering temple-pyramids built of limestone and faced with lime stucco; multiroomed structures which have sometimes been called "palaces"; rooms spanned by the corbel or "false arch"; causeways connecting groups of structures within cities, and sometimes even cities themselves; masonry ballcourts; monumental inscriptions on stelae, on the altars sometimes associated with them, and on wall panels, hieroglyphic stairways, and occasionally on the buildings themselves; and very elaborate interments in building substructures, with rich offerings.

In contrast the highland Maya during the Classic span had no writing whatsoever (although they had a notable development of it in Late Formative times), no stone architecture, and of course a total absence of the corbel arch. Their culture, both in the Guatemalan uplands and in much of highland Chiapas, is very different from that of the lowlands, and in many respects hardly rates the designation "Maya." We shall now examine this culture as it was manifested at one of the great and ancient Mesoamerican centers.

Early Classic civilization at Kaminaljuyú

It will be remembered that Kaminaljuyú, on the western edge of modern Guatemala City, was a precocious center for Formative and what was to become Maya civilization. Its strategic location athwart the meeting place of the Atlantic and Pacific watersheds probably made it a strategic entrepôt for the shipment of such vital materials as

Above Kaminaljuyú stela II, Late Preclassic Miraflores phase in the Guatemalan highlands. Stelae from Cerro de las Mesas in Veracruz and Izapa on the Guatemalan Pacific coast share similar motifs of the long-lipped god and plumed headdress, foreshadowing Classic lowland Maya themes and suggesting close ideological ties over a wide geographical area.

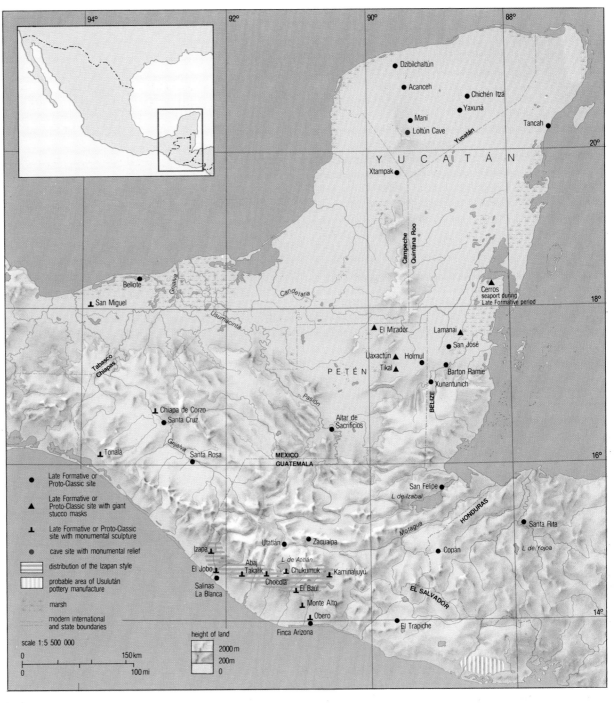

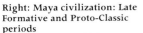

Right: Maya civilization: Late Formative and Proto-Classic periods

Complex ceremonial life among the ancient Maya began in the southern highlands and in the piedmont zone between it and the Pacific Coast. Here are a number of large mound sites with monuments carved in the Izapan style, so named from the type site of Izapa in Chiapas. Some of these sculptures have dates in the Long Count system, as at Abaj Takalik and El Baúl, although even earlier dates are known at Tres Zapotes in the Olmec area, and at Chiapa de Corzo.

During the Late Formative, after about 200 BC, Izapan culture was transmitted, via Kaminaljuyú, to the northern Petén lowlands, where Maya populations were burgeoning. There early monuments are seemingly absent, but in northeastern Petén and northern Belize there are some very large and important sites, such as Tikal and El Mirador, in which the stairways of great temple platforms were faced with gigantic stucco masks of the Maya gods. It was not until the end of the Proto-Classic, however, that dated stone monuments appear in the lowlands (stela 29 at Tikal, 292 AD).

The "index" pottery of the Late Formative in the Maya area is Usulután, an orange-slipped ware decorated with wavy parallel lines produced by a negative technique. It was probably manufactured in southeastern El Salvador.

obsidian to many areas of southeastern Mesoamerica. During the Early Classic, at about 400–500 AD, it attracted the attention of the great city of Teotihuacan in the central Mexico highlands, then the mightiest power in Mesoamerica. A substantial portion of the Guatemalan capital was remodeled along Teotihuacan architectural lines, even though the local craftsmen had to work with clay and tufa rather than the fine building stone of Mexico. Two mounds excavated by the Carnegie Institution of Washington in the early 1940s threw much light on this Teotihuacan presence in the Guatemalan highlands. Each of these consisted of a series of superimposed temple platforms with frontal stairways, capped by now-disappeared superstructures of pole and thatch; the platforms themselves were of the familiar batter-and-entablature type. The occasion for each rebuilding was the interment of a great personage underneath the staircase of the new building. In a tour de force of archaeological dexterity, A.V. Kidder and his assistants revealed a

sequence of incredibly rich tombs.

It is logical to ask, who were these people, and why the strong Teotihuacan cast to their culture? Some of those most familiar with the problem, such as William T. Sanders, feel that they formed part of an elite merchant-warrior group from Teotihuacan who had taken over the highland Maya area, perhaps marrying local noble women to establish their legitimacy. If so, then their hegemony was not confined to that area, but is confirmed by many objects in Teotihuacan style, especially composite incense burners, from the Pacific coast of Guatemala which they probably also controlled. As we shall see, Teotihuacanos were very much present in the Maya lowlands as well: there was apparently a *Pax Teotihuacana* over most of Mesoamerica in the latter centuries of the Early Classic.

The Early Classic in the Maya lowlands
The Early Classic or Tzakol period in the Maya lowlands was conveniently held to have begun at

about 300 AD, since the Leiden Plate—an incised jade plaque found in a Post-Classic context on the Caribbean coast of Guatemala (now in the Rijksmuseum voor Volkenkunde, Leiden)—bears what was once thought to be the earliest Long Count date acceptable to Mayanists. This was 8.14.3.1.12, a day in the year 320 AD. However subsequent excavations in the city of Tikal, where the Leiden Plate was probably executed, have disclosed stela 29, with an associated date falling in 292 AD. Thus by the last decade of the 3rd century after Christ the Maya in the Petén region had at last adopted the ''Maya'' calendar that had been developed centuries earlier outside the Maya area proper.

Tikal and its neighbor to the north, Uaxactún, early established the cultural primacy of the northern Petén. Underneath the Late Classic buildings of Tikal's Central Acropolis lie massive structures of Tzakol date. These had been built over elite tombs which had been cut into bedrock. Within these the rulers of Early Classic Tikal had been interred with dozens of ceramic vessels, some of which were Thin Orange ware from Teotihuacan, stuccoed and painted in the Teotihuacan mural style.

A new light was thrown on the Teotihuacan presence in the Early Classic Petén by the discovery of stela 31, a deliberately mutilated monument which had been deeply buried in a Tzakol structure at Tikal. This bears a long and very important dynastic text; the principal figure is a richly bedecked Maya ruler nicknamed by the epigraphers ''Storm Sky,'' carrying in the crook of his left arm a personified Tikal ''Emblem Glyph.'' Flanking this personage are two warriors wearing purely Teotihuacan costume, including shields with Tlaloc faces. There is no unanimity on the subject, but many scholars are convinced that by the year of the stela's carving, 435 AD, Tikal and probably other Petén centers had fallen under the shadow of warrior-merchant groups from Teotihuacan, as had Kaminaljuyú in the highlands. The presence of these central Mexicans is documented even in the northern lowlands, such as the site of Acanceh in Yucatán.

What were the Teotihuacanos after? The lowland Maya rulers probably had access to large amounts of the much-prized blue-green quetzal feathers from the Alta Verapaz, as well as other tropical products unknown on the Mexican plateau. In return, they brought with them the excellent green obsidian from the Pachuca mines, which were controlled by Teotihuacan, as well as elite vessels like stuccoed bowls and tripod cylinders. With control over all parts of the Maya area, including even the cacao-rich Pacific coastal plain, the Teotihuacan empire seems to have been as much mercantile as political.

When Teotihuacan declined—and fell—its power and presence ceased to exist among the Maya. Its demise must have caused ripples, even disruption, all over the Mesoamerican world, including the Maya. From 534 to 593 AD no new monuments were carved and erected in the southern Maya lowlands, and new construction ceased, indicating a profound political and economic crisis. Following this hiatus, at the beginning of the Late Classic, Maya civilization soared to new heights, freed from what may have been Teotihuacan shackles.

Tikal

Lying in the heart of the Petén rain forest, the Mayan city Tikal sprawls over 16 square kilometers. Once thought to have had only ceremonial purposes, because of its scaring temple pyramids and elaborate palaces concentrated in the center, Tikal has been shown to have had a substantial suburban population. Construction at the ceremonial center began in Formative times on a modest scale and increased in complexity during the Early Classic period to reach, in the 8th and 9th centuries, the architectural grandeur that is seen today. Inscriptions on stelae (the latest date is 869 AD) record temporal and dynastic information, both of which were seemingly obsessions with the Maya. Relations with other Maya centers are noted on stelae, and it is during the Early Classic period that ties with faraway Teotihuacan were particularly strong. Tikal's eminence faded in the Late Classic, part of the mysterious Maya ''collapse.''

Below Maya artistic excellence ranged from finely worked small objects to monumental architecture. This pottery effigy censer, identified by missing teeth and sunken cheeks as representing the Old God, holds a human head on a plate, probably an offering. The censer was recovered from burial 10 in the north acropolis (group A), dated by archaeologists to 450 AD. The grave contained not only the remains of a priest and exotic offerings, but of nine other humans, presumably ritually sacrificed.

Below right Seen from the air, temples seem to float on the forest canopy. Pyramids built in the 8th century (temples I–IV), rise to over 45 m.

Left Plan of Tikal's center. Temples I and II flank the Great Plaza which was lined with intricately carved stelae. The north acropolis (group A), most complex of all the groups of buildings and covering about a hectare, overlooks the Great Plaza. Rich burials underlay most structures. Causeways and ramps link the heart of Tikal's ceremonial center with outlying shrines and temples.

Below This jade pendant, Late Classic, was part of a rich offering in burial 77 in the west plaza. A human face wears a deity headdress, and earspools similar to those shown surrounding the pendant.

Maya Writing and the Calendar

The Maya script was the only *complete* writing system in the ancient New World: that is, only the Maya could express in writing everything that was in their language. It was a complex mixture of ideographic and phonetic elements, similar in structure to certain scripts of the Old World, such as Sumerian, Egyptian and Japanese. Since the system included a complete syllabary (i.e. a symbol for each syllable), they could in theory have written everything phonetically, but like the Japanese they did not because the ideographs continued to have immense prestige and probably even religious overtones. The Maya scribes often displayed their virtuosity by varying ideographic with phonetic writing, often taking advantage of the fact that there are many homonyms in Mayan languages: for example, the signs for "sky," "four," "snake" and "captive" could be substituted for each other since all four words are pronounced *chan* (Cholan) or *can* (Yucatec).

Maya hieroglyphic writing appears on a wide variety of materials. From the last decade of the 3rd century AD until the Classic downfall, there are hundreds of inscriptions on stelae, wall panels, lintels and other stone monuments which are now proven to be dynastic records, including the births, accessions to power, marriages, victories and deaths of the elite caste that ruled the lowland cities. There must have been thousands of codices—folding-screen books of bark paper coated with gesso—but all those of Classic date have disappeared, with only four surviving from the Post-Classic period. In addition, vast numbers of painted or carved funerary vases contain hieroglyphic texts, some as long as those on the monuments.

The rather block-like Maya hieroglyphs are to be read (with rare exceptions) in double columns, from left to right and top to bottom. As with ancient Egyptian public monuments, the stone texts are extremely parsimonious and usually

closely tied to the picture of an important event, such as the taking of a captive or ceremonial bloodletting. Like a Hemingway short story, the Classic inscriptions eschew adjectives and adverbs. The "skeleton" on which dynastic inscriptions are fleshed out is the Long Count calendar, which the Maya did not invent but took to its ultimate degree of refinement.

The Long Count consists of the cumulative total of five kinds of time cycles, along with the numerical coefficients by which they are to be multiplied. These cycles are: baktun, 144 000 days; katun, 7200 days; tun, 360 days; uinal 20 days; kin, 1 day. A Long Count date was to be calculated by adding this total to the putative starting date of the calendar, which was most likely considered to be the creation date of our present era. Thus, using modern notation, the Long Count date 9.8.9.13.0 would be 1 357 100 days since the starting point, reaching a Calendar Round position of 8 Ahau (in

Below The Maya number system operated with only three symbols: a stylized shell for zero or completion; a dot for one; and a bar for five. The system was largely vigesimal (base 20) and positional. However, unlike our horizontal Arabic numeration, Maya numbers were arranged

vertically, with the lowest-value positions at the bottom and the highest at the top. Most Maya numbers record elapsed days in the Long Count, for which the 360-day tun was basic. The third position is thus 18 × 20, rather than 20 × 20.

Below In a typical Long Count date in the Classic inscriptions, each cycle is expressed by a glyph, usually ideographic, with a different numerical value; baktun, 144 000 days; katun, 7200 days; tun, 360 days; uinal, 20 days; kin, 1 day. These values are to be multiplied by the bar-and-dot coefficient preceding the cycle glyph, and the whole added up to express the number of days since the starting point, 13 August 3114 BC.

Introducing Glyph   baktun   katun
tun   uinal   kin

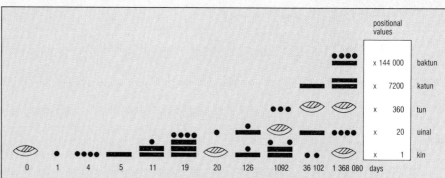

	positional values	
	x 144 000	baktun
	x 7200	katun
	x 360	tun
	x 20	uinal
	x 1	kin

0   1   4   5   11   19   20   126   1092   36 102   1 368 080   days

Right A Rabbit God shown as a scribe on an 8th-century painted vase. He holds a brush pen in one hand, and is writing a folding-screen codex with jaguar-skin covers.

Left Detail of a Late Classic vase from Yucatán, showing a Monkey-Man scribal god with a folding codex.

Below At the heart of the Maya calendar was the ancient 260-day count or almanac. This consisted of the coefficients 1–13 permutating against 20 named days. Still surviving in some

parts of the Maya highlands, in Classic times it was probably the major factor in determining the luck of a particular day, whether the birth or accession of a ruler, or the baptizing of a child.

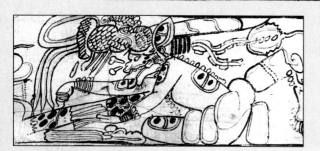

Right Part of a lintel from the Maya center of Yaxchilán, carved with calendrical glyphs.

Right Part of a lintel from the Maya center of Yaxchilán, carved with calendrical glyphs.

the 260-day count), 13 Pop (in the 365-day count). This system was, of course, ideal for recording historical events, for they could be placed in a cycle not just of 52 years but of more than five millennia.

Every significant moment in time had its astrologically based auguries, and these were carefully noted. Many personages and events in Classic texts are improbably remote in the past, and must concern divine ancestors of Classic dynasts.

It has often been claimed that all of this knowledge, and the writing system itself, was in the hands of a priesthood during the Classic period. Yet it is now clear that if any group controlled epigraphic, astronomical and historical information it was a caste of scribes (*ah dzib*) who had their own patron deities: Itzamná, the Creator God and legendary inventor of writing, and the Monkey-Man gods of the *Popol Vuh*. The scribes must have been of extremely high rank.

Operating along with the 260-day count was an approximate or "Vague Year" of 365 days, consisting of 18 months of 20 days each, with an extra five-day period called Uayeb falling at its end. (*Below* are the signs for the months and Uayeb.) While the Classic Maya knew that the tropical year was actually 365¼ days, they did not reckon with leap years. Among its other deficiencies, the Vague Year was always gaining on the seasons, thus making it difficult to coordinate agricultural activities with important dates. The permutation of the two cycles produced the Calendar Round, an interval of 52 × 365 days. This was a pan-Mesoamerican calendar, with roots going back to the Olmec.

pop	uo	zip	zotz	tzec	xul	yaxkin
mol	chen	yax	zac	ceh	mac	kankin
muan	pax	kayab	cumku	uayeb		

Below Names could usually be written several ways. The name of the 7th-century ruler of Palenque, Pacal or "Hand-shield," could be written in several ways: (a) ideographically, with picture of a hand-shield, preceded by the title *mak'ina*; (b) with picture of a hand-shield postfixed with *l(a)* as a phonetic reinforcer; or (c) syllabically as *pa-ca-l(a)*.

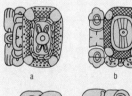

a   b

c

Left Some grammatical signs: (a) *u*, the third person singular possessive; (b)-*ah*, a verbal suffix; (c) *ah*, honorific prefix for males; (d) *na*, honorific prefix for women.

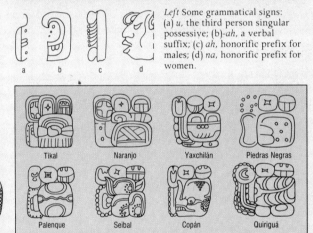

Tikal	Naranjo	Yaxchilán	Piedras Negras
Palenque	Seibal	Copán	Quiriguá

Above Every politically important Classic city in the southern Maya lowlands was represented in the inscriptions by one or more emblem glyphs, which probably represent the lineages (the "blood of kings") which ruled these sites. Each glyph consists of a distinctive main sign, surmounted by two signs standing for *ahpo* or "ruler," the combination being prefixed by the symbol for self-sacrificed blood. It was the recognition of emblem glyphs that led to the understanding of Classic Maya monuments as historical records.

Bishop Diego de Landa's *Relación* of 1566 gives a so-called "alphabet," along with examples of how it was to be used, but this is now recognized as a partial syllabary. It has been greatly enlarged by recent scholarship, largely through the analysis of glyphic substitutions. Words and names could be written completely phonetically, in which case the final vowel of the last syllabic sign was silent; by an ideograph reinforced by one or more syllabic signs; or by means of ideographs alone. So far, scholars agree upon the readings of between 40 and 50 syllabic signs (*below*), but many more may yet be identified.

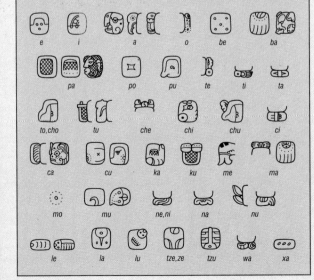

e	i	a	o	be	ba
pa	po	pu	te	ti	ta
to,cho	tu	che	chi	chu	ci
ca	cu	ka	ku	me	ma
mo	mu	ne,ni	na	nu	
le	la	lu	tze,ze	tzu	wa	xa

Right The birth dates of rulers, and even of their divine ancestors, were frequently celebrated on Classic monuments. Accession to power was marked by mighty rituals which included human sacrifice and probably self-sacrifice. The ritual shedding of blood, by male rulers from the penis and by their queens from the tongue, had its own ideographic signs and iconography. Since warfare between cities was so important a feature of Classic Maya culture, it is not surprising that a number of glyphs, both ideographic and phonetic, refer to this activity. Other recently recognized signs relate to parentage, marriage and titles.

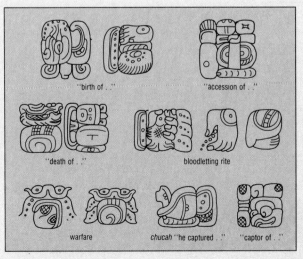

"birth of . ."	"accession of . ."
"death of . ."	bloodletting rite
warfare	*chucah* "he captured . ." "captor of . ."

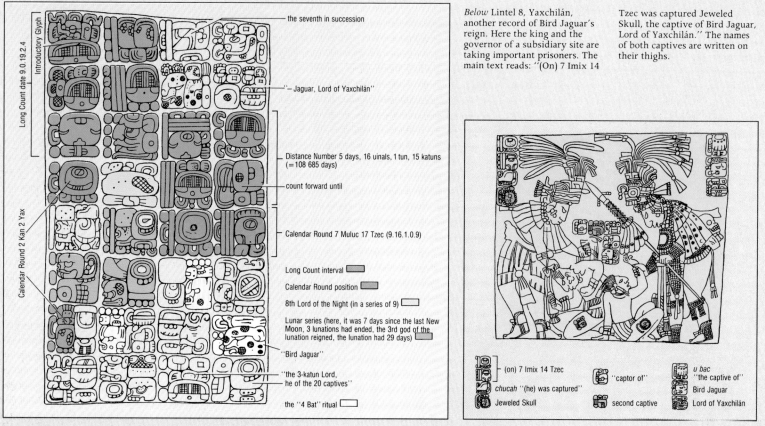

Long Count date 9.0.19.2.4

Introductory Glyph

Calendar Round 2 Kan 2 Yax

- the seventh in succession

"– Jaguar, Lord of Yaxchilán"

Distance Number 5 days, 16 uinals, 1 tun, 15 katuns (= 108 685 days)

count forward until

Calendar Round 7 Muluc 17 Tzec (9.16.1.0.9)

Long Count interval ▭

Calendar Round position ▭

8th Lord of the Night (in a series of 9) ▭

Lunar series (here, it was 7 days since the last New Moon, 3 lunations had ended, the 3rd god of the lunation reigned, the lunation had 29 days) ▭

"Bird Jaguar"

"the 3-katun Lord, he of the 20 captives"

the "4 Bat" ritual ▭

Below Lintel 8, Yaxchilán, another record of Bird Jaguar's reign. Here the king and the governor of a subsidiary site are taking important prisoners. The main text reads: "(On) 7 Imix 14 Tzec was captured Jeweled Skull, the captive of Bird Jaguar, Lord of Yaxchilán." The names of both captives are written on their thighs.

(on) 7 Imix 14 Tzec

chucah "(he) was captured"
Jeweled Skull

"captor of"

second captive

u bac "the captive of"
Bird Jaguar
Lord of Yaxchilán

Above This is lintel 21 at Yaxchilán, a fairly standard Late Classic dynastic record, from the reign of Bird Jaguar of Yaxchilán. It opens with a Long Count calculation and Calendar Round expression, and includes a notation indicating the Lord of the Night who ruled on that date, along with astrologically significant lunar calculations. At that time, a predecessor of Bird Jaguar, described as the seventh ruler, performed an unknown rite called "4 Bat" in his palace or temple. Some 297½ years later, Bird Jaguar went through the same ritual, by which date he had been king for over 40 years ("the 3-Katun Lord") and claimed the distinction of taking 20 captives.

Without the benefit of telescopes, the Maya nevertheless kept very accurate records of the length of the year and of the movements of the moon and the planets. These observations were largely but not entirely based upon the appearance, disappearance and north–south motions of these bodies as seen along the horizon. While the ultimate purpose of their calculations was astrological, the Maya closely approached true science. The eclipse pages of the Dresden Codex, for instance, are based upon the formula that 405 lunations equal 11 958 days, giving a synodic month of 29·52592 days, only 7 minutes away from the modern value. The Codex also contains a five-page Venus table, along with other tables suggesting that they were keeping close track of Jupiter, Mars and Mercury.

Right Page 49 from the Venus Calendar, Dresden Codex. While the Dresden Codex was produced in the Early Post-Classic, inscriptions show that the Venus Calendar already existed in the Classic. In fact it is clear that the apparent motions of Venus against the background of the stars often determined the dates of important battles between cities. The Maya calculated the synodic period of the planet to be 584 days (very close to its actual period of 583·920 days). The fact that 5 × 584 = 8 × 365 led them to arrange the Venus Calendar across five pages of the codex, so as to correlate Venus with the approximate solar year.

The Dresden Codex divides the synodic period into Morning Star (236 days), Superior Conjunction (90 days of invisibility), Evening Star (250 days), and Inferior Conjunction (8 days of invisibility). Times of heliacal rising of the planet (first appearance as Morning Star) were particularly feared, when the rays of Venus were conceived of as a god spearing a victim representing a class of Maya society. Page 49 shows this in graphic detail.

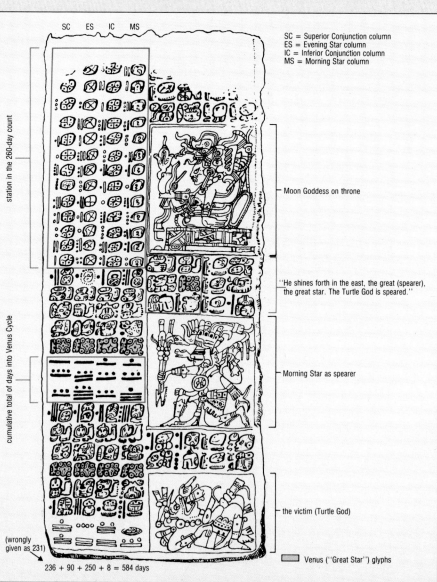

SC   ES   IC   MS

SC = Superior Conjunction column
ES = Evening Star column
IC = Inferior Conjunction column
MS = Morning Star column

station in the 260-day count

cumulative total of days into Venus Cycle

Moon Goddess on throne

"He shines forth in the east, the great (spearer), the great star. The Turtle God is speared."

Morning Star as spearer

the victim (Turtle God)

Venus ("Great Star") glyphs

(wrongly given as 231)

236 + 90 + 250 + 8 = 584 days

Yaxchilán

Yaxchilán

Below Yaxchilán follows the natural contours of the river bank landscape; temples and palaces were set on the top of ridges and knolls. The east group had a spectacular view of the river.
Right Lintel 24 from structure 33. The imposing figure of Shield Jaguar accepts atonement from a kneeling woman who passes a cord with thorns through her tongue. Graphic scenes of penitence carved in stone are unique at Yaxchilán.
Below right Interior partitions within structure 33 provide space for a series of lintels placed on the ceiling of each doorway.

Yaxchilán lies on the bank of the Usumacinta River, and with its neighbor, Piedras Negras (45 kilometers downstream and on the opposite side in Guatemala), forms the nucleus of middle river centers. Distinctive of each place, apart from geographical location, is the execution of low-relief carving on stelae and lintels. Early and late styles have been defined for Yaxchilán, as well as for Piedras Negras.

The stela cult began about 292 AD. At 760 (9.16.10.0.0.) figures appear in profile rather than frontally, and narrative themes are reiterated on carved stone. Inscriptions date Yaxchilán to the Late Classic period, and document the epochs of Shield Jaguar and his successor, Bird Jaguar.

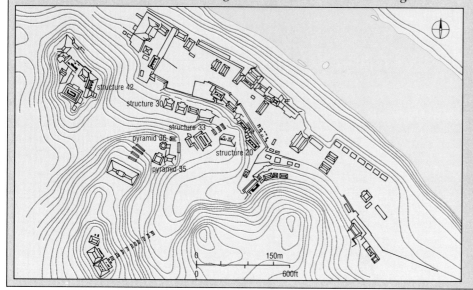

structure 42
structure 30
structure 33
pyramid 36
structure 20
pyramid 35

0   150m
0   600ft

Late Classic Maya civilization

An earlier generation of archaeologists spoke of Classic Maya civilization in the southern lowlands as the "Old Empire." We now know that there was never any such thing: the Maya lowlands were fractionated into a series of independent entities resembling the city-states of Sumer and Greece. No single city had hegemony over all the rest, although at times Tikal, the largest Classic Maya city, seems to have controlled certain centers along the Pasión drainage.

A quarter century of rapid advances in the decipherment of the Classic Maya inscriptions has enabled us to speak with some confidence about the nature of Maya politics and about the concerns of the elite who ruled the great Maya centers. They appear to have been in a constant state of war, with the taking of captives of high status, not territorial aggrandizement, the principal objective. The ultimate destination of these unfortunates was sacrifice, usually by decapitation, and often after lengthy torture which probably included sexual mutilation.

Another obsession of the Maya lords was lineage and royal descent. The presiding deity of the royal house was a somewhat reptilian creature known to

archaeologists as God K. Royal dynasts, both male and female, displayed God K's image at regular intervals, often holding it as a kind of scepter.

Like the elite of other Mesoamerican civilizations, including the Aztec, the Classic rulers of the Maya lowlands were believed to have descended from the gods themselves. This is made clear by the great inscription on the tablet of the Temple of the Cross at Palenque, which celebrates the ancestry of Chan-Bahlum, the eldest son of the great king Pacal. Because the rulers held within their bodies the very essence of divine descent—their own blood—it was necessary to shed it publicly at appropriate moments. Males drew blood from the the penis by perforating it with a sting-ray spine or bone awl (so important was this instrument that it was deified), while females passed a cord set with thorns through a hole in the tongue, a rite graphically depicted on two magnificent lintels from Yaxchilán.

Rulers were generally male, although a few females do occur in the succession records of some sites. Women, however, played an enormously important role, especially in establishing marriage alliances between cities. Succession to rulership seems to have been from father to eldest son,

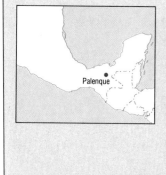

Palenque

Palenque, located in the western lowland Maya area approximately 50 kilometers from the lower Usumacinta River, is notable for its graceful architecture set in wooded hills overlooking alluvial plains, which stretch toward the Gulf of Mexico. The site was inhabited in Early Classic times, but it was not until the Late Classic period, beginning with the reign of Lord Pacal, that the major structures seen today were built. Palenque seems to have come into its own after the disruptions in the southern Maya lowlands of about 600 AD. Pacal's accession to the throne (aged 12) is recorded as 615; he ruled for 68 years, and was buried in the famous tomb inside the pyramid of the Temple of the Inscriptions. He was succeeded by his son Chan-Bahlum II (aged 48) whose great contribution to architecture was the construction of the Temples of the Cross, the Foliated Cross and the Sun. Inside the temples, intricately carved on limestone panels, are scenes and text legitimizing his authority and the lineage through his father from Palenque's patron deities. At his death after an 18-year reign, the throne passed to his younger brother, Kan-Xul II (aged 57), who continued the expansion. The palace was much enlarged and a tower was added. Three rulers of short and perhaps interrupted reigns followed, nonetheless contributing architectural refinement. In the late 8th century Palenque's control of at least its regional domain weakened. The last recorded accession date of a ruler of Pacal's lineage is that of Kuk in 764.

Below Two life-size stucco heads, finely fashioned and certainly portraits, were recovered from Lord Pacal's tomb, from underneath his sarcophagus which rested on six stone blocks. The head shown here was long thought to represent Lord Pacal's wife. Recent study, however, suggests a portrait of Pacal, aged 12, at his accession.

Left Maya hieroglyphs were occasionally expressed in human and animal form, referred to as full-figure glyphs. The calendrical notation for "zero days" is seen here in the form of the god of zero on the left, identified by the floral designs on his arm, and the anthropomorphic Monkey God representing day. In other contexts the long-eared monkey is patron god of scribes. This full-figure glyph, part of the Initial Series giving the birthdate of Kan-Xul II at 9.10.11.17.0 (643 AD), is inscribed on the Tablet of the Palace, which commemorated his accession.

Above A view of Palenque's ceremonial center, looking east from the Temple of the Cross. In the background the Temple of the Inscriptions (left), the bulk of its pyramid base buried in dense vegetation, overlooks the palace complex. Noteworthy of Palenque architectural design is the latticed roof comb and stucco sculpture on mansard roof facades, especially well preserved on the Temple of the Sun (foreground). To Western sensibilities the small, cramped rooms of Maya temples and houses contradict the large open spaces around them. The ancient Maya no doubt appreciated their warm tropical temperatures as much as contemporary residents and visitors do, when spending much of the day out-of-doors.

Above This mosaic jade mask was found lying on top of the lid of Pacal's sarcophagus with other small ritual items, placed there by the ancients. Perhaps intended to represent Lord Pacal, its rigid geometric lines contrast strikingly with the more realistic stucco portrait opposite. The Maya ideal of beauty it represents—a flattened forehead and prominent aquiline nose—was achieved in life by keeping an infant's skull between two boards until the bones had hardened.

The palace at Palenque served many functions, both sacred and secular, as is attested by dedicatory plaques, stucco representations of gods and humans and by the architecture itself. The tower was undoubtedly used for astronomical sightings.

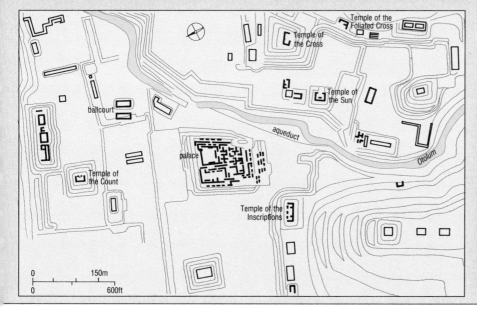

although a few cases of fraternal succession are known. Accession to the throne, which probably took place on an astrologically auspicious date, was a great ceremonial occasion, marked by the sacrifice of captives.

We know very little about social classes beneath the rulers and their families. There was a class of nobles who fulfilled important ceremonial and military offices in the palace hierarchy, and there was a special rank of governors of subsidiary sites. Among the high-status individuals who provided the palace infrastructure must have been the scribes, painters and carvers; these even had their own supernatural patrons, a pair of monkey-men deities who are shown on pottery vessels in the act of writing in screen-fold books with jaguar skin covers. The scribes in particular must have been repositories of knowledge about hieroglyphic writing, astronomy, history, and mythology. Curiously while there was a class of priests (called *ah kin*, "he of the Sun") in Yucatán just before the Spanish conquest, there is no evidence that priests existed in earlier times; their function must have been exercised during the Classic by scribes and perhaps by the rulers themselves.

Society and the economy
There must have been an enormous number of highly skilled artisans in each city to supply the elite with the sumptuous goods that their status required. The Late Classic Maya art style, particularly in the southern lowlands, was delicately refined and quite naturalistic, and was applied to a wide variety of materials, including wood (most of which has perished), bone, shell, jade (the most precious substance), stucco walls and books, pottery, obsidian and even chipped flint knives (the so-called "eccentric flints"). The ultimate destiny of much of this finery was to accompany the dead lords on their final journey. The deceased ruler of each city was interred in his own funerary pyramid—the towering Late Classic temple-pyramids are therefore mausoleums. Most of these seem to have been built following his death, but in the case of the Temple of the Inscriptions at Palenque, the pyramid was constructed by the ruler Pacal himself to house his own remains. Other members of the ruling family and the nobles were buried in other structures.

The major structures of a Late Classic Maya city thus reflect the concerns and ideology of the elite. Each center had two to three masonry ballcourts and, as in Classic central Veracruz, the game was closely associated with human sacrifice and the Underworld. The successful outcome of a war was apparently commemorated by a hieroglyphic staircase, such as the enormous one at Copán which was constructed following its conquest in 737 AD by the far smaller city of Quiriguá. Exactly what activities took place in the multiroomed "palaces" is not fully known, but some rooms contain thrones which were exactly that: carved stone benches on which the rulers could receive their insignia and display their power.

The mass of the population lived in cities and in smaller concentrations of population down to hamlet size, scattered through the countryside. They undoubtedly were mainly employed in farming, although probably subject to periodic corvée labor in the construction and maintenance of the great cities: quarrying and transporting limestone, masonry work, digging the reservoirs, constructing the causeways and so forth.

The exact size of the lowland Maya population, or for that matter of any Maya city during the Late Classic, is a matter of conjecture. Estimates of the size of Tikal, for example, vary all the way from 20 000 to 125 000 people, but the lower figure is probably closer to the truth. It is impossible even to guess at the total lowland population, but it may have been more than 3 million persons.

Because the predominant form of cultivation since colonial times in the Maya lowlands has been of the swidden, or slash-and-burn, type, it was long assumed by archaeologists that this was the only form of working the land in Classic times. However it has become increasingly apparent that other kinds of cultivation were known and used by the ancient Maya. Raised field agriculture was widespread in lowlying areas, especially along river courses, in which there was poor natural drainage, while terracing of fixed fields was practiced in some of the hillier country of the southern lowlands. Crop yields must have been much higher than in those regions where shifting cultivation was the rule, and the potential for populations higher than previously estimated must be taken into account.

The collapse of Maya civilization in the southern lowlands
Late Classic Maya civilization—and probably ancient American culture in general—reached its apogee in the southern lowlands at the end of the 7th century AD and continued through the 8th. Beginning about 800 AD a vast and inexplicable malaise began to be felt over the southern Maya cities.

Throughout the subsequent century, center after center ceased to carve and erect the stone monuments that celebrated the ancestry and deeds of those who had directed the Maya realm for the past six centuries. By 900 AD use of the Maya Long Count had virtually ceased, to be replaced in the Post-Classic of the northern lowlands by a truncated version called the Short Count. There is at this time clear-cut evidence of a paroxysm of destruction, as profound as that which had swept over the Olmec millennia earlier. Construction ceased at most sites, and the cities, which were abandoned by their inhabitants, reverted to the tropical forest.

Where did the people go, and what had brought about this terrible cataclysm? No one knows, in spite of endless speculation. Although there is some archaeological evidence that some of the cities continued to support a population and culture of sorts into the Post-Classic period, the elite and their concerns had surely been eliminated. All sorts of hypotheses have been proposed, generally centering either on ecological causes, such as agricultural collapse brought about by climatic change of overuse of the land, or sociopolitical ones, such as social revolution probably brought on by the supposed disgust of the masses with their thoughtless rulers. Suffice it to say that there is as yet no general support for any of these many rival hypotheses.

Copán

Copán, one of the southernmost of the major Maya sites, lies by a river of the same name in the Motagua Basin of Honduras. Metropolitan Copán probably covered an area of 13 by 3 kilometers; today one sees only a small part of that, with ruins of temples, plazas and above all three-dimensionally carved stelae—the hallmark of Copán. John Lloyd Stephens, traveling with artist-architect Frederick Catherwood in 1839, bought the site for 50 dollars, so they could uninterruptedly uncover and record the ancient monuments. Intensive restoration work was carried out in the 1930s by the Carnegie Institute, not the least of which was to divert the Copán River because it had eroded a gigantic chunk from a pyramid complex.

Right Viewed from the Temple of the Inscriptions, Copán's beauty can be appreciated in the graceful lines of the ballcourt (foreground) and the elegant freestanding statuary in the main court beyond.

Below right Unique at Copán is the absence of military or violent scenes. Personages carry insignia of rank, not weapons. Sculptured serenity is seen in the countenance of the young Maize God.

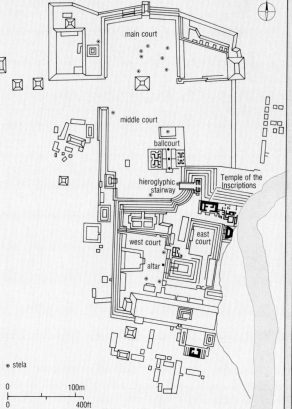

Left The romantic atmosphere of Catherwood's "Fallen Idol" (stela C) belies the precision and accuracy executed in his drawings. Stela C and the 37 others, now upright again, depict lords (and one lady) of Copán in full regalia. Each holds a ceremonial bar, wears clothing and jewelry of intricate complexity, and is accompanied by hieroglyphic text. Decorative details are released from the stone (trachyte) block, making the stelae fully carved, unlike the two dimensions rigidly adhered to at Yaxchilán and Piedras Negras. Deity-zoomorphic altars were placed in front of the stelae.

92° 90° 88°

GULF OF MEXICO

Y U C A T Á N

Dzibilchaltun
◻ Mérida
Acanceh ● Izamal
▲ Chichén Itzá
Oxkintok ● Cobá ▲
Yaxuná ●
Uxmal ▲ Mul-Chic ● Chacchob ●
Jaina ▲ Kabah ▲ Tancah ◻
Xcalumkin ● Sayil ▲ Labná ▲ Chacmultún ●
Keuic ▲ Yucatán
◻ Campeche Xcichmook ●
Xtampak ●
Edzná ▲ Dzibilnocac ● Huntichmul ● Felipe Carillo Puerto ◻
Hochob ●

N O R T H E R N   A R E A

Campeche │ Quintana Roo

Laguna
de Términos

Candelaria

Comalcalco ▲
◻ Villahermosa
Tortuguero ▲
Balancán ●
Palenque ▲ Pomoná ●
Chinikihá ▲

Becan ▲ Xpuhil ●
Hormiguero ▲ Pasión del Cristo ●
Oxpemul ● Uaacbal ● Río Bec ● Cohunlich ●
La Muñeca ● Nohmul ●
Calakmul ▲ Pared de El Palmar ●
los Reyes ● Altamira ●
Ucal ● Balakbal ● Colhá ●
MEXICO Lamanai ● Altún Ha ●
GUATEMALA El Mirador ● Naachtún ● Río Azul ●
C E N T R A L   A R E A La Honradez ● San José ●
Xultún ● Belize City ◻
El Porvenir ● El Perú ● Uaxactún ▲ Holmul ●
Piedras Negras ▲ Tikal ▲ Nakum ● Baking Pot ● Belmopán ◻
El Cayo ● P E T É N Uolantún ● Naranjo ● Xunantunich ●
La Mar ● Motul de San José ● Yaxhá ●
Toniná ▲ Yaxchilán ● Flores ◻ L. Petén
◻ Tuxtla Gutiérrez Itzá Mountain
Lacanhá ● Caracol ● Cow ●
Bonampak ● Itzán ● Actún M A Y A Pomona ●
Agua El Cayo ● Balam M O U N T A I N S
Escondida ● La Amelia ● Seibal ● Sacul ● Nimli Punit ●
Santa Elena Altar de Sacrificios ● Dos Pilas ● Nah Tunich ● Lubaantún ●
Poco Uinic ● Aguateca ● Ixtutz ● Pusilhá ●
Machaquilá ● BELIZE
Chinkultic ● Cancuén ●
◻ Quen Santo Salinas de los
Nueve Cerros ●
Lagartero ●

MEXICO
GUATEMALA

Grijalva

Chamá ● L de Izabal
Cobán ◻ ◻ San Pedro Sula

Nebaj ● GUATEMALA
HONDURAS
Quiriguá ▲
Los Higos ●
S O U T H E R N   A R E A El Paraíso ●
Zacualpa ● Copán ▲ L de Yojoa
San Agustín
Acasaguastlán ●
L de Atitlán
Kaminaljuyú ◻ Guatemala City
Amatitlán ●
El Baúl ● Pantaleón ● Asunción
Tiquisate ● Mita ●

EL SALVADOR
Tazumal ▲
◻ San Salvador

Legend

▲ major Classic center
● minor Classic center
● cave site
▢ Puuc style
▨ Chenes style
▨ Rio Bec style
▨ Cotzumalhuapan sites
→ trade route

intensive cultivation in Northern and Central Areas
▨ raised fields
▥ stone-faced terraces
marsh
— · — modern international
and state boundaries
◻ modern city or town

--- city state boundary 790 AD

scale 1:3 400 000

0   150 km
0   100 mi

The Classic cities of the north

Just as earlier scholars, such as the late Sylvanus Morley, had championed the now untenable model of a Maya "Old Empire" in the southern lowlands, so did they espouse the idea of a "New Empire" in the Yucatán Peninsula to the north of the Petén. This would have been founded by refugees from the south following the Classic collapse. This notion was discredited when it was found by archaeologists that the northern cities had been built and occupied in the Late Classic.

The northern cities are generally classified by their architectural styles. Beginning in the south, the Río Bec style just to the north of the Petén featured multiroomed structures with "false-front" towers superficially resembling the temple pyramids of cities like Tikal (with the exception that the "stairways" cannot be climbed). Further north, in southern Campeche, are sites of the Chenes style, with ceremonial structures entered through gigantic monster-masks, perhaps faces of the celestial double-headed dragons of the "ceremonial bars" carried by southern rulers.

The most splendid architectural monuments of Classic Maya civilization are the cities of the Puuc, an area of northern Campeche and the state of Yucatán that centers on a V-shaped, low range of hills. Sites like Uxmal, Kabah, Sayil and Labná are among the most perfect known to students of the past, and their buildings have influenced even modern architects like Frank Lloyd Wright. The style emphasizes finely cut plates of limestone placed over rubble cores, with the employment of thousands of mosaic-like carved elements on upper facades; often these form the impressive face of the celestial divinity (the so-called "Long-nosed God") stacked up in multiple form like a totem pole.

The further one moves into this peninsula, the thinner the soils, the drier the conditions, and the

Left: Classic Maya civilization
For over five centuries, beginning about 290 AD. Classic Maya cities flourished in the tropical forests of the Central and Northern Areas. Many Classic centers were linked through royal marriages, but no city had hegemony over the others, not even the great Petén city of Tikal. Most were basically independent, and engaged in frequent intercity warfare. In the southern lowlands 22 independent polities can be identified c. 790.

Throughout the 9th century center after center failed to glorify its rulers with stone monuments.

Shifting slash-and-burn agriculture was probably the norm in the Maya lowlands, but this alone could never have supported the huge populations that existed there in Classic times. There is increasing archaeological evidence that two forms of intensive agriculture, in which permanent fields were cultivated throughout much of the year, were found in some

parts of the Central and Northern Areas: raised fields and stone-faced terraces. These may have been responses to population pressures.

Right A contemporary Maya house is neighbor to an ancient Maya palace.
Above An exuberant example of Puuc architecture is the Palace of the Masks at Kabah. Repetitive rain god (Chac) masks in stone mosaic entirely cover the 46-m.-long facade.

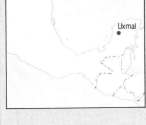

Uxmal

Uxmal is renowned as the architectural jewel of the Yucatán peninsula; archaeologically it remains virtually unknown. Restoration work has been carried out on the major buildings, yet "greater Uxmal" has not been properly mapped. Sources of information available in other Mesoamerican regions—dated stelae, long hieroglyphic texts, codices—are lacking, as is mural painting depicting historical events. A preliminary ceramic study, undated stelae, and a date (909 AD) painted on a capstone have been used to establish a temporal context for Uxmal. More conclusive yet is the distinctive Puuc architectural and decorative style incorporated on buildings at many sites.

Evidence points to a Late Classic occupation, probably ending with the Mexican invasions into the peninsula. Uxmal design is based on Puuc tradition accented with foreign motifs, giving it a cosmopolitan flavor.

Below Geometric designs, Chac masks and stylized naturalistic forms are combined over the principal doorway of the Palace of the Governor (a detail from a lithograph by Frederick Catherwood). A similar but less ornate pattern continues on all four sides of the building (which measures 100 m. long). Large Chac masks are set over each of the 11 doorways and are stacked at a 45-degree angle at the corners. The frieze (3·5 m. high), like those of the Nunnery buildings, is made up of small, probably mass-produced, mosaics, so carefully cut that they need no stucco coating to hide imperfections.

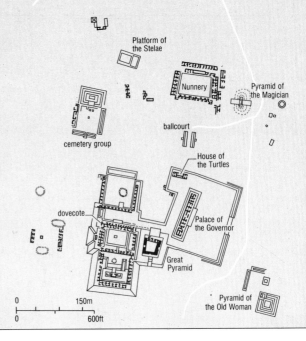

north group

Platform of the Stelae

Nunnery

Pyramid of the Magician

ballcourt

cemetery group

House of the Turtles

dovecote

Palace of the Governor

Great Pyramid

Pyramid of the Old Woman

0   150m

0   600ft

Low horizontal lines of the Nunnery quadrangle (*left*), with the House of the Turtles in the right foreground, contrast with the towering bulk of the Pyramid of the Magician (*below*). The Nunnery (early explorers thought the small rooms resembled nuns' quarters) exhibits pure Puuc architectural features of vertical walls divided horizontally with undecorated lower facades and elaborate upper registers.

Unique at Uxmal is the elliptical base of the Pyramid of the Magician. Studies during restoration show five construction stages, all of which follow Puuc canons of design, as do the temples at its base and summit.

As surface water-sources are practically nonexistent in Yucatán, early inhabitants in the eastern region settled around sink-holes (*cenotes*) in the limestone shelf. However, there are no natural wells in the west, and residents had to rely on collecting seasonal rainfall to supply their needs during the six dry months. The man-made underground cistern, *chultun*, is perhaps the greatest innovation of northern Maya genius. Nonetheless, scarcity of water was a prime concern: multitudes of Chac (rain deity) masks decorate building facades.

Above left The motif of skull and crossed bones is repeated around the top edge of a platform in the cemetery group—an example of highland Mexican design used to decorate a Puuc structure.

Above Feathered serpents entwine over geometric mosaics on the west frieze of the Nunnery quadrangle.

Left Uxmal's buildings, covering 100 hectares, seem to have been laid out as much to create a dramatic landscape as to adhere to an astronomical alignment (the slightly east-of-north axis may be noted). The Palace of the Governor is considered to be the most perfect example of Puuc architecture extant. Built upon two superimposed platforms, its main entrance overlooks a large plaza toward the Pyramid of the Old Woman, possibly the oldest building at Uxmal. To the north, the monumental corbel vault archway is the entrance to the Nunnery quadrangle. A complex of four disconnected buildings set around a courtyard (75 by 60 m.), the Nunnery conveys the idea of spaciousness rather than enclosure.

Art of Jaina Island

Jaina is a small, marly island off the Campeche coast. It is famed for the beauty of its clay figurines which accompany the hundreds of Late Classic burials that have been found on the island. These are hollow and are usually fitted with whistles at the back. Depicted are lords and ladies, enthroned rulers and deities, all of whom are engaged in a variety of activities. The richness of the Jaina burials suggests that the island was a cemetery for the elite which ruled the nearby Puuc sites.

The so-called Fat God (*right*) is often found in Jaina figurines, as well as carved in stone on the facades of Puuc buildings. Of probable Teotihuacan origin, his role in the Mesoamerican pantheon remains unknown. Here he wears a feathered war costume and carries a shield in one hand. Some figurines showing everyday activities, such as a young Maya lady weaving with a backstrap loom (*left*), may be deceptive, for it is likely that this is the young moon goddess shown as patroness of weaving. A bird is perched upon the post from which the loom is suspended, and two other birds are found below. Many Jaina figurines are miniature portraits (*below*), giving an excellent idea of Late Classic Maya costume. The figure seated tailor fashion is a nobleman wearing a mirror-like object on his chest, while to the right is a robed and bejeweled woman holding what also seems to be a mirror. Mirrors were closely connected with the idea of rulership, for a great Maya lord was held to be "the mirror of his people."

Below Some Jaina figurines are extraordinarily expressive, the artist having been allowed more freedom than those who carved the public monuments. This personage, perhaps a ruler, is shown in the midst of an ecstatic dance.

Bottom Far more hieratic is this figure of a ruler seated upon a circular throne. While facial hair is rare in Classic Maya monumental sculpture, Jaina rulers, like this one, often have goatees. In his left hand he holds a bag for copal incense.

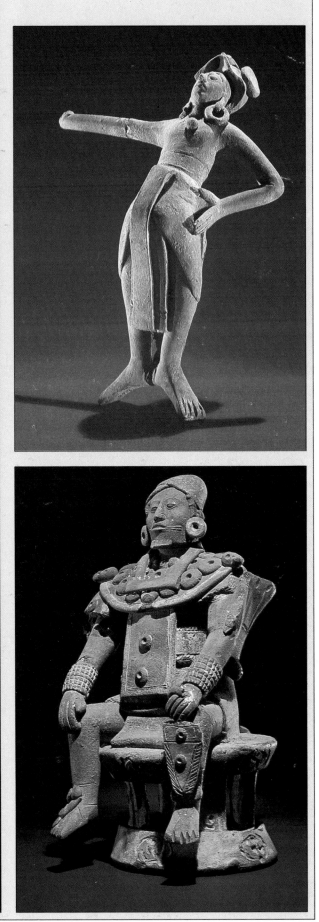

more scarce ponds, lakes and flowing water. The Puuc sites, including their easternmost extension at Chichén Itzá, are strongly tied to the only source of drinking water. Maize agriculture becomes more precarious in the north, and trade in salt and honey may have been the mainstay of the economy.

While it is doubtful if any migrations from the south into the Puuc sites ever took place with the demise of the southern sites, it is probable that these cities maintained their populations and ceremonial life well past 900 AD. They were important contributors to the hybrid Toltec-Maya civilization that flourished at Chichén Itzá after the Toltec takeover of Yucatán towards the end of the 10th century AD, and Puuc artists and architects played an important role in the sudden burst of creative activity at that great Post-Classic center.

The Maya in central Mexico

It used to be thought that the Classic Maya were cultural "stay-at-homes," having little cultural influence on other areas, and certainly never moving beyond Maya borders. In recent years some striking evidence has come to light that confirms the Maya presence in the highlands of central Mexico during the last century or so of the Late Classic period.

To understand the nature of this presence it is necessary to turn to the Putún. At the time of the Spanish conquest these were a Chontal-Maya-speaking group occupying the swampy coastal region of Tabasco and southern Campeche. This land was known to the Aztec as Acallan or "Land of Canoes," a tribute to the extensive maritime trading network run by the Putún all along the coastline from Honduras to Veracruz. They were also known by the Nahuatl name Olmeca-Xicallanca. Now there are compelling reasons for believing that the Putún had moved into the power vacuum created by the collapse of the Petén cities beginning about 800 AD.

The large hilltop site of Cacaxtla lies on the border between the states of Tlaxcala and Puebla, in the dry highlands to the east of the Valley of Mexico. Strong historical traditions indicate that this was a stronghold of a dynasty of Olmeca-Xicallanca, that is Putún Maya, origin. Confirmation of the tradition came in 1974 through the chance discovery by looters of an extraordinary palace complex of Late Classic date, with magnificent and brilliantly colored murals, all of obvious Maya derivation; more specifically, they are in the style of the late stelae of Seibal.

Another site showing bearing on the Late Classic Maya presence in central Mexico is Xochicalco, an enormous hilltop complex in western Morelos, southwest of the Valley of Mexico, where there is not only a platform with Feathered Serpents enclosing within their undulations purely Maya seated figures obviously copied from Late Classic Maya jades, but also a network of causeways surely based on the *sacbeob* ("white roads") of lowland Maya cities.

These Maya intrusions came at a time of troubles for the cities of the southern lowlands, and at least Cacaxtla was the product of a people who are known to have taken advantage of the chaos resulting from the breakup of the New World's greatest civilization.

Far left Cotzumalhuapa is the name given to the unique sculptural design on more than 200 carved stone monuments from the Pacific coast of Guatemala.

Each stela in the series features a male dressed in the paraphernalia of a ballplayer, here seen on monument 6 reaching up, one arm extended, toward a diving god. The stelae are carved in low relief except for the deity heads which seem to push out from the background. Iconographical elements (death heads, decapitated human heads, flowering vines, anthropomorphic cacao-pods, celestial serpents, among others) are repeated throughout the series, but occur in various combinations on each stela.

Left Detail of a Cotzumalhuapa stela: a priest, dressed as a ballplayer, holds a man's head in one hand and a sacrificial knife in the other. The snakes symbolize blood.

The enigma of Cotzumalhuapa

One of the most puzzling of Mesoamerican civilizations during the Classic period is the one called Cotzumalhualpan, from the type site of Santa Lucía Cotzumalhuapa on the Pacific plain of Guatemala. Within a very compact region in what used to be one of the richest cacao-producing areas in Mesoamerica are a number of small sites with fairly rustic, cobble-covered architecture but with a plethora of carved stone monuments. These are in a style and have an iconography that are neither Mayan nor Mexican, but a combination of both. A number of deities are clearly central Mexican, such as Tlaloc, the goggle-eyed Rain God, and Mictlantecuhtli, Lord of the Land of the Dead. Calendrical hieroglyphs relating to the 260-day Count are shown in a fashion thus far unique in Mesoamerica. Ballgame imagery is ubiquitous, and so are ballcourts, suggesting a connection with the Classic Veracruz culture of the Gulf Coast, but Cotzumalhuapa cannot obviously be derived from it, nor from Teotihuacan, which had a powerful presence on the Guatemalan coast during the Early Classic. Even the dating of the culture is in question, although the leading expert on the subject, Dr Lee Parsons, feels that it falls in a "Middle Classic" straddling the end of the Early and the beginning of the Late Classic. Certainly its flowering can be explained by the riches attendant upon successful cacao production.

Who were these people? At the time of Spanish contact the Cotzumalhuapa region was occupied by a non-Maya group called the Pipil, who spoke a language of the Nahua group distantly related to Nahuatl, the Aztec tongue. Most authorities feel that the Pipil were responsible for Cotzumalhuapan culture during the Classic, and that they may have arrived on the coast, perhaps from central Mexico, by the 6th century AD. They nevertheless remain something of a mystery.

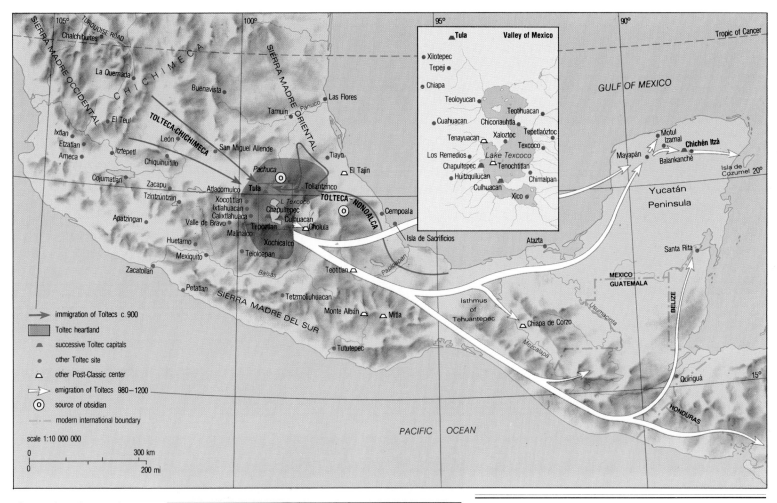

Legend:
- → immigration of Toltecs c. 900
- ▨ Toltec heartland
- ▲ successive Toltec capitals
- • other Toltec site
- △ other Post-Classic center
- ⇨ emigration of Toltecs 980–1200
- ⊙ source of obsidian
- — · — modern international boundary

scale 1:10 000 000

0 ——— 300 km
0 ——— 200 mi

Above: The Toltec empire
The Toltec era occupies a legendary position in Mesoamerican mythology: late Maya and Aztec rulers consistently laid claim to Toltec ancestors, believing that their reigns like those of their precursors would be eras of ubiquitous prosperity. As the map shows, much of Mexico felt the influence of Toltec power, which was perpetuated even after the empire's demise by wandering émigrés from Tula. Yet the Toltecs had humble beginnings, being partly descended from nomadic tribes of the Chichimeca Desert that had been driven south by drought and starvation.

Right Xipe Totec, the flayed god, is represented by an almost life-size terracotta hollow figure. God of vegetation and harvest, his human impersonator wore the flayed skin of a sacrificial victim.

THE RISE OF
THE TOLTEC STATE

The era from 900 AD to the Spanish conquest is called the Post-Classic, and it is distinguished from everything that preceded it in Mesoamerica by being historical: that is, there are written annals and histories which were compiled after 1521 by both Spaniards and by native intelligentsia which apply to the period.

To be sure the Classic Maya had a written history, but it is extremely parsimonious in content—restricted to the doings of the elite. Many of these histories which apply to the Post-Classic, however, are full of ambiguity and must be treated with caution.

There is one other striking difference between the Classic and Post-Classic: the arrival of metallurgy. This art almost surely diffused from South America, probably the coastal region of the Peru–Ecuador border; perhaps the Intermediate Area, where fine gold and copper casting by the "lost wax" process has old roots, also contributed. Most Mesoamerican metallurgy was confined to ornaments, however, and bronze, known in the Andean area at this date, never made an appearance. The Post-Classic was no age of metals.

The Toltec-Chichimeca
When the Spaniards arrived in Mexico and Central America the native dynasties which then ruled, and their colonial descendants, spoke of an earlier people called the "Tolteca," who had created in a place called "Tollan" (later corrupted to "Tula") or

"Place of the Reeds" a wonderful culture. The Tolteca or Toltecs were marvelous artisans and architects, and Tula was a kind of never-never land, with palaces created from jewels. The Aztec emperor, Motecuhzoma Xocoyotzin, himself claimed descent from Toltec ancestors.

There are many extant traditions about the Toltec, and some of them have a grain of historical truth, although the so-called histories are not easy to interpret.

Lying beyond the northern border of Mesoamerica was the great desert plateau contained between the two arms of the Sierra Madre mountains. Beyond the agricultural "pale," this was the haunt of the Chichimeca—nomadic hunting-and-gathering peoples who followed a way of life inherited from the Archaic period of Mesoamerican prehistory. It was probably through them that the bow and arrow entered Mesoamerica from the north in Early Post-Classic times, for the only bowmen in the Aztec armies were Otomí mercenaries of Chichimec affiliation.

These nomads had probably irrupted south across the Mesoamerican frontier at various times in the past, but at the close of the Classic one group, led by a chieftain called Mixcoatl ("Cloud Serpent"), had established itself at what was to become Tula, joining with another group known as the Toltec. This hybrid people developed a new culture, certainly in part influenced by the Mayanized central Mexican centers like Xochicalco—for instance, the ballcourt at Tula exactly replicates in all its dimensions and details the I-shaped playing field at Xochicalco. Tula eventually became the capital during the Early Post-Classic Tollan phase (900–1200 AD) of a far-flung kingdom or even empire. It also became the model for the Late Post-Classic states of Mesoamerica, for not only the Aztec but the very late Maya ruling houses claimed descent from the Tula rulers.

Toltec influence is to be found over wide areas of Mesoamerica, including the Gulf Coast of Mexico. The Toltec presence there and in the capital itself is signaled by a fine, glazed pottery known as Plumbate Ware, produced to Toltec standards on the Pacific coast of Chiapas and Guatemala, and widely traded wherever the Toltec went. In fact it is likely that far-flung trading networks were initiated by Tula, for fine polychrome pottery from Costa Rica has been found at the capital, and sites such as La Quemada and Chalchihuites were probably established by the Toltec in the Mesoamerican northwest to bring in elite goods like turquoise from Southwest trading stations such as Casas Grandes.

The Toltec in Yucatán

The legends concerning the downfall of Quetzalcoatl at the hands of the evil Tezcatlipoca ("Smoking Mirror") also tell of his flight from Tula and his journey with his retinue down to the Gulf Coast. One version has the Feathered Serpent performing an act of self-immolation, while the other has him journeying on a raft of sea serpents over the Gulf of Mexico to the east, destined to return some day to reclaim his own land.

It is the latter version that finds confirmation in archaeology and ethnohistory. In a *katun* (time cycle) that ended in 987 AD a man calling himself

Tula, capital city of the Toltecs, lies about 65 km. northwest of present-day Mexico City. The archaeological remains of Tula are far less grandiose than those of Teotihuacan but nonetheless bespeak the seat of government of a far-flung empire. Atlantean figures (*below*) on the top of pyramid B have become almost symbolic of Tula. By far the largest sculptures at the site (4·6 m. high, whereas the pyramid is slightly more than 10 m.), they are the focal point for the militaristic element that became dominant in representational Post-Classic art in the Central Highlands.

Tula

Below The Serpent Wall (Coatepantli). This freestanding wall, 2·6 m. high, is carved in repetitive designs including human skeletons being swallowed by rattlesnakes. Tula iconography combines the Feathered Serpent, Venus and military orders—components of the Quetzalcoatl myth.

Below Detail of one of the four Atlantean figures. The strong planes of the typical, or perhaps idealized, Toltec face (compare with the Chac Mool, *below right*) are reflected in the technique of the sculpture. Each consists of four sections. They were carved of basalt and tenoned into one column forming a roof support. Square columns at the rear of the pyramid of figures dressed in similar military garb, carved in bas relief, continue the archtectonic device.

Tula, in the state of Hidalgo, is represented today by the remains of a large city, smaller than the earlier Teotihuacan but impressive nonetheless. The center of the site is dominated by several squat but sizable temple pyramids, such as pyramid B, which was probably dedicated to Quetzalcoatl, the Feathered Serpent. Its substructure is faced with reliefs of prowling jaguars and coyotes, and eagles eating hearts, probably a reflection of the warrior orders who dominated the city. According to legend Tula was ruled by a semimythical king who had the title of Quetzalcoatl, and who had been bewitched, ruined and driven from the city by the dread god Tezcatlipoca, the patron of sorcerers and warriors.

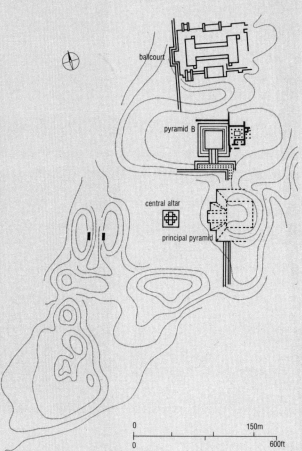

Left Pyramid B, seen here from the southeast, was fronted by a colonnaded hall. The base of the pyramid is decorated with jaguar and eagle profile figures devouring hearts, and a frontal view of a human head emerging from the jaws of a feathered creature, associated with Venus and known by the Nahautl name Tlahuizcalpantecuhtli.

Above right Plan of Tula. The I-shaped ballcourt is located behind pyramid B. It has exactly the same dimensions and orientation as that of Xochicalco. Adjacent to the pyramid is the Palacio Quemado ("Burned Palace").

Right A Chac Mool, thought to be a sacrificial stone. Six similar sculptures were recovered, all mutilated.

Kukulcán ("Feathered Serpent," i.e. Quetzalcoatl) arrived in Yucatán with his followers and conquered the Maya. The culture that was taken over and channeled along Toltec political lines was Puuc. Most Puuc sites, however, were abandoned at this time, with one notable exception: Chichén Itzá.

There are hardly any other sites of the Early Classic Toltec-Maya period in Yucatán, suggesting that the new rulers had depopulated the countryside and concentrated the northern Maya at Chichén Itzá, so as to control them better. The only other important site of the period is Balankanché, a cave not far from Chichén, with an underground ritual chamber dedicated to the worship of the Toltec Rain God, Tlaloc.

Post-Toltec developments in the northern Maya area

By 1224, when a Katun 6 Ahau ended, Toltec hegemony had disappeared in the northern lowlands (in fact, the great Tollan phase at Tula was over), and the Toltec became only a glorious memory over much of Mesoamerica. Shortly afterwards the Itzá had settled at Chichén Itzá, where they established or perhaps heightened the cult of the Rain God at the Sacred Cenote or Well of Sacrifice, into which human victims were thrown to appease the divinity.

During the second half of the 13th century the Itzá founded Mayapán, about 100 kilometers west of Chichén, and this remained their capital until its overthrow and destruction a century later. Mayapán was a teardrop-shaped city enclosing some 2000 structures within its walls. The Carnegie Institution of Washington, which excavated Mayapán over a period of years, estimates that between 11 000 and 12 000 people lived there. We know from histories that most of these were prominent families of northern Yucatán, held hostage to ensure a steady flow of tribute to the Cocom family overlords who controlled the peninsula at that time.

Excavations in the more elaborate dwellings have disclosed numerous shrines, along with pottery incense burners in the form of the deities worshiped there. These idols include many gods of central Mexican origin, as well as the indigenous Maya Rain God, Chac.

By the time of the Spanish invasion of Yucatán, Mayapán was in ruins, as was of course Chichén Itzá.

The peninsula was then divided into 16 independent statelets, probably not so very different in their political and social organization from the independent city-states of the far earlier Classic Maya; the absence of an overall supreme authority made these Maya far more difficult for the Spanish to subdue than the very centralized empire of the Aztec.

The Late Post-Classic in the Maya highlands

The archaeology of highland Guatemala and Chiapas is very poorly known following the decline of Teotihuacan influence after 500 AD at important centers like Kaminaljuyú. When the formidable Pedro de Alvarado conquered this area, accompanied by native mercenaries from Tlaxcallan in central Mexico, the Guatemalan highlands were

Chichén Itzá

Left View from the Temple of the Jaguars (on the lower east-facing section of the ballcourt). A jaguar throne looks toward the central pyramid, the Castillo. The pyramid (24 m. high), dominated by Feathered Serpent themes, derives from the last phase of construction. Most buildings at Chichén Itzá demonstrate a blend of Maya and Toltec design.

Below This sculpted likeness of a skull rack (*tzompantli*), around the sides of a platform in the later-built section of Chichén Itzá, repeats a Toltec motif.

Chichén Itzá was strategically located in the center of the Yucatán peninsula. According to the standard interpretation of Yucatecan prehistory, Toltec invaders made this their new capital, enlisting Puuc Maya architects and artists to create a more grandiose and opulent Tula. The Temple of the Warriors at Chichén, while based on the model of pyramid B at the old capital, is far larger and more ambitious than the latter, and the ballcourt at Chichén outstrips anything at Tula. Among the more characteristic Toltec sculptures at Tula are the reclining-figure statues called (for very obscure reasons) Chac Mools. A number of these have been found at Chichén, but they dwarf the Toltec originals. Chichén's most striking structure, however, the great four-sided temple pyramid known as the Castillo, has no obvious parallels at Tula. Its only antecedent would seem to be the four-sided pyramids erected during the Late Classic period at Tikal and Copán.

There remains a great deal of unresolved controversy over the chronology of Toltec-Maya culture at Chichén, in part caused by the ambiguous dating system in use in Post-Classic Yucatán. Thus, for example, one school of thought is able to advance the idea that the "Toltec"-like buildings of Chichén Itzá actually predate the supposed prototypes at the admittedly less impressive Tula, in far-off Hidalgo. Certainly much "dirt" archaeology will have to be done at Chichén to resolve this controversy.

Above This small jade plaque in Maya-style carving is one of thousands of objects recovered from the Well of Sacrifice, a sacred waterhole (*cenote*). It was the scene of ritual activity which included the offering of jade, pottery and metal, as well as human sacrifice. Metal disks found there, embossed with scenes of Toltec and Maya conflict, probably record historical events.

Below Monumental architecture at Chichén Itzá covers about 3 by 2 km. Puuc-style buildings in the south predate by centuries "New Chichén" in the north. Notable examples of highland Mexican ideas are processions of warrior figures, the Chac Mool, Feathered Serpent themes, human sacrifice and jaguar-eagle cults.

Left Temple of the Warriors and Court of the Thousand Warriors are similar in design to pyramid B and the Patio Quemado at Tula, but grander in concept and scope. The columns are carved on each side with a warrior figure, each of which has an individual combination of insignia. Monumental serpent roof supports are seen again on the upper temple overlooking the ballcourt.

Right A human face emerges from the jaws of an animal (shown here sculpted in stone), a representational theme with beginnings as least as early as Teotihuacan. It grew increasingly important among eagle-jaguar warrior societies in the Toltec epoch, and even continued into historically documented Aztec times.

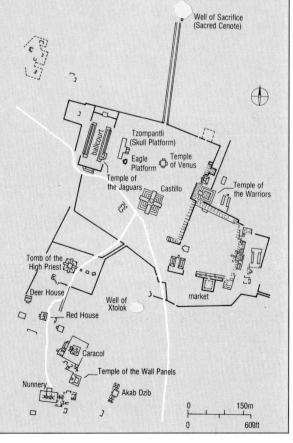

A View into the Maya Underworld

Classic Maya pictorial ceramics were painted or carved as an accompaniment for the deceased's journey to the Underworld or Xibalbá ("Place of Fright"). A detailed account of Xibalbá was preserved after the conquest in the *Popol Vuh*, the sacred book of the Quiché Maya. In it two young men named 1 Hunahpu and 7 Hunahpu are summoned by the Underworld lords (all of whom have the names of mortal diseases) to play a ballgame, are put through a set of trials and are finally defeated, suffering decapitation. The head of 1 Hunahpu, placed in a calabash tree, magically impregnates Blood Lady, daughter of a Xibalban lord. After exile to the earth's surface she gives birth to the Hero Twins, great blowgunners and ballplayers named Hunahpu and Xbalanque. Eventually these also are called to play ball with the chthonic deities, but through subterfuges they survive to overcome the Underworld rulers and rise up to become the sun and the moon. While these and a number of other episodes in the *Popol Vuh* are explicitly referred to on Classic Maya pottery, many scenes have no counterpart in recorded mythology.

Below Photographic rollout of a 7th-century polychrome cylinder from the Petén region. Two ballplayers square off before a match, each carrying a ball, in front of a stepped structure. These might be 1 Hunahpu and 7 Hunahpu, or the Hero Twins, or one of these and an Underworld lord. The fantastic birds to the right recall the magic owls that were sent by the rulers of Xibalbá to summon the earth-surface people for a ballgame in the Underworld. The glyphic text at the top has yet to be deciphered, but probably contains the names and titles of the deceased for whom the vase was painted.

In the *Popol Vuh*, half-brothers of the Hero Twins climb into a tree at the Twins' behest to bring down birds that the Twins had shot; they are trapped there, and the Twins turn them into monkeys. On this vase (*left*) the monkey men are shown as patrons of writing, pointing to codices covered with jaguar skin. The Underworld scenes on many Maya ceramics, however, cannot be directly related to the *Pool Vuh*. On a codex-style vase (*right*) a lord holds a tube-enclosed serpent, from whose jaws emerges an aged god blowing a shell trumpet.

Below A rollout of an 8th-century cylindrical vase from the northern Petén, Guatemala. An obviously pregnant young woman appears before Xibalban lords, who dance in what seems to be anger. The *Popol Vuh* legend suggests that this is Lady Blood, laden with the future Hero Twins.

Before her is a sinister deity with an almost phallic nose, perhaps meant to be her enraged father; this oddly shaped appendage and the fan held in one hand lead one to believe that he is Ek Chuuah, the god of merchants, who certainly had Underworld associations. The two other male figures would be his

subordinates. Arranged in two columns are what may be the name glyphs of the protagonists.

Although it used to be thought that the artists who produced pictorial ceramics were illiterate artisans ignorant of the esoteric concerns of the Classic elite, it is now generally recognized that they were the

same ones who produced the codices, carved the monuments and painted the great murals such as those at Bonampak.

In a rollout of a codex-style vase (*below*), God GI (lord of sacrifice and rain) and the skeletalized Death God dance in triumph over the infant Jaguar God of the Underworld. On the right is a torch-bearing firefly and a monstrous dog, bearer of souls into the Underworld.

A polychrome vase (*bottom*), depicts a young Maize God.

Right: Post-Classic Maya civilization

The Chontal-speaking Putún dominated a trading network that extended into the heart of the Petén, and by boat around the Yucatán Peninsula to trading centers like Nito on the Río Dulce and Naco in Honduras. The canoes filled with traders and their merchandise seen by Columbus off the Yucatán coast in 1502 were probably Putún Maya. Their great commercial center was Xicallanco, an international "port of trade," where Aztec long-distance merchants exchanged goods with traders from the Maya area. It is generally thought that the Itzá of Chichén Itzá and, later, Tayasal, were Mexicanized Putún by origin.

Following the downfall of Mayapan in the mid-15th century, the Northern Area fell into political disarray, with the rise of 16 independent statelets, each vying for power with its neighbors. In spite of this, there was some degree of centralization on the ceremonial level, since the ruling family of each statelet kept up a royal cult at the Temple of the Feathered Serpent in Maní. Yet the prevailing political "balkanization" made it very difficult for the Spaniards to conquer northern Yucatán, since there was no overall authority to topple as in central Mexico.

Important Post-Classic centers
Mayapán Capital of Yucatán from 1283 until the mid-15th century.
Chichén Itzá This old Puuc-style center was taken over by Toltecs from central Mexico in the late 10th century. It became the Toltec-Maya capital of the entire Yucatán Peninsula until its eclipse after 1200.
Balankanché An underground cavern containing numerous incense burners in the form of Tlaloc, the Toltec Rain God.
Tulum A small coastal town occupied from the Late Post-Classic until the conquest.
Isla de Cozumel This island was occupied by the Putún Maya, who made it a storage point for goods moving by their maritime trade network.
Tayasal Island capital of the Itzá Maya after they had left Yucatán. Although visited by Cortés, it did not fall to the Spaniards until 1697.
Nito A Late Post-Classic trading center on the Río Dulce.
Naco A large commercial settlement during the Late Post-Classic, with ties to the maritime trade carried on by the Putún Maya.
Zacaleu A Classic and Post-Classic center, capital of the Mam Maya at the time of Alvarado's 1525 conquest of the Maya highlands.
Utatlán Capital of the powerful Quiché Maya kingdom, burned to the ground by Pedro de Alvarado's forces.
Iximché Chief town of the Cakchiquel Maya during the Late Post-Classic.
Mixco Viejo Pokomam Maya capital. Surrounded by steep gorges, it was almost impregnable, but fell to Alvarado's army through treachery.

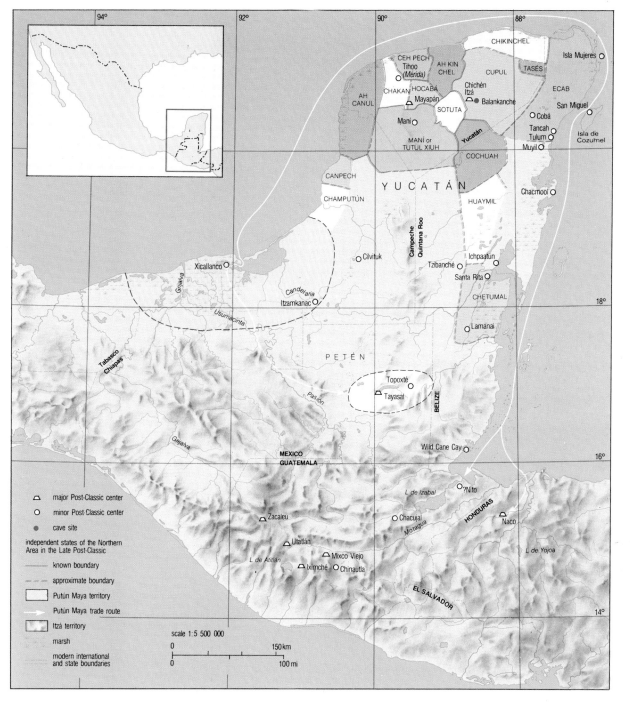

dominated by the Cakchiquel and Quiché Maya, who had major states with great capitals, and to a lesser extent by the Tzutuhil (on the south shore of Lake Atitlán) and Pokomam. In the west, bordering on the Tzeltal and Tzotzil Maya of Chiapas, were the Mam, with their capital at Zacaleu. The ruling dynasties which led these highland Maya groups usually claimed to have descended from migrant tribes originating in Tula, the great Toltec capital, but their annals (such as the Quiché *Popol Vuh*) prove that their culture was still heavily native Maya in character.

The most striking legacy of these highland nations is their literature. This was written down in the early colonial period, but surely harkens back to hieroglyphic originals. In particular, the great Quiché Maya epic known as the *Popol Vuh* ("The Book of the Mat") and the *Annals of the Cakchiquels* provide a window into preconquest Indian thought that is unique for the entire New World.

OAXACA IN THE POST-CLASSIC

The Mixtec of the western third of Oaxaca made their appearance on the Mesoamerican scene in the late Post-Classic, after the downfall of the Toltec as a pan-Mesoamerican power, but their roots must go much further back. Unfortunately, Mixtec archaeology is only in its infancy. The abundant data on these people come from the Mixtec themselves, in the form of eight pre-Spanish codices or screenfold books written on deerskin covered with gesso. Most of these contain genealogical and other historical information on the dynasties that ruled the Mixtec realm and carried out their extensive conquests.

Since the Mixteca is a fairly mountainous region, the Mixtec overlords took advantage of the terrain and constructed their principal towns on defensible hilltops: the hieroglyph for a particular place-name usually includes the sign for "mountain." After 1200 AD, probably under the influence of old and prestigious centers in neighboring Puebla such as Cholula, the Mixtec developed a style of painting, and perhaps even architecture, that has been called "Mixteca-Puebla."

By the 14th century the Mixtec had begun involving themselves with the old Zapotec domain, in particular the Valley of Oaxaca. In a familiar Mesoamerican pattern, Mixtec lords had taken over Zapotec statelets by a judicious combination of military might and royal marriages. Apparently the local Zapotec powerbrokers were only too willing to go along with this arrangement to cash in on the tribute accruing to the new power.

It will be remembered that Monte Albán was the ancient Zapotec capital, from Middle Formative times onward. In the last centuries before the Spanish conquest the abandoned hilltop site was decisively usurped by Mixtec rulers.

The Aztec conquest of Oaxaca began under the fourth ruler, Itzcoatl (1427–40), continued under Ahuitzotl (1486–1502), and concluded with Mote-cuhzoma Xocoyotzin (1502–20). Sometimes the Mixtec and Zapotec put aside their differences to

Left A Mixtec terracotta censer representing the Rain God. Recovered in large numbers from the Mixteca Alta (the mountainous kingdom of the Mixtecs), these hollow figures with holes in the tops were intended to be placed over fires, with smoke issuing from mouth or headdress. Goggled eyes and fangs identify this example as Tlaloc (the god's Aztec name); others lack such deity characteristics.

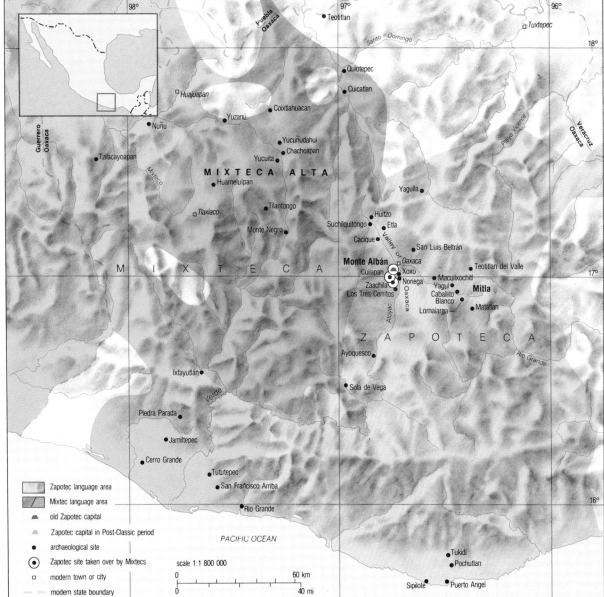

Left: Mixtecs and Zapotecs in Post-Classic Oaxaca
It is the survival of eight preconquest codices that has enabled us to know more about the Mixtecs than any other people who occupied what is now the state of Oaxaca in southern Mexico. These codices chronicle the rise of the Mixtec aristocracy from under Toltec domination late in the Post-Classic period. By 1350 AD much of the mountainous country in the western portion of this map was under their control, and covetous eyes were turned toward land further east, in particular the beautiful Valley of Oaxaca.

The Zapotecs had lived there for centuries, undisturbed by outsiders. Now their capital, Monte Albán, and other important towns fell easily into Mixtec hands as princes and princesses were married stategically into Zapotec courts. By the time the Spaniards arrived, Zapotec sites everywhere had come under Mixtec influence. Oaxaca towns came to reflect their cultural duality: Zaachila was a Zapotec capital and had a Zapotec king, but some remarkable polychrome pottery in the Mixtec style has been uncovered at tombs excavated there. Mitla, one-time center of Zapotec civilization, where Zapotec nobles and heroes are said to be buried in a secret chamber beneath the city, also displays architecture in the Mixtec-Puebla style.

Mitla

Below Step fret mosaics, Hall of the Columns, Mitla. One hundred and fifty panels on exterior as well as interior walls were decorated with variations of eight basic geometric patterns, some set in mosaic and others carved into lintels. Step fret decorated cruciform tombs and lintels painted in codex style typify Mitla art and architecture.

Below right In Monte Albán V times the urban zone of Mitla would have covered between 1 and 2 sq. km. with a sustaining hinterland of 20 sq. km.

Mitla is by far the most important site in Late Post-Classic Oaxaca, located in the southeastern arm of the valley. It consists of five magnificent palace groups which are masterpieces of architecture. Each group consists of long buildings arranged around an inner courtyard, rather similar to the Puuc architecture of Late Classic Yucatán, to which it may be related.

It is still uncertain whether Mitla was a Zapotec or Mixtec site, although no one doubts that the style is Mixteca-Puebla. The town today is purely Zapotec, but Mixtecs and Zapotecs are so interwoven in the Valley of Oaxaca that the question may not be answerable.

logically, this impressive site is dominated by an enormous rectangular masonry platform which supports five great *yácatas*. These are stepped, circular "pyramids" joined to stepped platforms, all faced with very fine, perfectly worked and joined, masonry slabs recalling the Inca stonework of Peru. The *yácatas*, which are also found at other Tarascan sites like the former capital Ihuatzio, seem to have been funerary monuments containing the remains of past Kasonsis and their retainers.

The *Relación* gives us extraordinarily detailed information on the structure of the Tarascan royal court and how it functioned. There was an incredible variety of retainers and palace craftsmen, some of whom were sacrificed on the death of a Kasonsi. Separate from the palace was a large group of non-celibate priests, headed by a supreme high priest; their duty was to lead the worship of the Tarascan gods, which included the sun and the moon.

While the Aztec state was swallowing up rival Mesoamerican states throughout the Late Post-Classic right through to the Spanish conquest, the Tarascans successfully defended their frontiers against the Aztec onslaught; the Kasonsi was therefore treated as an equal by the Aztec emperor.

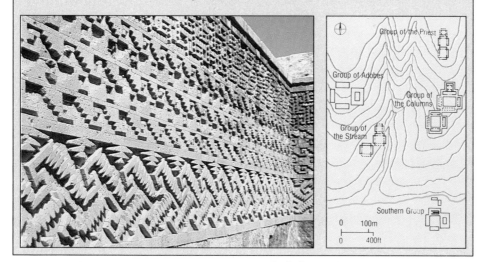

present a united defense, but there were times when the latter had to go it alone. In particular, the Zapotec put up a spirited and successful resistance to the Aztec armies at the hilltop fortress of Guiengola, so that at least some Zapotec princedoms maintained their independence.

THE TARASCAN KINGDOM

The prehistory of Michoacan in western Mexico, homeland of the Tarascan or Purépecha people, is poorly known. It is thus difficult to know how much we can rely on traditional Tarascan history, as recorded in the *Relación de Michoacan*. They claimed that at least some of their forebears had been Chichimec, wandering from the north into the fertile basin surrounding the beautiful Lake Pátzcuaro, which abounds in fish. Other settlers of Michoacan spoke the Nahuatl language. But the ruling families were speakers of Tarascan, a language with no known affiliation to any other in the hemisphere.

From the *Relación* it seems that the Tarascan royal house, headed by the king or *kasonsi*, established successive capitals during the Late Post-Classic, with the last at Tzintzuntzan, overlooking Lake Pátzcuaro. Only partially explored archaeo-

THE AZTEC EMPIRE

Aztec civilization is the best known of the New World's pre-Spanish cultures, not so much from the archaeological research, which has been minimal, but from the incredible number of documents written after the conquest in Nahuatl and in Spanish. For example, the great 12-volume encyclopedia compiled by the early friar Bernardino de Sahagún from testimony of Nahuatl-speaking informants covers almost every aspect of Aztec life, both material and spiritual. For no other New World people do we have such richness of data.

Aztec origins
The Aztec had two distinct origin legends, both of which stress that they were *not* native to the Valley of Mexico. The Aztec liked to talk of their rude ancestry, and claimed affiliation with the Chichimeca, but it is likely that at an early stage they were an agricultural people who in some way or another had absorbed traits of the old Toltec culture, particularly its religious beliefs and practices.

The Valley of Mexico that they entered in the early 13th century was a thoroughly populated place with old traditions. The leading powers were the Tepanec of Atzcapotzalco, on the northwestern shores of the Great Lake; the Toltec-derived state of Texcoco to the east of the lake; and the powerful and cultivated city of Culhuacan in the south, whose rulers claimed to be descended from the Tolteca-Chichimeca of Tula. A tribal prophecy had foretold the Aztec that their great capital and the future center of the world was to be established on a swampy island, where there would be an eagle seated on a prickly-pear cactus holding a serpent in its beak. After many vicissitudes, during the course of which the Aztec acted as vassals or mercenaries for one or another power in the Valley, the prophecy reached its fulfillment in 1325 when the Aztec settled at Tenochtitlan ("Place of the

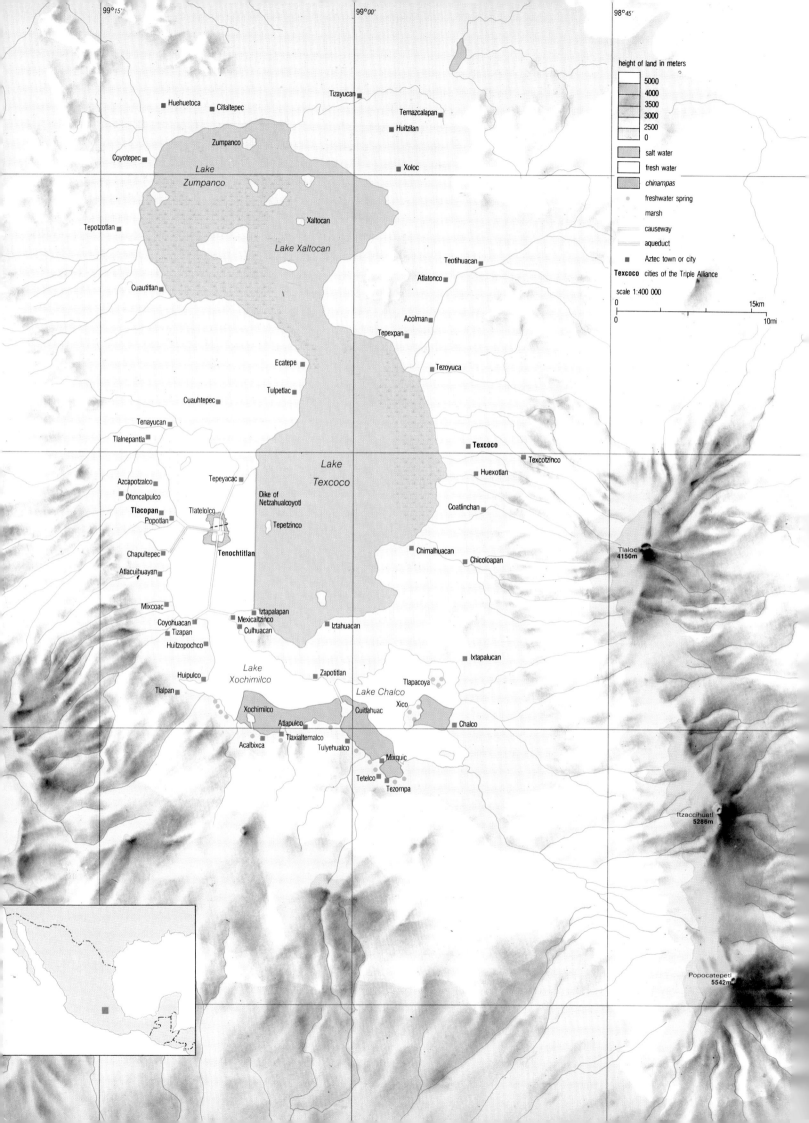

99°15'   99°00'   98°45'

height of land in meters

5000
4000
3500
3000
2500
0

salt water
fresh water
chinampas

freshwater spring
marsh
causeway
aqueduct
Aztec town or city
Texcoco cities of the Triple Alliance

scale 1:400 000

0   15km
0   10mi

Huehuetoca
Citlaltepec
Tizayucan
Temazcalapan
Huitzilan
Zumpanco
Xoloc
Coyotepec
Lake Zumpanco
Tepotzotlan
Lake Xaltocan
Xaltocan
Cuautitlan
Teotihuacan
Atlatonco
Acolman
Tepexpan
Ecatepe
Tulpetlac
Tezoyuca
Cuauhtepec
Tenayucan
Tlalnepantla
Texcoco
Texcotzinco
Azcapotzalco
Tepeyacac
Huexotlan
Otoncalpulco
Tlacopan
Tlatelolco
Lake Texcoco
Dike of Netzahualcoyotl
Coatlinchan
Popotlan
Tepetzinco
Chapultepec
Tenochtitlan
Chimalhuacan
Chicoloapan
Atlacuihuayan
Tlaloc 4150m
Mixcoac
Iztapalapan
Coyohuacan
Mexicaltzinco
Tizapan
Culhuacan
Iztahuacan
Huitzopochco
Ixtapalucan
Huipulco
Lake Xochimilco
Zapotitlan
Tlalpan
Tlapacoya
Lake Chalco
Xico
Xochimilco
Cuitlahuac
Atlapulco
Chalco
Tlaxialtemalco
Acalbixca
Tulyehualco
Mixquic
Tetelco
Itzaccihuatl 5286m
Tezompa
Popocatepetl 5542m

Left: The Valley of Mexico under Aztec rule
Since in preconquest times the Valley of Mexico was without exterior drainage, it contained a broad, shallow lake known as the Lake of the Moon; most Aztec cities and towns were located near its margins, and thousands of boats daily plied its surface, engaged in commerce. In its western part, where the island capital of Tenochtitlan-Tlatelolco was located, and in the south (Lakes Xochimilco and Chalco), the lake was fresh, being fed by abundant springs. It was there that the raised-field plots known as *chinampas* were found. Occasionally these would be inundated and ruined by salty waters coming in from Lake Texcoco during the rainy season. To protect the chinampa zones, which were the "breadbasket" of the Aztec state, the mid-15th-century poet-king of Texcoco, Netzahualcoyotl, constructed a great dike separating the two waters.

The Aztec state was theoretically an alliance between the rulers of Tenochtitlan, Texcoco and Tlacopan (modern Tacuba), but it was dominated by Tenochtitlan. Texcoco, however, had great prestige because of the antiquity of its traditions and through the learning and culture of its rulers. The Texcocan monarch's pleasure gardens and rock-cut baths were built on a hill at Texcotzinco, and were a marvel in their day. Tlacopan had little power, and its role was poorly defined.

Prickly-pear Cactus").

Their military experience as mercenaries had given the Aztec a formidable knowledge which they soon exercised in overturning the suzerainty of their former overlords, the Tepanec. And after their alliance with two other city-states, Texcoco and Tlacopan (the Triple Alliance), they soon gained supreme dominion over the entire valley. The basis had been laid for the Aztec conquest of Mexico.

The Aztec imperial expansion

By the mid-14th century the Aztec kings had created what amounted to an empire, beginning with Itzcoatl, continuing with Motecuhzoma Ilhuicamina (1440–68), and extending to the reign of the sixth ruler, Axayacatl (1469–81); it was during the latter's reign that Tenochtitlan subdued its close neighbor to the north, Tlatelolco. Henceforth the capital was a twin city, Tenochtitlan-Tlatelolco.

One of the least comprehensible Aztec institutions to modern eyes is that of the "Flowery War," which was instituted between Tenochtitlan on the one hand and the rival states of Tlaxcallan and Huexotzinco, on the other. This was a pact not of peace but of eternal hostilities, the purpose of which was to provide a never-ending stream of captive warriors for the sacrificial knife. "Flowers" in Aztec poetic imagery was a metaphor for human blood, and the battlefield was conceived of as a field of flowers. There is some evidence that Tlaxcallan was considerably weakened and embittered by this perpetual cycle of violence, and its rulers and army readily took up the Spanish side when Cortés entered Mexico.

Aztec armies were very large, and were organized under war chiefs or officers who had risen to prominence by the taking of captives. Aztec warriors were gorgeously arrayed, especially those who belonged to the warrior orders—the Jaguar or Eagle knights. Battles were fought with formidable weapons, particularly the terrible *macahuitl* or flat sword-club, edged with obsidian blades set in slots. Even the Spaniards were terrified of these. The atlatl-propelled dart was one of the principal weapons, but mercenary Otomí tribesmen acted as bowmen for the Aztec state.

Conquered enemy states were organized as tribute-producing provinces of the Triple Alliance, under the immediate rule of large Aztec garrisons. A vast bureaucracy, which included grim tax-collectors, was in place to see that the system ran smoothly. Small wonder that many of the conquered provinces welcomed the Spaniards as saviors.

City, state and society

The temporal and spiritual heart of the empire was the island capital of Tenochtitlan-Tlatelolco, and more specifically, its ceremonial precinct and Great Temple. Crisscrossed by canals paralleled by streets, it was described by the *conquistadores* as "another Venice." Like that mighty Adriatic power, the ready access of water transport made heavy commerce a reality. It is said that about 200 000 canoes could be found on the Great Lake in the early 16th century.

It is difficult in the extreme to state the population of the city in 1519, when Cortés first arrived, but it could not have been less than 100 000 souls, while the entire empire may have controlled more than 10 million people. Although the Aztec in earlier times may have been on a tribal level of social and political organization, by 1500 they had reached the level of class society. At the bottom of the heap were slaves, who were well treated, and the serfs who worked the private lands of the nobility. The bulk of the population were commoners or *macehualtin*, who lived on and worked commonly held lands by right of usufruct. These freemen and their families belonged to localized kin groups called *calpulli* or "big houses," each of which had its own lands, "clan" leaders and temple. There were about 20 of these in Tenochtitlan-Tlatelolco. Above them were the hereditary nobility or *pipiltin*, who supplied the top bureaucrats in the Aztec imperial system, and from whose ranks was formed a council which advised the emperor and elected his successor from the ruling lineage.

The supreme leadership of the empire was vested in the royal house. This leadership was more complex than the Spaniards assumed, for they dealt principally with the man holding the

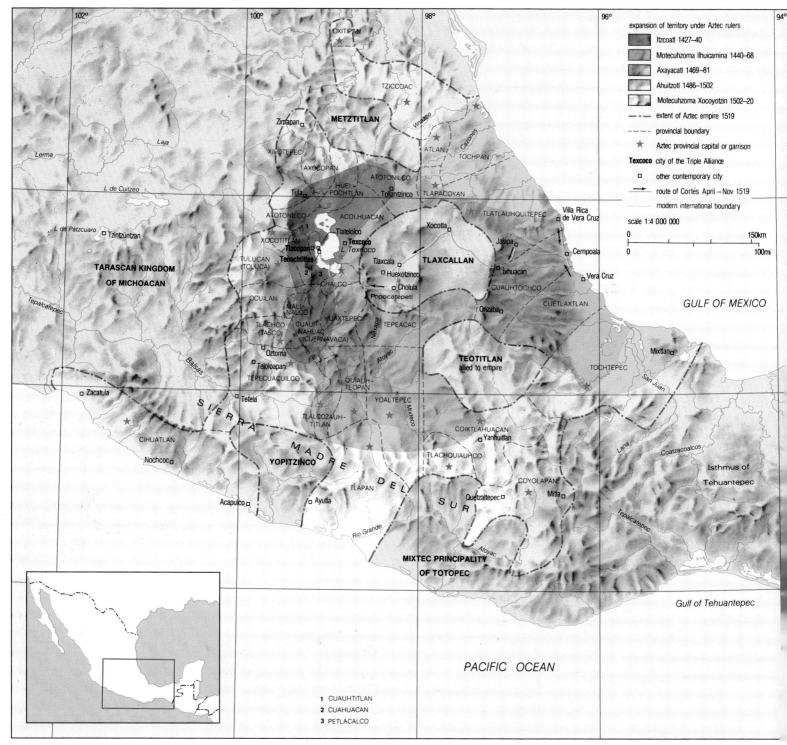

expansion of territory under Aztec rulers

Itzcoatl 1427–40
Motecuhzoma Ilhuicamina 1440–68
Axayacatl 1469–81
Ahuitzotl 1486–1502
Motecuhzoma Xocoyotzin 1502–20

— · — · — extent of Aztec empire 1519
— — — provincial boundary
★ Aztec provincial capital or garrison
Texcoco city of the Triple Alliance
□ other contemporary city
→ route of Cortés April–Nov 1519
— · · — modern international boundary
scale 1:4 000 000

0   150km
0   100mi

1 CUAUHTITLAN
2 CUAHUACAN
3 PETLACALCO

title of *Tlatoani* (or "Speaker"), whom they called the emperor. In 1519 this was the ill-fated Motecuhzoma Xocoyotzin ("Montezuma" to the *conquistadores*). A close analysis of the documents shows that the Tlatoani was mainly concerned with the external relations, peaceful or otherwise, of the city and empire. Unbeknown to the Spaniards there was a parallel ruler, also a member of the royal lineage, with the title of *Cihuacoatl* ("Female Serpent"). He had jurisdiction over the internal affairs of the Aztec capital. Thus, when Cortés had eliminated the Tlatoani, the resistance of the city to the invaders only increased rather than diminished.

An economic institution which has long puzzled scholars is that of the *pochteca*. This was a kind of hereditary guild of long-distance merchants who traded for luxury goods in foreign markets, often traveling at night or disguised so as to avoid the possibility of ambushes in unfriendly territory.

The Aztec economy

Apart from the incredible tonnage of foodstuffs which arrived twice yearly in the capital, along with manufactured items which might have been "farmed out" to *pochteca* merchants for barter in distant ports of trade like Xicallanco in Putún Maya territory, the Aztec state was dependent upon the food production of the Valley of Mexico. Central to this was the system of *chinampas* or raised fields which included not only the surviving zones of Xochimilco and neighboring towns in the southern part of the Great Lake but also most of the island of Tenochtitlan-Tlatelolco itself, away from the ceremonial areas. Apart from the wet-rice cultivation of eastern Asia, probably no system of agri-

Above: The Aztec empire
This map is based upon data gleaned by the late R.H. Barlow from the *Matrícula de Tributos*, an Aztec book listing the conquered provinces and their towns, along with the tribute due from each province to the members of the Triple Alliance, especially Tenochtitlan, the Aztec capital, which took the lion's share of the goods.

Annual tribute to the Triple Alliance was very heavy, and enforced by local rulers appointed by the Aztec state, and by special tax collectors, who were much feared. The province of Cuauhtitlan, for instance, which lay to the north of Tenochtitlan, had to provide 1200 cotton mantles, 62 warriors' costumes along with feathered shields, 4000 reed mats, 4000 reed seats, and one

huge bin each of maize, beans, *chian* (sage seeds) and amaranth.

Tlaxcallan (modern Tlaxcala) was an independent state within the empire, and no attempt was made to conquer it. However, a special state of perpetual hostilities, known as the "Flowery War," prevailed between it and the Aztec state.

Xoconocho (called Soconusco by the Spaniards) was the most distant Aztec province. Conquered at the close of the 15th century by Ahuitzotl, it comprised the rich coastal plain and piedmont zone of southeastern Chiapas and neighboring Guatemala.

Right A detail of the Codex Cospi. Although of disputed origin, it is representative of the books kept by Aztec priests.

Aztec Deities

In Aztec religion a distinction has to be made between a more ancient religious system, which the Aztec inherited from the Toltec or Toltec-derived states of Post-Classic Mexico, and a system which was closely geared to the ideology of the expanding Aztec state. The latter was based upon a solar myth centered upon the miraculous birth of the tribal God of the Sun, Huitzilopochtli. His mother, the earth goddess Coatlicue, who had previously borne the 400 stars of the night sky and their sister the moon goddess Coyolxauhqui, became impregnated by a ball of feathers as she was sweeping her house or temple on Coatepec, or "Snake Mountain." The son-to-be was Huitzilopochtli. Furiously jealous, the nocturnal luminaries cut off Coyolxauhqui's head, but Huitzilopochtli was born anyway, fully grown and fully armed, and slew his half-siblings. This obviously refers to the daily destruction of the moon and stars by the sun's rays.

At dawn on every day the solar deity was reborn, rising to noon on the back of a Fire Serpent; thereupon, the dread Cihuateteo, the souls of women who had died in childbirth, took him down to the Underworld below the western horizon. Unless he was constantly nourished by the hearts and blood of brave captives, Huitzilopochtli, the Sun himself, would fail to emerge once more at dawn to bless mankind with his life-giving rays. Thus the constant human sacrifices in the Aztec capital. The older tradition concerns the first moment of creation, involving an old, androgynous deity, dwelling in the uppermost of 13 stratified heavens.

Coatlicue or "Serpent Skirt" (*above*) was mother of the Aztec tribal god of the sun, Huitzilopochtli; she had been magically impregnated by a ball of feathers as she was sweeping her house. Her other children, the 400 stars of the southern sky, and her daughter Coyolxauhqui, the moon, cut off her head in jealous anger, but Huitzilopochtli sprang forth fully armed and slew his rivals—obviously an astronomical myth of the defeat of the nocturnal luminaries by the sun's rays. Tonatiuh (*left*) was an older solar deity whose role was largely usurped in Aztec times by Huitzilopochtli. He bears on his back the day-sign Ollin or "Earthquake," symbol of the end of the present age or "Sun," when the universe will be destroyed by earthquakes.

culture is more productive than the raised fields of the valley.

Due to the varied nature of the central Mexican terrain and climate, seasonal production of food-stuffs was also highly varied and markets were spaced throughout the Aztec realm to ensure that goods were evenly distributed in the population. The greatest market was in Tlatelolco.

Aztec religion

The Aztec were the recipients and interpreters of a tradition of thought which goes back to the Olmec, and which was reinterpreted by every subsequent civilization, including the Classic Maya. Of course there were always regional differences and special-izations, including tutelary divinities for each pre-Spanish nation and city. But the general outlines for all native Mesoamerican religions were the same.

The worship of all these supernaturals was under the control of a celibate priesthood, who had studied for their profession in a *calmecac* or semi-nary. Their task was to keep count of the daily rituals of the 260-day calendar recorded in screen-fold books of leather and to supervise the offerings and sacrifices at the *calpulli* and state temples, of which the most important was the Great Temple. The latter, which had been rebuilt a number of times since the arrival of the Aztec on the island, was a huge double construction dedicated to the cult of the old Mesoamerican Rain God, Tlaloc, and to Huitzilopochtli, the life-giving sun.

The Aztec themselves had predicted the death of their civilization. Every 104 years, when the 260-day and 365-day counts, and the cycle of the planet Venus (584 days) coincided, they were in fear and trembling that the Fifth Sun (our own creation) would be terminated, and took the utmost precautions to prevent this by sacrifices to the Fire God. There is a great deal of surviving Nahuatl poetry, and it has a bittersweet, decidedly re-strained quality to it, such as these pessimistic lines attributed to the poet-king of Texcoco, the great Netzahualcoyotl (Fasting Coyote):

> Even jade is shattered,
> Even gold is crushed,
> Even quetzal plumes are torn . . .
> One does not live forever on this earth:
> We endure only for an instant!

A number of sources attest to the deep despair of Motecuhzoma Xocoyotzin, Tlatoani of the Aztec empire when the Spaniards arrived. Unnerved by predictions of the downfall of his people, terrified by all sorts of strange omens and portents which had appeared during his reign, and held in thrall by the legend that Quetzalcoatl, the great Toltec ruler-king, was to come back at last to reclaim his realm—Motecuhzoma was basically demoralized by the arrival of the Spaniards in 1519.

Hernán Cortés was no fool, nor was his Indian mistress and interpreter Malintzin or Doña Marina. Treated as the returned Feathered Serpent, he dar-ingly took his troops, augmented by disaffected tributaries of the Aztec state, into the very heart of the capital and eventually overthrew the last and one of the greatest New World civilizations. In April of 1521, in a ruined city reeking with the corpses of its brave defenders, 3000 years of Mesoamerican civilization came to an end.

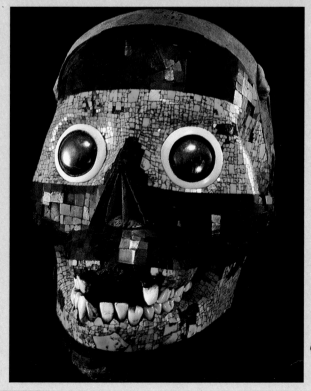

Xipe Totec (*above*) was the god of springtime and the coming of the rains. The new layer of vegetation and the sprouting crops were symbolized by priests donning the skin of flayed sacrificial victims. The supreme divinity was Tezcatlipoca or "Smoking Mirror" (*left*). This is the skull of a captive who had impersonated him for one year. Tezcatlipoca's cosmic antagonist was Quetzalcoatl ("Feathered Serpent") (*below*).

Tenochtitlan

Right Canals cut through swampy ground at Tenochtitlan. *Chinampa* agriculture is a system of land reclamation and irrigation, by which garden plots are formed and enlarged by mud dredged from the bottom of canals. Vines or trees were planted at the edges to contain the rich soil.

Center right Tzompantli in stone. Rows of skulls decorate a recently excavated platform in the north patio of the Templo Mayor. Archaeologists interpret this platform as a shrine—not the base of a skull rack (*tzompantli*) as no bones were recovered there.

Below Dismembered moon goddess, Coyolxauhqui. The monolith (3·25 m. in diameter; estimated weight 5–8 tonnes) remains in situ where it was excavated at the base of the Templo Mayor on the south side. It dates from the reign of Ahuitzotl (1486–1502).

Tenochtitlan, capital city of the Aztec, is virtually obscured nowadays by modern Mexico City. Cortés and his followers methodically razed the temples, replacing them with churches. Domestic architecture underwent the same fate, as the Spanish objective was to colonize as well as conquer. The great twin temple pyramid in the city's center (Templo Mayor), dedicated to the gods of Rain (Tlaloc) and War (Huitzilopochtli), was dismantled to provide building material for the Metropolitan cathedral. Tenochtitlan's prime real estate was usurped for palatial Spanish residences. In order to enjoy the fruits of conquest, the Spaniards had to maintain a work force. Once the power structure was broken with the death and dispersal of the highest-ranking Aztec leaders, Spanish control was strengthened by utilizing geographical territory already associated in the minds of the Aztec with governmental and religious administration. Most of what is know of ancient Tenochtitlan comes from reports written shortly after the conquest. Obviously, archaeological work to show the entire scope of the city cannot be carried out in a densely populated urban area. Historical accounts of the Templo Mayor, describing it as the physical and cosmological center of the Aztec world, have been confirmed by recent extensive excavations of the leveled pyramid (five construction layers) and its surrounding shrines.

Right An early European conception of Tenochtitlan is seen in Benedetto Bordone's plan of 1528. Houses are drawn to resemble European, rather than Aztec, style. The ceremonial precinct comprised not only the Templo Mayor, but palaces, schools and shrines; every Aztec deity was commemorated in architecture and/or sculpture. Aztec social and political organization, highly stratified and rigidly controlled, seems to be reflected in the geometric layout of the city. Tenochtitlan city-planners imposed a grid system of causeways and canals upon their island's topography.

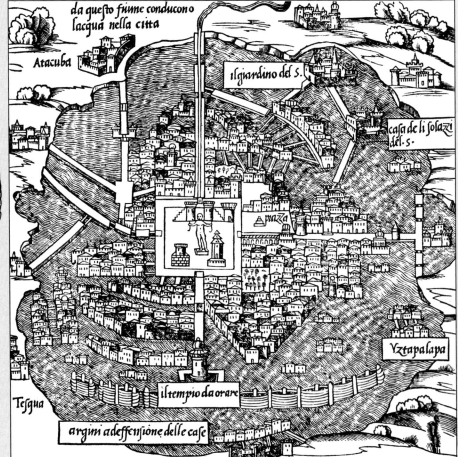

PART FIVE
SOUTH AMERICA

Cuba   Hispaniola

Yucatán
Peninsula

G r e a t e r   A n t i l l e s

CARIBBEAN   SEA

ATLANTIC
OCEAN

Guajira
Peninsula

L e s s e r   A n t i l l e s

G of
Darien

Trinidad

Nicoya
Peninsula

G of
Panama

Orinoco

L l a n o s

GUIANA HIGHLANDS

Equator

Japurá

Negro

Marajo I.

G of Guayaquil

Amazon

Sechura
Desert

Madeira

Tapajós

C São Roque

Marañón

Ucayali

S e l v a s

Xingu

Araguaia

Parnaíba

C a a t i n g a

São Francisco

A
N
D
E
S

L Titicaca

Altiplano

C a m p o s

B R A Z I L I A N   H I G H L A N D S

PACIFIC
OCEAN

Atacama Desert

G r a n

C h a c o

Paraguay

Paraná

C Frio

of Capricorn

Salado

A
N
D
E
S

Colorado

P a m p a s

Rio de la
Plata

P a t a g o n i a

Chiloé I.

Vegetation of South America

Many different kinds of cultural
and ecological adaptations have
been motivated by the
tremendous range of South
American vegetation, wild and
domesticated. The most
successful cultures have
clustered along the west coast,
where climatic extremes lie close
together. These civilizations
developed where vegetation is
naturally less rich than in the
lowlands to the east. On the west
coast crops are raised in virtually
vegetationless natural desert
with the use of water from the
mountains.

Throughout millennia, plants
have provided food, housing
materials, clothing, utensils,
drugs, dyes, ornaments and
trade goods for New World
peoples. Lists of indigenous
plants were made by
missionaries and other early
European visitors.
Archaeologists have found traces
of ancient plant remains—in
burials and caves, for example.
A number of recent studies by
paleobotanists and
ethnobotanists have added to the
information and speculation
concerning plant origins, use
and diffusion in ancient times.

Magellan Strait

Tierra del Fuego

C Horn

mountain summits

Andean "puna" vegetation (sparse, coarse grassland)

mountain tropical forest

thorn forest, scrub steppe and semidesert

tropical rainforest

temperate and subtropical forest

alluvial floodplain

grassland

desert

scale 1:30 000 000

0   600km

0   400mi

GEOGRAPHY AND RESOURCES

Below The bleak landscape of the Bolivian Altiplano lies between the central and western cordilleras of the Andes at the height of some 4000 m. This plateau above the timberline is a region where llama and alpaca herds (or nowadays sheep) have long been kept, for this "inhuman" environment has long been inhabited. Root crops are important here, and maize and cotton can be grown in protected areas, but they are subject to hail damage. This plateau has interior drainage, with salt marshes and salty lakes, as well as the sweet-water Lake Titicaca.

South America is a continent of contrasting superlatives. The Andes are among the highest mountains in the world, rising to heights of about 7000 meters. To the west of them lies the world's driest coastal desert, which adjoins what is normally the world's richest fishing ground, the Humboldt Current. To the east of the mountains lies the largest, and one of the lushest, forests on earth, and the world's greatest river system.

South American climates range from the steaming Tropics to snowy, oxygen-rare altitudes. Precipitation rates are extreme: some regions have virtually no rainfall; the Pacific coast of Colombia annually receives 10 000 millimeters of rain. Climate can change enormously within a few kilometers. Changes of seasons in much of Central and South America, however, are marked not by temperature but by rainfall differences. In the highlands there is more temperature change within 24 hours than from season to season.

The Antilles and Central America are generally rugged, sometimes volcanic. Northwestern Costa Rica has a chain of volcanoes down the center, with

plains on either side. The chain of mountains that becomes the Andes begins in eastern Costa Rica, where the coastal plains are narrow (as they are along the adjacent Atlantic coast of Panama). There are few rivers along this coast of sandy beaches and rocky bluffs. The rainfall is so high in some places along the coast of Panama and in the mountains that agriculture is virtually impossible.

The north coast of Colombia has moist lowlands, river floodplains with streams, swamps and lagoons, rainy and dry seasons. The Guajira Peninsula, however—the northernmost spur of South America, shared by Colombia and Venezuela—has only 200 millimeters' annual rainfall; its dry season makes it an almost barren desert. In Ecuador, at least in modern times, there has been a generally semiarid coastal climate. In the past, however, there were mangrove swamps along this coast. They probably continued down to the Sechura Desert, a riverless expanse in northern Peru. Below the Sechura the coastal desert is interrupted by rivers. Nevertheless, along the entire cost of Peru and northern Chile a narrow strip of desert lies

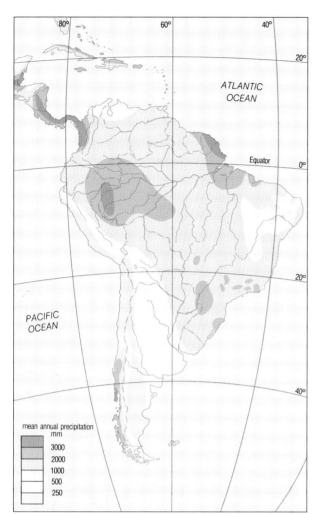

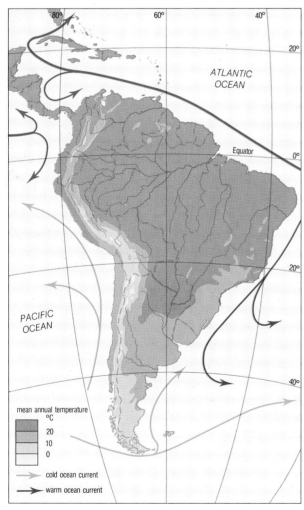

between barren mountains and the sea. There are also dry intermontane valleys.

In the north the Peruvian coast is watered by relatively regularly spaced rivers coming down from the mountains, perpendicular to the coast. The longest river is the Santa. The northern rivers discharge more water than the southern ones. The north coastal plain also has more arable land than the south coast.

The Amazon Basin is yet another world. The South American lowland tropical forest, which includes most of the Amazon Basin and a northward extension to the mouth of the Orinoco River, covers more than 2·6 million square kilometers. Over 1000 tributaries feed the Amazon; 17 of these are over 1500 kilometers long, and two of them rank third and fourth in volume among all the world's rivers. In places the Amazon achieves a width of about 15 kilometers. Many of its tributaries rush powerfully down from the Andes, but through the Amazon Basin the pace is slow; the rivers meander, forming serpentine curves and oxbow lakes.

South of the Amazon system there are woodlands, steppes and prairies, as the mountains shrink to the west and the continent tapers off towards the end—the barren, windswept plains of Tierra del Fuego.

Resources

This part of the world has a great range of plant species, both wild and domesticated. (It has been noted that if one stands in an Amazon forest, it is difficult to see two trees of the same species.) Maize (of various varieties) is generally the staple crop in the western lowlands of South America, and manioc is the basic crop in the east.

Manioc was probably first cultivated by the tropical-forest peoples of eastern Venezuela, and the agriculture of the Amazon-Orinoco lowlands is still based chiefly on slash-and-burn manioc farming. Narrow stretches of floodplain along the river system are fertilized by silt brought down from the mountains in yearly inundation. These fields can be used continuously, because their nutrients are replaced, whereas the slash-and-burn farmers away from these floodplains must move their fields every few years, because they become unproductive. Back from the rivers the forest is high with a canopy so dense that the forest floor is fairly clean under it.

In the highlands the potato is the staple food, especially at altitudes where only root crops can be grown. Maize can be raised at fairly high altitudes, but often at great risk from hail and frost. Other important food crops were beans, squash, peppers and peanuts. Cotton was raised in the lowlands from very early times, and gourds were an important crop for utensils.

The peoples of the Peruvian and Ecuadoran coasts were developing irrigation agriculture by about 2000 BC. Since the river valleys not only bring water but also serve as communication channels with the mountains and the forest beyond, goods from the sierra and the far slopes of the mountains were available through trade. The coastal peoples also had the sea as a source of food and were able to exploit offshore guano islands for fertilizer.

Left: Climate of South America Maps show the extremes of the South American climate, with its immense variation in rainfall and temperature and ocean currents that affect the land. The west-coast desert is caused by a combination of circumstances. Moist winds from the Amazon Basin are blocked by high mountains on the east. To the west, the Peruvian, or Humboldt, Current flows in a deep trench. (From its deepest part to the highest Andes peak measures some 15 km.) Cold waters from the Antarctic condense moisture offshore. Because sea life is most abundant in cold waters, this is normally

one of the world's richest fishing grounds. A warm current from the north—known as El Niño because it usually flows south at Christmas, the time of El Niño, the Christ Child—sometimes flows for prolonged periods, not only affecting fishing but changing climate over a wide area.

Above Pre-Columbian peoples altered their landscape to meet both practical and symbolic needs, as in the circular terraces at Moray, an Inca adaptation of natural declivities in the highlands of southern Peru.

In the highlands there are few broad valleys for agriculture. The largest level area in the Andes is the altiplano, on the Peru–Bolivia border, nearly 4000 meters above the sea. Among the few sizable valleys are the Callejón de Huaylas, the Bogotá plateau and the valleys around Cuzco. Most farming in the sierras was done on agricultural terraces.

There were various adaptations to cultivation needs, e.g. ridged fields, that is the use of ditches to provide drained cultivation areas, could be used during flood times. Domesticated plants existed in much greater quantity and variety than animals. The only animal domesticates were llamas, alpacas, guinea pigs, ducks and dogs. Llamas were used in the highlands for a multitude of purposes: they were the only pack animal in the New World; they were also good for wool, for food and for medicine. Dogs were raised for food and for hunting. The rivers of eastern South America contained a great variety of fish, as well as water turtles, caymans and manatees. Some creatures had other uses as well—manatee tusks and turtle shells, for example. In the Initial period, on the coast of Peru, and at the same time in Ecuador, increasing dependence on the sea developed. Middens at coastal sites have yielded mollusks and gastropods, and remains of fish, birds and sea mammals.

Ways of life developed in adaptation to different environments, and, gradually, to the complex interaction between environments.

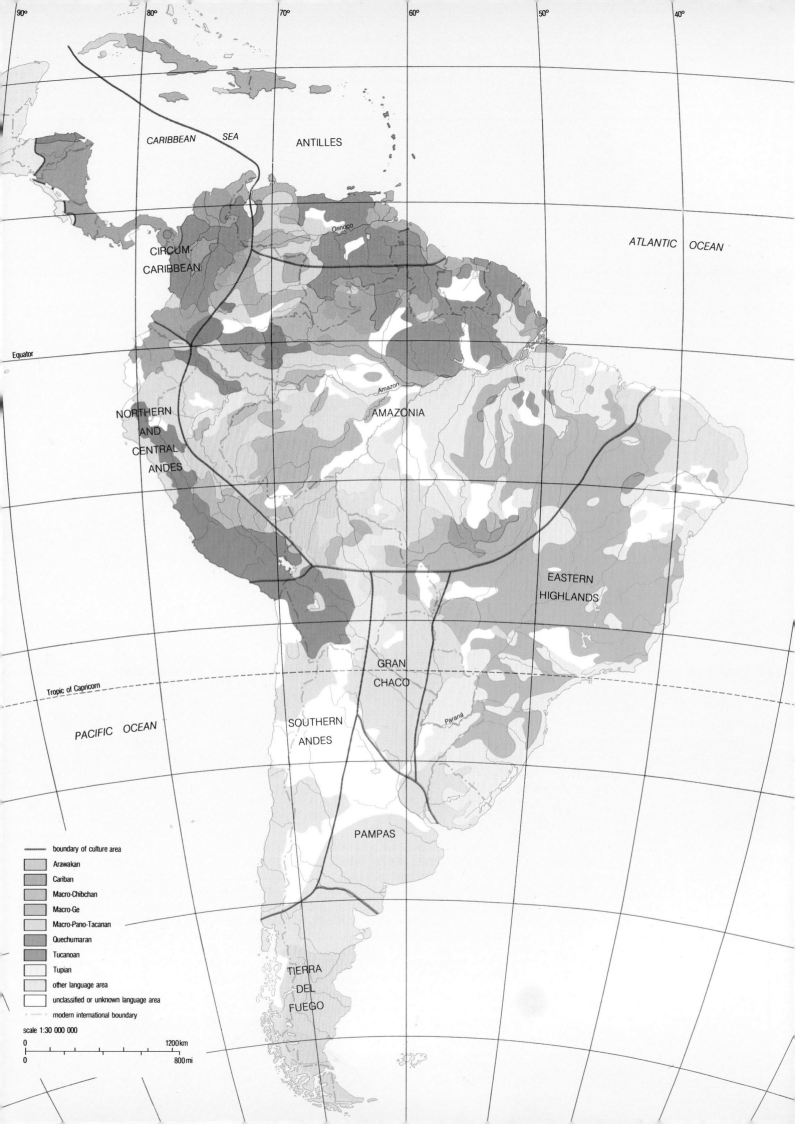

90° 80° 70° 60° 50° 40°

CARIBBEAN   SEA   ANTILLES

ATLANTIC   OCEAN

CIRCUM-
CARIBBEAN

Orinoco

Equator

NORTHERN
AND
CENTRAL
ANDES

Amazon

AMAZONIA

EASTERN
HIGHLANDS

Tropic of Capricorn

GRAN
CHACO

PACIFIC   OCEAN

SOUTHERN
ANDES

Paraná

PAMPAS

boundary of culture area

Arawakan

Cariban

Macro-Chibchan

Macro-Ge

Macro-Pano-Tacanan

Quechumaran

Tucanoan

Tupian

other language area

unclassified or unknown language area

modern international boundary

scale 1:30 000 000

0   1200km

0   800mi

TIERRA
DEL
FUEGO

CULTURES AND BELIEF

It is impossible to draw a simple diagram of South American cultures, for their developments function organically. A chart cannot show precisely the interrelationships of cultures within the entire area or with areas outside, nor can it indicate the unevennesss of the timing of periods or the time lags of influences.

The rough general scheme that seems to work best is the following. The Antilles form one region, related to eastern Venezuela. Lower Central America (eastern Nicaragua, Costa Rica and Panama), western Venezuela and northern Colombia form a circum-Caribbean region. The region of the Northern Andes comprises southern Colombia and Ecuador. Lower Central America, Colombia and Ecuador are sometimes called the Intermediate Area (intermediate between Mesoamerica and the Central Andes). Most of Peru is combined with the adjacent part of Bolivia to form the Central Andes. Amazonia is a separate region. The Southern Andes region consists of northern Chile and northwest Argentina. Patagonia is considered as a separate entity.

None of these regions is isolated from its neighbors. All were subject to different influences at different times, and within each region individual areas experienced different influences. Cultures were closely interrelated. Reference to modern political boundaries is, of course, for convenience only. It is largely by their art styles that we know archaeological cultures: the iconography of deity depictions, the shapes and wares and means of decoration of ceramics, the types of architecture—these are the surviving indications of the status of religion, politics and society.

The Central Andes

The highest cultural development in South America took place in the Central Andes. This complex archaeological region is divided into cultural subareas of the Northern Highlands, North Coast, Central Highlands, Central Coast, Southern Highlands and South Coast. In the Central Andes there must have been, from the beginnings of civilization, interaction between the fish-rich coast, the river-watered coastal agricultural valleys, the mountains, which provided resources lacking on the coast, and even the tropical forest on the other side of the mountains.

The Central Andes is divided chronologically by most archaeologists into periods that alternate between "horizons," times when an art style is found over a very wide area, and intermediate periods, when regional art styles indicate an absence of widespread movements.

The Initial period (c. 2000–1400 BC) is just that: a time when civilization was just beginning, when nomadic peoples had settled and established villages with ceremonial centers, when agriculture and pottery- and textile-making were in their early stages.

The Early horizon (c. 1400–400 BC) shows marked architectural development, culminating in the spread of the style called Chavín, after the type site at Chavín de Huantar on the eastern slopes of the Andes (although the style seems to appear earlier at certain other sites).

The Chavín art style influenced much that developed after the power that motivated it had died out. The following Early Intermediate period (400 BC–500 AD) was a time of regional styles, although some of these styles were clearly the expression of expanding political chiefdoms, the Mochica for example.

The Middle horizon (500–900 AD) is defined by the Tiahuanaco-Huari expansion, from the southern highlands to the far north coast and to Cajamarca in the northern highlands. The spread of the style and the architecture that intruded into the captured regions indicate an imperial administration thought by many to have been a forerunner of the Inca expansion—well organized, ambitious and successful (at least for a time) in conquest.

After the Huari strength faded, there was another period of regional styles, the Late Intermediate period (900–1476 AD). A kingdom like that of the Chimú, however, was not merely a local chiefdom but a sizable state, aggressive and tightly knit. It ruled the entire north coast. When the Inca marched on the north coast they confronted a power of almost equal strength.

Each time the pendulum swung, the horizon became wider, the territory larger. In the Late horizon (1476–1534 AD) the Inca provided the last example of indigenous New World imperialism, a state that radiated out from Cuzco north to the Ecuador–Colombia border and south into Central Chile and northwest Argentina.

A tendency to form empires is characteristic of the Central Andes. In reality there was obvious aggression and conquest, and in many art styles warfare is an important theme. Outside the Central Andes smaller chiefdoms were the usual form of government. The chieftain or ruler was usually in charge of warfare, the growing and distribution of food and religious ritual; he was at the top of the hierarchy that made decisions on these important matters. Rulers were probably considered to have supernatural powers. In many cases the perhaps mythical ruler at the beginning of the lineage was deified, or at least ranked as a demigod. Most iconography can be explained in terms of agriculture, royal power and the political manipulation of religion.

The recurrent empire-forming tendency must have been motivated not entirely by aggression, ambition and aggrandizement but also by the geography of western South America—by its diversity, its potential, the need or desire it fostered for acquiring things from other places within it, and by the enormous varieties of resources within short, if difficult, distances.

Architecture and water

One of the most important forces for interaction and conquest was water. The requirement for irrigation in the coastal desert, and therefore the need for control of the rivers that came down from the sierra, led to the greater social and political organization that distinguishes high cultures. And as societies expanded, more irrigable land was needed. (Water control was not limited to coastal deserts; it occurs in many circumstances in virtually every high civilization. Sometimes it is functional, sometimes symbolic, religious or ritualistic.)

Evidence for irrigation has been found at the 3rd-millennium BC site of La Galgada up in the Santa River drainage. The earliest known highland use of masonry channels for an apparently ritual use of water is found near Cajamarca, in the northern highlands, in the 2nd millennium BC. Waterworks are not limited to the major centers, nor to the Central Andes. Ridged fields and irrigation ditches have been found in Bolivia, Peru, Ecuador, Colombia and Venezuela, and water was ritually channeled in Costa Rica. Water was essential: its use and religious meaning are probably not always separable.

Complex stone architecture begins in the 3rd millennium BC in the Central Andes. In general, stone architecture and sculpture are highland traits, and the use of sun-dried adobe bricks or *tapia* (large adobe slabs) a coastal trait. The shape of adobe bricks changes through time and can be used as a dating aid; *tapia* is usually a later material. Perhaps because of the lack of stone for impressive iconographic statements, coastal peoples became remarkable metallurgists at an early stage and made exceptional pottery and textiles.

Religion and ritual

Sources of knowledge about religion are sacred architecture, the depictions on works of art, burial patterns and contents, the early Spanish chronicles—and practices that continue today.

In general, South and Central America had similar religious practices, with almost infinite variations. The gods were those of the forces of nature, controlling water, sky, earth, mountains and sea. In most regions there was a creator god, associated with origins and ancestors, and often with the sun, the sky and with the mountains that touch the sky and are also the sources of rivers and the entrances to the earth and to the underworld. The Andean civilizations saw the sun rise from the mountains, which are the source of water for agricultural irrigation. East and west were particularly important directions—the origin and terminus of the sun's path.

In the Central Andes Viracocha is the god concept most frequently encountered. At Chavín de Huantar deity representations are probably prototypes of Viracocha. The god may have even earlier origins. The figure on the Gateway of the Sun at Tiahuanaco and on Huari-style pottery is also undoubtedly a precursor of Viracocha. The major Mochica god must have belonged to this class of deities, who were associated not only with origins of the tribe but also with those of the sky and the sea. Bochica, the major god of the Muisca, in Colombia, had similar aspects.

Ritual usually had a calendrical organization, celebrating moments in the liturgical calendar of heavenly bodies, of agriculture or, in some instances, of fishing. The movements of the sun, especially solstices and equinoxes, the rising of the Pleiades, moon phases, and the synodic cycle of Venus were likely occasions for ceremonies. Also celebrated were times for planting and harvest, and the beginning of the good fishing season.

One widespread ritual practice on the west coast and in the highlands was the chewing of coca leaves. In the pre-Columbian Quimbaya culture of Colombia some of the finest gold objects were containers for the lime that was chewed with the leaf. It is obvious from hundreds of Mochica ceramics that the coca-chewing ritual was not only an important and complex one with many stages but one that was associated with war and sacrifice.

There is some evidence for the ritual use of the San Pedro cactus as a hallucinogen in the Chavín and Mochica cultures. Its use may have been wider, for it also grows, for example, in Ecuador. Peripheral peoples used *Piptadenia, Banisteriopsis* and *Datura* as ritual hallucinogens, and tobacco was smoked in ceremonies in the northern lowlands.

To judge from the depictions in pre-Columbian art, ritual sacrifice by beheading was at the top of the list of offertory practices. Nude male figures with hands tied behind their backs are a frequent theme in art, undoubtedly awaiting sacrifice. This is sometimes depicted. Virtually every culture has a sacrificer figure, who stands holding a knife in one hand, a human head in the other. These heads are generally referred to as "trophy-heads," and iconographers tend to speak of "trophy-head cults" although the head was probably thought of more as food for agricultural gods than as a cult object in itself. Throughout the pre-Columbian high cultures there was the belief that the forces of nature vital to the growing of crops had to be fed with human blood or with human heads. Human sacrifice may have been one of the motivations for warfare—to take prisoners for sacrifice.

Other sacrifices were also made, often by burning. A hallmark of 3rd-millennium-BC ceremonial architecture is a hearth for burnt offerings. Sacrificial remains have been found in archaeological excavations, among them chili peppers. Chroniclers in the 16th century wrote that offerings of llamas, guinea pigs, coca leaves, cloth, food, sea shells, quartz crystals and various other substances were still being made.

Rituals and offerings were celebrated not only at special times, but also in special places. Certain places were sacred to early nomads—rocks, mountains, springs. Such places continued to be sacred, and are still among the things that are considered *huaca*. A huaca is a holy thing—a natural object, the remains of an ancestor, a small stone or piece of quartz. In Inca times huacas were given offerings of food and drink; they were offered cloth or dressed. The Inca are said to have covered sacred rocks with sheet gold.

Early sedentary peoples located a temple at, or directed toward, such a place. The temple, the sacred house, was probably one of the first structures built by such people—if not the first. As the village grew, as the community became more pow-

Above The central figure on the Tiahuanaco Gate of the Sun is a deity who probably took various names and forms throughout the Andes, but was generally a sky god.

Below On the temple walls at Cerro Sechín, Peru, severed heads with closed eyes, flowing hair, and blood streaming from the neck are a characteristic Chavín motif.

symbolic objects. Women are often accompanied by weaving paraphernalia. Sometimes grave offerings are arranged in patterns; vessels may represent certain themes rather than others. Burial customs are also indicators: flexed burials are often a highland trait, whereas extended burials are usually a coastal trait.

Depictions of skeletal figures are common in Andean art. These may show the realm of the dead or they may portray priests or shamans imitating the dead or visiting the underworld. Figures with skeletal faces often have live sexual organs, or "dead" figures may embrace women. The numerous scenes of sexual activity often include skeletal figures. Again there is the association of death and fertility; the underworld-earth is the source of life.

Common artifacts

Garments throughout the Central Andes were generally similar. A rectangle of cloth was woven in various sizes and used in various ways. The most commonly encountered garment is the tunic or shirt, in which two rectangles were sewn together with slits left for the head and the arms. The poncho or tabard was a very similar form, with the sides open. Loincloths and kilts were common, and a kind of trouser is seen on infrequent occasions; the major Mochica deity seems to wear boxer shorts. There were also mantles, such as those found in Paracas burials, and capes, worn in certain specific ways for specific occasions in Mochica pottery depictions—the coca rite, for example.

A major diagnostic element of dress is headgear. From carefully wrapped cloth headbands to elaborate gold crowns or semicircular frontal pieces with an animal head, headdresses mark status—human or divine—and ritual occasions. Important people everywhere wore ear ornaments, usually of precious metal, which fit through a hole in the earlobe. The most common form has a circular frontal piece. Forms vary, however, according to the identity of the wearer and the occasion. Gold or silver nose ornaments fit over the septum; in some cases it is better to describe these as mouth-masks, for they are more a means of covering the mouth than of decorating the nose. South-coast deities wear sheet-metal brow-masks as well; actual brow-masks have been found in graves.

Sound-making objects were made almost everywhere. Many ceramic vessels have rattles (pebbles or bits of clay) in the base or in the feet. Whistling vessels, double- or single-chambered, are common in many cultures; flowing liquid pushes air through holes in the vessel to make a whistling sound. Many gold or copper objects were rattles with pellets inside. Musical instruments were also plentiful. The most prevalent were drums, flutes, panpipes, trumpets, ocarinas and conch shells.

The pre-Columbian cultures had many shared traits, yet each culture is distinctive. Most of the objects from these cultures that appear in museums are easily identifiable as belonging to a fairly specific time and place. And yet because there was interaction and interchange, invention, creativity and constant development, there are many puzzles. With increasing knowledge, there are new problems to be solved.

erful; as chiefdoms developed, the major visual display of power was the ceremonial center, the lavish sacred place of the people. It was not only the house of the gods, a numinous space for the priest and the ritual, it was also a sign of the strength of the local gods to be seen by the outside world. Each village or center was, of course, the center of the world.

All pre-Columbian peoples seem to have been disposed toward viewing rocks as particularly sacred, but this was especially true in the Andes where many ceremonial centers incorporate a rock or rocks in the site plan. This is true of some of the very early ceremonial centers, of the Mochica sites of Pañamarca and Moche, and most obviously of Inca sacred places.

Burial places were also huacas, since ancestors were sacred, and death and the Underworld were major themes of preoccupation—perhaps largely because of the association of the underworld with the agricultural earth. Many of the richest artifacts are found in graves; the burial without grave goods is the exception. Grave goods give clues about religion and status, for they tend to be high-quality, surplus objects—fancy pottery rather than everyday ware, unusual objects rather than common ones. Chieftains are buried with many

CULTURE AREAS

THE ANTILLES: ARAWAK, CARIB AND THEIR PREDECESSORS

It was Arawak Indian territory into which Christopher Columbus sailed when seeking a sea route to Asia. In October 1492 he made his first landfall in the New World, on an island in the Bahamas which he called San Salvador; its Arawak name meant Iguana. Columbus was greeted by naked Indians wearing elaborate feathered accessories. Within a century of the Spanish arrival these Island Arawak were wiped out, victims of imported diseases to which they had no immunity, and of Spanish aggression against which they had no defense.

The Arawak had come northward to the Caribbean Islands in long, slow, sea migrations from Venezuela via Trinidad. Their remains are found in the Lesser Antilles—the chain of smaller islands, from Curaçao to the Virgin Islands—and in the larger, more northerly islands of the Greater Antilles—Puerto Rico, Hispaniola (Haiti and the Dominican Republic), Jamaica and Cuba—as well as the Bahamas. At the time of the Spanish conquest the Arawak dominated the Greater Antilles.

The Arawak exploited sea and shore resources—fishing gear and spearthrowers have been found. Their most important artifact, however, was the canoe. The value of canoes to these people cannot be overemphasized. The Arawak were dependent on canoes for migration, trade, fishing and hunting and gathering along rivers and coasts. They had numerous dugout or compound canoes of enormous size. The Arawak were also farmers, cultivating maize, beans, sweet potatoes, squash and, surely most important, bitter manioc. Also raised were peanuts, peppers, pineapples and fruit trees. Useful nonedibles were gourds, cotton and plants from which body paint was obtained. Year-round provision of food was achieved by putting different kinds of plants in garden plots—in a dry part of Hispaniola there was irrigated agriculture. Wooden digging sticks were used for planting, and a wooden broadsword was employed for cutting brush and digging, as well as for a weapon.

People lived in bell-shaped thatched houses and slept in hammocks. They made cotton cloth, amulets of stone, bone and shell, and fine ceramics with a great variety of decoration—vessels, figurines and masks—as well as functional pottery, notably griddles for baking cassava bread from manioc. There were musical instruments: trumpets of *Strombus* shell, wooden trumpets and drums,

Left A European engraving illustrates a story from Columbus's fourth voyage. The admiral gathered together the chieftains of Hispaniola to chide them for their failings in Christian eyes— especially their negligence in giving food and support to the Spaniards—and then he predicted an eclipse of the Moon as a warning to them from the Christian God that they should mend their ways. When the eclipse occurred, the awed Indians quickly brought provisions to the Spanish ships and promised to serve them and their God faithfully in the future. Priests of higher New World cultures probably exploited their own people with the same techniques.

Above: Cultures of Lower Central America and the Antilles
The map reflects the patterns of movement of peoples. The exodus from northeastern South America to the Antilles took place in stages by canoe, with the Windward and Leeward Islands serving as stepping stones to the larger islands of the

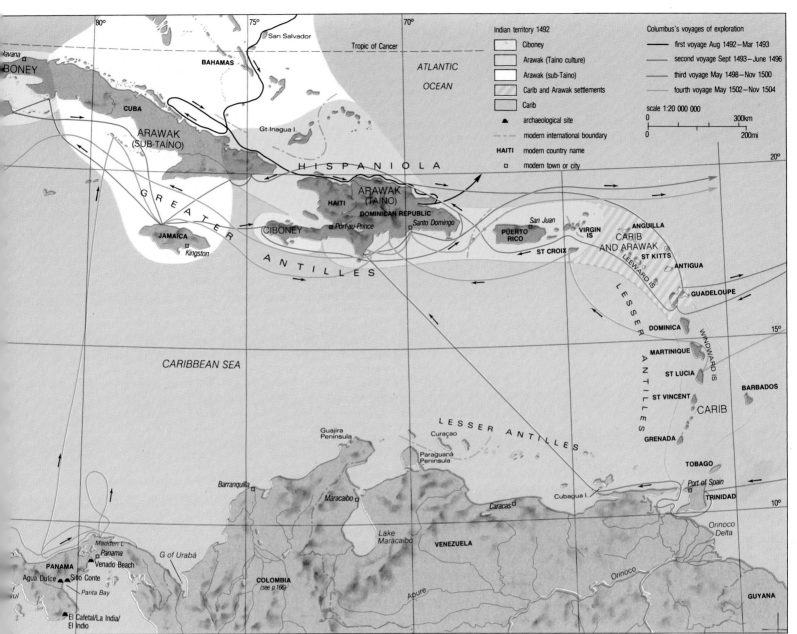

Greater Antilles. The Ciboney, the early migrants, went or were pushed over to the far west of Cuba and the most remote part of Hispaniola. The Arawak, or Taíno, achieved the highest culture in the very center of this region, largely on Hispaniola, settling Puerto Rico on one side of Hispaniola and, on the other side, the nearby region of Cuba. The Carib, the Johnny-come-latelies, were still in the process of pushing north from the mainland at the time of the arrival of Columbus on San Salvador, to the north of the Taíno region. Although western Cuba is very close to the Yucatán Peninsula of the Maya region, there seems to have been little contact. Hispaniola became a center of operations for Columbus's activities in the Caribbean. He was also on Cuba, but did not reach Yucatán.

bone whistles and flutes, maracas, rattles and clay ocarinas. Many artifacts of perishable materials—wood, fibers and cane—have not been preserved.

The highest Arawak culture of the Antilles was that now called Taíno, found on Hispaniola, Puerto Rico and parts of Cuba. The most advanced Taíno areas were in the highlands of Santo Domingo, which was to become a major Spanish colony.

Columbus and his companions, however, were little interested in Indian culture: they were looking for gold. They met with chieftains (or caciques) who wore gold ear ornaments and gold-trimmed woven belts and sat on carved wooden seats trimmed with sheet gold; their daughters wore gold nose ornaments. The Arawak however valued gold less than they valued tumbaga, or guañín, a gold-copper imported from the mainland. Objects of guañín had value because they were imported, possibly from the land of the ancestors, because the mainland had finer metallurgists and because of the richer color of this alloy. The copper in this alloy also produced an odor which may have enriched its meaning for the Indians. Above all, however, the Arawak prized finely worked objects of bone and shell.

Village and ritual

Arawak deities were called zemí. This word seems to have been similar in meaning to huaca (sacred) in the Andes, for many things could be zemís: gods, idols or symbols of the gods, remains of the dead and the powers of sky, sun, moon, wind and earth. They were the gods of an agricultural people. The representations of these gods took various forms, often carved with great skill and sophistication. The body painting noted by Columbus depicted zemís. In Puerto Rico, the Dominican Republic and Haiti a three-cornered idol of stone or conch shell was common in the late period. The form may derive from that of a volcano cone; it apparently represented the god who was the donor of manioc. (Since plants were often thought to come from earth deities, and earth deities were thought to live in mountains and volcanoes, it would be logical to depict a mountain with a face.) According to early Spanish chroniclers the idols were used in a ritual in which the shaman took psychoactive Piptadenia snuff with tobacco and conversed with the zemí to find out weather and crop predictions. The zemí was not only an image of a god, but an intermediary between men and gods, an oracle.

The Arawak social system was stratified. Chieftains, who controlled economic matters, ruled over regions greater than their immediate village. There were five such chiefdoms on Hispaniola, for example, with a hierarchy under each chieftain. The chieftains had elaborately accoutred entourages, whose members wore cloaks and headdresses of red or white feathers, according to their duties. Columbus described one *cacique* who was carried on a litter.

Although their heritage was derived from northeastern South America, the Arawak seem to have had influence from Central America and Mesoamerica as well, sharing with the cultures of the mainlands such customs as burial with grave goods, the ritual use of tobacco and other practices.

Large Arawak villages were centered around a public plaza, sometimes simply a clearing, sometimes a circle or rectangle with earthen embankments or upright stones and paving or cobbling. In some places two parallel embankments made an enclosure. The house of the chieftain facèd the plaza, and there were often petroglyphs nearby. (Petroglyphs are also found near water sources and caves.)

Dances and funerary rites were probably held in the plazas or enclosures. The most significant ritual, however, seems to have been a ballgame, which may have come from Mesoamerica. (Yucatán is only 195 kilometers from Cuba, but there is little hard evidence for contact.) The ballgame was known in northern South America— the Venezuelan game is similar to the island one—although it was not so developed there as in Mesoamerica. Early Spanish chroniclers describe the place in the center of each town that was set aside for the game. The larger villages also had peripheral *bateys*, as the plazas or enclosures are called. This type of court developed in the Antilles sometime after 500 AD. The most elaborate ballcourt, in Puerto Rico, dates from about 1200 AD. The Arawak ballgame was played with rubber balls and involved human sacrifice. It also apparently functioned in agricultural predictions, and seems to have had a relationship to water, probably to rain.

Origins and enemies

The Antillean settlers had come from northeast Venezuela, through Trinidad, "the gateway of migration," and the archaeology of these regions is closely related. On Cubagua Island, off the Venezuelan coast, there are remains from about 5000–1000 BC of a people who may have had a part in the early occupation of the Antilles. Between about 1000 and 500 BC groups of Arawak-speaking peoples came down the Orinoco River to the delta —incipient agriculturalists, whose staple crop was manioc. Indeed, manioc may have been first cultivated in Venezuela. These people, the ancestors of the Island Arawak, begin to appear in Puerto Rico about the time of Christ, and spread out through the Antilles in the succeeding centuries.

The Island Arawak had all but driven out an earlier group of Indians called the Ciboney, who date back to about 2500 BC. At the time of the Spanish conquest a few Ciboney remained in southwestern Haiti and parts of Cuba. These preceramic people, who had also come from Venezuela, left shell middens and other faunal remains—tools, pendants and a few human burials. Even these early people had canoes, or at least rafts of balsa wood, and they had probably arrived in the Antilles through fishing in coral reefs, and hunting and gathering in the many mangrove swamps that were well stocked with food.

In the late period the Island Arawak were threatened by the Carib of the Lesser Antilles (from whose name derives not only the word Caribbean but also "cannibal"). Like the earlier invaders the Carib had originally come from northeastern South America. The early Spaniards found evidence of Carib man-eating activities, but they also admired the bravery of the Carib. For the Carib, warfare was a basic principle of social organization; they were always at war or preparing for war or raids, and the war chieftain was a prominent and powerful member of the community. The Carib used bows and arrows, rather than the more sophisticated spearthrower. Carib culture was less highly developed than that of the Arawak, and their society less structured. Religious images were made of wood and cloth, rather than of stone and shell; few have been preserved.

The early Spaniards, however, may have somewhat simplified the Arawak-Carib situation. For them the distinction was easy: the submissive Indians were Arawak, the fierce ones Carib. Modern scholars, on the other hand, have found a more complex pattern of migration, intermarriage and language-borrowing, for while the men captured on Carib raids were eaten, the women were taken as wives. Despite Carib threats the Arawak had long dominated the Greater Antilles by the time the conquering Spaniards arrived in the New World. It was their culture that impressed the early explorers. There are still Arawak in the Guianas, but they have long since vanished from the Caribbean Islands. There are still a few Carib on reservations in the Leeward Islands.

CHIEFDOMS OF THE INTERMEDIATE AREA: LOWER CENTRAL AMERICA, COLOMBIA AND VENEZUELA

Columbus's fourth voyage took him along the coasts of Panama and Costa Rica. He found the Talamanca Indians in Costa Rica wearing gold "eagle" pendants and the Guaymí Indians of Panama wearing gold disks. The Spaniards saw large villages arranged around a central plaza that was ringed by royal residences and by tombs of royal ancestors. They saw *voladores* ("flying" men attached to a pole) and *patolli* (a game using maize kernels on a board), traits also found in Mexico.

At the time of the conquest the circum-Caribbean groups had communities of 1000 or more inhabitants and a hierarchy of chieftains, the topmost of whom had authority over a region beyond their own village. That society was stratified is evidenced in part by differences in grave goods. Chieftains had elaborate burials; other interments had simple grave goods. These circum-Caribbean groups had also developed patterns of warfare and a hierarchical religion with depictions of idols in stone, wood or shell placed in special temple structures tended by a professional priesthood.

A single language phylum, Macro-Chibchan, dominated the area from Nicaragua through

The Central Highlands of Costa Rica produced stone ''flying-panel'' *metates* (grinding tables), with full-round figures of birds, crocodilians, jaguars and anthropomorphs engaging in acrobatic feats beneath the surface. These denizens of tropical environment and myth supported the surface on which maize might be ground. The sculptures, standing about 0·5 m high, are among the most intricate in pre-Columbian Central America. Many are edged with trophy heads, and some have a woven border design, a motif that in Mesoamerica was a sign of kingship. In the Central Highlands a corpse was sometimes laid out on three adjacent *metates*. Other Costa Rican stone sculpture includes finely carved mace heads and beautifully worked pendants of jade or jadelike stone.

Panama to coastal Colombia and Venezuela. The geography of the area provided many small environmental niches and access between them. Routes ran along the coasts and through river valleys to and from the highlands. Gold was widely exchanged, and there was also commerce in a wide range of commodities which traveled along the coasts and up and down the river valleys. The region from El Salvador through northwest South America had generally similar ecological adaptations, with agriculture based on maize, manioc (bitter manioc in Venezuela, sweet manioc elsewhere) and sweet potatoes. Ceramic crafts and metallurgical technology were advanced.

The trade patterns observed by the first Spaniards probably had a long history. Many of the earliest preceramic remains, as well as early pottery, are found along this coast and down the connecting strip of coastal Ecuador. However, there are also important preceramic sites inland in the highlands. Early sites had similar living patterns. After an initial dependence on tropical-forest hunting and gathering, primitive agriculture and marine or riverine gathering gradually provided a background for intercourse and exchange.

It is estimated that early man, in his migrations, passed through lower Central America before 20 000 BC. Paleo-Indian points found in Turrialba, in the Atlantic watershed of Costa Rica and at Madden Lake in Panama date from before 5000 BC. There have been fairly frequent finds of percussion-flaked tools in shell middens at Cerro Mangote, in Panama (c. 4800 BC), and in numerous caves and rockshelters, often associated with animal bones. In Puerto Hormiga, one of the many shell middens on the Caribbean coast of Colombia,

a quantity of pottery has been encountered, dating to about 3000 BC. For a time it was considered to be the earliest yet found but it seems to be a blend of two traditions, and even earlier pottery has recently been found in the region. Although ceramics usually accompany agriculture, there are no clear-cut signs of food cultivation with these finds.

Until about 2500 BC many circum-Caribbean people gathered food; tools for processing food, and tools for making such tools, have been found in rockshelters and caves. Root-crop agriculture developed probably in Venezuela in the 4th millennium and seems to have traveled along the Atlantic coastline. So-called Barrancoid pottery spread from the lower Orinoco region toward the northern coast of Venezuela, then up into the Antilles and along the mainland coast to the west in the 2nd millennium BC, one of the many stages of cultural travel through this region. In Chiriquí, Panama, there is evidence for the beginnings of manioc cultivation late in the 2nd millennium, and in the Turrialba Valley, at the La Montaña site, clay griddles have been found, dating from about 1500 BC. These implements are commonly associated with manioc processing. The La Montaña site has five carbon 14 dates between 1500 and 300 BC, associated with the griddles and with monochrome pottery in a variety of forms. Maize cultivation seems to have begun somewhat later than that of manioc.

Lower Central America is geographically a narrow bridge between the vast continents to the north and south. It was influenced by them in various ways at various times, yet it had an individual development, which varied according to place and time. Until recently there has beeen little information available about lower Central America

before 1000 BC, but new excavations and surveys have been turning up a great deal of preceramic material, especially in Panama, inland from Parita Bay, where some 200 sites have been found. Beginning with the period c. 1000 BC - 500 AD there is a large store of artifacts.

Costa Rica

Costa Rica has three basic archaeological zones. In the west is Greater Nicoya which includes the Nicaraguan Isthmus of Rivas, between Lake Nicaragua and the Pacific Ocean, as well as the province of Guanacaste and the Nicoya Peninsula in Costa Rica. The central part of the country consists of the Atlantic watershed and Central Highlands. In the southeast the archaeology of the Diquís Delta is related to that of the adjacent Panamanian province of Chiriquí. These zones have quite distinct traits, with considerable overlap—or variations on a single theme.

A great increase in the number of archaeological sites around the time of Christ indicates an expanding population and, with it, greater social stratification. Large ceremonial centers with monumental sculpture are rare, but there are columnar monoliths from the islands of Lakes Nicaragua and Managua and neighboring sites. Similar sculpture is found in Guanacaste.

In Costa Rica the most widely found important stone artifacts are tripod *metates* — grinding tables for maize. In the Guanacaste-Nicoya zone these are of curving rectangular stone, often with carving on the bottom. Somewhat later examples have a feline or jaguar head at one end to zoomorphize them. Some show signs of wear and may be accompanied by *manos* (handstones) for working the maize. They are found in high-status burials.

It is likely that the elaborate *metates* had a number of functions: as ritual maize-grinding tables; as seats of the ruler who was responsible for the processing and distribution of food; as burial equipment that symbolized transformation — both the transformation of the maize into flour and the transformation of the deceased. The carving

Above Lake Guatavita, high in the mountains not far from Bogotá, was the dwelling-place of a mountain-sky-water god. The round lake, 37 m. deep and 4 km. in circumference, must have been formed by the impact of a meteor, an event that would have given it special significance if the ancestors of the Muisca had seen the glowing meteor plunge out of the sky into the earth to create a repository for water. The gold offered to the lake may have imitated the natural event for the purpose of ensuring the continuance of precious water.

beneath the *metates* evokes the underworld and the fertility of the earth, and gives the sculpture significance as a cosmological model.

In the 500 years before the arrival of the Spaniards many changes took place. *Metates* decreased and once-common mace heads disappeared. Ovoid polychrome vessels, often with a feline head and forelegs in high relief, became a common ceramic form. In the highlands, sites with circular mounds built on stone foundations, plazas and cobbled causeways were constructed. The large and complex site of Guayabo de Turrialba has stone-lined aqueducts. Flagstones are used as bridges, floors and tomb lids, and stone cist tombs are common. Tall stone slabs with carved border designs may have served as funeral biers.

Greater Chiriquí

The Diquís Delta has produced artifacts different from those of the other regions of Costa Rica: it is part of the zone known to archaeologists as Greater Chiriquí. Fine and distinctive metalwork comes from this region, which is also notable for stone work and sculpture. Enigmatic, large stone ''balls'' are found there. Probably the most important center in this region was Barriles, under the Barú Volcano, in Panama, not far from the Costa Rican border. Named for the barrel-shaped sculpture encountered there, the site has yielded a great deal of large sculpture of volcanic stone. Low, stone-faced platforms were constructed in ceremonial sites, and burial grounds had cobble platforms and walls.

Central Panama and Darien

Like Costa Rica, Panama is divided into three archaeological zones, which blend at the extremes with the adjacent zones of the modern political entities. While the western zone is related to the Diquís Delta, the eastern zone is allied with the region of Colombia around the Gulf of Urabá.

The central zone produced brilliant and very individual art styles. Burial sites such as Sitio Conte and Venado Beach have yielded quantities of various kinds of fine cast and sheet-gold objects, as well as handsome polychrome ceramics. The two media often feature similar motifs, compound creatures who are sometimes two-headed or appear paired in the design.

The earliest known metalwork in Panama appears in the first centuries of this era, and becomes common about 400 AD. Some of the early pieces must have been imported from Colombia, and those made locally show strong Colombian influence. Although Panamanian styles are distinct, with a high degree of craftsmanship and individuality, Panama belongs essentially to the Colombian goldworking tradition.

Northern Colombia

The Sierra Nevada de Santa Marta, in the northeastern corner of Colombia, is a mountain chain independent of the Andes. Here a people known as Tairona produced one of the most impressive of New World civilizations. More than 200 Tairona sites, with stone structures and urban traits, are distributed from the coastal lowlands up to alti-

Right El Dorado, the Gilded One, is shown here as a large figure seated on a stool or throne on a raft, wearing jewelry and accompanied by smaller attendants. On taking royal office the gold-clad Muisca ruler made offerings at Lake Guatavita. Attempts to drain the lake for gold were made as early as the 16th century. Although objects have been retrieved, Guatavita has never been successfully drained. This unusually elaborate *tunjo*, or offering piece, is more than 18 cm. long. Most *tunjos* are flat, with thread-like detail. Unlike many gold figures, these offerings do not have rings for suspension.

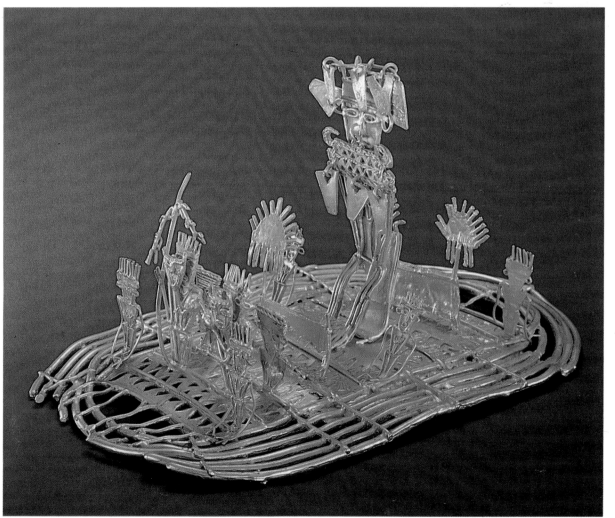

tudes of about 2000 meters.

The recently investigated site of Buritaca 200—it was not discovered until 1975—was constructed in the 14th century. Now surrounded by forest, it stands almost 1000 meters above the Buritaca River. Once one of the largest centers in this region, it has curving, stone-faced, hillside house platforms; stone stairways; retention walls; canals and drainage systems; a ceremonial plaza; and roads.

Some 260 house sites have been found, as well as 500 kilometers of stone roads nearby, for this was a junction of trade routes from Colombia to Central America, Venezuela and Ecuador. It was also an important gold-mining center. Tairona goldsmiths achieved work of such remarkable quality that it is admired with envy by modern smiths.

The Tairona began to consolidate their strength in the early centuries of the Christian era, achieving their full development some time after 1000 AD. They must have attained a powerful political and social structure, with a hierarchy of sites—Buritaca would have been in the top ranks. These Indians held out against Spanish invading forces for about 100 years. The Kogi Indians, who inhabit this region today, are descended from the ancient Tairona.

In the lowlands to the west the culture called Sinú was located in the lower Sinú and Magdalena River Valleys. The Sinú had an economy that was a happy mixture of root-crop agriculture and gathering from the rich resources of the rivers, the sea and the tropical lowlands. The most impressive remains of their culture are cast and hammered gold ornaments.

Central Colombia

The Muisca (or Chibcha) Indians of the Bogotá highlands had an attitude toward metallurgy different from that of other Colombian aborigines. They seem to have had little interest in the workmanship, the clever casting and fine finishing of the Tairona, the Sinú and others. Rather they made small, often crude objects of *tumbaga*, cast in multiples with little attention to finishing.

It was in Muisca territory that the El Dorado legend reached the ears of the gold-hungry Spaniards. The ceremony that inspired the legend took place at Lake Guatavita, north of Bogotá, on the accession of a new Muisca ruler. After having been secluded in a cave (caves are often sacred places), he journeyed to the lake. A reed raft was set afloat, with burning torches and incense, and the ruler-to-be was stripped and covered completely with clay to which gold dust adhered. Then "the gilded one" boarded the raft, where piles of gold and emerald offerings were placed in front of him. He was accompanied by chieftains, wearing only golden jewelry, who also had piles of precious offerings. To the sound of musical instruments the raft set out for the center of the lake, where the gold and emeralds were offered to the god, who must have been a water-mountain-and-earth deity. In such manner was the reign of the new ruler initiated.

The Quimbaya goldsmiths, who inhabited the slopes of the Cordillera Central, took great pains to make large, intricately cast and finely polished objects. Among the rich objects produced by the

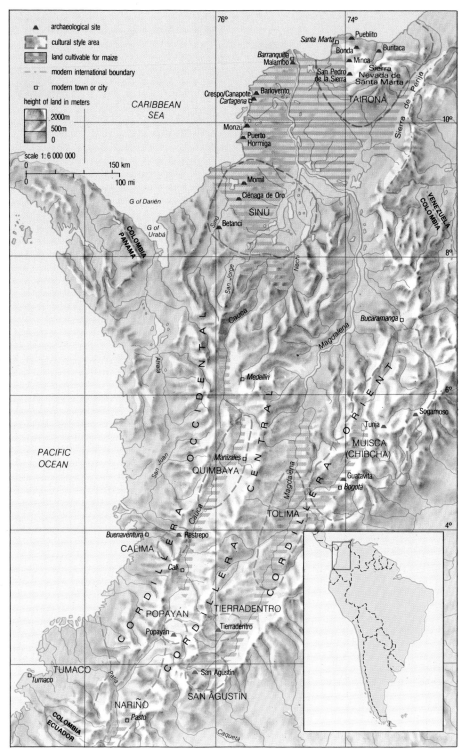

Quimbaya were gold or tumbaga lime containers for the coca ritual, masks, spearthrower tips, lizard and crocodile pendants, and hammered, repoussé helmets. Distinctive pottery also comes from this region.

Calima goldsmiths cast pendants and pin ornaments showing masked figures. Pins are found unusually frequently in this gold oeuvre. Other Calima gold objects are of cut and embossed sheet gold: tweezers and ear ornaments and pectorals, diadems and nose ornaments with multiple light-catching danglers. Goldwork of the Tolima style comes from the middle Magdalena Valley. Typical of Tolima cast gold pectorals is a distinctive design of an abstract figure with outstretched, angular arms and legs, and sometimes even a forked tail.

Above: Colombia
The combination of rugged landscape with relatively easy environments for producing food probably explains the fact that ancient Colombian peoples did not go afield to create empires. Groups remained in relatively small areas, creating distinct art styles, but little of the architecture and monumental sculpture that are the showpieces of kingdoms that had wide influences. On the other hand, north–south river valleys and coastal lowlands permitted travel and trade; goods and ideas flowed along them. Goldworking techniques and styles traveled from Colombia into Panama, and there were interactions with Ecuador to the south.

San Agustín

At San Agustín raised platforms, drainage ditches, burial mounds and stone-cist shaft tombs cover some 500 square kilometers. No other site in the Intermediate Area has such sculptural riches; more than 300 statues, reminiscent of sculpture of the Central Andean highlands, have been found there. Anthropomorphic figures often have the feline canines or fangs that signify sacredness or supernaturalness in Andean art.

Right Major sites around San Agustín. Lush hills and valleys surround the town of San Agustín, about 1800 m. above sea level. Nearby begins the Magdalena, an important river, which flows north to the Atlantic. One of the major sites in this region, Las Mesitas, has rectangular chambers of vertical megaliths with capstones, covered with earth to heights of some 4 m. and diameters of about 25 m. One or more sculptures are found in each of these probable burial chambers. At Alto de los Idolos, a semicircular artificial mound yielded stone tombs, trough-like sarcophagi, and sculpture.

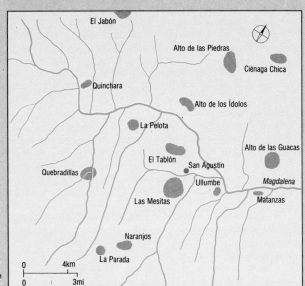

Above This stone sculpture comes from a site in the San Agustín complex. The sculptures often depict figures holding trophy heads, weapons or figures so small that they emphasize the supernaturalness of the monumental figures. Some sculptures are in their original positions, but many have been brought to the archaeological park (*left*), where the large tenons that secured them in the ground are exposed. Some sculptures apparently show women.

Southern Colombia

The highlands of southwestern Colombia were inhabited by maize-growing peoples who lived in perishable houses built on terraces on the slopes above valleys. San Agustín, situated near the headwaters of the long Magdalena River, in a series of lush valleys and hillsides, is the most spectacular Colombian site, or group of sites.

The San Agustín region was occupied in the last millennium BC but the great earthwork projects were not started until after the beginning of the Christian era, when, apparently, a new group of people came in.

The goldworking style of the upper Cauca Valley, called Popoyán, produced relatively few examples of spread-winged bird pendants in a distinctive style. As the styles to the northwest merged over modern political boundaries, so they did to the south. Gold abstract pendants and disks with faces in relief are ear-ornament types found in the Nariño zone of Colombia as well as in northern Ecuador. Like their neighbors to the south, the Nariño and Tumaco smiths used platinum and silver as well as gold and copper. The goldworking of Tumaco is the oldest in Colombia, dating back to about 325 BC.

AMAZONIA

The Amazon River is part of a complex river system with many tributaries. Eastern Colombia, Ecuador, Peru and Bolivia are part of the system, as are Brazil and eastern Venezuela. Along much of the river there is a narrow floodplain, whose soil fertility is maintained by annual flooding. In many areas away from the major streams slash-and-burn farming is used today, but with this method land can be cultivated for only a few years at a time. The forest is often dense, with a tremendous range of species of flora and fauna, and an upper canopy that rises about 45 meters above the forest floor. The forest produces trees that supply thatch, rope, barkcloth and rubber. Simple early hunting societies probably kept close to the rivers, for in the dense forest hunting circumstances are far from ideal. There were some inhabitants along the river by about 5000 BC.

The Amazon Basin is usually considered as divided culturally into Upper, Middle and Lower Amazon. The Upper Amazon can be said to extend downstream to the mouth of the Madeira River, the Amazon's greatest southern tributary (just below the Negro River, which is its greatest northern tributary).

Many languages are spoken in the Amazon Basin —evidence for influx of many peoples. Among the tongues is an Arawak language, of the same stock as that of the Taíno of the Antilles. It is thought that the Arawak-speaking people developed downriver and fanned out to the Upper Amazon and to the Orinoco (it is possible to reach the Orinoco from the Amazon by canoe), whence they settled downstream and then spread out along the coast and on to Trinidad and the Antilles. Arawak languages had a greater geographical range than those of any other language stock or family. There are also Carib-speakers in the basin.

South American Metallurgy

The earliest evidence for metallurgy in the New World, dating from before 1500 BC, consists of bits of thin, worked, gold foil, found in the hands of a man in a grave in the southern highlands of Peru. Nearby lay what was probably a tool-worker's kit. The oldest extant elegant goldwork is of the Chavín style, dating from about 800 BC. In the ensuing centuries metalworking slowly spread, southward to northwest Argentina and northward to Colombia, toward the end of the last millennium BC, and to Central America in the early centuries AD.

Metallurgical techniques or emphases vary from place to place, but there is a general similarity of workmanship. Much of the finest work was done on the north coast of Peru, in the early centuries of the Christian era, by Mochica smiths, who were surely some of the most sophisticated and experimental craftsmen.

Despite the depredations of the Spanish conquerors, who "mined" pre-Columbian burials for gold objects which they melted down in vast quantities and sent back to Spain, gold-surfaced objects remain the most abundant and spectacular of pre-Columbian metals. All that glitters is not pure gold, however: gleaming artifacts were usually made of alloys, although all were gold on the surface. Some silver was worked; copper was widely used for simpler objects; there were also silver-copper alloys.

Gold deposits were found in alluvium-rich rivers of the highlands, and quartz veins were sometimes worked for gold. Portable furnaces and crucibles were used for smelting with blowpipes. In the earliest technology metal was hammered into a sheet with a metal or meteoric iron tool over a cylindrical stone anvil, and then worked. Casting developed later and became the principal method in Central America and northern Colombia, while worked sheet metal continued to be preferred in the Central Andes, Ecuador and southern Colombia; some objects combine both techniques. In time metallurgy became complex and sophisticated, with the development of various methods of using different metals on the same object.

Although tools and weapons were made, metal was used principally for objects that symbolized supernatural power, and, by identification with this power, lordly status. Mythological beings and motifs were often depicted—intermediaries between man and the forces of nature. Gold was an important trade item, and metal objects known by their style to have been made in one place have been found in quite distant sites, yet gold had little market value in itself; what was valued was the life-giving way it was worked. Its symbolism was usually associated with the sun, hence with life and agricultural generation. It was important that metal imitated celestial light. Early sources tell us that the Inca thought of gold as "the sweat of the sun," and of silver as "the tears of the moon."

Metallurgy reached great sophistication under Inca aegis, particularly bronze-working. Metals had been used in combination before Inca times, but the technique of inlaying was developed only shortly before the Spanish conquest. A 12·5 cm.-high bronze mace head (*above*) is fashioned in the form of a bird with copper and silver inlaid stripes for the feather markings. Such mace heads take various animal forms. The bird here belongs to the order Pelecaniformes, and is probably a cormorant or anhinga; it seems to be eating a fish. Sea birds were generally important in Andean iconography, as were condors and Harpy eagles.

Andean goldwork can be impressively intricate. Knives, or *tumis*, with lavishly worked handles come from the Sicán culture of the Peruvian north coast (*above*). This handle shows a sky or moon god with repoussé face and a semicircular headdress with dangling hummingbirds. Beads and filigree were added, and the figure was inlaid and painted. Blade shapes were incorporated into many pre-Columbian art forms. Some of the finest ancient goldwork comes from the Tairona culture in northeast Colombia. The anthropomorphic pendant (*right*), 13 cm. high, has a complex headdress with two full-round birds, profile animals and scrolling vegetation motifs. The intricate mask represents a bat with a nose leaf. Danglers and bosses were added after lost-wax casting.

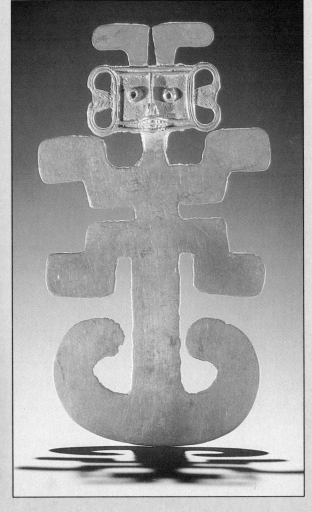

In the Lambayeque Valley, on the north coast of Peru, wide, relatively flat masks have been found in burials, one mask placed on the tomb occupant and several more on bundles. This painted example (*above*) is 50 cm. wide, made of a single sheet of gold, with raised facial features and danglers attached by wires. The eye wires may once have held precious stones. The mask probably depicts the major Sicán deity, whose visage is seen on ceramics as well as on several kinds of gold objects—for example, the knife on p. 168 and hammered gold beakers that were also placed in burials in great numbers. The wide face and the teardrop-shaped eyes are diagnostic of the Sicán style.

Stylized pendants of cast gold are typical of the Tolima culture of southern Colombia (*left*). The angled arms and legs of a splayed human body make a symmetrical, geometrical, flat design. To this is added an anchor-shaped tail and a square head with raised features. Like many pre-Columbian gold ornaments, this has a loop for suspension at the rear.

The peoples of the tropical forests of South America used dugout canoes. All the waters of the Amazon Basin are rich in marine life, but the rivers that flow down from the Andes are particularly rich. The first explorers reported dense populations in houses made of cedar planks along the floodplain stretches. An estimate of 5 million inhabitants has been made for the Amazon Basin in the mid-16th century. The inhabitants made hammocks for sleeping, large palm-leaf mats, painted cotton garments, feather cloaks, and musical instruments—flutes, rattles and drums. They hunted and fought with spearthrowers, used shields for defense, deformed their skulls and made elaborate burials with grave goods. Their pottery was much admired by the early Spaniards.

Below In the lush forests of eastern Ecuador, streams rush down mountainsides in clouds of spray. This region of Ecuador has dense vegetation and an annual rainfall of more than 3000 mm. Here the Río Quijos falls a spectacular 145 m. in its journey to the Río Coca, which drains into the Río Napo, an important tributary of the Amazon. Finds of pre-Columbian objects of the Integration period have been made in this region, and there are still Indian populations.

These people cultivated manioc and other crops, and also exploited river resources: they kept turtles in corals, to eat and for making axes and adzes from the shells. Manatee meat also was eaten. Fish were hunted from the shore or from canoes with spearthrowers. Today, in various places, bows and arrows and blowguns with curare are used for hunting. Many insects are eaten, and the honey of forest bees is a valued food.

Each village had a chieftain, and above him there was a chieftain for a whole "province." In at least one instance the name or title of the chief was the word for "god," and it was written by the early explorers that he was greatly revered for a long distance along the river. Chieftains undoubtedly drew some of their importance from the fact that the planting and harvesting schedules had to be carefully planned to adapt to the rising and lowering of the river. Weather and agricultural deities were also important, because the river might flood beyond its normal boundaries, or might not flood enough to fertilize the fields. The gods had to be consulted and venerated. In the forest the trophy-head cult of the Andes sometimes took the form of headshrinking and cannibalism.

The middle Orinoco has yielded ceramics dating to 3600 BC. Securely dated pottery from about 3100 BC has recently been found at the mouth of the Amazon, and similar pottery occurs at a number of places in the Amazon Basin. Archaeological sites found in the Lower Amazon include the late-period Marajó Island in the mouth of the river. Here over 100 mounds have been found—dwellings, substructures and tombs.

The Upper Amazon

The Upper Amazon concerns us most, however, for it long had ties with high cultures elsewhere. A tropical forest culture developed here, dependent on the exploitation of water resources and on root-crop agriculture, particularly the cultivation of the vegetable bitter manioc. Ceramic objects associated with the processing of manioc have been found by archaeologists—griddles and fire-dogs and vats for brewing beer. (Plant remains have not survived.) The beginnings of manioc cultivation may have been as early as 7000–5000 BC. Other root crops (that is, roots, tubers and rhyzomes) were the sweet potato, the New World yam, arrowroot, jíquima and *Xanthosoma*. The peanut was probably first cultivated here. Other non-root-crop foods were pineapple and Brazil nuts, various chili peppers, beans and the yield of palm and fruit trees. Tobacco probably originated here. Achira was grown for use as a dye, and cotton and bottle gourds were important.

Sites such as Tutishcainyo show ceramics from around 2000 BC, which do not look like initial efforts at ceramic-making. Ground-up sherds of much earlier ceramics were used by the early Tutishcainyo potters. Ceramics and stone axes, indicating land-clearing for agriculture, are among the relatively few material remains in the Upper Amazon. However, many artifacts would have been made of wood. Upper Amazon culture did not reach the high levels of cultures to the west, but many of its motifs are the same as those of the high cultures, and some must have originated in the forest.

ECUADOR: CROSSROADS OF THE AMERICAS

Ecuador fascinates archaeologists, for many reasons. It has notably early achievements in many cultural developments. The Las Vegas culture of the Santa Elena Peninsula dates back to about 10 000–6600 BC, and the El Inga site, near Quito, in the highlands, is dated to about 9000–8000 BC. Ecuador produced some of the earliest New World ceramics, textiles and metalwork. The use of ceramic molds is apparently earlier there than elsewhere. Moreover it is literally a crossroads for northerly and southerly ocean currents and for intermontane valleys to the north and east. There is also a route along its Pacific coast. It is, therefore, also a crossroads for people. Its northern archaeological zones merge with those of southern Colombia. Similar traits are found in both the Carchi culture of Ecuador and the Nariño culture of Colombia, for example, pedestal bowls and coca-chewing men seated on stools. The Tumaco culture of southern Colombia is the same as that of nearby La Tolita. There are also associations with neighbors to the south. La Tolita metalwork is very similar to that found in the far north of Peru. In Peruvian myths the creator god Viracocha disappeared over the sea at Manta, on the central Ecuadoran coast. There were many connections with other places. The Chorrera culture (1200–300 BC), for example, had widespread influence.

Most intriguing is the possibility of relationships between Ecuador and Mesoamerica. A number of similar objects and traits are found in both regions —for example, garment types, shaft tombs, raised fields, copper axes and shoe-shaped pots. It is thought that balsa rafts were used in the past for travel along the Pacific coast. If this travel was based on trade, there must have been a two-way street, but it seems that more Ecuadoran traits are found in Mesoamerica than the other way around.

The major focus of the trade may have been *Spondylus*. This is a bivalve found on the Ecuadoran coast. The demand for it was widespread. It seems to have been traded inland as early as Valdivia times (3000–1500 BC). *Spondylus* is shown on the sculpture and ceramics of the Chavín culture, early in Peru's cultural development. It became particularly important in later times. The legendary ruler of the later Sicán people of the Lambayeque Valley was said to have walked only on *Spondylus*, and mantles of *Spondylus* have been found in Sicán burials. *Spondylus* is represented with supernatural beings in Chimú art. Early Spanish sources tell that the shell, whole or ground, plain or burned, was the food of the gods. With heavy demands over long periods of time it is possible that the Ecuadoran shores may have been fished out. The genus ranges as far as Baja California in Mexico, however, and Ecuadoran shell-divers (it is found only at depths of 18–50 meters) may have gone north for it after "overfishing" on the Ecuadoran coast.

The early cultures

The coastal region of Ecuador is the best known archaeologically. Today it is semiarid scrub land, apparently a development of the last few centuries,

In the Regional Development period, the La Tolita culture of coastal Ecuador produced fascinating, finely made objects. A gold mask or figurine head (*far left*) has inlaid eyes and wears separately made nose and ear ornaments. Gold objects of a similar style are found in the far north of Peru. A strange deity image in clay has a mouth with feline canines (*left*). Half of the face is—or is obscured by—a coiled snake. Split faces—half one creature and half another—appear with some frequency in pre-Columbian art. This figure also wears a snakehead necklace.

Above House models, a common Regional Development form, possibly represent sacred houses or cosmological diagrams.

Below An important Manteño sculptural form is a stone seat or throne, sometimes supported by a jaguar and sometimes by a crouching human, who may have a skeletal face. A "skyband" is incised on the U-form of some examples. The seat may well be related to the *metate*-throne form found in lower Central America and elsewhere.

Right Figures—sometimes quite large ones—were made of clay by the people of the Bahía culture, who inhabited the coast of Ecuador near the modern city of Manta in the Regional Development period. Some of these were mold-made, some made by hand. Both male and female figures appear. The faces and the helmet-like headdresses are very distinctive. This figure wears ear ornaments and a nose ornament clipped on the septum; these were attributes of important people throughout the Andes. A large figure holding a small one is a common Andean theme. Often described as "mother and child," they are more apt to be sacrificial offerings, for children were often considered to be especially valuable sacrifices. Sometimes, on the north coast of Peru, a clay figure held a sculpture or a human-effigy pot.

for early Spanish accounts indicate that it was once forested. There are still small pockets of forest, some of them lush, but for the most part the only remains of past forest are the ceiba trees which stand out dramatically in the inland scrub.

On the Santa Elena Peninsula, north of the Gulf of Guayaquil, there are preceramic Las Vegas sites with shell middens and posts for thatched houses. There is even some evidence for the cultivation of maize and bottle gourds before 6600 BC. As in other places, a shift can be noted from the hunting of land mammals to an emphasis on sea resources and the beginnings of plant domestication. North of the Santa Elena Peninsula, Valdivia and other later coastal sites of the Formative period have produced textile remains, small, abstract stone figures, and ceramic figurines, bowls and wide-mouthed jars. The pottery is simple, decorated with a modest variety of techniques. The early communities tend to be close to the coast, near bays or harbors and curving beaches, with gently rising ground behind them, which could be used for agriculture. At Río Alto, a Valdivia-related site on the Santa Elena Peninsula, phytoliths of maize were found dating to about 2450 BC. The scarcity of shell middens at Valdivia also suggests the possibility that maize or other agriculture was more important as a food source than sea-gathering, and recent work at inland Valdivia sites confirms this.

Valdivia has been the focus of an argument that a Japanese vessel introduced pottery and other traits there; but this proposal is complicated by the existence of contemporary or older pottery elsewhere, from Loma Alta, up the Valdivia river valley, from Puerto Hormiga and Monzú in Colombia, and from the Amazon Basin. Moreover, the very early preceramic societies in the Valdivia region argue for a background from which ceramic societies could develop.

Today modern fishing villages overlie the sites of the Santa Elena Peninsula and the Valdivia culture. In the past, fishing, gathering and hunting would have been possible, along with agriculture. In ancient times coastal salt flats were surrounded with mangroves, where marine gathering could be accomplished. Although the mangroves have disappeared, salt works are still found along the coast;

in the past, salt would have been used to preserve fish as well as to season food. Balsa trees (*Ochroma* species) grow in parts of this region, as do other trees (for example, the ceiba) whose wood might have been used for rafts.

Toward the end of the Formative period the Chorrera phase spread over a much wider area than the earlier phases. The type site of Chorrera is inland, upriver from Guayaquil. The Chorrera people utilized farm lands away from the sea for raising maize and manioc. Chorrera-style objects, however, also appear along the part of the coast that was inhabited by the earlier cultures and much further north, up into Esmeraldas. The sophisticated pottery shows innovations in form, including a bridge-handled spout, which endured through the following phases.

The later periods
The Regional Development period, 500 BC–500 AD, produced a number of local styles—along the coast, in the sierras and in the Amazonian region. Particularly notable are the coastal cultures, from north to south, of La Tolita, Jama-Coaque, Bahía, Guangala, Guayaquil and Jambelí. In the more northerly cultures metalworking arrives on the scene, mostly goldwork, with some copper and platinum as well. Many new ceramic forms appear at this time, for example, polypod vessels, pedestal bowls with rattles and head rests.

The Bahía phase, found from La Plata Island north to the Bahía de Caráquez, appears to have been highly developed socially and politically. Rectangular platform mounds have been found, some of which were faced with uncut stones and had ramps or staircases. La Plata Island seems to have been a pilgrimage place— there are structural remains but no evidence of housing. Jama-Coaque and La Tolita, to the north, also achieved high levels of development, with the La Tolita artisans distinguishing themselves by producing some of the finest New World metalwork.

The Integration period, 500–1535 AD, saw the rise of the Manteño and Milagro-Quevedo phases in eastern Ecuador, spreading over wider areas than the earlier styles had covered. There were also a number of distinctive cultures to the east.

The Manteño, or Manteño-Huancavilca, culture, which dominated the central region from the coast inland to the Guayas River, was a society of sea-going farmers who raised maize, sweet manioc, beans, potatoes, peppers and other foods, as well as guinea pigs and ducks, and traveled on large rafts with cotton sails. They used stone in building, as well as in several distinctive sculptural forms. The Manteño craftsmen also made delicate gold, silver and copper objects.

The Milagro-Quevedo phase, which is found from the Peruvian border, east of the Gulf of Guayaquil and the Guayas River, on a northeasterly diagonal almost to the Colombian border, achieved the largest territorial expansion in pre-Inca Ecuador. The culture is also memorable for its fine metalwork and for its chimney tombs of stacked burial urns.

In the highlands the late styles are overlaid by fairly abundant remnants of the Inca intrusion, which began about 1463. Numerous artifacts found in Ecuador, the northernmost stronghold of the Inca empire, have Peruvian forms and motifs, although modified by local traditions. The Inca never succeeded in integrating coastal Ecuador into their empire, however, and virtually no Inca-style artifacts remain there.

Ecuador lacks spectacular pre-Inca architecture, but there is evidence of earth-moving and of stone structures or facings, often on hill or mountain tops near village sites. Some of this activity suggests alteration of the environment for cosmological reasons. There are reports of solstice rituals from the time of Spanish contact, and some structure alignments indicate that there were earlier ideas of the same sort. The early Spanish chronicler Cieza de León noted that the people of the Manabí coast were "addicted to sacrifices and religious rites." There are indications of sky, volcano and mountain worship from various sources. Like their Peruvian neighbors, the early Ecuadorans had a sense of *huaca*, or sacredness, in aspects of nature, and altered their world to accord with it.

A number of Ecuadoran sites have very long sequences. Although a single site may not have been continuously in use, the coast generally has been occupied for at least 12 millennia.

THE CENTRAL ANDES: THE BEGINNINGS OF CIVILIZATION

The earliest inhabitants of the Andes were hunters, but fishing and farming gradually became more important than hunting. Summer fishing camps, dating from the mid-4th to the mid-3rd millennium BC, have been found on the coast of Peru at Chilca and Ancón. However, serious settlement had already begun, and by about 2500 BC there were villages with permanent buildings on the coast, as well as in the highlands, and also a more complex way of life, in which fishermen traded with farmers for food.

A number of preceramic sites with monumental architecture date from about this time in the north-central highlands and along the central and lower-north coast, from the Moche Valley south to the Mala. Although there are early sites on the south coast, architectural remains are lacking. Sites from

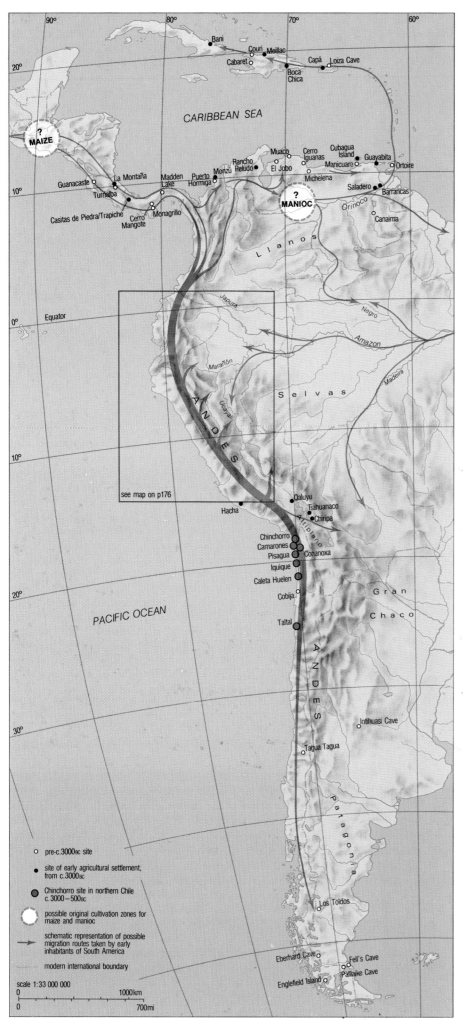

Left: Early settlements in South America

Early man entered America from a Bering Strait land bridge and worked southward and eastward on the American continents in his search for food. The inhabitants of South America came initially from North America, down through the narrow isthmus of Panama. It is possible that there was some traffic by boat, as there was later in the Antilles and along the South American coasts and in the Amazon system. Some groups went as far as Tierra del Fuego. Others moved around the coasts of the South American continent, often traveling inland. The Amazon Basin was a great nexus of watery highways for such migrations.

The earliest ceramics yet found come from various places around the northern part of South America. As archaeologists work more widely and deeply, and as archaeological techniques become more refined, the dates of man in the New World become increasingly early. People moved to, and eventually settled, where there was food. Rivers and lakes were sources of food as well as transportation.

The high Andes seem an inhospitable environment for people with relatively simple cultures. In the steep valleys below snow-capped peaks nights

are cold; yet for millennia people have used these environments. Remains from c. 10 000 BC have been found in a number of caves. Early hunting-and-gathering sites are increasingly found in the high plains, where hunting around lake shores was good—fish, waterfowl, deer and camelids. The vicuña was apparently an important food animal for early peoples, and the guanaco then ranged in this region. The area around Lake Titicaca (*above*), at some 4000 m. elevation, has produced very early cultural remains.

this period include Huaricoto, up in the Callejón de Huaylas, La Galgada, not far away on the Tabladera River, and Los Morteros. Early structures tended to be relatively small, but by the early 2nd millennium some were enormous. Aspero became a huge preceramic center by about 2000 BC, with seven known mounds and six other structures—the earliest construction there dates to about 2600 BC, the upper structures to about 2300–1900. Many sites are known from this period of settlement and growth; there are, for example, 30 pre-2000 BC sites between the Chicama and Nazca Valleys.

By 2000 BC widespread building activity on the central coast featured stone complexes, with at least one platform and a sunken court or pit, often a round one. Early highland sites also have sunken

circular courts, a feature that continued into the 2nd millennium BC; the court at Las Haldas is a coastal example.

On the coast during the 2nd millennium U-shaped stone complexes were constructed, with mounds arranged around three sides of a plaza or patio, as at El Paraíso (Chiquitanta) at the mouth of the Chillón River. Dating from about 1600 BC, this site is the largest preceramic complex of monumental architecture yet known in South America, with at least six mounds constructed mainly of cut stone, set with clay mortar and plastered with clay. The two largest mounds are over 300 meters long. Running parallel to each other, they form a patio, with a temple structure at one end. The structures have numerous interior rooms.

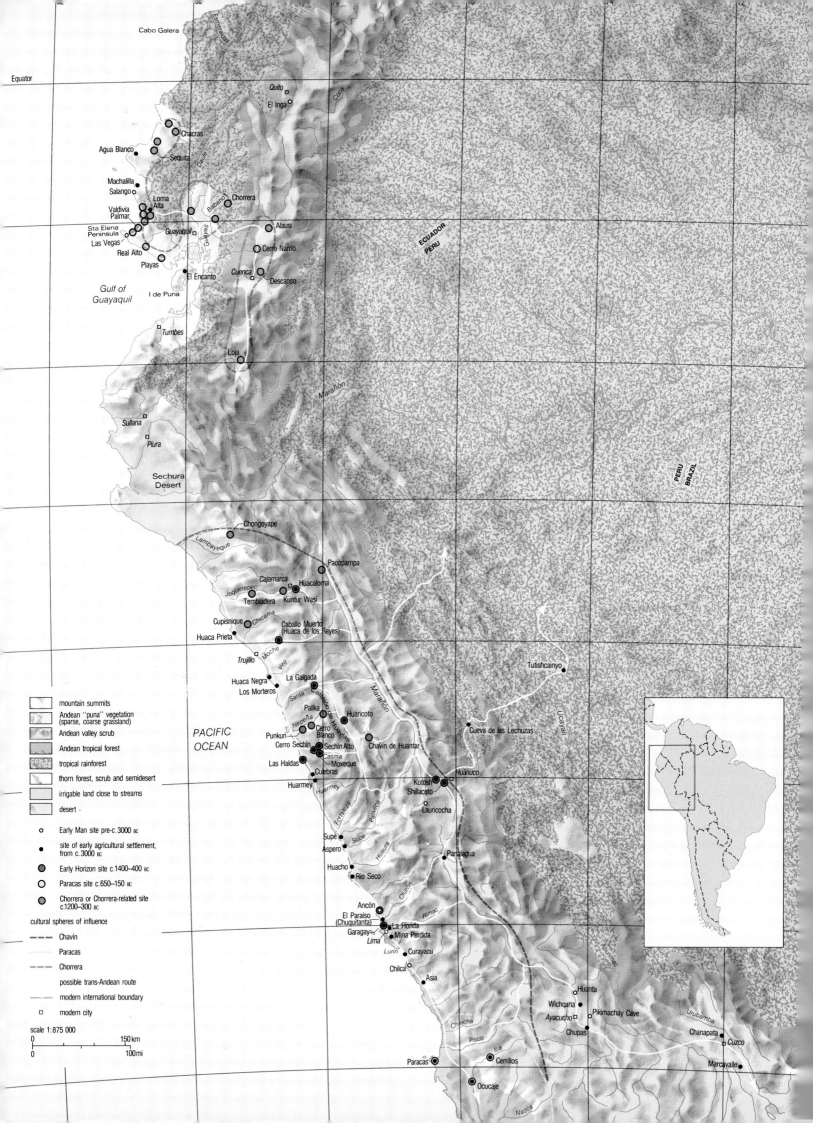

Cabo Galera

Equator

Esmeraldas

Quito □
El Inga ●

●Chacras
Agua Blanco ●
Sequita

Machalilla ●
Salango ○
Loma Alta
Valdivia
Palmar
Sta Elena Peninsula
Las Vegas
Real Alto ●
Playas ●

Guayaquil

Chorrera ●
●Alausi

●Cerro Narrio

El Encanto ○
Cuenca □
Descanso

Gulf of Guayaquil
I de Puna

ECUADOR
PERU

Tumbes □

Sullana □
Piura □

Loja □

Sechura Desert

Marañón

PERU
BRAZIL

●Chongoyape

Lambayeque

●Pacopampa

Cajamarca □
Huacaloma ●
Jequetepec Kuntur Wasi ●
Tembladera ●

Cupisnique ○
Chicama
Caballo Muerto
(Huaca de los Reyes) ●
Huaca Prieta ●

Trujillo *Moche*
Virú

Huaca Negra ●
Los Morteros ●
La Galgada ●
Huaricoto ●
Pallka ●
Cerro Blanco ●
Punkuri ●
Cerro Sechin ●
Sechin Alto ●
Chavín de Huantar ●
Las Haldas ●
Moxeque ●
Culebras ●
Huarmey

Callejón de Huaylas
Nepeña
Casma

Tutishcainyo ●

Cueva de las Lechuzas ●

Ucayali

PACIFIC OCEAN

Huarmey
Fortaleza
Pativilca
Kotosh ●
Shillacoto
Huánuco
Lauricocha ●

Supé ●
Supe
Aspero ●
Huacho ●
Rio Seco ●
Huaura
Paramonga ●

Ancón ●
El Paraíso (Chuquitanta) ●
La Florida ●
Garagay Mina Perdida ●
Lima
Chillón
Rímac
Curayacu ●
Lurín
Chilca ●
Asia ●

Chincha
Huanta ○
Wichqana ●
Ayacucho □ Pikimachay Cave ●
Chupas ●

Unubamba
Chanapata ●
Cuzco □

Pisco
Ica ○
Cerrillos ◉
Paracas ◉
Ocucaje ◉
Marcavalle ●

Nazca

Legend

- mountain summits
- Andean "puna" vegetation (sparse, coarse grassland)
- Andean valley scrub
- Andean tropical forest
- tropical rainforest
- thorn forest, scrub and semidesert
- irrigable land close to streams
- desert

○ Early Man site pre-c.3000 BC
● site of early agricultural settlement, from c.3000 BC
⬤ Early Horizon site c.1400–400 BC
◎ Paracas site c.650–150 BC
⬤ Chorrera or Chorrera-related site c.1200–300 BC

cultural spheres of influence
– – – Chavín
········· Paracas
– – – Chorrera
possible trans-Andean route
modern international boundary
□ modern city

scale 1:875 000
0 ——— 150 km
0 ——— 100 mi

Huaca Prieta, on the north coast, yielded thousands of fabrics of cotton and other fibers from the 3rd millennium BC. The drawing (*above*) shows one of their designs. Huaca de los Reyes is the name given to a U-shaped complex (*right*), the largest of eight *huacas* that form the site of Caballo Muerto, 17 km. from the sea up in the Moche Valley. The structure, dating from about 1300 BC, is decorated with 39 low-relief sculptures of clay over stone matrices. Their iconography is very similar to that of Chavín de Huantar, but they predate the florescence of that site.

Left: Early cultures in the Central Andes
As man settled he not only used the food resources of shorelines, river valleys and lakes, but he cultivated fields and exchanged goods; there was interaction between the very varied environments of the Central Andes. He began to make pottery and other artifacts, which would have encumbered his migratory ancestors. Developing civilizations had a momentum that permitted increased populations with an adequate food supply, more "consumer goods" and a religion—or a relationship with agricultural gods—which, along with hard labor, maintained that supply. Early man must have always recognized sacred places, but in the Early Horizon the concept of sacred places became architecturalized, and the great ceremonial centers were constructed.

The open end of the U-shaped complexes usually faced toward the northeast, toward the mountains and river sources. The major platform, at the base of the U shape, faced this opening. Although the sunken courts and the U complexes tend to be found separately, some sites have both features, for example Sechín Alto.

The major architecture at these sites is ceremonial. The orientation toward mountain peaks and their restricted, sacred inner spaces suggest this. Moreover these mounds are often built over the tombs of ancestors. Dedicatory caches have been found in sites like Aspero. Few of the sites have architectural sculpture: lowland exceptions are Cerro Sechín, the Huaca de los Reyes at Caballo Muerto, and Garagay. Kotosh, in its earliest phase, has the single highland example: crossed arms (perhaps a cosmic symbol) in relief on the outside of its temple.

An outstanding feature of many highland sites of the preceramic period is a ritual hearth: fire was undoubtedly a major ceremonial feature. At Huaricoto, in the Callejón de Huaylas, which began about 2800 BC, 13 ceremonial hearths have been found from its two millennia of occupation as a ceremonial center. Other sites relatively near each other and near Huaricoto also have hearths—Kotosh, nearby Shillacoto, La Galgada and Huacaloma, near Cajamarca. The religious-hearth cult in the mountains seems to have been widespread. Hearths have yielded burned offerings of marine shells, quartz, meat and plant material, notably chili peppers. The eye-watering burning of chili peppers may have been part of a ritual to invoke rain by sympathetic magic.

Interaction

The quantity of sites, and of some their size and indicated stratification, evince developing social organization, chiefdoms, group or corporate labor, religious ceremonialism, an expanding economy and interaction with other groups—in sum a groundswell toward civilization. Considerable labor would have been pooled to construct some of the sites—Caballo Muerto, for example, or La Florida—and their situations indicate growing interaction.

Caballo Muerto lies in the Moche Valley, which in later eras was the center of the Mochica chiefdom or state, and later the center of the kingdom of Chimor. Many of the sizable early sites are clustered around modern Lima, with access along the coast as well as up the Rimac Valley. The Casma, Fortaleza and Santa Valleys give access to the Callejón de Huaylas and thence over the Andes; there are early sites in all of these valleys.

These ceremonial centers were also markets or terminals for trading between farmers and fishermen; most of them would have depended on such commerce.

Las Haldas lies on the coast in the desert south of the Casma River Valley. It would probably have existed by trading fish and marine products for edible produce and cotton grown in the valley. Evidence from excavations shows that, by the late 3rd millennium BC, there was long-distance intercourse between the coast and the sierra. Fishmeal from anchovetas was likely to have been an important trade substance; marine shells are found in highland sites; highland tubers and even Amazonian feathers are found on the coast.

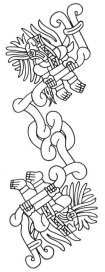

Ceramics

The earliest ceramics known in the New World have been found not in the Central Andes but in the central Amazon Basin, at the mouth of the Amazon, at Puerto Hormiga and Monsú on the Atlantic coast of Colombia, and at Valdivia, dating variously between about 3600 and 3000 BC. Pottery appears on the coast of Peru some time after 2000 BC, at different sites at somewhat different times, depending on the development stage and the needs of the site. It appears at about the same time as maize. Maize and pottery are the two main indicators of New World civilization. Cultures are identified in terms of being "ceramic" or "preceramic": the manufacture of pottery marks the transition into civilization. Maize was the staple of the high civilizations of the New World.

It took the Central Andes about two millennia to develop the constituent elements of civilization —agriculture, water control, monumental architecture, ceramics and textiles. These things were developed interconnectedly, as part of the same momentum of progress and, concomitantly, of increase in population and social organization.

CHAVÍN DE HUANTAR AND THE CHAVÍN STYLE

The Chavín type site lies adjacent to the modern town of Chavín de Huantar in a small valley on the eastern slopes of the Andes. The modern town lies over at least part of the support area for the site. Although it seems remote, Chavín de Huantar is accessible by routes from the coast and from highland points, as well as from Amazonia.

For many years archaeologists believed that the so-called Chavín style spread from Chavín de Huantar through the highlands and down to the coast, and that it marked a spectacular beginning of civilization in the Andes. Chavín was surely a great religious center, the grandest of the early ones, not in size (others are much larger) but in architectural sophistication, masonry and quantity of sculpture—more than 200 finely worked stone sculptures have been recovered from its sacred area, and there were undoubtedly more. With new carbon 14 dates and the investigation of early structures elsewhere, however, Chavín de Huantar has lost the temporal priority that it was once considered to have. The dates of Chavín de Huantar are now put at 850–200 BC with the period of florescence and outward influence being about 400–200 BC. The site of Kotosh, not far away in the highlands, has an earlier Chavín-style stratum (of 1200–870 BC). La Galgada and Shillacoto have produced jewelry and objects of Chavín style in a pre-Chavín context. Of the coastal sites Huaca de los Reyes has architectural sculptures from about 1200 BC, with iconography very similar to that of Chavín; the Cerro Sechín architectural stone carvings are dated to about 1300 BC; Ancón has produced Chavinoid objects from about 1000 BC; Garagay has Chavín-like mural decorations of about 1000 BC. Other sites, earlier than the Chavín site, have the U-shaped configurations and sunken courts of Chavín architecture. Chavín de Huantar is the glorious culmination of a development, not the origin of it.

Above A steatite tumbler carved with a pair of figures that somewhat resemble those on the Black-and-White Portal at Chavín de Huantar. The continuous design traverses the bottom of the vessel. Later Mochica vessels show figures holding cords, and Inca cord-holding rituals are described. Here the cord-holders are clearly supernatural. This vessel, 10 cm. high, comes from the north coast.

Above left A hollow figurine, about 20 cm. high, representing a flute-player wearing pendant-disk ear ornaments and a jaguar headdress; the rest of the jaguar hide forms a cape at the rear. This ceramic style, with incised lines marking color zones, is typical of the Jequetepec Valley on the north coast, but it is also similar to the Paracas mode of decoration on the south coast. Incised designs are also found on stone objects at about the same time.

Early agriculture

Twined-cotton fishing nets and textiles were found at the early fishing camps at Chilca and Ancón. Cotton, used for string, netting and textiles, was cultivated by at least 3500 BC and seems to have been a major crop in the coastal valleys, and even upland at La Galgada. The heddle loom may have come into use for weaving about 2000 BC. Gourds, used as containers for food and drink and also for fishing floats, were domesticated by at least the 4th millennium. Cane would have been used for various construction purposes, and perhaps for fire-lighting. *Tillandsia,* a plant related to pineapple, would have been gathered for fuel.

The early agriculturalists managed flood farming or farming near springs, but as populations increased and settled life evolved it was necessary to control the river waters that came down into the desert, so irrigation systems began to be developed. The central plazas of the U-shaped structures at some sites might have been irrigated or flooded, and it is possible that crops were grown in this space. The large ceremonial complexes were usually placed adjacent to cultivated fields.

Few animals were domesticated, but guinea-pig remains earlier than 1800 BC have been found in Culebras, and llamas and alpacas were under domestication in the highlands at about this time. Fish remains have been found in quantity in coastal middens, as well as remains of sea mammals, sea birds and land snails. Sea life continued to be vital to livelihood throughout succeeding millennia.

Chavín de Huantar

The temple structure of Chavín de Huantar, which contains interior galleries with stone-block ceilings, stairs, ramps, niches and air vents, faces out over a large, square, sunken plaza; a mound on each long side of the temple gives the whole a U shape. At the side of the temple a staircase leads down to a sunken circular court, lined with stone blocks incised with jaguars and anthropomorphic figures. The oldest part of the temple structure is a small U configuration. Inside the center of the base of the U is a cruciform space lying at the junction of two galleries. This sacred space is nearly filled by a massive, stone sculpture 4·5 meters high, known as the Great Image of the Lanzón (because of its lance-like form). The figure is characteristic of the inconography of the style known as Chavin.

In its final stage the Chavín temple facade was embellished with the Black-and-White Portal, so called because its steps are black (limestone) on the north side, and white (rhyolite porphyry) on the south side. Two columns incised with winged polymorphs (combinations of human, feline, avian and serpent elements) supported a carved lintel. The outside walls of the main part of the temple, constructed of finely worked ashlars in rows of alternating sizes, displayed heads tenoned into the wall: each head is different, but most have the same general facial features. These tenoned heads, which are virtually the only examples of sculpture in the round at Chavín, may refer to the trophy-head cult, although they are surely supernatural heads.

Recent archaeological work has revealed a system of canals running through the temple, which were probably constructed to permit the ritual use of water from the glacially fed Huachecsa River. Water could run through the large platform and beneath the circular sunken court, so that the galleries, echoing the rushing sound of the water, would make the temple literally roar.

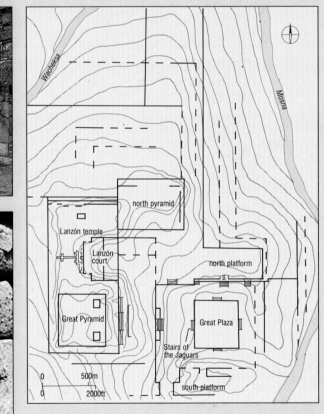

The facade of the temple at Chavín de Huantar (*above center*) is now only partially covered with finely worked facing stones. In a room in the interior of the temple stands the Great Image (*above left*), a powerful stone carving depicting a Chavín god with a fanged mouth, round eyes with a high pupil, prominent nostrils, and hair and eyebrows of snakes. This deity appears in other sculpture at Chavín, and traits like the intermeshed fanged heads above the figure and on the garment are seen in objects of the style found elsewhere. At the Early Horizon coastal site of Cerro Sechín, trophy heads and dismembered bodies are seen along with figures of warriors, set in the walls of the temple.

Above Plan of Chavín de Huantar.

Left One of the tenoned heads on the exterior of the Lanzón temple at Chavín de Huantar.

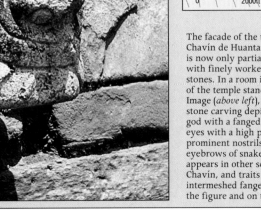

Artifacts

The composite cosmological creatures seen on Chavín sculpture are made up of the telling attributes of powerful creatures in nature. Sometimes the motifs are repeated in modules, as if to emphasize their power in an incantation.

Figures from the Chavín pantheon, or their individual attributes, are depicted on sculpture, small stone and bone objects, pottery, painted cloth and worked sheet gold, sometimes in punning ways—a face that can be read right-side-up or upside down, for example. All media of Chavín art show essentially the same kinds of designs presented in very similar ways.

The problems of Chavín

Many of the Chavinoid motifs on portable objects seem to be essentially replicas of those at Chavín de Huantar. Painted textiles, for example, found preserved in arid conditions on the south coast, bear motifs almost identical to those of the sculpture at Chavín. There has long been a proposition that the Chavín style might have been carried to the south coast by means of the highly portable textiles. The fact that their yarns are not spun in the characteristic south-coast manner suggests that they might have originated elsewhere. In the past it was believed that the textiles might have come from Chavín; it is now considered that they may have been made on the north or central coast.

With information now available from earlier sites it is evident that the Chavín style originated earlier than the type site. Some of the Chavinoid material was copied during the short span of influence of the site itself but, according to radiocarbon dates, much of it is earlier. So where did the Chavín tradition come from? Where did it have its greatest early manifestation? How did it travel?

A number of sites, some of which had been built at least 1000 years earlier, were apparently strongly influenced at a certain stage by Chavín itself or, perhaps more likely, by the "Chavín" style that existed before the construction of the great temple. Pacopampa, in the northern highlands, over 400 kilometers from Chavín de Huantar, was an early site and clearly an important ceremonial center in pre-Chavín times. It has a Chavín-style stratum on top of this early occupation. Closer to Chavín de Huantar, Kotosh and Shillacoto, for example, show a pattern of pre-Chavín importance, and then a strongly influenced Chavín-period layer. In some of the older sites the "Chavín" influence was absorbed in a syncretic way; it did not displace the older religion but was blended with it. This was apparently the case at Huaricoto.

The valley of Chavín de Huantar seems to be isolated from the coastal action, but it is a nexus of north–south routes through the mountains and east–west routes to the coast and the Amazon Basin. It would have had the virtues of a node on a well-traveled route, as well as the merits of a sacred site. The pattern of distribution of Chavín-related sites suggests that the visual message of Chavín iconography may well have come from early coastal sites; some of the most important of these may have been later destroyed by tidal wave or river flooding, a possibility that has recently been discussed.

The sacred features of Chavín iconography derive largely from creatures of the tropical forest—the iconography had an early appearance at highland sites not far from the Amazon Basin. Chavín de Huantar itself is on the downward slopes, and undoubtedly there had been traffic through the passes for a long period. The Amazon region developed early and could well have been a source of religion and artistic motifs. One fact weakens the argument for a direct Amazonian or *ceja de montaña* source, however: it is that virtually all pre-Spanish Latin American iconography is based largely on lowland forest creatures. The habitat of significant creatures does not, however, necessarily identify an immediate source of iconography.

The legacy

The influence, wherever it came from and however it spread, was felt for a long time after the waning of the power that motivated it. Many Chavinoid forms are prominent on the north coast in cultures of the succeeding centuries, notably in Mochica art, where the major deity strongly resembles a Chavín god. The south-coast Oculate Being bears a strong resemblance to the "smiling" Chavín god. Later highland art, especially that of Tiahuanaco and Huari, was affected by the Chavín heritage; on certain Chavinoid objects, profile figures face a staff-carrying god shown frontally, as they do on the Gate of the Sun at Tiahuanaco. All deities of the succeeding generations in the Central Andes look more or less like the god in the temple at Chavín de Huantar.

PARACAS CULTURE

On the south coast of Peru the Paracas Peninsula protrudes into the rich fishing grounds of the Pacific Ocean—a barren windswept spit of sand between two bays. ("Paracas" means "wind storm" in Quechua.) Now a desolate landscape, the peninsula was once populous. Because of the rich finds there the peninsula has given its name to the early culture of the entire region.

A striking landmark in the pale desert is Cerro Colorado, a rosy hill of granite porphyry. In the 1920s, in its sandy slopes, three cemeteries known as Cabeza Larga, Cavernas and Necropolis were investigated by the Peruvian archaeologist J.C. Tello. Paracas Cavernas yielded the oldest materials, although the sites overlap in time. Cavernas dates from the late Early horizon (600–400 BC); the Necropolis and Cabeza Larga sites begin in the 6th century BC and extend into the Early Intermediate period. Other burials with grave goods of similar styles have been found in the nearby coastal valleys of Ica, Pisco, Chincha and Nazca.

The Cavernas style is named for the bottle-shaped shaft tombs, or "caverns," dug into the summit of Cerro Colorado. These burials each contained 30–40 individuals, interred with varying, but generally not large, quantities of grave goods. Subterranean dwellings were also uncovered at the site. Some of the Necropolis burials seem to have been dug into Cavernas refuse dumps.

Virtually all of the skulls in the Cavernas burials,

male and female, were deformed, and nearly half had been trepanned. The cranial operation of trepanation has been found in a number of Andean cultures. It was performed with several techniques: by making cuts to form the corners of a rectangle or square and then removing the defined piece, by drilling the outline of a circular cut, or by gouging away the bone.

Tied on the outside of the Cavernas mummy bundles were woven cotton masks, with a frontal head or figure painted in dark brown, purple, red and/or gray, in a style suggesting influence from south-coast Chavinoid textiles.

Paracas Necropolis was clearly the high-status burial place for the dominant people of its place and time, and contained numerous funerary bundles. Some of these contained over 100 cotton garments, elaborately and colorfully embroidered with wool. Tello found 429 of these bundles placed in walled structures or house foundations; many others have been found by looters. The conical bundles vary greatly in size. A large one can measure up to 1·5 meters at the base and in height, and may have three or four times as many items inside as the small ones. Each bundle is different in details, but the general procedure of its preparation is the same.

There has been argument about whether a mummification procedure was used, for Tello suggested that brains and viscera had been removed. This has been contested, but the bodies may have been dried or smoked. The body was arranged in a tight fetal position and tied. Sometimes a loincloth or jewelry might be worn, but the body was essentially naked. A small piece of sheet gold was often placed at the back of the mouth, and a gourd bowl with food offerings between the chest and the legs. Other offerings could also be put next to the body, for example, brow, nose or ear ornaments of thin sheet gold.

A coarse cotton cloth was wrapped around all this, and the bundle was placed in a mat or basket. The spaces in the basket were filled with garments and other objects, and the whole was covered with one of the huge (2·5 meters or more long) embroidered mantles, which are the hallmark of the Paracas culture.

The major motif at the Necropolis is a creature known as the Oculate Being, a large-eyed, frontal figure with streaming appendages ending in trophy heads; often the head is heart-shaped, and sometimes a little head sprouts Athena-like from the top of it. This figure, which came in with the Paracas Cavernas style, is the only figure shown on Cavernas painted masks.

Ceramics

Grave goods also included ceramics. The brilliantly embroidered Necropolis bundles were accompanied by vessels with monochrome slip, ovoid, double-spout-and-bridge forms, which were gadrooned or animal-shaped. In other burials, however, polychrome vessels and negative-painted vessels were found. Best known is the large group found inland at Ocucaje, the earliest examples of which have motifs derived from Chavín iconography. There are several examples of the stirrup-spout form from the earliest phase. This is a diagnostic northern form, and these vessels may have

Above As if to create vegetation in the desert, this candelabra-like tree was fashioned, at an unknown time, on a hill near the entrance to the modern Paracas harbor. It faces the sea and rocky islands, inhabited by sea lions and thousands of sea birds, which used to be a rich source of guano fertilizer.

Left Detail of an embroidered garment found in a Paracas Necropolis mummy bundle. It shows the Oculate Being wearing a headband of a kind that has actually been found in burials, made of sheet gold. This supernatural figure is often shown horizontally, upsidedown or crouching. This one has, at the end of its long, serrate tongue, a human figure, also wearing a headband.

been imported. The most prevalent pot form has a bridge which, in earlier phases, connects a spout and a bird head (a blind spout) and later connects two matching spouts. Many of the earlier examples are whistling jars. The Chavinoid faces are replaced in later phases by the Oculate Being, seen on both Paracas and Cavernas textiles.

The earliest phases of Paracas have strong Chavín influence and probably date from the initial appearance of the Chavín style in the region. A distinctive style develops out of the introduced one, with changes to meet local religious and cultural requirements, but with a strong Chavín flavor. At one end of the time scale the Paracas style evolved easily and distinctively out of the Chavín style; at the other end, it evolved naturally into the Nazca style.

NAZCA CULTURE

The dominant art style on the south coast during the Early Intermediate period (c. 370 BC–450 AD) is called Nazca. It took over from the Paracas style. The transition from Paracas to Nazca was smooth. Painted plain-cloth Nazca textiles showed figures not unlike those on Paracas garments. The preferred textile was tapestry with designs that had roots in motifs on the earlier embroidered mantles, although embroidered mantles continued to be made in a somewhat different style, and brocading and featherwork are also found. Early Nazca or proto-Nazca ceramics have color zones and details designated by incising; in later Nazca designs the incising is replaced with painted outlines. Many Nazca motifs are very similar to those seen in Paracas art. A descendant of the Oculate Being appears, sometimes called the Anthropomorphic Mythical Being. The double-spout-and-bridge vessel of the Paracas period becomes the predominant Nazca vessel shape.

The transition between Paracas and Nazca is basically marked by a change from resin paint applied after firing to fired slip paints, and by a shift from textiles to ceramics as the most important medium for expressing important subject matter. Nazca potters produced some of the most brilliant polychrome ceramics in the New World, using six or seven colors.

The trophy-head cult was particularly strong in the Nazca culture. Caches of severed trepanned heads have been found in Nazca cemeteries; effigy vessels may take the form of a trophy head; and some vessels are decorated entirely with painted repetitions of these heads. Anthropomorphic condors or hawks have trophy heads drawn on their wings, and sometimes they have trophy heads in their mouths. The Anthropomorphic Mythical Being is most often shown with a human body, wearing a loincloth and camouflaged by an array of supernatural attributes. In some depictions he holds a trophy head to his mouth, as if to eat it.

The remains of cities
The Nazca florescence took place essentially in the region occupied by the people who made Paracas-style art; for example, large finds of Nazca pottery

have been made at Ocucaje, which was known also for its Paracas material. There was a slight shift to the south, however, with a greater concentration of sites in the region of the Nazca River and its five major tributaries and in the Acarí Valley to the south, possibly as a result of military conquest. The pattern of expansion and contraction, or at least of power shifts, seems to be indicated in these valleys as some sites are abandoned and others begun.

Few Nazca architectural structures remain. There is evidence of irrigation canals, but there was little stone building. Important structures were usually made of adobe, and residential structures were of tied cane. The ceremonial center of Cahuachi, in the Nazca Valley, may have been the capital of an early expanding chiefdom, which later waned in importance. Cahuachi had a stepped pyramid, an adobe-faced natural rise, 20 meters high, one of the few large structures from this period and region. Around it were plazas and adobe rooms and tombs. This site was abandoned before the end of the Early Intermediate period, as were several of the other large early sites. In the last period other large sites developed.

In the last phase, Nazca influence reached further to the north and south and up into the highlands toward Ayacucho, perhaps preparing the way for the Huari–Nazca relationship of the Middle Horizon.

Above The bay of Paracas is one of the most prominent indentations on the Peruvian coast, although its combination of ocean and desert is found along the entire coast of Peru and down into Chile. This sandy landscape, near the Cerro Colorado burial grounds, has preserved many relics of the past. Paracas is still an important fishing area, as it was in pre-Columbian times.

Above right A late Nazca cylinder vase design of hunters with spearthrowers and parrots. The liveliness and the border of snake heads may reflect influence from contemporaneous Mochica culture on the north coast.

Right A Nazca effigy jar in which the Anthropomorphical Mythical Being is associated with trophy heads: it shows the complexity of mythical motifs that could be combined using the rich polychrome favored by Nazca potters.

Potters made vessels in the form of trophy heads with closed eyes and mouths pinned shut—just as they are found in caches of Nazca trophy heads. The triangles on the cheeks may depict face paint, a common pre-Columbian trait.

Lines in the Desert

Perhaps the most fascinating archaeological site in the Americas is spread out over some 500 square kilometers near the modern town of Nazca, on the south coast of Peru. Over 1000 years ago figures, lines and geometric forms were drawn on the earth by removing the dark surface gravel to reveal the light-colored stratum below and neatly piling the gravel or stone along the edges. Anthropomorphs, animals, birds and flowers are found along with straight-line, trapezoidal and other abstract forms, as neat as if they had been made with a ruler.

These markings have given rise to wildly imaginative speculation as well as to serious scholarship. The lines can be seen properly only from the air, and a number of scholars have suggested the possibility of astronomical alignment or significance, which some markings seem to have, although this has not yet been proved for the whole complex. The lines may also have been sacred ritual pathways. Some lines go dead-straight for long distances; others converge on a single point.

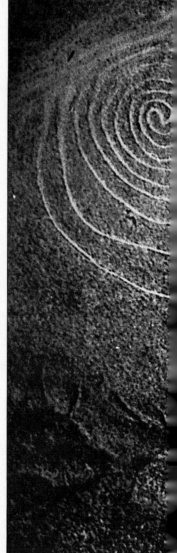

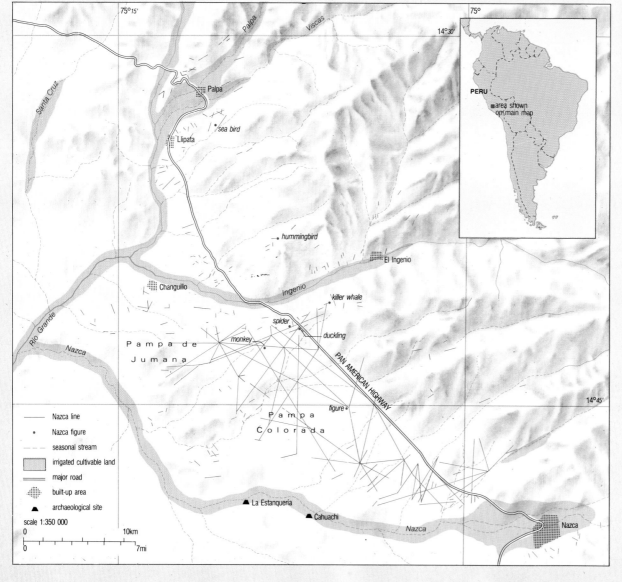

The ground markings of the region northwest of Nazca in southern Peru run straight across the uneven plains of arid desert, near but not on irrigable land, as can be seen in the map (*left*). Sometimes lines converge on a center (*above left*), which may have had special sacred associations; offerings were possibly made there. The spectacular Nazca markings, as great a tribute to pre-Columbian gods and pre-Columbian skill as a gigantic pyramid, are the best-known examples of this art form, but similar markings, or geoglyphs, have been found elsewhere near the Peruvian coast and in Chile (see opposite).

The markings were probably made primarily as offerings to ancestors, or to sky or mountain gods (which shared overlapping identities). Mountain/sky gods controlled precious water in the coastal desert and had strong fertility associations.

Left One of the most intriguing figures on the Nazca plains is a monkey with splayed fingers and a great, tight coil of a tail. Monkeys are creatures of the Amazon forest, not of the desert coast, yet they are important motifs in coastal iconography.

Below This close-up view of part of a Nazca "drawing" reveals the monumental scale of the desert works. Lines were made by removing dark surface gravel to expose underlying light-colored rock.

Left A hummingbird is drawn with long, straight lines on the plain above the El Ingenio Valley. This bird was significant in myth for its fierceness, its beauty and its sun associations. It appears frequently on Nazca ceramics. Other bird forms are also found among the Nazca markings.

Above This giant anthropomorph, about 90 m. in length, lies at Cerro Unitas in northern Chile where there are markings similar to those at Nazca some 800 km. away. At Cerro Unitas the markings are also associated with irrigated fields. A smaller, less carefully made version of this figure can be found at Nazca. These figures might be images of fertility gods, or they may be supine figures placed as offerings to the sky.

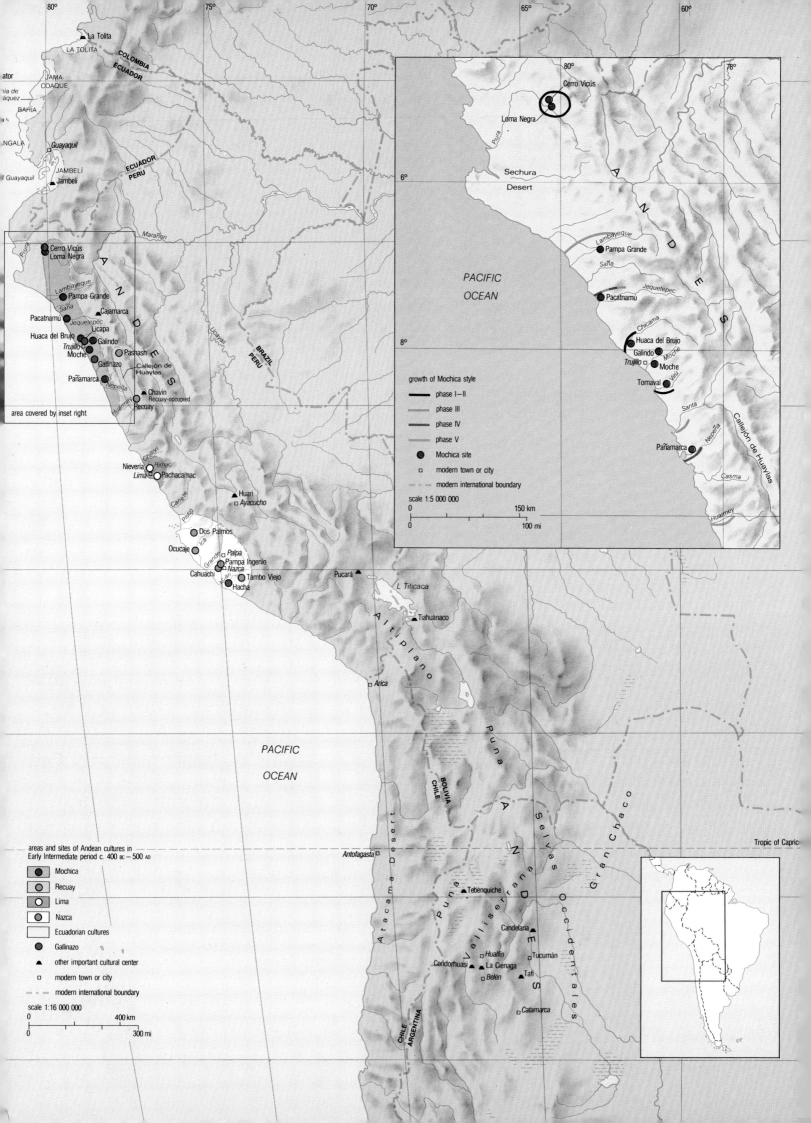

Inset (top right):

PACIFIC
OCEAN

Cerro Vicús

Loma Negra

Sechura
Desert

Pampa Grande

Lambayeque

Saña

Jequetepec

Pacatnamú

Chicama

Huaca del Brujo

Galindo

Trujillo

Moche

Viru

Tomaval

growth of Mochica style

—— phase I–II

—— phase III

—— phase IV

—— phase V

● Mochica site

□ modern town or city

— · — modern international boundary

scale 1:5 000 000

0 _____ 150 km

0 _____ 100 mi

Pañamarca

Nepeña

Callejón de Huaylas

Casma

Huarmey

Main map labels:

La Tolita

LA TOLITA

COLOMBIA

ECUADOR

JAMA-
COAQUE

BAHÍA

bahia de
íquez

NGALA

Guayaquil

JAMBELÍ

Guayaquil

Jambeli

ECUADOR
PERU

Marañón

Cerro Vicús
Loma Negra

Piura

A
N
D
E
S

Lambayeque

Pampa Grande

Saña

Cajamarca

Pacatnamú

Jequetepec

Licapa

Huaca del Brujo

Galindo

Trujillo

Pashash

Moche

Gallinazo

Callejón de
Huaylas

Pañamarca

Nepeña

Huarmey

Chavin
Recuay-occupied

Recuay

Ucayali

BRAZIL

PERU

Nieveria

Lima

Rimac

Pachacamac

Chillón

Huari

Ayacucho

Cañete

Pisco

Dos Palmos

Ocucaje

Ica

Grande

Palpa

Pampa Ingenio

Nazca

Cahuachi

Tambo Viejo

Hacha

Aja

Pucará

L. Titicaca

Altiplano

Tiahuanaco

Arica

Puna

PACIFIC

OCEAN

Atacama Desert

Antofagasta

BOLIVIA

CHILE

Puna

A
N
D
E
S

Selvas

Gran Chaco

Occidentales

Valliserrana

Tebenquiche

Candelaria

Huaflin

Tucumán

Condorhuasi

La Ciénaga

Belén

Tafi

Catamarca

CHILE
ARGENTINA

Tropic of Capric

areas and sites of Andean cultures in
Early Intermediate period c. 400 BC – 500 AD

● Mochica

◑ Recuay

○ Lima

◐ Nazca

□ Ecuadorian cultures

● Gallinazo

▲ other important cultural center

□ modern town or city

— · — modern international boundary

scale 1:16 000 000

0 _____ 400 km

0 _____ 300 mi

area covered by inset right

MOCHICA

Neighbors and precursors

On the north coast of Peru the Chavín phenomenon was followed by the Salinar and Gallinazo cultures. Salinar produced relatively simple pottery with spout-and-strap handles. Gallinazo was part of a widespread fashion of negative-painted pottery, found from Hacha, in the south, where it seems to appear earliest, to the Piura region (Vicús) in the north.

Negative- or resist-painted ceramics also characterize the Recuay culture, in the Callejón de Huaylas, above the Mochica coastal valleys. Named for a town in the Callejón, not far from Chavín de Huantar, the Recuay style had some roots in Chavín art but showed very individual characteristics. After the end of Chavín dominance the temple at Chavín de Huantar was occupied by Recuay people. The Recuay style probably began somewhat before that of the Mochica, but is essentially contemporary. A number of Mochica art motifs seem to have been borrowed from the Recuay style —there must certainly have been contact, for river water for irrigation in Mochica valleys had its source in Recuay territory. The motifs borrowed from Recuay are used in Mochica scenes depicting the coca ritual and related activities. At least some Mochica coca must have come from or through Recuay lands at some point in their history.

Considering the geographical proximity and obvious contact, the differences between Mochica and Recuay are interesting. Recuay produced dippers, effigy vessels and pots with "deck" figures, which are Mochica forms. In general, however, vessel shapes are different: typical Recuay traits are urns with everted necks, ring vessels, globular pots with wide-flaring spout rims, and a spout jutting up from the deck of a pot like a funnel. Although some of the same motifs are used, they seem to carry different meanings. Some of the shared non-coca-associated motifs are: house forms, figures holding vessels, a man with a feline, a figure pecked by vultures and the so-called moon-animal.

The region and the sites

The site of Moche, near the modern city of Trujillo, was the ceremonial and administrative center of the Mochica (or Moche) people for at least a substantial part of their period of importance, from about the time of Christ until about 600 AD. The Huaca del Sol, or Pyramid of the Sun, an enormous adobe structure 40 meters high and at least 350 meters long—the largest solid adobe structure in the New World—was probably built over several hundred years and was much larger than it is now. What stands today is perhaps only a third of its original size. Today it looks out on irrigated fields on the river side and across pale, bare desert on the other side. Across a large open space the pyramid faces the Pyramid of the Moon (Huaca de la Luna), which is situated just below a prominent hill, Cerro Blanco; the man-made mountain of the Pyramid of the Sun faces the natural mountain. A long formation of "living rock" frames the inland side of the site at the end of the two major structures. Remains

between the large pyramids are now covered by sand.

In this valley and in others along the coast the Mochica grew cotton, maize, potatoes, peanuts and peppers, by irrigating the coastal desert. Fishing was, of course, also a major source of livelihood. It provided food for immediate consumption by the coastal people and goods for trading with inland peoples.

Mochica ceramic styles have been seriated in five phases. Moche I and II are found above the Gallinazo stratum in the Moche, Chicama and Virú Valleys from about the time of Christ or a little before. The earliest phase to be encountered in the Santa Valley is Moche III; this would indicate that expansion southward took place at that time. The splendid site of Pañamarca in the Nepeña Valley, with mural paintings and Moche IV traits, marks the furthest southward point of known Mochica architecture, although there is ceramic evidence for a Mochica presence as far south as Huarmey. The situation to the north is more complex. Mochica burials have been found at Pacatnamú, which would indicate a normal northward expansion. But in the far north, in the Piura Valley, very early Mochica pottery has been found, as well as some of the finest Mochica-style metalwork. A vast burial ground, known as Loma Negra, has yielded hundreds of examples of fine work in gold, silver and copper. Also found in this region, apparently from about the same date (although it is not known if they are found together), are resist-decorated ceramics related to those found in the Virú Valley. This leaves open the possibilities that the Mochica people may have come to the Moche Valley from the north, that there may have been an early northern colony of people from Moche, or that the peoples of the Piura and Moche Valleys may have originated in a third, undiscovered place, perhaps in between. Whatever the explanations, there had been a Mochica presence in the northern valleys about the time of Christ, and there was an abandonment of the Moche site and a definite power shift to the Lambayeque region about 600 AD.

Art and religion

The Mochica artisans were among the best in the New World. They included ingenious goldsmiths who subtly gilded silver and copper, fine weavers —as the few remaining textiles attest—and remarkable potters. Ceramic decoration includes modeling in high relief, low relief created by stamping and scenes painted on a flat surface. Some vessels were made in molds; many were hand-modeled. There was a variety of shapes, but a stirrup spout was appended to most "fancy" ceramics. Not only do the vessels show a wide variation in form and decoration, they reveal more about Mochica myth and ritual than do the artifacts of any other Andean civilization.

The basic iconographic system seems to be one of clusters of subject matter, which sometimes overlap (as in the modern symbol for the Olympic Games). For example, one cluster has to do with the ritual chewing of coca leaves (a theme found in Ecuadoran and Colombian art as well). Sometimes the bag for the coca leaves and the gourd and stick for the lime that was used with the leaves are

Left: Andean cultures in the Early Intermediate period
Among the numerous diverse art styles that developed in the Early Intermediate period, the style of the central coast and the Rímac Valley is called by various names—among them Lima, Early Lima and Nievería. It is less well known than other coastal styles, partly because much of it lies under the capital of Peru, Lima, or under the remains of later pre-Columbian cultures. It was influenced by Nazca and Mochica styles, although it was less distinctive and fine. At Pachacamac a Lima adobe pyramid is preserved, with murals that were retouched in later times. Pachacamac was an important site, which became politically powerful toward the end of the Middle Horizon and had a famous oracle in Inca times.

In the highlands in the Early Intermediate, the Huarpa style throve in the Ayacucho region, which later became the seat of Huari power; the Tiahuanaco style was also developing.

The inset shows wide Mochica influence, but its extent in the peripheral areas is not clear. Although objects of Moche style have been found as far south as the Huarmey Valley, there was probably no serious political influence here. Quantities of Mochica-style objects have come from the Piura Valley in the far north, but there are no architectural remains. Although the Mochica were clearly an aggressive people— this is clear not only from their geographical spread but from the quantity of war motifs in their iconography—probably much of what we see as their influence came from that of their art.

Moche

Below The portrait of a Mochica god forms the body of this stirrup-spout vessel. The fanged, angular mouth, lidded eyes, ear shapes and the snakes on the head derive from Chavín deity depictions. Such vessels have been found in graves and were probably made for burial.

The archaeological site of Moche lies in the shelter of a bare, sandy hill. From the top of its huge main pyramid, there is a view across the desert toward the sea and across the cultivated valley; it also looks up the valley, whence the river descends and where the mountains close in. Most Andean sites are located close to a hill—a sacred place but also a strategic place from which to see the surrounding world. The first archaeological work at Moche was done in 1899 by Max Uhle, who discovered paintings in the Pyramid of the Moon (which have since disappeared) and burials in the area between the two pyramids. Other projects have been undertaken more recently.

Toward the end of the Early Intermediate period, Moche was abandoned; Galindo, up the valley, became the important local center. There is still a community near Moche, whose customs were studied earlier in the 20th century for remnant patterns of pre-Columbian ancestors.

Below A vase scene shows coca-leaf chewing in a night ritual. The figure at left, standing under a serpentine sky band, has an angular supernatural mouth. The distinctively dressed human figures have gourds and sticks for the lime that was chewed with the leaves, which were carried in bags.

Above This painted gilt-copper mask has shell-inlay eyes and holes in the earlobes for ornaments. It was found in a burial in the Pyramid of the Moon. It may be a portrait of the deceased.

Right The Pyramid of the Moon, seen looming over the irrigated fields of the Moche Valley.

Above A stirrup-spout effigy vase showing an owl man with a trophy head in his left hand. This could be either a man dressed up as an owl or an owl god.

depicted, sometimes they are not. But, when these items are absent, the figures are still recognizable as belonging to the coca ritual by their distinctive dress. Certain battle scenes show figures in coca-ritual clothing. War and the taking of captives for several sacrificial beheading rituals are prominent themes in the art.

The major god of the Mochica was Chavín-derived, as were so many Andean gods. He had feline canines and a belt with snakehead extensions. Sometimes depictions of him show the figure-eight ears of Chavín art, or curiously lidded eyes found on some Early Horizon pottery.

The end of Moche
At the end of phase IV there seems to have been a virtual abandonment of the site at Moche. The real center of power seems to have been moved to Pampa Grande, in the Lambayeque Valley, a former Early Horizon site. There is some evidence for a major sand sheet having moved in on Moche and the canal system around it, disrupting agriculture and forcing a movement away from the site. The Huari expansion, beginning about this time, may well have motivated some changes. Certainly there are changes in style and subject matter in Moche V art. The stirrup-spout form changes

slightly, but that is not surprising, considering the evolution of the form throughout earlier phases. Color is more restricted, and painting is generally less skillful. One major style change is a kind of pictorial agoraphobia, in which painted scenes are so cluttered with filler material that it is hard to read the major elements. New subject matter is introduced, old matter dropped. During the final Moche phase, perhaps contemporary with the Moche V vessels, Huari motifs and style of painting were mingled with Mochica motifs and vessel shapes. Even in the pure Moche V vessels, iconographic details—a drawing of an eye, the form of a headdress ornament—suggest the beginnings of the Lambayeque and Chimú styles.

TIAHUANACO AND HUARI

Tiahuanaco is a large site with handsome stone architecture and sculpture. It is located about 20 kilometers from Lake Titicaca and nearly 4000 meters above sea level, on the great altiplano that stretches from Bolivia into southern Peru. The Bolivian site was known to the Inca; some versions of their origin myths take place on an island in Lake Titicaca, and there are Inca remains on the lake.

Titicaca is the highest navigable lake in the world, and Tiahuanaco the highest urban settlement, certainly of the ancient New World. The altiplano, lying above the timber line, is rimmed by mountains—a desolate, inhuman-seeming landscape; yet it is the largest expanse of level, arable land in the Andes, and has been occupied for millennia. By various means a fairly large population can be supported. Ridged or drained fields recently discovered near Lake Titicaca were undoubtedly used to help feed the denizens of Tiahuanaco by conserving, distributing and draining water. The high plain is good not only for growing tubers, which could be freeze-dried, but also for grazing herds of llamas and alpacas.

Tiahuanaco was occupied from 1500 BC to 1200 AD; its great period was 500–1000 AD. The major structures and also some sculptures were probably put in place before 500 AD, but at about that time the structures were refurbished and new and striking sculpture and architectural details were added. The Gateway of the Sun dates from this time, which is called the Classic Tiahuanaco period.

Tiahuanaco and Huari
Tiahuanaco shared with the site of Huari, near the city of Ayacucho in the southern highlands of Peru, an iconography of certain figure types, such as those on the Gate of the Sun. The motifs seem to have appeared in both places about 500 AD. At Conchapata, near Huari, a cache of large urns was found bearing these motifs and dating from this time. This ceramic style is found along with the local pottery types that had preceded it. The Ayacucho Valley has a very long history of occupation; there are remains dating back to beyond 7000 BC. At the time of the introduction of the new iconography it was occupied by a culture known as Huarpa.

There is still debate about the mechanisms by which the new motifs appeared in the two sites.

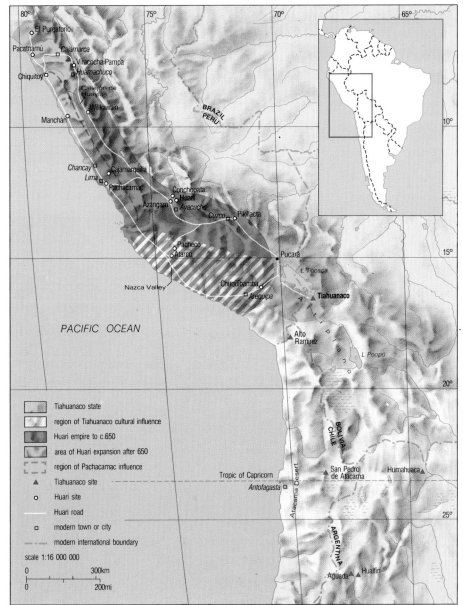

Tiahuanaco state

region of Tiahuanaco cultural influence

Huari empire to c.650

area of Huari expansion after 650

region of Pachacamac influence

▲ Tiahuanaco site

o Huari site

Huari road

□ modern town or city

modern international boundary

scale 1:16 000 000

0   300km

0   200mi

Tiahuanaco

The most important features of Tiahuanaco cluster around the Akapana, an enormous stone-faced platform mound, which measures 200 meters on each side and stands 15 meters high. Some of the ashlars of andesite or sandstone weigh over 100 tonnes; they were quarried at places away from the site and brought by raft and overland. Adjacent to the north side of the Akapana is a semisubterranean temple, reminiscent of very early Andean sunken plazas, with walls in which projecting heads of volcanic tuff have been tenoned, a feature suggestive of remote Chavín influence. Next to it stands the Kalasasaya, the largest and most important architectural complex and the principal temple, a rectangular precinct with walls of sandstone pillars alternating with smaller, rectangular blocks of ashlar masonry. Close by is the Putuni, a building complex thought to have been a palace compound. There are stone drainage systems in some of the structures. At a distance stands the

Pumapunku, another huge stone-faced platform, measuring 5 meters high with walls 150 meters long. The Katatayita, the administrative center, also stands away from the Akapana.

Megalithic gateways led to the Kalasasaya, the Pumapunku and the Akapana. The Gateway of the Sun, at the Kalasasaya, is the best-known Tiahuanaco sculpture. A cosmological model, it has a central panel above the opening on which is carved a large, frontal figure; at either side three rows of smaller, winged, profile figures run toward it; below is a row of frontal heads.

Monolithic sculpture found at various places in the site often takes the form of columnar figures with human faces, holding ceremonial objects. These statues, ranging from 1·5 to 7·6 meters tall, are clothed with garments rendered by fine incision; their faces and limbs are carved in low relief. Some still stand *in situ* in the Kalasasaya. Stelae and wall plaques are also found at the site.

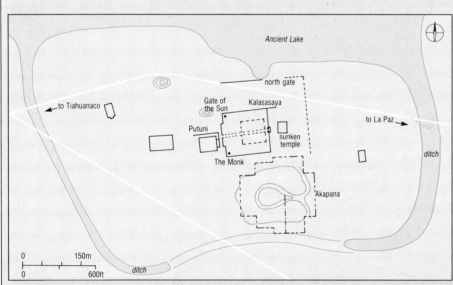

One of the finest sculptures at Tiahuanaco (*left*) stands just inside the Kalasasaya. The full figure rises c. 3·5 m. above the ground. A columnar monolith with intricate, low-relief incising, it characterizes the compactness and symmetry of Tiahuanaco sculpture. It also demonstrates the complex iconography of Tiahuanaco art. The mask-like face with squarish, staring eyes and cheek-panels is typical. The monument, dating from the second half of the 7th century AD, is known as the Ponce Monolith, after the Bolivian archaeologist who has worked most at Tiahuanaco. A short distance away, at Lake Titicaca, fishermen and Indian commuters still use reed rafts like those made by the inhabitants of Tiahuanaco in pre-Columbian times (*right*).

Tiahuanaco (*above*) lies on the plain between La Paz and the south shore of Lake Titicaca. The earliest description of the ancient city was written by Cieza de León, a Spanish soldier who was much impressed on his visit there in 1549. The magnificent Kalasasaya has been restored. Part of one wall of its huge sunken courtyard is seen (*right*), with one of the great gateways of Tiahuanaco behind it. The Gateway of the Sun stands nearby. Monolithic sculpture is found free-standing in the center of the courtyard and also set into the wall along with tenoned heads. This structure, 135 by 130 m., would have been the ceremonial heart of the city.

The two cities may have developed for the most part independently, with some contact and cross-fertilization and a common source for religious motifs. One school of thought believes that the motifs came to both Tiahuanaco and Huari from a third place, which would have preserved motifs from the earlier, Chavín-influenced art of Pucará (200 BC–220 AD), which lies between Tiahuanaco and Ayacucho.

At Tiahuanaco the frontal god and the winged profile figures appear on a major stone monument; they are rare, if present at all, on pottery. On the other hand, the motifs appear in elaborate form on Huari and provincial Huari ceramics. It would seem possible that the portable objects were copied from the monument. Yet there are variations in the motifs that might be explained by derivation from a third site. The difference in medium may reflect a difference in emphasis, which is apparent in other aspects of the two cultures. Huari sculpture was certainly simpler and cruder than that of Tiahuanaco, and its religion was probably less developed. Tiahuanaco seems to have had a more ceremonial bent and Huari a more secular one, but both cities, after 500 AD, were expanding and beginning to establish confederations.

Another possible interpretation of the Huari-Tiahuanaco relationship is that they were dual capitals, with Huari controlling the northern lands and Tiahuanaco those in its neighborhood and to the south. The strong contemporary influence from this region in northern Chile and northwest Argentina, for example, appears to come from Tiahuanaco. Huari had colonies in the Nazca Valley, some 300 kilometers toward the coast. The Nazca region, however, was associated with both Huari and Tiahuanaco.

Some scholars believe that Tiahuanaco was the real power behind all the expansion, and that Huari was the center of Tiahuanaco political and military control in the north. Whatever the pattern, both cities were expanding shortly after 500 AD.

The characteristic motifs

The standing, frontal deity, often shown on a stepped platform bearing a staff or other symbolic objects in either hand, is found in Pucará, Tiahuanaco, Huari and provincial art. The figure has a mask-like face with radiant forms, sometimes serpent-ended; it wears a tunic, belt and kilt. It probably represents a prototype of the deity later called Viracocha, a pan-Andean sky and creator god. Profile figures, often winged and running, kneeling, flying or floating, accompany the frontal figure or are seen independently. The two figure types share attributes such as snake hair and similar garments. These figures are associated or interchangeable with a sacrificer holding an ax and a trophy head. Trophy heads are a prominent motif. It has been suggested that Tiahuanaco and Huari imitated older art so that their rulers might associate their power with a venerated culture.

Architecture and the expanding Huari empire

The Middle Horizon is defined by the Huari expansion. Huari came to life shortly after 500 AD, when the new art style suddenly appeared in the Ayacucho Valley. The following period, around 600 AD,

Left Mirrors are found in several pre-Columbian cultures. This Huari-Tiahuanaco example, 24 cm. high, has a reflecting surface of pyrite pieces and a mosaic back showing a central face with cheek panels terminating in small heads, like those on Tiahuanaco sculpture, and two small disembodied faces at either side.

Andean cultures in the Late Intermediate period

In the Late Intermediate period the Chimú expanded in both directions along the coast from their capital, Chan Chan, and were, before the incursions of the more aggressive Inca, empire-builders in their own right. Most other sites on the map date from this period. Chiquitoy, in the Chicama Valley, is a Late Horizon site although its architecture resembles that of the Chimú. Manchan, which is now being investigated by archaeologists, was the southern administrative capital of the kingdom of Chimor. South of the fortress of Paramonga there is evidence of Chimú presence and/or control. Among the groups conquered by the Chimú were the people of the culture known as Chancay. Chancay graves have yielded many remarkable textiles, some of which may have been imported from Chan Chan.

Activity on the south coast in the Late Intermediate centered in the Ica and Chincha Valleys. La Centinela, in the Chincha Valley, is an adobe pyramid complex from this period. This site and another large pyramid nearby are decorated with geometric friezes. Ica-style vessels, apparently valued trade objects, have been found up in the sierra and as far north as Ancon. A distinctive Ica artifact was a tall wooden digging board, resembling a center- or leeboard, which was used as a grave-marker. In the highlands at this time, between the south coast and Cuzco, there were several small groups of peoples, known generally as Chanca, which were later overrun by the Inca.

was a time of conquest extending to Chancay on the coast and to the Callejón de Huaylas in the highlands.

Large architectural complexes, built in a style previously unknown in the Andes, appeared in strategic locations. Enormous walls enclosed houses, streets, plazas and structures with hundreds of rooms. There were buildings for civil administration and military garrisons; there were storage facilities, habitation sites for support staff, and quarters for artisans and workers. Nearby religious shrines were taken over. The architecture was regular, rectangular, symmetrical, indicating not only orderly minds but planned, single-stage construction—not the accretion or agglutination found in so many pre-Columbian structures. The architecture was designed to have an impressive presence and to centralize the occupying forces. The building of an empire was in progress.

The evidence for Tiahuanaco's southern influence is based largely on finds of equipment for using hallucinogenic snuff, which was, throughout Andean time and space, an essential part of religious ritual. Tiahuanaco's geographical position, between the selva, where hallucinogens like *Piptadenia* grew, and the coast, where they were used, favored the ritually centered trade and reinforced Tiahuanaco's religious influence, which is seen in small objects rather than in architecture. The influence on the Quebrada de Humahuaca, in northern Argentina, and on San Pedro de Atacama, in Chile, may have been direct, whereas that found in the Hualfín Valley, in Argentina, may have come second-hand through the other sites.

After the period of Huari expansion there was apparently a crisis which caused an abatement of building and conquest patterns and the abandonment of some villages in the Ayacucho Valley. At this time the coastal center of Pachacamac became important, possibly even rivaling Huari's power. Pachacamac later developed a sphere of influence of its own, overshadowing Nazca; in Inca times its temple and oracle had great importance and prestige. The Huari engine of conquest had carried the power of empire, for a short time at least, to the far northern coast of Peru and to Cajamarca in the highlands.

Before 800 Huari was abandoned; the great period of conquest ended apparently abruptly. Its art style, however, continued to be influential. Tiahuanaco continued to thrive for a time, adding new colonies in the south.

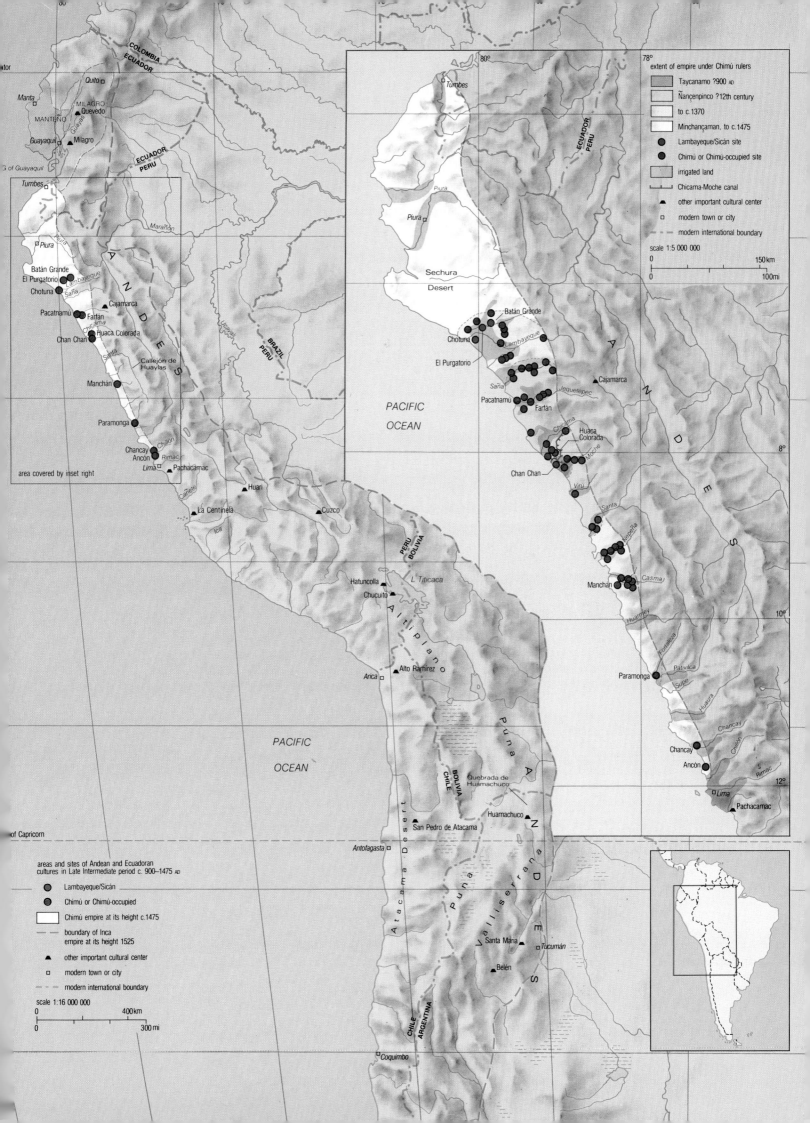

THE CHIMÚ

The Chimú, or Chimor, story can begin with the Classic Lambayeque or Sicán style, which evolved in the first half of the 8th century AD, with distinctive blackware ceramics, and within the next century with religious architecture. The grandest and best-known phase of this style comes from Batán Grande, between the La Leche and Pacora Rivers, at the northern edge of the Lambayeque Valley. Batán Grande, an archaeological complex which includes some 50 sites, had a history dating from about 1500 BC. Remains of a U-shaped temple from that time are still visible. The Mochica had intruded into this region in their last period, with a center at Pampa Grande, in the Lambayeque Valley; but their power ended about 700 AD. There followed a period of influence from Huari and Pachacamac, to the south, and from Cajamarca, in the mountains to the east. Some of the traits introduced in the southern intrusion remained throughout succeeding periods—the beaker, or *kero*, shape for example, and the double-spout-and-bridge vessel, initially a south coast form.

From the Sicán heyday of 850–1050 AD there are at Batán Grande at least 17 major constructions of adobe, along with large shaft tombs and other architectural features. The enormous complex was, apparently, not an urban center but a place for ritual and burial, which had mural paintings and some of the richest tombs known in the New World. Some tombs contained over 200 objects of gold or silver. There is evidence of metalworking activity in the complex. The nearby site of El Purgatorio probably became a center for the Lambayeque government until the Chimú conquered the Lambayeque Valley around 1350 AD.

Ethnohistorical sources tell more about the north coast than about most pre-Inca regions in the Andes. For example, an early post-conquest legend tells of Ñaymlap, who was said to have arrived by balsa raft in the Lambayeque Valley, where he established a royal lineage; it was not known whence he came. He was perhaps mythical, but his line was thought to have ruled Lambayeque until the Chimú conquest. There was then, presumably, a new lineage with royal status but no political power, a situation that continued through the Inca occupation of the north coast.

The kingdom of Chimor

There was also a legendary Chimú ruler, Tacaynamo, who arrived by balsa raft and founded the city of Chan Chan. His heirs, in two major expansion thrusts, to the south and to the north, created the kingdom of Chimor. (Chimor was the ancient name for the Moche Valley.) The Chimú ultimately controlled a territory from Tumbes, on the far north coast, down to the Chillón Valley, north of Lima. The kingdom of Chimor was expanded through conquest and clever administration. It was a well-organized operation under the guidance of a semidivine ruler—the first ruler had undoubtedly been deified, a pattern common in pre-Columbian America. Like most pre-Columbian rulers the Chimú lord had responsibility for agriculture and the well-being of his people through his supernatural connections.

Legend tells something of Chimú religion, of the moon goddess Si, the principal deity, who was thought to be the protector of public property, perhaps because, watching at night, she could see and spotlight thieves in the darkness. The moon traveled westward over the sea, which was thought of as a deity called Ni, also important in the lives of these coast-dwelling fishing people. We are told by early sources that the ancestors of the coastal people were four stars, two of which created the kings and nobles, while the other two created the common people. This mythical caste system seems to have been quite real in the stratified society of Chan Chan.

Chan Chan lies on the opposite side of the Moche Valley from the older site of Moche, across the river, at the edge of the sea, close to the almost adjoining, larger Chicama Valley. Irrigation systems had been established in this part of the coast millennia before the Chimú occupation, but the Chimú extended the systems and built a canal some 65 kilometers long, to carry water from the upper Chicama Valley to Chimú fields in the Moche Valley—though whether this was actually finished and used has been a matter of considerable debate.

It is not known just when the first Chimú ruler arrived in his raft or what new ideas he brought with him. The Chimú art style basically merges Mochica and Middle Horizon (Huari) elements. The great walled compounds and a frontal deity figure are reminiscent of Huari traits; the architecture is similar to that of Huari, certainly very different from that of Moche. On the other hand Chimú artisans retained some of the vessel forms and some of the motifs of the Mochica culture, although the repertoire of Chimú subjects and shapes is much more limited. Sea motifs prevailed; complex ceremonial scenes were rare.

Sometime between 1462 and 1470 the Chimú conflict with the Inca began and was resolved by the inclusion of the kingdom of Chimor within the rapidly expanding Inca empire. The Chimú themselves were imperial and as highly developed as the Inca—indeed, they probably had deeper roots and longer development—but they gave in to the force of the southern highlanders. It is ironic that Chimú-style artifacts were found more widely distributed after the Inca conquest than before. This may have been related to trading or taxation networks, and/or it may have had to do with the great respect that the Inca had for Chimú craftsmanship. Chimú metalsmiths were taken to Cuzco to work for the Inca. Chimú textiles of this period, however, are inferior to earlier ones.

The south coast

On the south coast at this time there were important and interrelated cultures in the Ica and Chincha Valleys, with the Cañete Valley linked to Chincha. Clay-walled pyramids, with friezes similar to those at Chan Chan, and handsome pottery and textiles, with small, all-over, geometric designs, distinguish these cultures.

These valleys, which had been of lesser importance in Early Intermediate times, and had then been under Huari domination, apparently submitted easily to the Inca conquerors.

The adobe walls of Chan Chan have various decorative motifs. Some seem to be functional; others are decorative or symbolic. A single design is usually repeated, but sometimes the compositions are complex. These squirrel-like designs (*below*) are unusual; creatures of the sea—birds, fish and men in boats—are more common at this coastal site. Some functional patterns of ornamentation can also be seen (*bottom*), in this case open diamonds and checkerboard designs. Unfortunately most of the walls within the *ciudadelas* have been destroyed.

Chan Chan

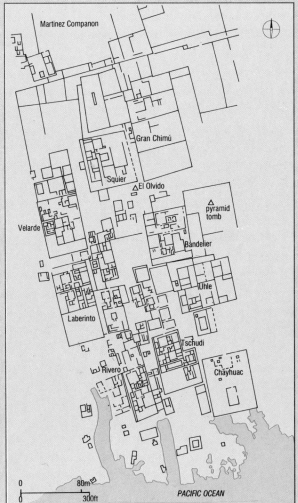

Below The *ciudadelas* were built progressing inland from the sea. Variations in the basic interior plan are shown. The enclosures, which were abandoned around 1470 AD, are named mostly for archaeologists or travelers who worked at or visited the site in the 19th century.

The great city of Chan Chan covered about 6 square kilometers, accommodating ten huge walled adobe compounds, as well as smaller elite structures and simple living quarters and workshops. The compounds are all rectangular, with an approximately north–south orientation and roughly the same inner layout. The largest compound, or *ciudadela* ("little city"), contained 221 000 square meters of floor space; the outer compound walls might be as high as nine meters, and one of the enclosure walls was 650 meters long. The thick adobe walls usually had cobblestone foundations.

These *ciudadelas*, the royal palaces of Chimú rulers, were entered by a single door in the high north wall, which opened onto a corridor leading to a vast entry court. On the south wall of this court a ramp sloped up to a long bench. Excavations in these ramps yielded burials, probably made at the dedication of the structure. The maze-like buildings of the compound included smaller courts, storerooms and *audiencias*, the latter being small, U-shaped structures, the form of which may have been a token reference to the large U-shaped coastal buildings of the ancient past. *Audiencias*, which had a floor space of 5–6 square meters, have

been described as possible centers for the distribution and control of goods. The fact that burials have been found in or near them suggests a ritual function, however, as does their shape as a house model or cosmic niche.

This entire northern section of the compound was approximately square. Attached to it, again approached through a single door in its north wall, was another enclosed square of roughly equal size, with more storerooms, a few *audiencias*, and living quarters.

The most important feature of this sector was a burial platform for the royal family, usually the last structure to be built in each compound. Nine of the ten compounds contain, at the southeast end, this truncated pyramid, within which are multiple cells, entered from above after approach through a special court. A central, larger cell must have held the body of the ruler.

The Chimú king-lists name ten kings; there are ten palatial walled structures at Chan Chan. Archaeologists today believe that each *ciudadela* was a particular king's residence and the center for administration of the great Chimú kingdom. On the demise of the ruler, his residence became his sealed mausoleum.

extent of territory under Inca rulers

▨	Manco Capac c.1220
▨	Yahuar Huacac to c.1400
▨	Pachacutec 1438-63
☐	Pachacutec and Tupac Yupanqui 1463-71
☐	Tupac Yupanqui 1471-93
☐	Huayna Capac 1493-1525

— ·— boundary of Inca empire 1525

— — boundary of empire quarter

◢◣ Inca road

■ Inca town or city

Huánuco □ known provincial capital

Lima □ modern name/modern city

— · — modern international boundary

scale 1:16 000 000

0   400km

0   300mi

PACIFIC OCEAN

Tropic of Capricorn

Left The vast Inca empire required tight organization, which was maintained partly through the use of large roadside hostels and storage depots, such as Tambo Colorado on the south coast, seen here.

THE INCA

Andean empire-building had its grand climax in the century before the arrival of the Spaniards in the New World, when the Inca empire spread from Cuzco, in the southern highlands, down into Chile and northwest Argentina and up through Ecuador. One aspect of the Inca phenomenon often noted is its brevity: the Inca state lasted for 90 years or so, and the Inca empire for little more than 50 years, before the Spaniards arrived to end it. It was, however, in the nature of Andean empires or large states to be short-lived after serious expansion. There was already fighting over accession to power at the time of the Spanish arrival.

The Inca people had started as a small chiefdom in the Cuzco area, gradually building up local strength. Sometime around 1440, after successful expansion in the neighborhood, they began more serious conquests under their ruler, the Inca Pachacutec, the "great man" of Inca history. (The word Inca originally referred to the ruler, who was considered to be the son of, or the earthly incarnation of, the sun. It has come to be applied to the conquering Quechua-speaking people.) Pachacutec also reorganized the economic and political structure of the chiefdom into a centralized, stratified state, and rebuilt Cuzco from a wood-and-thatch town to the city that so impressed the Spaniards and made Inca architecture world-famous.

The Inca are notable for many traits, but perhaps particularly for city-building and fine stonework. Their mortarless masonry of enormous, irregularly cut, pillowy stones, fitted so that a knife blade could not pass between them, is legendary. The Inca built not only Cuzco but other cities throughout the empire. Sometimes they built from scratch, sometimes they renovated existing buildings. Huge blocks of stone were laboriously quarried, pecked and hammered with stone tools, and then dragged on log rollers or sledges with ropes—by a vast amount of manpower. Ramps of earth and stone, on which the stones could be raised, were built against the wall under construction. The final cutting and grinding were accomplished with the stone in place; but the lifting, cutting and lowering must have been done many times before the perfect fit was achieved. An early chronicler, Pedro de Ondegardo, stated that it would take 20 men an entire year to dress each of some of the larger stones. The Inca had plumb-bobs, two-stick slide rules, bronze and wooden crowbars and levers, and bronze chisels (the Inca did pioneer work in bronze-casting), but the bronze tools were of little use in stone-cutting. The stone was worked with stone hammers and polished with stone or wet sand.

Much labor was expended in the construction of agricultural terraces and waterworks. Cuzco has wide valleys around it, but there is generally little flat, arable land in the Andes, so crops are grown on hillside terraces, some of remarkable steepness. The terraces were constructed with stone retaining walls and with gravel beds under the earth to ensure drainage. Stone-lined drainage systems were built through the terraces.

Social and cosmic structure

Like many ancient cities Cuzco was the "navel" of the world—such is the meaning of the name. The Inca empire was called Tahuantinsuyu, "world of the four quarters." World directions were important to pre-Columbian peoples, and the Inca were no exception. For them, however, east and west were the dominant directions, for they marked the course of the sun. The Inca tended to divide both the world concept and the populations into quarters or halves.

In theory—and to a large extent in practice—Inca society was rigidly structured. At the top of the structure was the semidivine Inca ruler. Like the empire, the city of Cuzco was divided into four quarters, and there were strict social and duty divisions for each. The quarters of Tahuantinsuyu were divided into provinces of varying sizes, with a capital in each, and the provinces were divided into moieties. The ruling officials for each of the four quarters lived in Cuzco. There was also a governor for each province. These officials were all nobles, who were likely to be relatives of the Inca ruler.

Within the provinces the population was, ideally, divided decimally and led by a hierarchy under the governor, who had responsibility for more or less 10 000 souls. Lesser officials controlled lesser decimal counts.

To make such a system work it was necessary to move peoples for various reasons. If one group seemed restless under the Inca yoke they might be moved to another place, where their opportunities for mischief-making might be fewer. If labor was needed it was moved according to the demand; the opening up of new territory or the intensification of agriculture or the use of other resources might occasion such movements. Often these groups of so-called *mitmac* labor were brought to Cuzco, where the people from one place, organized in its traditional *ayllu* or lineage and wearing the garments of their homeland, were put in a part of the city or its environs with others of their own group. They retained their own languages, but Quechua was the official language, the lingua franca. There are still Quechua place-names today as far away as Ecuador.

Taxation largely took the form of labor. In general a third of all food or goods produced went to the Inca, or to the state, a third to the gods (this probably also went to the state), and a third remained for the use of the producers.

Agriculture was, naturally, of primary importance. Inca rituals were largely geared to the agricultural calendar. The ruler himself initiated the planting season. As the population grew, and the power sphere was enlarged, the production and control of food distribution became increasingly important. The identification of the ruler with the sun may well have been a way of emphasizing politically the ruler's control over agriculture.

Records were kept by means of the *quipu*, a string, abacus-like device on which calculations could be made by making unit-value knots in decimal-value positions. These have been used in the 20th century for everyday record-keeping; in the past, they may well have had more esoteric uses, perhaps being employed for astronomical or religious purposes.

Sacred Stone

All pre-Columbian peoples seem to have had sacred or special stones, but the Inca went further with this practice than any other people. The feeling for stone seen in the architecture is reflected in myth. There are a number of variations of Inca origin myths found in 16th-century chronicles. One version tells that the creator god made men from stone. In another version, having failed to make man successfully, the creator turned the product of his experiment into stones. One story tells that the original Inca people were four brothers and four sisters who emerged through a stone door—that is, out of a cave—on an island in Lake Titicaca, not far from Tiahuanaco. (In other myths the sun was born from a sacred rock on this island.) One of the four brothers returned to the cave and was never seen again; two of the others were turned to stone; the fourth was Manco Capac, the first Inca ruler, who, having founded Cuzco, is said to have marked off the land by throwing four slingstones toward the four corners of the earth. It was believed that Manco Capac himself eventually turned to stone and, as such, was carried into battle by later Inca warriors.

All around Cuzco sacred stones fan out from the city, some plain and weathered, some natural rocks carved with step motifs, serpentine forms and other designs. These were "owned" by groups of people, and rituals were held at them.

Dramatically situated on the top of a steep hill above the Urubamba River, and surrounded by higher mountains, Machu Picchu is a strategic site on the edge of the Inca empire, but it is also a sacred place, containing many carved living rocks that the Inca considered *huaca*. The most prominent, the thronelike Intihuatana, "hitching post of the Sun," is placed at a high point, approached by steps hewn in rock (*far right*). A series of finely carved basins channels water down through the site (*right*).

Trapezoidal doors or niches, characteristic of Inca architecture, are found in fine masonry buildings of the King's Group at Machu Picchu (*above left*) and at Tambomachay, just east of Cuzco. The four niches at Tambomachay (*left*) may refer to the four brothers emerging from caves in Inca origin myth, for stone, caves and ancestors are intimately connected. The terraces and walls of this site, one of the shrines that lay along lines that radiated from Cuzco, enclose and channel a sacred spring. From early times, religious structures were built around springs. According to an early Spanish source the Inca ruler stayed at Tambomachay when hunting, an ancestor-related ritual activity. The wall supporting the niches is of finer stonework than the lower walls. Such contrasts are frequent.

Left The Inca marked nature with man's skill. Prominent natural rocks were often partially worked with precise carving. Many have a tripartite design, and the step motif was common. This rock, called the Throne of the Inca, is a feature of a large limestone outcrop, which includes other carvings—niches, stairways, and passages—as well as an unusual natural formation of igneous rock. The Throne, oriented to the east, faces Sacsahuaman, an immense structure above Cuzco, which catches the morning sun before it lights the valley below. The stone could have been a throne or altar as well as a sacred stone. Legend tells that the Inca ruler came to sit on this stone on certain occasions. Astronomical meaning has also been suggested for it.

Cuzco

Below The church of Santo Domingo was built on part of the destroyed Temple of the Sun, the Coricancha or "Golden Enclosure," the most important Inca structure, the ceremonial heart of the city. Its walls were covered with sheet gold and silver. Some of its interior spaces have now been restored.

Cuzco lies in a valley nearly 3500 meters above sea level, at the junction of the Chunchullmayo, Tullumayo and Huatanay Rivers. East of the city flow the headwaters of the Urubamba, which eventually drain into the Amazon. The valley of Cuzco is small and protected, but the river valleys give it access to the former Inca empire.

In legend, the city was founded by Manco Capac on the site that later held the Inca Temple of the Sun, and now the church of Santo Domingo. According to one early Spanish source, Pedro Sarmiento de Gamboa, the Inca ruling family lived on this site in simple houses until the city began to grow. Separate royal residences were then built.

It was Pachacutec who made the city splendid. One story tells that this Inca ruler visited the earlier city of Tiahuanaco and was so impressed by it that he rebuilt Cuzco of stone. Handsome stone architecture was, however, a highland tradition, and the architecture of Cuzco has little relationship to that of Tiahuanaco. Moreover, there were examples of fine buildings closer to home. Pikillacta, for example, is a large and handsome Huari site on the Collasuyo road, not far from Cuzco. Pachacutec built a handsome new Temple of the Sun; it is the remains of this that one sees today. He constructed stone temples, palaces for officials and a convent for the Chosen Women, who wove the finest cloth and had duties in connection with various rituals. Pachacutec also started the construction of Sacsahuaman, the magnificent temple-fortress above the city.

Pedro Sancho, Francisco de Pizarro's secretary, and Pedro de Pizarro, the nephew of the conqueror, left accounts of the city before Spanish plundering and the battles for its possession largely destroyed it. Monumental walls of enormous Inca stones cannot easily be destroyed or displaced, however, and many of them remain in Cuzco as the foundation of the modern city.

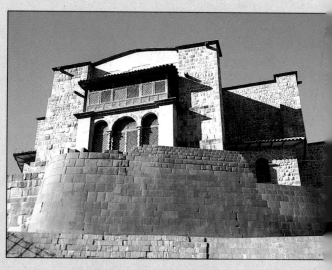

Below Illustrations by the Belgian Théodore de Bry were more European than American. Never having seen Cuzco, he drew it as a walled European city in a perfect grid. The drawing does reflect the four quarters of the Inca empire and cosmos, and the Inca did put three concentric walls around certain places; the drawing also shows the city's rivers. Cuzco was not walled, however, and its shape was not so regular.

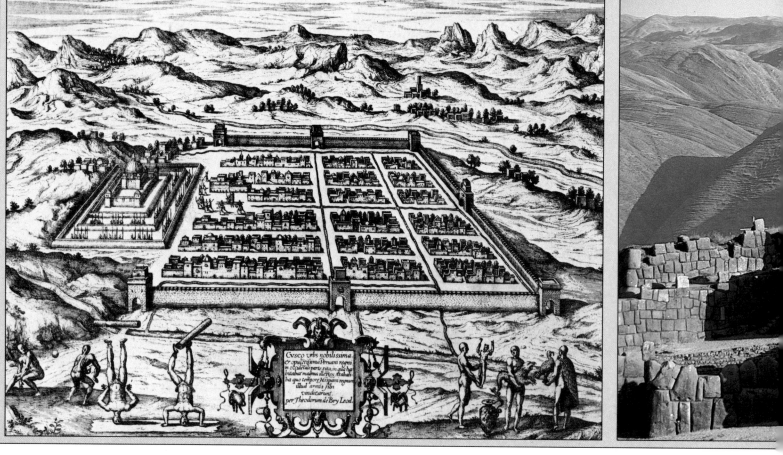

Cvsco vrbs nobilissima & opulentissima Peruani regni in occidentali parte sita, in qua hac initabat maxima ille Rex Atabalipa quo tempore Hispani regnum illud armis sibi vindicarunt per Theodorum de Bry Leod.

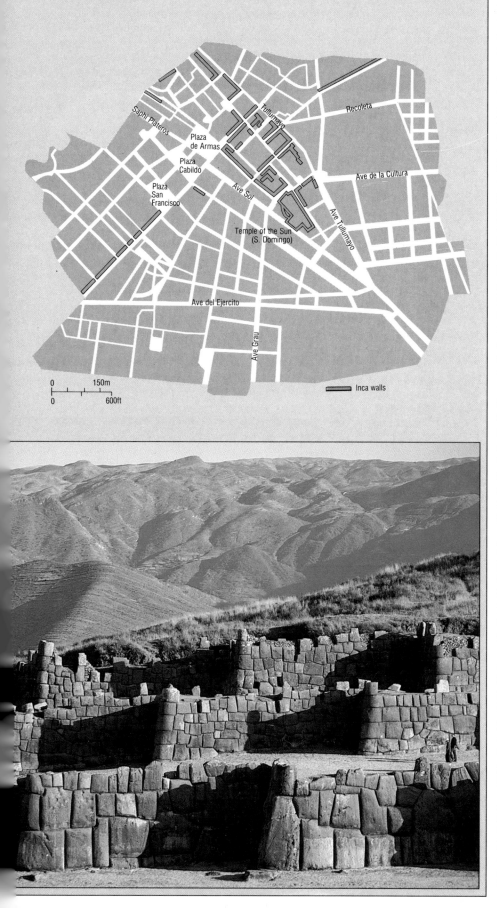

Below The colonial city of Cuzco was built on Inca remains. Much of the Inca plan survives, as do many Inca walls. Cuzco is probably the oldest continuously occupied city in the New World.

Bottom Sacsahuaman lies beyond the top center of the plan, to the west. This huge site, on a steep hill above the city, was begun by Pachacutec in the mid-15th century and almost completed by the time of the Spanish conquest. It is guarded by three immense, zigzagging walls that now stand about 16 m. high, and were once even taller. It is said that 10 000 souls—most of the population of Cuzco—could have gone inside the walls for refuge; Sacsahuaman was the scene of battles at the time of the Spanish conquest. It was also a place that was sacred to the Sun, and rites were apparently held there.

The road system

The lifeline of the Inca empire was a system of roads, the length of which is still unmeasured, but which probably totaled about 40 000 kilometers. The main road ran through the Andes from Cuzco to Quito; many Inca centers lay along it. The northern extension led to present-day southern Colombia. Another highland road went from Cuzco south into northwest Argentina and Chile, beyond Santiago. There was also a coastal road, which was connected at various points with the mountain roads, and there were roads linking all the towns.

When possible, road-builders avoided difficult terrain—high altitudes, swamps and desert—but they had remarkable ways of coping when necessary. Because wheeled traffic did not exist—there were no draft animals—construction was adapted to the geography and the use to which the road was put. Width ranged from about 1 meter to 16 meters, though in a few places the road might be wider. Sometimes a road was not formally constructed; it was merely a worn path. In many places pre-Inca roads were utilized. There were Middle Horizon roads, for "Inca" roads connected many Huari and Tiahuanaco sites, and there is some evidence for roads as far back as the Early Horizon. The Inca mountain roads sometimes narrowed along a cliff face. The coastal roads were broader and straighter, with low walls of stone, adobe or tapia, or rows of wooden posts on either side to keep out desert sands. Roads through agricultural regions were lined with high side walls. Causeways, drainage canals and stone pavements were used when the road passed through wetlands.

Inca suspension bridges over deep chasms are renowned. There were also bridges with wood or stone superstructures that rested on stone footings, a few examples of the use of natural stone bridges, and, in the region of Lake Titicaca, bridges on pontoons of reeds. In some instances the traveler was carried across a river in a basket on cables, and some streams had ferries of balsa wood, gourds or reeds. On some occasions the traveler was expected to cross water by swimming.

Along the roads were *tambos*, structures of varying sizes which served as lodgings and storage places, and were probably also seats of local administration and centers for various other activities. There were probably at least 1000 *tambos* of various sizes and architectural forms, the larger ones in the towns and smaller ones spaced at about a day's journey along the roads.

Roads were not for the use of ordinary tourists. An important means of controlling the empire, they could be traveled only on imperial orders. A royal litter might be carried on one of these roads. On them the Inca moved populations from one place to another and armies were marched to control the populations of the vast empire. Trains of llamas—each animal can carry up to 45 kilograms—carried goods from one part of the empire to another.

Overleaf This view of Machu Picchu shows its complex structures, its varied stonework and its dramatic setting. The "hitching post of the Sun" is within the masonry enclosure at center left, above agricultural terraces.

Andean Textiles

Cloth was of primary significance to the ancient Peruvians: it was a form of wealth; it was presented in exchanges between rulers; it was employed in ceremonies and given, burned or sacrificed as an offering; its use marked changes in life cycles, and it was placed in burials in great quantities. A symbolic substance, made by a symbolic process, it bore the most important religious motifs. Garments, usually woven ones, indicated status and ritual; certain clothes were worn by certain people performing certain acts on certain occasions.

Pre-Columbian Peruvian weavers, using a variety of techniques, were some of the finest in the world. The back-strap loom was the most common weaving mechanism: a narrow loom, with one end tied around the weaver's waist and the other end tied to a tree or house post.

Weaving probably began with cactus fiber used for looping and netting. Cotton is found in textiles of the 3rd millennium BC from northern Chile, Peru and Ecuador. Cotton was one of the earliest crops domesticated in the valleys of the west coast of South America. In the Central Andes an early phase is often called the Cotton Preceramic, because, although people had not yet started making pottery, they raised and used cotton. Textiles from the early Early Horizon are mostly cotton plain-weave. Toward the end of this period, camelid fibers—from llama, alpaca, guanaco or vicuña—were introduced and used for the colorful embroidery of Paracas garments (wool takes dye better than cotton) and for some of the early south-coast tapestries.

Garments were not tailored. Tunics (shirts) were woven in two rectangular, loom-width panels and stitched together at the sides and down the front, with openings left for the head and arms. This garment, through time and space, took on many variations of the basic form.

Early sources tell of the hierarchy of Inca weavers: the cloistered women who wove the finest cloth for cult images, for the Inca ruler and for ritual sacrifices; the wives of officials, who sent garments to the Inca each year; and the specialist male weavers whose labor-tax obligation was fine cloth. The keeping of camelids from whom the wool was gathered was also controlled by the government. In the late period vicuña wool was used only for the garments of the ruler himself.

When the last Inca ruler, Atahualpa, met Pizarro in Cajamarca, he is quoted as having reproved the Spaniard, saying, "I know what you have done along this road. You have taken the cloth from the temples, and I shall not leave until it has been returned to me."

In the Andes today, older Indian women still have a spindle in hand much of the time. The need to make cloth is still so deeply bred into the highland people that young women in modern dress can be seen knitting as they walk across a town plaza.

Left An embroidered creature on a garment from the Paracas Necropolis has a cat head and a bird tail. Small figures fall from the tips of its upper appendages. Within its stomach is a quadruped, which has in its stomach another creature. Paracas embroideries are full of such complex iconography.

Bottom left Large painted textiles were common on the coast in the Late Intermediate period, and a figure standing beneath a sky-band serpent is a frequent motif. This textile is 1·25 m. high.

Four-peaked caps of pile cloth—"Peruvian velvet"—are characteristic of Huari-Tiahuanaco ritual costume. This example (*below left*) is unusual because of the height of its body. Bird feathers attached to cotton plain-weave were used for special garments like this neck-piece with Chimú designs (*below*).

A Nazca mantle (*left*), 255 by 95 cm., is embroidered with figures in a single color, in contrast to the earlier Paracas mantles with multicolored embroidery. The repeated design seems to show a *huaca*, a sacred hill with plants growing out of it and a crowned head to designate its spirit; a cave entrance may reveal a spring. In front of it, two figures grab a central figure, one holding the hair—a sign of conquest in the Andes—and the other holding the wrist, perhaps to tie it. This may be a captive about to be sacrificed. A supernatural animal appears in pairs, one right side up, the other upside down. Such mantles were probably made primarily for burial. The cotton cloth would likely have been woven on a back-strap loom, like the one in the drawing (*above*), with its end tied to a tree, shown on a Moche pot.

THE SOUTHERN ANDES AND TIERRA DEL FUEGO

The archaeological area known as northwest Argentina, which was the most highly developed culture area south of the Central Andes, was composed of three regions: the Puna (high tableland), the Valliserrana (intermontane valleys) and the Selvas Occidentales (the western forests), with a cultural concentration in the intermontane valleys. Northwest Argentina was a meeting place for the people already established there with peoples and influences from northern Chile, the Central Andes, the Chaco to the east—the last were nomadic peoples with a rudimentary economy—and hunter-gatherer peoples of the Patagonian pampas regions to the southeast.

The Early or Formative period, 500 BC to 650 AD, was a time of development. In the first 300 years of this period there was incipient agriculture. After about 200 BC pottery-making and metalworking began with the early Condorhuasi culture in the central valleys and the Candelaria culture to the northeast. The Condorhuasi culture, probably a mixture of peoples of Andean origin and those of a lower cultural level from the Chaco or the tropical forest, was found in the low valleys. The craftsmen of Condorhuasi villages made modeled polychrome pottery of high quality, stone sculpture and simple pendants of gold and silver.

By the beginning of the Christian era there was a florescence of the cultures of Condorhuasi and La Candelaria, as well as of those of La Ciénaga, Tafí and others clustered in the provinces of Catamarca and Tucumán, between the forested plains of the Chaco, the eastern border of the Andes and the High Puna. In the Puna to the west the Tebenquiche culture was developing, a culture of altiplano llama shepherds and potato-planters with small villages and a relatively advanced technology of weaving and pottery. Increasing social stratification might help explain the presence of gold ornaments in this culture.

The Middle period, 650–850 AD, includes the Aguada culture, which was influenced by Tiahuanaco but had a distinct ceramic style of incised figures on rounded vessels, some of the handsomest pottery in the region. The culture also produced fine metal objects; Tiahuanaco *kero* forms were made in sheet gold or silver. New plant varieties were introduced at about this time.

A Late or Regional Development period, lasting from about 850 to 1480 AD, featured the Santa María and Belén cultures, notable for large, polychrome funerary urns. The final period was a time of Inca domination and influence (1480–1535).

The peoples of northwest Argentina had chiefdoms with confederations led by one or more leaders. A special house in the village was used as a temple, but architectural accomplishments were few. There was intensive irrigation agriculture, domestication of animals and food surpluses. Artisans painted petroglyphs and made good-quality ceramics, modeled or painted with two or three colors; they worked gold, silver, copper and bronze, and made textiles and baskets. Little is left of their wooden sculpture

Chile

The Atacama Desert of the northern Chilean coast is one of the driest places in the world. The region just south of Arica, on the far-north coast, is particularly rich archaeologically. Its cemeteries have yielded hundreds of well-preserved burials, including some with bodies mummified in highly sophisticated ways. The Chilean coast becomes semiarid at the Tropic of Capricorn, near modern Antofagasta, and moist as it approaches Chiloé Island. In the semiarid region of the central coast, near Coquimbo, in the Late period, the Diaguita culture flourished. The Araucanian Indians, who inhabited the moist coastal strip of Chile in the late periods, defied first the Inca invasion and then that of the Spaniards and Chileans. Farmers, who cleared land with stone axes and practiced slash-and-burn agriculture, cultivated maize, squash, potatoes, beans, chili peppers and quinoa. They had dugout canoes and reed rafts, and used llamas as pack animals on land. The Mapuche, one group of Araucanians, were semisedentary hunters of guanaco, deer, foxes and birds, and gatherers of plants. An early Spanish chronicler gave a vivid description of these Indians lining a riverbank, slapping the water and then, with a three-pronged pole, hooking the abundant fish.

A stone mask with geometrized features; 11 cm. high. Tafí culture of Northwest Argentina.

The Early period of hunters and gatherers had begun by about 10 000 BC with the pursuit of now extinct fauna; by about 7000 BC modern species were being hunted, gathered and fished for. Toward the end of this period a "shell/fish-hook" culture appears, remains of which have been found around Cobija. Around 3000 BC the Initial period or Chinchorro tradition began, which lasted until about 500 BC. On the coast Chinchorro is found as far south as Taltal. This preceramic culture lacked agriculture, but had basketry, hunting and fishing tools, some textiles (cotton and later wool) of natural color or with red dye, and elaborate feather and fiber headdresses.

The Intermediate period or altiplano tradition, showing contact with Tiahuanaco and southern Bolivia, lasted from that time until the late era of Inca influence and control. In the early part of this period, the Alto Ramírez phase, village sites had developed although with minimal architecture. Maize, beans, calabash and capsicum (peppers) were raised. Simple pottery was made, and weaving was advancing.

A bronze ceremonial ax from the Late or Regional Development period of Northwest Argentina.

Patagonia, Tierra del Fuego and southern Chile

Man had found his way to the furthest tip of the South American continent by at least as early as 9000 BC. Archaeologist Junius Bird found remains of early man from this approximate date on the mainland side of the Straits of Magellan, at Fell's Cave and Palliaike Cave, camping sites of hunters who used stone projectile points in the pursuit of now extinct horses and ground sloths, as well as the still-extant guanaco. Still earlier remains (of c. 9400 BC) have been found further north on the coast of Chile, at the Laguna de Tagua Tagua, a lakeside camp where hunters could wait for animals to come to drink. At about the same latitude, inland, Intihuasi Cave yielded remains dating from before 6000 BC.

Strictly defined, Tierra del Fuego is the large island north of the archipelago at the southeastern tip of South America between the Straits of Magellan and the Beagle Channel, but the name is used loosely for the entire archipelago, and the Fuegian culture continues up the archipelago of western Chile as far as Chiloé Island. Glaciers come down from the mountains to the west; the Andean slopes are densely forested; to the east, there are rolling grasslands. Charles Darwin described Tierra del Fuego as having a wretched climate with natives in a miserable condition. The climate of Tierra del Fuego, however, is not as extreme as that of some inhabited parts of the northern hemisphere. There is timber, abundant wildlife for hunting and the possibility of limited agriculture. A sizable population could be supported. Yet Indian culture there, despite its early start, remained at a very low level. Even in the 20th century there was no pottery and no weaving; the spearthrower, ax and drill were missing, as were cooking containers.

There were four Indian groups in the region, two land-oriented (Foot Indians) and two sea-oriented (Canoe Indians). Both groups were hunters and gatherers. Remarkably little clothing was worn—capes, penis sheaths, waterproof moccasins, feather-and-fiber headdresses and jewelry. For ritual occasions they painted "clothing" on themselves.

Those closest to the sea, the migratory Yahgan and Alacaluf, had canoes, paddles, bailers and mooring rope, but lacked fishhooks. They caught fish by spearing or by baiting and taking the fish by hand. Whale meat was a great delicacy, and they ate sea birds, especially ducks, and fish. They killed seals as their main food.

The nomadic Ona and the smaller group of Haúsh gathered plants and hunted (with the help of a now-extinct Fuegian dog) guanaco and foxes which they used for food and for hides to make cloaks and bags. Windbreaks were constructed of hide or bark supported by poles. Sea mammals were hunted from the shore, and fish were gathered from pools at low tide. Ona myth closely resembles that of peoples to the north: there was a creator god or a first man, who became a god at the origin of the world and created certain elements in it. This mythic pattern is found throughout much of the New World. Ona origin myth also tells of the first people coming down from the sky on a rope, a myth also found among peoples to the north. To the northwest the Chono hunted and gathered seafood along the Chilean shore. They also wore little clothing, but had long cloaks of guanaco hide and waterproof moccasins.

Patagonia lies north of Tierra del Fuego and east of the Andes. Here dry plateaus flatten out into the pampas, the grasslands to the north. These prairies were the homeland of the Puelche and Tehuelche, small nomadic bands of 50–150 people who hunted guanaco, fox and small game. These Indians had stone tools for preparing skins and for weapons. They decorated hide mantles, made masks and baskets, and carved objects from bone. Like their neighbors to the south they painted themselves. Some of the later groups made a little pottery of poor quality.

Since the beginning of the 20th century, the Indian populations have been virtually eliminated. Like many other Indian groups, the Fuegians were wiped out by the Europeans and their diseases.

PART SIX
THE LIVING HERITAGE

Clash of Cultures

It can be argued that contact between Indian and European cultures still continues, and that divisions remain deep. However, the contacts of the 16th century were special, for they were sporadic and involved cultures that had no prior experience upon which to base mutual understanding. The cultures of America and those of Europe (there were many on both continents) were founded on very different and often conflicting principles. Initial contacts were often soured in the eyes of all parties by misunderstood gestures and inadvertent offenses.

The exchange of goods was seen by most Europeans as commerce, by most Indians as reciprocity. Soon, however, each side adapted to the customs of the other. European traders began manufacturing the goods most desired by the Indians, goods such as brass kettles, beads, guns and axes. For their part the Indians stepped up the hunting of fur-bearing animals in order to supply the Europeans with what they wanted.

It was inevitable that the Europeans would seek to acquire and settle Indian lands. The process was rapid in the Caribbean. The empires of Mexico and Peru fell to the Spanish soon thereafter. But it took a century or longer for other parts of the Americas to come under European domination. Exploration and tentative attempts at colonization sparked the sporadic epidemics that would eventually grow and engulf the Indian nations. The Europeans brought diseases that had been spawned centuries earlier in the Eastern Hemisphere, often mutations from diseases of the much more numerous domesti-

cated animal species found there. The diseases, to which the European populations had already gradually adapted, struck the American Indians forcefully, sometimes in concert. Such afflictions as smallpox and other crowd infections were able to reduce Indian populations by as much as 90 percent over the next century or two. Thus the clash of cultures was not played out just in social and political terms; unintentional biological warfare played a major role.

Sixteenth-century engravers in Europe borrowed heavily from graphic sources coming from all parts of the Americas. This illustration of a massacre of Indians in their village (*left*) could easily illustrate any of several narratives of such events from both American continents.

Some South American Indian cultures have persisted relatively untouched until recently (*top left*). However, the mixed blessings of attention from traders and missionaries have undermined traditional culture,

and disease has reduced their numbers even in recent decades.

An engraving illustrating treatment of natives in 16th-century Virginia (*above*) borrows from South American sources. Curers use fumigation and shamanistic techniques to combat unknown disease—fundamentally not unlike European practices of the same time.

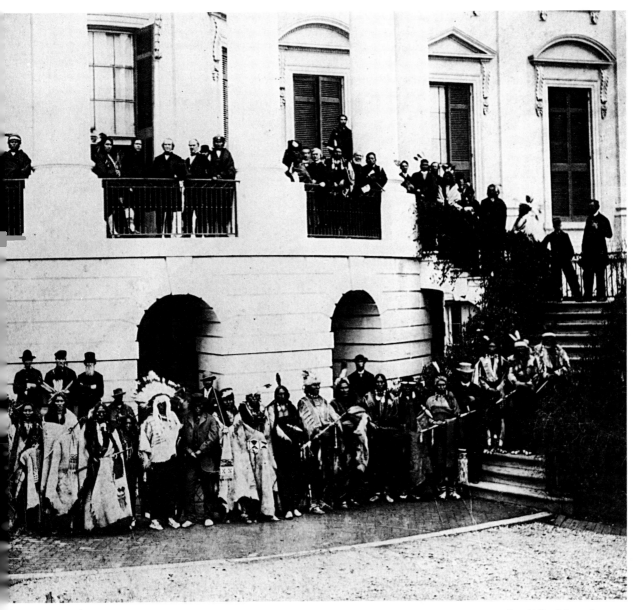

Below This ridicule pole is a poignant reminder that sanctions often fail to work across cultural boundaries. In this case, a white trader (seen here at the top of the pole) is ridiculed for having cheated—a powerful device for social control within this Northwest Coast culture, but one having no effect on the departed trader.

By the middle of the 19th century the US government was dealing regularly with the Indian nations of the West. Most, but not all, of the Indian wars were past, and treaty protocol was well established. Occasionally Indian delegations visited Washington, D.C. Here (*above*) a delegation of Indians visits President Andrew Johnson at the White House in 1867.

The U.S. constitution forbids states and other public and private entities from entering into separate treaties with Indian nations, and requires that Indian nations be treated as if they were sovereign even though they may live entirely within the United States. These provisions have led to the invalidation of several treaties between particular states and Indian nations, and cases to settle land and other claims made by modern Indian nations may still be in litigation when the 20th century ends.

Eskimo communities were among the last to experience pervasive conversion of traditional culture. Many traditions continue, but motorboats and snowmobiles have largely replaced the dogsleds and kayaks photographed by early explorers (*left*).

Eskimo Life

The Eskimos and their Aleut relatives are relatively recent arrivals, having moved into the American Arctic from Siberia between 4000 and 5000 years ago. They were and are distinct from American Indians in many ways—biologically, linguistically and culturally. They brought with them an advanced lithic technology, which they elaborated as necessary to allow them to penetrate the hostile and treeless Arctic.

Eskimo technology has been described as gadget-ridden. In some cases, as with the toggling harpoon, the kayak and the dog sled, their tools are highly sophisticated, to the point that they could probably not be substantially improved within the constraints of traditional raw materials. Some implements, like the wolf-killer or the sealskin float, are simple but ingenious. The wolf-killer is a double-pointed strip of whale baleen, coiled and frozen in a lump of blubber; when gulped down by a hungry wolf it melts, springs open and kills the animal. The sealskin float is used by kayakers on harpoon tethers; harpooned seals and walrus pull

against the float rather than fragile kayaks until they tire and die.

Clever tools, oil lamps and sea mammals allowed bands of Eskimos to penetrate and survive in the world's most hostile environment. The adaptation allowed little room for error, but the long Arctic night provided time for amusement and crafts.

Eskimo life has proved resistant to 20th-century pressures but modern equipment has largely replaced traditional tools.

Right Polar Eskimos use dog teams to haul killed walruses onto the ice for butchering. Above the tree line harnesses allowed the dogs to fan out as shown here. Where trees might split the team and wreck the sled, dogs were harnessed in a more complicated arrangement of pairs in tandem. Strong dogs were essential, particularly in winter, and it is doubtful that any prehistoric culture could have adapted to the Arctic without this tough breed.

Below Birds were taken for food and feathers by several means: spears, nets and even bolas were used to kill or capture them.

Below The bow drill permits the quick drilling of precise narrow holes in tough materials. Before the introduction of trade iron, Eskimo craftsmen used stone, copper and meteoric iron for bits. In this early 20th-century photograph a man drills holes in a walrus ivory cribbage board.

Below right The snow house is only one kind of igloo, but the ingenious snow and ice structure is the form that most captures the imagination of non-Eskimos. Skin tenting, sod and rock served in other seasons, for even in the Arctic winter does not last forever.

Left A man waits motionless at the edge of the ice. With a short stick in one hand he bobs a lure to attract char, an Arctic relative of trout. The other hand holds a leister like the spare in the foreground. A central spine will impale the fish while the two arms of the device spread to trap the fish. Spines set backwards in the arms prevent the fish from wriggling free.

Above A modern Greenland Eskimo scoops an auk out of the air with a long-handled net. Greenland Eskimos descend from the great Thule Eskimo expansion eastward across the American Arctic. The expansion 1000 years ago also drew the Norse westward to Greenland, but only the Eskimos stayed in the long run.

Hopi Ritual Drama

How is it that the approximately 6500 Hopi survive as a viable cultural group in a modern nation-state of 231 million people? The answer cannot be a tight-knit political organization, for each of the Hopi villages is essentially self-governing, with its own village chief and its system of matrilineal, landholding clans. What really holds this culture and society together is a ceremonial cycle of ritual dramas in which virtually every Hopi is a participant, and the religious and philosophical underpinning to the dramas.

Basic to Hopi ceremonialism are the kachinas; these are spirits of the benevolent dead, that is ancestors, impersonated by masked dancers. There are about 335 different kachinas, each with a distinct personality and mask, living in their own supernatural village with their own chiefs. They arrive in each Hopi village in December, and spend the winter, spring and part of the summer with the people, blessing them and ensuring rain for the crops. Finally, in July they return to the Kachina Village in the mountains.

The underground heart of everything Hopi is the kiva, a rectangular chamber with a ladder in the roof to the world above. The kiva is the Earth Mother, and a hole in its floor (the *sipapu*) the Place of Emergence through which the Hopi ascended from previous worlds. Most ritual dramas begin in the village kiva, and some end in it. Succcess of the prayers offered before kiva altars is ensured by the use of feathered pray-sticks, sacred cornmeal and tobacco.

As in other Pueblos, clowns are an integral part of the performance. Painted in black-and-white horizontal stripes, they provide ribald humor, mimicry, burlesque and cutting social comment, sometimes at the expense of white spectators. They are an important safety valve for "letting off steam" in this highly conformist society.

All ceremonies and public dances are announced by a Crier Chief. In kachina dances the chanting participants are led into the plaza by "grandfather," accompanied by drummers, all moving counter-clockwise with the dance leader at the center; in purely social dances the singers and the drummers remain separate.

In contrast to what happened in post-conquest Mesoamerica, Pueblo ritual drama is almost purely indigenous, with little or no Spanish influence or syncretism. We have here not only a direct descendant of the religion and ceremonies of the Classic Pueblo period of the American Southwest, but also an indication—on a smaller scale—of what the great calendrical performances of Aztec Tenochtitlan might have been like before 1521.

Right During alternate years the Flute and Snake Societies hold important rituals to bring rain clouds to the village, and to ensure water for the tanks and cisterns. The Flute ceremony begins here at the main village spring, with two Flute Maidens and the Flute Boy, followed by the Flute Priests.

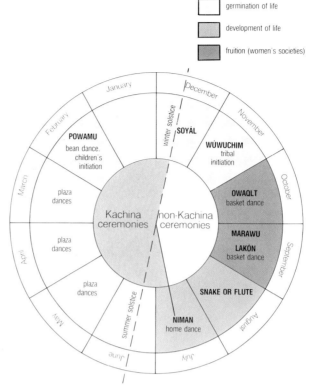

THE HOPI CEREMONIAL CALENDAR

☐ germination of life

☐ development of life

☐ fruition (women's societies)

Left The Hopi year of ritual dramas is set by the sun and the stars. It begins with Wúwuchim, a 16-day ceremony celebrating the creation of the universe, during which a New Fire ritual is performed by various religious societies in their own kivas, and young men are given final initiation. At Winter Solstice, during Soyal, the first kachina suddenly appears in the village, masked in a turquoise helmet and tottering like a very young child; he, and the ceremony, symbolize new life being reborn. Powamu ("purification") marks the last of three phases of the creation of germination ceremonies. Bean seeds are forced in the kivas and miraculously sprout in the dead of winter; this is also the time when Hopi boys and girls are initiated into the tribal societies by the kachinas.

In July, when the maize and other crops are ripening, a great dance is held to mark the return of the kachinas to their own home. In mid-August the spectacular Snake or Flute ceremonies are held in the alternate years to ensure rain for the crops.

Finally, in September and October it is time for the women's societies, which also play a part in curing, to mark the fruition and harvesting of the crops by their own dances. It has been forbidden since 1911 to take photographs of Hopi sacred performances. However, around the turn of the century a few non-Hopi visitors did manage to make photographic records, usually of the Snake Dance. From 1904 to 1906 a young man named Joseph Mora, who was also a talented watercolor artist, took a remarkably fine series of views of Hopi ritual drama, some of which are shown here.

Below Niman is a 16-day ceremony held in July, in which the kachinas dance for the last time in the year, before returning to their spirit home. They will not return to the villages until December. Here in the plaza at Walpi a line of green-faced Kuwan Heheya kachinas, their masks marked with rain clouds, dance to the music of rasps. They are watched by a group of striped Hano clowns.

212

Below Led by the Kaletaka, or warrior, the Flute Society procession wends its way up the mesa flank. As the chanting group enters the village plaza, they will walk over symbolic rain clouds drawn in sacred white cornmeal.

Above During or after the Powamu rite, a group of monsters appears in the village, visiting each house to demand food, and terrorizing children who have misbehaved by threatening to eat them. They are seen here calling down a kiva hatch for the kiva chief to give them fresh meat, or they will devour him too.

Below In the autumn the three women's societies celebrate the fruition of the crops by dances and by the public distribution of food and household goods. This Basket Dance is being held by the Lakón Society in the plaza at Walpi, on First Mesa. To the right can be seen Snake Rock, a natural formation.

Below Hopi kachinas of the Powamu or "Bean-planting" ceremony, photographed in 1893. These are the most important actors in the Bean Dance, which is performed in February, generally late at night. Although the kachinas are both male and female, the roles of the latter are acted out by men.

Right A mid-19th-century wooden Hopi doll, c. 20 cm. high. Its eyes represent the rain clouds and its eyelashes the rain.

WALPI   Hopi village

☐   Eastern Pueblo

■   Western Pueblo

limit of Hopi reservation

limit of Navajo reservation

land over 2000m

road

☐   modern town or city

scale 1:3 000 000

0   80km

0   60m

The origin legend of the Hopi

All Pueblo societies have their origin myths. These are the unwritten charters for ceremonial and social behavior. Similar to other New World peoples, such as the Aztec, the Hopi (an abbreviation of Hopituh Shinumu, "The Peaceful People"), believe that there have been earlier, imperfect underworlds or creations, and that their ancestors have passed through these in succession, in the case of the Hopi through a *sipapu* or world-vagina. Each underworld is associated with a specific direction, color, mineral, plant and bird. This concept is probably of Asiatic origin.

The first world, "Endless Space," was a pure and happy universe containing the First People. However, it was eventually destroyed by fire as dissension and war, so alien to the Hopi ethic, took place. In the second world, "Dark Midnight," on account of renewed conflict, the universe was brought to an end by cold and ice, the Chosen People surviving in an anthill. These climbed up a ladder into the third world, but the same scenario again took place, with great floods as the destructive force; Spider Woman saved the ancestors by hiding them in reeds and floating them to dry land. In the fourth world, our own, "The World Complete," Masau'u the Fire God and the giver and taker of life is caretaker. This emergence through the *sipapu* saw the migration of the Hopi clans to the mesa-top villages where they are found today.

Below: Indian Pueblos and the Hopi and Navajo reservations.
There are actually eight Hopi villages, distributed on three mesas; only four villages are shown here. Zuni is the largest of the Pueblos, with a population in 1970 of 5460. The total Pueblo population is more than 35 000. In contrast, there were over 125 000 Navajos in 1970, and their number is rapidly increasing.

Taos is the northeasternmost of the Eastern Pueblos, and is situated near the southern edge of the Great Plains. In fact, the Taos people have taken over some aspects of Plains culture, in certain features of costume, music and dance; there is even a small herd of buffalo on the Pueblo's lands.

Right Hopi kachina "dolls" are given to children not to play with, but so that they may recognize them in real performances. This is a "doll" depicting the Hemis kachina, the principal character in the Niman Kachina dance.

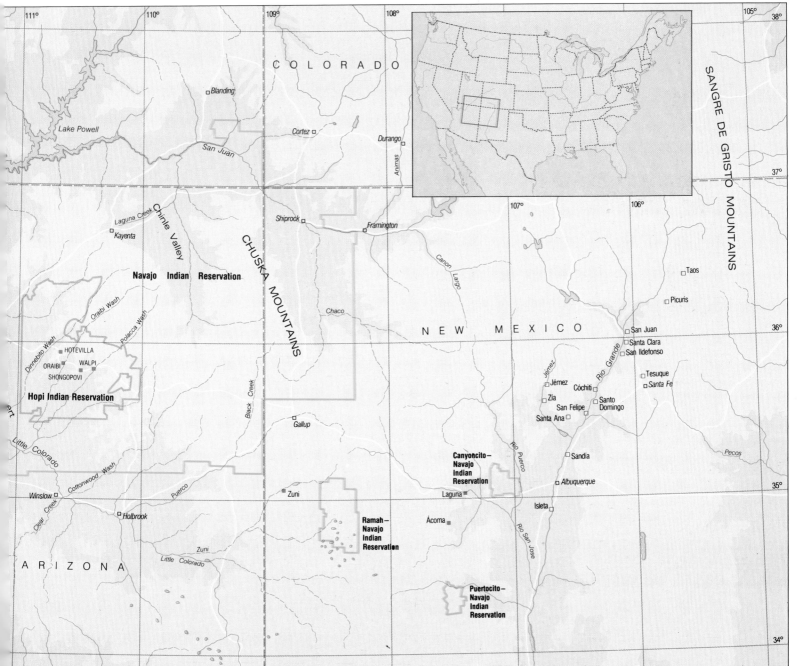

Life on the Plains

The colorful mounted nomadic tribes of the Great Plains are comparatively recent cultural developments. Horses were not available to American Indians until they began to escape or be stolen from 16th-century Spanish outposts in the Southwest. However, by the 18th century many tribes had adopted the horse, and had adapted to full- or part-time buffalo-hunting and a nomadic way of life on the vast grasslands of the West.

As the native cultures of the Prairies and Plains were developing, Euro-American attitudes about American Indians were also changing. By the early 19th century romanticized positive images had replaced earlier more negative attitudes. As the West opened up to exploration and immigration, these new developments converged, and the scene was set for the establishment of the myth of the Plains Indian as the romantic archetype of all American Indian culture.

Nineteenth-century painters, for example, Karl Bodmer and George Catlin, and later photographers traveled with early explorers and brought their romantic vision to their Indian subjects. The paintings, drawings, and photos that resulted are often our only visual access to these cultures.

Above An engraving of a Plains village after a painting by the Swiss painter Karl Bodmer (1809–93). He accompanied the German prince Maximilian of Wied-Neuwied on an expedition up the Missouri River in 1833.

Far left George Catlin (1796–1872) painted Mah-to-toh-pah (Four Bears), second chief of the Mandan, in 1832. Small painted figures and locks of human hair on his shirt tell us that he had killed or scalped several enemies. A painted hand indicates that he had killed an enemy in hand-to-hand combat.

Left Mandan and other Plains tribes conducted buffalo dances to draw the animals magically to the hunters. Young men danced day and night, relieving each other from time to time, until scouts announced that bison were in range.

Right A Minnetaree (Hidatsa) scalp dance depicted by Bodmer. The Hidatsa remained settled farmers but maintained many of the cultural conventions of the Plains nomads.

Ritual Masks of the Northwest Coast

Below This shaman's rattle shows more of the curvilinear embellishment commonly found in Northwest Coast art. Such rattles were commonly made in two hemispherical pieces, their two half-round handles being lashed together to form one.

Right This northern Kwakiutl mask is unusual for its simple lines and lack of painted decoration. It might represent a heavenly body.

The abundant vegetation of the Northwest Coast permitted the development of large villages without there being even simple horticulture. The temperate rain forests of the region supplied cedar trees that could be felled and split into broad planks with wedges and mauls. Thus in spite of lacking both domesticated animals and plants and iron tools the Northwest Coast Indians built large communities of substantial wood houses.

Before contact with Europe, iron tools may have been fabricated from pieces found in Pacific flotsam. After contact, iron tools of European manufacture quickly gained acceptance and there followed an explosion of creativity. Many of the works produced retain their vitality.

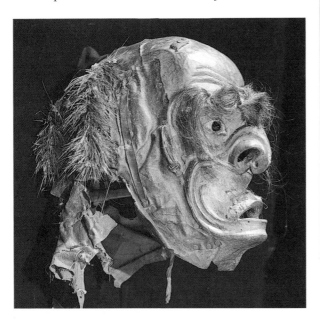

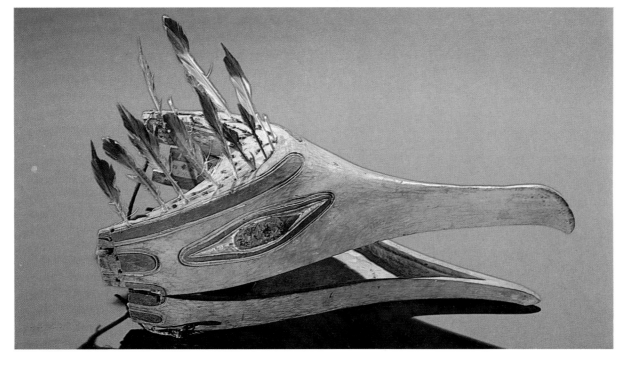

Above left Most Northwest Coast Indians feared the ghosts of the dead. Even the ghosts of people who were beloved while alive were feared. This fascination gained expression in the rituals of the Kwakiutl dancing societies. This mask represents Bowkus, the chief of the dead.

Left The Indian world of the Northwest Coast was full of supernatural beings. Public rituals frequently depicted these beings within the larger theme of supernatural experience, turning belief into theater. This Nootka bird mask with its movable jaw gave substance to a supernatural being in public performance.

Below This unpainted grave effigy from a village near Kitimat, British Columbia, has the look of driftwood. The Kwakiutl piece deliberately conveys the essence of death in the treatment of eyes and mouth.

Bottom A painted Bella Coola mask illustrates the curvilinear motifs that abound in Northwest Coast art. Although there is a tendency for all available space to be filled, the design seems to flow uncluttered.

Survivals
Everyday Life:

In many parts of Latin America, ancient basic patterns are reflected today. Important plants remain much the same, and ways of processing them have changed little. Introduced domestic animals have made some differences. For example, in the Andes, llamas have been largely replaced by sheep, and there are generally many more animals for food. Yet Indians are not heavy meat-eaters.

Markets exist almost everywhere, selling vegetables, fruits, herbs, pottery and other goods of ancient markets. Women are sometimes seen carrying produce to market in baskets or bundles on their heads. In larger towns, modern mass-produced articles or bright-colored synthetics are also sold, but the old things are basic.

In the highlands of both Mesoamerica and the Andes weaving is important. Many regions still produce idiosyncratic designs and garments that identify the wearer—and often the weaver.

Simple architecture has changed little. Thatch is still a prevalent roofing material; cane and adobe are used. A few Inca bridges are in use, and some roads, perhaps pre-Inca, are traveled.

These things occur in underdeveloped regions, it is true. It is also true that things are often done in ancient ways because that is how they are done best. Past methods are still valid. Practical criteria to do with environment or materials long ago determined methods that remain effective today.

An early drawing by Guaman Poma shows the Inca ruler initiating the spring planting (*above*). He and the men behind him use a foot-plow, related to the Mesoamerican digging stick. Contemporary farmers (*right*) are seen with a foot on the same kind of curved tool on an agricultural terrace in Peru. Similar implements are still used in many places in the Americas, for in conditions of shallow soil, these simple implements work better than the plow we know.

Carrying objects with a tumpline—a cloth around the brow and down over the shoulders—is an ancient method that is still used. The 17th-century drawing (*left*) shows sacks being carried to storage during Inca times. (The foreground chickens, introduced by the Spaniards, are anachronistic.) Faraway, in the highlands of Chiapas, Mexico, a modern Maya woman carries her firewood in the same way (*above*).

Far left A typical Indian market occurs once a week in Chinchero, a town near Cuzco, which has extensive Inca stone ruins and was once an important gathering place. The women wear distinctive hats with a four-quarters-of-the-world design.

Left A rarer custom today is face- and body-painting, a trait formerly more widespread. Like the first Indians Columbus saw, many Amazonian groups wear no clothing but have brightly painted bodies. In most cases, body paint is applied only on special occasions. For feasts, Yanomamö women paint themselves with red designs.

Grinding tables, or *metates*, can take many forms (*below*). The basic household job of grinding maize for tortillas or gruel is usually carried out by women. *Metates* are normally smaller than this one and used by only one person. Grinding stones also come in many shapes. The rough stones held here pulverize the substance they are rocked across. Hallucinogenic drugs for ritual use are sometimes ground by shamans on a *metate*.

The back-strap loom, in ancient times the most commonly used weaving device in the Andes (*left*), is still in service today (*far left*). The woman here works in conservative Chinchero, which has unusual, Inca-cut rocks. Such looms are in use in many places today. They are easily portable, and one end can be tied to any convenient vertical.

Survivals: Rituals

A striking aspect of ritual survival in Latin America is its intermeshing with Catholicism. There are many elements in the mixture, some of them used by early missionaries to facilitate conversion—for example, the cross, a significant Maya symbol. The Sun—anciently an important god throughout Latin America—is merged with Jesus Christ in many Indian minds. The Virgin Mary is often identified with the Moon (by the Maya) or with the Earth Goddess (in the Andes). The Thunder God was important to the Inca; this god is now confused with Saint James, Santiago, the patron of the gunpowder-equipped Spanish soldiers. Feast days of saints are celebrated at churches with masked dances.

There are also rites held away from the churches. Early Spanish accounts report that offerings and sacrifices were made to sacred places at certain times in the year. There are still such places—mountains, springs, caves—and offerings and sacrifices are still made to them, often in connection with Christian ceremonies. Mountains are particularly sacred. The high, young mountains of the New World produce earthquakes and volcanic eruptions. The earth trembles and the stones move by themselves. The mountainside falls in a cascade of water and rocks, or the sky explodes with the fire of a volcano.

In addition to the animism that catastrophe lends to nature, the basic cosmological frame is still there. The Sun rises from the sacred mountains, where rituals are still held, and dies in the west, the place of the dead.

The Inca presented to *huacas*, or sacred places, offerings—often burned—of fermented maize liquor, food, cloth and coca. Llamas were among the most important offerings (*above*), and they are still sacrificed in certain rituals—for example, those to mountain gods. At El Calvario, a hill above La Paz (*right*), people come to burn incense and pray, raising the fragrant smoke and other offerings toward the snow-capped mountains across the valley.

The Tarahumara Indians of northern Mexico stage a Holy Week Dance of the Pharisees (*far left*). They paint their bodies and wear turkey- or chicken-feather crowns as they dance with a stuffed Judas figure to the sound of drums and reed whistles. Food is offered to the saints in the church.

In festival dances throughout Mesoamerica, dancers wear the costumes of anciently important animals, deer, monkeys, and—the most powerful one—the jaguar, the great predator of the lowland rain forests. In Guerrero two jaguar-suited men engage in mock combat (*left*).

November, known as Ayamarca to the Inca, was the month of the dead, when mummies were removed from their resting-places and carried on litters in procession (*above*). For the living, the litter indicated high status; its use for the dead demonstrates the sacredness of ancestors. In the Christian world, 1 November is the Day of the Dead, celebrated with particular vividness in Mexico.

Like the officers of most peoples in the world, New World officials carried staffs of office in the past, and still do today. An officer of Upper Cuzco was also related to the Inca (*above*), for he wears an Inca crown and partly royal garments. In the highlands of modern Chiapas, Tzotzil Maya officials wear beribboned hats and formal clothing as they carry their staffs through the town (*top*).

The town of Paucartambo, near Cuzco, celebrates the Festival of the Virgin on 15 July (*left*). The statue of the Virgin is removed from the church and paraded under an Inca parasol of macaw feathers. Masked dancers accompany her procession. One dance performed at Paucartambo has dancers in old Spanish costumes holding ropes; cords were used in ancient Andean dances. The Virgin is associated with Mamapacha, the Inca earth goddess. The remains of Inca *chulpas*, or tombs, can still be seen at Paucartambo.

LIST OF ILLUSTRATIONS

ACKNOWLEDGMENTS
Equinox would like to thank Sue Scott of the Institute of Archaeology, University of London, and John Fisher of the University of Liverpool for their assistance. Elizabeth Benson would like to thank Patricia Anawalt, Elizabeth Boone, Richard Cooke, Hernan Crespo Toral, Alban Eger, Olga Fisch, Olaf Holm, Julie Jones, Nancy Mason, Gordon McEwen, Presley Norton, Michael Snarskis and George Stuart for aiding her research.

LIST OF ILLUSTRATIONS

BIBLIOGRAPHY

Part One: The New World
G. Ashe, T. Heyerdahl, H. Ingstad, J. V. Luce, B. J. Meggars and B. L. Wallace, *The Quest for America*. New York 1971.
J. D. Jennings (ed.), *Ancient Native Americans*. San Francisco 1978.
B. Landström, *Columbus*. New York 1967.
M. Magnusson and H. Pálson (trans.), *The Vinland Sagas: The Norse Discovery of America*. Baltimore 1965.
R. L. Wauchope, *Lost Tribes and Sunken Continents*. Chicago 1974.
G. R. Willey, *An Introduction to American Archaeology*, vol. 1 *North and Middle America*, vol. 2 *South America*. Englewood Cliffs, N.J. 1966.
G. R. Willey and J. A. Sabloff, *A History of American Archaeology*. San Francisco 1974.

Part Two: The First Americans
A. L. Bryan, *Paleo-American Prehistory*. Pocatello, Idaho 1965.
A. L. Bryan (ed.), *Early Man in America from a Circum-Pacific Perspective*. Edmonton, Alberta 1978.
D. Dincauze, "An archaeo-logical evaluation of the case for pre-Clovis occupations," *Advances in New World Archaeology*, vol. 3, pp. 276–323, 1984.
J. E. Ericson *et al* (eds.), *Peopling of the New World*. Los Altos, Calif. 1982.
W. S. Laughlin and A. B. Harper (eds.), *The First Americans: Origins, Affinities and Adaptations*. New York 1979.
K. Macgowan and J. A. Hester, Jr, *Early Man in the New World*. Garden City, N.Y. 1962.
R. S. MacNeish, "Early man in the New World," *American Scientist*, vol. 63, no. 3, pp. 316–27. New Haven 1976.
P. S. Martin and H. E. Wright, Jr, *Pleistocene Extinctions: The Search for a Cause*. New Haven 1967.
I. Rouse. "Peopling of the Americas," *Quarternary Research*, vol. 6, pp. 597–612, 1976.
Scientific American, *Early Man in America*. San Francisco 1973.

Part Three: North America
L. M. Alex, *Exploring Iowa's Past: A Guide to Prehistoric Archaeology*. Iowa City 1980.
J. B. Billard (ed.), *The World of the American Indian*. Washington, D.C. 1974.
D. S. Brose, J. A. Brown and D. W. Penney, *Ancient Art of the American Woodland Indians*. New York 1985.
L. Campbell and M. Mithun (eds.), *The Languages of Native America: Historical and Comparative Assessment*. Austin, Tex. 1979.
J. L. and K. K. Chartkoff, *The Archaeology of California*. Stanford, Calif. 1984.
L. S. Cordell, *Prehistory of the Southwest*. New York 1984.
—— "Southwest Archaeology," *Annual review of Anthropology*, vol. 13, pp. 301–332, 1984.
D. Damas (ed.), *Arctic*, Handbook of North American Indians, vol. 5. Washington, D.C. 1984.
P. Druker, *Cultures of the North Pacific Coast*. San Francisco, Calif. 1965.
P. S. Essenpreis, "Fort Ancient Settlement: Differential Response at a Mississippian–Late Woodland Interface," in B. D. Smith (ed.), *Mississippian Settlement Patterns*. Orlando, Fla. 1978.
W. W. Fitzhugh and S. A. Kaplan, *Inua: Spirit World of the Bering Sea Eskimo*. Washington, D.C. 1982.
F. and M. E. Folsom, *America's Ancient Treasures*. Albuquerque, NM 1983.
H. S. Gladwin, *A History of the Ancient Southwest*. Portland, Me. 1957.
J. B. Griffin, "Eastern North American Archaeology: A Summary," *Science*, vol. 156, pp. 175–191, 1967.
W. G. Haag, "The Bering Strait Land Bridge," *Scientific American*, 1962.
C. W. Hibbard *et al.*, "Quaternary Mammals of North America." in H. E. Wright, Jr, and D. G. Frey (eds.), *The Quaternary of the United States*. Princeton, N.J. 1965.
B. Hayden, "Research and Development in the Stone Age: Technological Transitions among Hunter-Gatherers," *Current Anthropology*, vol. 22, pp. 519–548, 1981.

R. F. Heizer (ed.), *California*, Handbook of North American Indians, vol. 8. Washington, D.C. 1978.
J. Helm (ed.), *Subarctic*, Handbook of North American Indians, vol. 6. Washington, D.C. 1981.
C. Hudson, *The Southeastern Indians*. Knoxville, Tenn. 1976.
A. S. Ingstad, *The Discovery of a Norse Settlement in America*. New York 1977.
J. D. Jennings, *Prehistory of North America*. New York 1974.
J. D. Jennings (ed.), *Ancient Native Americans*. San Francisco, Calif. 1978.
R. Kirk and R. D. Daugherty, *Exploring Washington Archaeology*. Seattle, Wa. 1978.
A. L. Kroeber, *Cultural and Natural Areas of Native North America*. Berkeley, Calif. 1963.
D. J. Lehmer, *Introduction to Middle Missouri Archaeology*. Washington, D.C. 1971.
R. H. and F. C. Lister, *Chaco Canyon*. Albuquerque, NM 1981.
R. J. Mason, *Great Lakes Archaeology*. Orlando, Fla. 1981.
J. T. Milanich and C. H. Fairbanks, *Florida Archaeology*. Orlando, Fla. 1980.
—— and S. Proctor (eds.), *Tacachale: Essays on the Indians of Florida and Southeastern Georgia during the Historic Period*. Gainesville, Fla. 1978.
W. N. Morgan, *Prehistoric Architecture in the Eastern United States*. Cambridge, Mass. 1980.
D. F and P. A. Morse, *Archaeology of the Central Mississippi Valley*. New York 1982.
A. Ortiz (ed.), *Southwest*, Handbook of North American Indians, vol. 9. Washington, D.C. 1979.
—— *Southwest*, Handbook of North American Indians, vol. 10. Washington, D.C. 1983.
J. Pfeiffer, "America's First City," *Horizon*, vol. 16, pp. 58–63, 1974.
D. B. Quinn (ed.), *North American Discovery Circa 1000–1612*. Columbia, S.C. 1971.
W. A. Ritchie, *The Archaeology of New York State*, Harrison, N.Y. 1980.
V. E. Shelford, *The Ecology of North America*. Urbana, Ill. 1963.
B. D. Smith (ed.), *Mississippian Settlement Patterns*. Orlando, Fla. 1978.
D. R. Snow, *The Archaeology of new England*. Orlando, Fla. 1980.
—— *The Archaeology of North America*, New York 1976. (Published in London as *North American Indians: Their Archaeology and Prehistory*.)
R. F. Spencer and J.D. Jennings (eds.), *The Native Americans*. New York 1977.
E. G. Squier and E. H. Davis, *Ancient Monuments of the Mississippi Valley, Comprising the Results of Extensive Original Surveys and Explorations*. Washington, D.C. 1874; reprinted New York 1965.
J. B. Stoltman "Temporal Models in Prehistory: An Example from Eastern North America," *Current Anthropology*, vol. 19, pp. 703–746, 1978.
J. B. Stoltman and D. A. Baerreis, "The Evolution of Human Ecosystems in the Eastern United States" in H. E. Wright, Jr (ed.), *Late-Quaternary Environments of the United States, Vol. 2, The Holocene*. Minneapolis, Minn. 1983.
G. E. Stuart, "Mounds: Riddles from the Indian Past," *National Geographic*, vol. 142, pp. 783–801, 1972.
B. G. Trigger (ed.), *Northeast*, Handbook of North American Indians, vol. 15. Washington, D.C. 1978.
W. R. Wood, *The Origins of the Hidatsa Indians: A Review of Ethnohistorical and Traditional Data*. Lincoln, Neb. 1980.
J. V. Wright, *Ontario Prehistory: An Eleven-Thousand-Year Archaeological Outline*. Ottawa 1972.
—— *Quebec Prehistory*. Ottawa 1979.

Part Four: Mesoamerica
A. F. Aveni, *Skywatchers of Ancient Mexico*. Austin 1980.
E. P. Benson, The Maya World. New York 1967.
—— (ed.), *The Olmec and Their Neighbors*. Washington, D.C. 1981.
I. Bernal, The Olmec World. Berkeley and Los Angeles, Calif. 1967.
R. E. Blanton, *Monte Albán: Settlement Patterns at the Ancient Zapotec Capital*. New York 1978.
D. S. Byers and R. S. MacNeish (eds.), *The Prehistory of the Tehuacan Valley*. Austin, Tex. 1967–77.
M. D. Coe, *Lords of the Underworld: Masterpieces of Classic Maya Ceramics*. Princeton, N.J. 1978.
—— *Mexico*. London 1984.
—— *The Maya*. London 1984.
M. D. Coe and R. A. Diehl, *In the Land of the Olmec*. Austin, Tex. 1980.
N. Davies, *The Ancient Kingdoms of Mexico*. London 1982.
—— *The Aztecs*. London 1973.
R. A. Diehl, *Tula, The Toltec Capital of Ancient Mexico*. London 1983.
K. V. Flannery (ed.), *The Early Mesoamerican Village*. New York 1976.
P. D. Harrison and B. L. Turner II (eds.), *Pre-Hispanic Maya Agriculture*. Albuquerque, NM 1978.
P. D. Joralemon, *A Study of Olmec Iconography*. Washington, D.C. 1972.
J. S. Justeson and L. Campbell (eds.), *Phoneticism in Mayan Hieroglyphic Writing*. Albany, N.Y. 1984.
M. E. Kampen, *The Sculptures of El Tajín, Veracruz, Mexico*. Gainesville, Fla. 1972.
D. H. Kelley, *Deciphering the Maya Script*. Austin, Tex., and London 1976.
J. Kelley, *The Complete Visitor's Guide to Mesoamerican Ruins*. Norman, Okla. 1982.
R. Millon, *Urbanization at Teotihuacan, Mexico*. Austin, Tex. 1973.
H. B. Nicholson and E. Quiñones, *Art of Aztec Mexico*. Washington, D.C. 1983.
J. Paddock (ed.), *Ancient Oaxaca*. Stanford, Calif. 1966.
E. Pasztory, *Aztec Art*. New York 1983.
W. T. Sanders, J. R. Parsons and R. S. Santley, *The Basin of Mexico: Ecological Processes in the Evolution of Civilization*. New York 1979.
L. Schele, *Notebook for Maya Hieroglyphic Writing Workshop at Texas*. Austin, Tex. 1986.
—— and M. E. Miller, *The Blood of Kings: A New Interpretation of Maya Art*. Austin, Tex. 1986.
M. E. Smith, *Picture Writing from Southern Mexico: Mixtec Place Signs and Maps*. Norman, Okla. 1973.
J. Soustelle, *The Olmec*. New York and London 1984.
R. Spores, *The Mixtec Kings and Their People*. Norman, Okla. 1967.
J. Eric S. Thompson, *Maya Hieroglyphic Writing: An Introduction*. Norman, Okla. 1971.
—— *Maya History and Religion*. Norman, Okla. 1970.
M. P. Weaver, *The Aztecs, Maya, and Their Predecessors*. New York 1981.

Part Five: South America
R. E. Alegria, *Ball Courts and Ceremonial Plazas in the West Indies*, Yale University Publications in Anthropology. New Haven, Conn. 1983.
G. Bankes, *Moche Pottery from Peru*. London 1980.
—— *Peru Before Pizarro*. Oxford 1977.
E. P. Benson, *The Mochica*. New York 1972.
—— (ed.), *Dumbarton Oaks Conference on Chavín*. Washington, D.C., 1971.
—— (ed.), *Pre-Columbian Metallurgy of South America*. Washington, D.C., 1979.
—— W. J. Conklin, J. B. Bird and S. J. Chavez, *Museums of the Andes*. New York and Tokyo 1981.
W. Bray, *The Gold of El Dorado*, London 1978.
D. Browman, *Advances in Andean Archaeology*. The Hague and Paris 1978.
B. C. Brundage, *Empire of the Inca*. Norman, Okla. 1963.
R. K. Burger, *The Prehistoric Occupation of Chavín de Huantar*, University of California Publications in Anthropology no. 14. Berkeley, Calif. 1984.
G. H. S. Bushnell, *Peru*. London and New York 1957.
C. B. Donnan, *Moche Art of Peru*. Los Angeles, Clif. 1978.
—— (ed.), *Early Ceremonial Architecture in the Andes*. Washington, D.C., 1985.
A. R. González, *Arte Precolombino de la Argentina*, Argentina 1977.
J. Henning and E. Ranney, *Monuments of the Inca*. Boston, Mass. 1982.
J. Hyslop, *The Inka Road System*. Orlando, Fla. and London 1984.
J. Jones, *The Art of Pre-Columbian Gold*. London 1984.

L. Katz (ed.), *Art of the Andes*. Washington, D.C., 1983.

P. Kosok, *Life, Land and Water in Ancient Peru*. New York 1965.

F. W. Lange (ed.), *Recent Developments in Isthmian Archaeology*. Oxford 1984.

—— and D. Stone (eds.), *The Archaeology of Lower Central America*. Albuquerque, NM 1984.

E. P. Lanning, *Peru Before the Incas*. Englewood Cliffs, N.J. 1967.

A. Lapiner, *Pre-Columbian Art of South America*, New York 1976.

D. W. Lathrap, *The Upper Amazon*, London 1970.

——, A. Gebhart-Sayer and A. M. Mester, "The Roots of the Shipibo Art Style," *Journal of Latin American Lore*, vol. 11. Los Angeles, Calif. 1985.

S. K. Lothrop, *The Indians of Tierra del Fuego*, Contributions from the Museum of the American Indian, Heye Foundation, vol. 10. New York 1928.

L. G. Lumbreras, "Excavaciones en el templo antiguo de Chavín," *Ñawpa Pacha*, vol. 15. Berkeley, Calif. 1977.

—— *The Peoples and Culture of Ancient Peru*, Washington 1974.

G. F. McEwan, *The Middle Horizon in the Valley of Cuzco, Peru*. Ann Arbor, Mich. 1984.

B. J. Meggers, *Amazonia*. Chicago 1971.

D. Menzel, *The Archaeology of Ancient Peru and the Work of Max Uhle*. Berkeley, Calif. 1977.

T. Morrison, *Pathways to the Gods*. New York 1978.

M. Moseley and K. C. Day, *Chan Chan*. Albuquerque, NM 1982.

J. V. Murra, "Cloth and Its Functions in the Inca State," *American Anthropologist*, vol. 64. Menasha, Wisc. 1962.

P. I. Porras G., *Arqueologia del Ecuador*. Quito 1984.

D. A. Proulx, "The Nasca Style," in L. Katz (ed.), *Art of the Andes: Ceramics from the Arthur M. Sackler Collections*. Washington, D.C., 1983.

R. Ravines (ed.), *Chan Chan*. Lima 1980.

G. Reichel-Dolmatoff, *Colombia*. London and New York 1965.

J. Reinhard, *The Hazca Lines: A New Perspective on their Origin and Meaning*. Lima 1985.

J. W. Rick, *Prehistoric Hunters of the High Andes*. New York 1980.

M. A. Rivera, *Prehistoric Chronology of Northern Chile*, Ann Arbor, Mich. 1977.

I. Rouse and J. M. Cruxent, *Venezuelan Archaeology*. New Haven and London 1963.

A. P. Rowe, E. P. Benson and A. L. Schaffer (eds.), *The Junius B. Bird Pre-Columbian Textile Conference*. Washington, D.C., 1979.

J. H. Rowe, *An Introduction to the Archaeology of Cuzco*, Papers of the Peabody Museum of American Archaeology and Ethnology, Harvard University, vol. 27. Cambridge, Mass. 1944.

—— *Chavín Art*. New York 1962.

—— *The Kingdom of Chimor*, Acta Americana vol. 6 1948.

C. Ponce Sangines, *Tiwanaku*, La Paz 1972.

A. R. Sawyer, *Ancient Peruvian Ceramics*. New York 1966.

J. H. Steward (ed.), *Handbook of South American Indians*, Bureau of American Ethnology Bulletin vol. 143, Washington, D.C., 1946–59.

—— and L. C. Faron, *Native Peoples of South America*. New York 1959.

K. E. Stothert, "The Preceramic Las Vegas Culture of Coastal Ecuador," *American Antiquity*, vol. 50. Washington, D.C., 1985.

J. C. Tello, *Chavín*. Lima 1966.

—— *Paracas: Primera parte*. Lima 1959.

—— *Paracas: II parte*. Lima 1979.

G. R. Willey, *An Introduction to American Archaeology*, vol. 2, South America. Englewood Cliffs, N.J. 1971.

Part Six: The Living Heritage

K. Birket-Smith, *The Eskimos*. London 1936.

D. Damas (ed.), *Arctic*, Handbook of North American Indians, vol. 5. Washington, D.C., 1984.

G. M. Foster, *Culture and Conquest*. New York 1960.

C. J. Frisbie (ed.), *Southwestern Indian Ritual Drama*, Albuquerque, NM 1980.

J. C. H. King, *Portrait Masks from the Northwest Coast of America*. London 1974.

C. Levi-Strauss, *La vie des mesques*. Geneva 1975.

R. H. Lowie, *Indians of the Plains*. New York 1954.

J. H. Steward and L. C. Faron, *Native Peoples of South America*. New York 1959.

F. Waters, *Book of the Hopi*. New York 1963.

G. Weltfish, *The Lost Universe*. New York 1965.

GAZETTEER

Canaima (Venezuela), 6°31′N 62°49′W, 174

Canapote (Colombia), 10°25′N 75°32′W, 166

Cancuén (Guatemala), 16°01′N 89°59′W, 126

Candelaria (Argentina), 26°04′S 65°07′W, 186

Candelaria R. (Mexico), 18°15′N 91°10′W, 115, 126, 141

Candy Creek (USA), 35°26′N 84°59′W, 51

Canete R. (Peru), 12°50′S 76°20′W, 186, 193

Canpech (state) (Mexico), 19°40′N 90°25′W, 141

Cantrell Mound (USA), 38°18′N 121°38′W, 80

Canyon de Chelly (USA), 36°07′N 109°20′W, 69

Canyonlands National Park (USA), 38°05′N 110°10′W, 69

Canyon Largo R. (USA), 36°25′N 107°30′W, 215

Capá (Puerto Rico), 18°29′N 66°57′W, 174

Capacha (Mexico), 19°00′N 104°08′W, 91

Cape Kent (Greenland), 78°32′N 71°00′W, 47

Cape Krusenstern (USA), 67°10′N 163°50′W, 46

Cape Nome (USA), 64°26′N 164°58′W, 46

Cape Russel (Greenland), 78°32′N 71°00′W, 47

Cappell Valley (USA), 38°09′N 122°12′W, 80

Caquetá R. (Colombia), 0°55′N 75°50′W, 166

Caracas (Venezuela), 10°35′N 66°56′W, 19

Caracol (Belize), 16°45′N 89°07′W, 126

Caráquez, Bahia de (Ecuador), 0°36′S 80°26′W, 186

Casa Grande (USA), 33°00′N 111°30′W, 69

Casas Grandes (Mexico), 30°22′N 108°00′W, 69

Cascade Range (USA), 43°00′N 122°00′W, 12, 67

Case Site (USA), 39°41′N 121°56′W, 80

Casitas de Piedra (Panama), 9°10′N 82°32′W, 174

Casma R. (Peru), 9°30′S 77°50′W, 176, 186, 193

Casper (USA), 42°50′N 106°21′W, 32

Catarpe (Chile), 22°55′S 68°10′W, 196

Catemaco (Mexico), 18°27′N 95°04′W, 105

Cato (USA), 38°23′N 87°11′W, 51

Cauca R. (Colombia), 7°10′N 75°40′W, 166

Cazones R. (Mexico), 20°30′N 97°30′W, 105, 146

Ceboruco, Volcán (Mexico), 21°06′N 104°30′W, 103

Ceh Pech (state) (Mexico), 21,15′N 89°25′W, 141

Cempoala (Mexico), 19°27′N 96°20′W, 133, 146

Century Ranch (USA), 34°13′N 118°38′W, 80

Cerrillos (Peru), 13°49′S 75°30′W, 176

Cerro Blanco (Peru), 9°09′S 78°19′W, 176

Cerro Cintepec (Mexico), 17°41′N 94°57′W, 95

Cerro de la Bomba (Mexico), 16°22′N 95°11′W, 91

Cerro de las Mesas (Mexico), 18°43′N 96°09′W, 91, 105

Cerro El Vigia (Mexico), 17°43′N 95°13′W, 95

Cerro Encantado (Mexico), 21°28′N 102°32′W, 103

Cerro Grande (Mexico), 16°11′N 97°57′W, 142

Cerro Iguanas (Venezuela), 10°58′N 68°22′W, 174

Cerro Mangote (Panama), 8°12′N 80°21′W, 174

Cerro Narrio (Ecuador), 2°29′S

79°11′W, 176

Cerros (Belize), 18°20′N 88°14′W, 115

Cerro Sanguey, Volcán (Mexico), 21°24′N 104°45′W, 103

Cerro Sechín (Peru), 9°30′S 78°12′W, 176

Cerro Vicús (Peru), 5°08′S 80°10′W, 186

Chacchob (Mexico), 20°19′N 89°15′W, 126

Chachalacas (Mexico), 19°18′N 96°17′W, 105

Chachoapan (Mexico), 17°33′N 97°17′W, 142

Chacmool (Mexico), 19°24′N 87°29′W, 141

Chacmultún (Mexico), 20°07′N 89°22′W, 126

Chaco Canyon (USA), 36°04′N 107°57′W, 69

Chaco R. (USA), 36°10′N 108°25′W, 215

Chacras (Ecuador), 0°47′S 80°16′W, 176

Chacujal (Guatemala), 15°19′N 89°49′W, 141

Chakan (state) (Mexico), 20°50′N 89°30′W, 141

Chalcatzinco (Mexico), 18°47′N 98°50′W, 91, 95, 105

Chalchihuites (Mexico), 23°39′N 103°45′W, 133

Chalchuapa (El Salvador), 13°46′N 89°51′W, 91, 95

Chalco (Mexico), 19°15′N 98°54′W, 144, 146

Chalco L. (Mexico), 19°17′N 98°58′W, 144

Chalk Hollow (USA), 35°05′N 101°40′W, 40

Chaluka (USA), 52°58′N 168°50′W, 46

Chamá (Guatemala), 15°38′N 90°33′W, 126

Champutún (state) (Mexico), 19°20′N 90°25′W, 141

Chanapata (Peru), 13°28′S 72°01′W, 176

Chancay (Peru), 11°38′S 77°22′W, 193

Chancay R. (Peru), 11°18′S 76°55′W, 193

Chance (USA), 42°35′N 74°26′W, 54

Chan Chan (Peru), 8°10′S 79°02′W, 193, 196

Chanchopa (Mexico), 18°51′N 103°52′W, 103

Chapala L. de (Mexico), 20°15′N 103°00′W, 84, 103, 105

Chapultepec (Mexico), 19°25′N 99°11′W, 133, 144

Chatsworth (USA), 34°17′N 118°14′W, 80

Chavín de Huantar (Peru), 9°18′S 77°19′W, 176, 186

Chetumal (state) (Belize/Mexico), 18°08′N 88°25′W, 141

Chiapa (Mexico), 19°43′N 99°33′W, 133

Chiapa de Corzo (Mexico), 16°43′N 92°59′W, 91, 105, 115, 133

Chicama R. (Peru), 7°45′S 78°55′W, 176, 186, 193

Chichén Itzá (Mexico), 20°39′N 88°38′W, 115, 126, 133, 141

Chicoloapan (Mexico), 19°24′N 98°53′W, 144

Chiconauhtla (Mexico), 19°37′N 99°01′W, 133

Chihuahuan Desert (Mexico), 28°00′N 104°00′W, 69

Chikinchel (state) (Mexico), 21°20′N 88°00′W, 141

Chilca (Peru), 12°33′S 76°40′W, 176

Chilecito (Argentina), 29°10′S 67°30′W, 196

Chillón R. (Peru), 11°30′S 76°50′W, 176, 186, 193

Chiloé Island (Chile), 43°00′S 74°30′W, 152

Chimalhuacan (Mexico), 19°25′N 98°56′W, 144

Chimalpan (Mexico), 19°22′N 98°56′W, 133

Chinautla (Guatemala), 14°40′N 90°29′W, 141

Chincha R. (Peru), 11°30′S 76°00′W, 176

Chinchasuyu (Inca quarter), 7°30′S 78°30′W, 196

Chinchorro (Chile), 18°39′S 70°13′W, 174

Chinikihá (Mexico), 17°26′N 91°41′W, 126

Chinkultic (Mexico), 16°07′N 91°50′W, 126

Chinle Creek (USA), 36°25′N 109°35′W, 215

Chinle Valley (USA), 36°40′N 109°50′W, 215

Chiquihuitillo (Mexico), 20°32′N 102°00′W, 133

Chiquito R. (Mexico), 17°20′N 94°44′W, 95

Chiquitoy (Peru), 8°02′S 79°10′W, 189, 196

Chiripa (Bolivia), 16°49′S 68°42′W, 174

Chiriqui, Gulf of, 8°00′N 82°00′W, 161

Chocolá (Guatemala), 14°37′N 91°23′W, 115

Cholula (Mexico), 19°03′N 98°22′W, 105, 133, 146

Chongoyape (Peru), 6°22′S 79°27′W, 176

Choris (USA), 66°20′N 161°25′W, 46

Chorrera (Ecuador), 1°31′S 79°34′W, 176

Chotuna (Peru), 6°42′S 80°02′W, 193

Chucalissa (USA), 35°05′N 90°00′W, 54

Chucuito (Peru), 15°59′S 69°48′W, 193, 196

Chugachik Island (USA), 60°00′N 149°57′W, 46

Chukumuk (Guatemala), 14°39′N 90°10′W, 115

Chupas (Peru), 13°21′S 74°00′W, 176

Chupicuaro (Mexico), 20°01′N 100°22′W, 91

Chuquiabo (Bolivia), 16°30′S 68°10′W, 196

Chuquibamba (Peru), 15°47′S 72°44′W, 189

Chuquitanta see El Paraiso

Chuska Mountains (USA), 36°30′N 108°55′W, 215

Ciénaga de Oro (Colombia), 8°54′N 75°39′W, 166

Cihuatlan (Mexico), 17°45′N 101°14′W, 146

Cilvituk (Mexico), 18°40′N 91°13′W, 141

Citlaltepec (Mexico), 19°49′N 99°08′W, 144

Claiborne (USA), 30°15′N 89°27′W, 40

Clasons Point (USA), 40°51′N 73°47′W, 54

Claypool (USA), 40°24′N 102°27′W, 32

Clear Creek (USA), 34°50′N 110°45′W, 215

Clemsons Island (USA), 40°32′N 76°58′W, 54

Closure (Canada), 62°51′N 69°49′W, 47

Coast Range (Canada), 55°00′N 130°00′W, 12

Coatepec (Mexico), 18°20′N 97°14′W, 89

Coatlinchan (Mexico), 19°27′N 98°53′W, 144

Coatzacoalcos R. (Mexico), 17°24′N 94°36′W, 95, 146

Cobá (Mexico), 20°29′N 87°47′W, 126, 141

Cobija (Chile), 22°32′S 70°15′W, 174

Coca R. (Ecuador), 0°03′S 77°40′W, 176

Cóchiti (USA), 35°40′N 106°18′W, 215

Cochuah (state) (Mexico), 19°50′N 88°35′W, 141

Coco R. (Nicaragua), 14°00′N 85°30′W, 84

Cohunlich (Mexico), 18°21′N 88°48′W, 126

Coixtlahuacan (Mexico), 17°44′N 97°20′W, 142, 146

Cojumotlan (Mexico), 20°08′N 102°51′W, 103, 133

Colhá (Belize), 17°53′N 88°21′W, 126

Colima (Mexico), 19°11′N 103°42′W, 105

Colima, Nevado de (Mexico), 19°34′N 103°38′W, 103

Colima, Volcán de (Mexico), 19°30′N 103°37′W, 103

Collasuyu (Inca quarter), 23°00′S 67°30′W, 196

Colorada, Pampa de (Peru), 14°46′S 75°08′W, 184

Colorado Desert (USA), 33°00′N 115°00′W, 69

Colorado Plateau (USA), 36°00′N 112°30′W, 69

Colorado R. (Argentina), 35°00′S 67°00′W, 152

Colorado R. (USA), 34°00′N 114°30′W, 37, 69

Columbia R. (USA), 45°45′N 121°00′W, 37, 67, 81

Comala (Mexico), 19°19′N 103°48′W, 103

Comalcalco (Mexico), 18°17′N 93°16′W, 105, 126

Comitán (Mexico), 16°15′N 92°04′W, 91

Comulco R. (Mexico), 18°19′N 97°10′W, 89

Conanoxa (Chile), 19°12′S 69°49′W, 174

Conchopata (Peru), 12°48′S 74°25′W, 189

Condorhuasi (Argentina), 27°28′S 67°47′W, 186

Conejo Rock Shelter (USA), 34°19′N 118°50′W, 80

Copales (Mexico), 19°07′N 103°31′W, 103

Copán (Honduras), 14°52′N 89°04′W, 91, 115, 126

Copiapo (Chile), 27°20′S 70°23′W, 196

Coquimbo (Chile), 29°57′S 71°25′W, 16

Corral Canyon (USA), 34°03′N 118°32′W, 80

Corral Falso (Mexico), 21°12′N 104°40′W, 103

Corralitos (Mexico), 19°14′N 103°30′W, 103

Corrientes, Cape (Mexico), 20°26′N 105°42′W, 103

Cotton Point (USA), 33°30′N 117°46′W, 80

Cottonwood Creek (USA), 59°58′N 151°58′W, 46

Cottonwood Wash (USA), 35°10′N 110°20′W, 215

Couri (Haiti), 19°54′N 72°58′W, 174

Cow Point (Canada), 45°53′N 66°24′W, 40

Coxcatlan Cave (Mexico), 18°11′N 97°08′W, 89, 91

Coxcatlan Terrace (Mexico), 18°12′N 97°08′W, 89

Coyohuacan (Mexico), 19°21′N 99°09′W, 144

Coyolapan (Mexico), 17°04′N 96°54′W, 146

Coyote Hills (USA), 37°24′N 121°56′W, 80

Coyotepec (Mexico), 19°46′N 99°12′W, 144

Cozumel, Isla de (Mexico), 20°20′N 87°00′W, 126, 133, 141

Crab Orchard (USA), 37°41′N 89°02′W, 51

Crag Point (USA), 57°48′N 152°50′W, 46

Craig Harbour (Canada), 75°00′N 80°02′W, 47

Crespo (Colombia), 10°25′N 75°32′W, 166

Criel Mound (USA), 38°24′N 81°50′W, 51

Crow Creek (USA), 44°00′N 99°20′W, 64

Crus del Milagro (Mexico), 17°24′N 95°01′W, 95

Crystall II (Canada), 63°42′N 68°33′W, 47

Crystal River (USA), 28°53′N 82°40′W, 51

Cuahuacan (Mexico), 19.38′N 99°27′W, 133, 146

Swift Creek (USA), 33°10′N 83°47′W, 51
Sylvan Lake (USA), 41°15′N 73°45′W, 40

T-1, T-3 (Canada), 64°10′N 83°10′W, 47
Taff (Argentina), 27°46′S 66°24′W, 186
Tagua Tagua (Chile), 34°49′S 71°13′W, 174
Takli Island (USA), 57°35′N 156°01′W, 46
Talca (Chile), 35°28′S 71°40′W, 196
Taltal (Chile), 25°26′S 70°33′W, 174
Tamaulipas Caves (Mexico), 23°15′N 98°22′W, 32, 91
Tamazula (Mexico), 19°43′N 103°11′W, 103
Tambo Colorado (Peru), 13°30′S 75°54′W, 196
Tambo Viejo (Peru), 15°08′S 74°21′W, 186
Tamuin (Mexico), 22°00′N 98°45′W, 133
Tancah (Mexico), 20°17′N 87°26′W, 115, 126, 141
Tanganhuato (Mexico), 18°10′N 100°30′W, 105
Taos (USA), 36°24′N 105°33′W, 215
Tapajós R. (Brazil), 6°00′S 57°00′W, 152
Tarma (Peru), 11°28′S 75°41′W, 196
Tasco see Tlachco
Tasés (state) (Mexico), 21°05′N 87°50′W, 141
Taxla (Mexico), 18°31′N 95°17′W, 91
Tayasal (Guatemala), 16°58′N 89°59′W, 141
Tazumal (El Salvador), 13°59′N 89°39′W, 126
Tchefuncte (USA), 30°29′N 89°59′W, 51
Tebenquiche (Argentina), 24°50′S 66°58′W, 186
Tecorral Canyon (Mexico), 18°22′N 97°25′W, 89
Tecorral Cave (Mexico), 18°23′N 97°24′W, 89
Tehuacan (Mexico), 18°29′N 97°22′W, 89, 105
Tehuacan Valley (Mexico), 18°25′N 97°25′W, 32, 91
Tehuantepec (Mexico), 16°21′N 95°02′W, 105
Tehuantepec, Gulf of (Mexico), 16°00′N 95°00′W, 84
Tehuantepec, Isthmus of (Mexico), 17°00′N 95°00′W, 84
Tehuantepec R. (Mexico), 16°40′N 95°35′W, 105, 146
Teloloapan (Mexico), 18°21′N 99°53′W, 133, 146
Temazcalapan (Mexico), 19°48′N 98°55′W, 144
Tembladera (Peru), 7°17′S 79°09′W, 176
Temecula Creek (USA), 33°35′N 117°09′W, 80
Tempoal R. (Mexico), 21°30′N 98°25′W, 105
Tenanco (Mexico), 19°08′N 99°32′W, 105
Tenayucan (Mexico), 19°32′N 99°11′W, 133, 144
Tenochtitlan (Mexico, Mexico), 19°25′N 99°08′W, 19, 133, 144, 146
Tenochtitlan (Veracruz, Mexico), 17°15′N 94°44′W, 95
Teoloyucan (Mexico), 19°48′N 99°19′W, 133
Teotihuacan (Mexico), 19°40′N 98°53′W, 91, 105, 133, 144
Teotitlan (state) (Mexico), 18°35′N 97°25′W, 146
Teotitlan R. (Mexico), 18°09′N 97°06′W, 89
Teotitlan del Camino (Mexico), 18°08′N 97°04′W, 89, 133, 142
Teotitlan del Valle (Mexico), 17°02′N 96°23′W, 142
Tepalcatepec R. (Mexico), 18°50′N 102°20′W, 103, 105, 146
Tepeacac (Mexico), 19°02′N 97°50′W, 105, 146

Tepecuacuilco (Mexico), 18°25′N 99°30′W, 146
Tepeji (Mexico), 19°52′N 99°20′W, 133
Tepetlaóztoc (Mexico), 19°33′N 98°48′W, 133
Tepetzinco (Mexico), 19°26′N 99°05′W, 144
Tepetzintla (Mexico), 21°10′N 97°51′W, 105
Tepexic (Mexico), 19°57′N 99°26′W, 105
Tepexpan (Mexico), 19°36′N 98°57′W, 91, 144
Tepeyacac (Mexico), 19°29′N 99°07′W, 144
Tepic (Mexico), 21°28′N 104°56′W, 103
Tepotzotlan (Mexico), 19°42′N 99°14′W, 144
Tepoztlan (Mexico), 19°09′N 99°00′W, 133
Tequixquiac (Mexico), 20°00′N 99°07′W, 91
Términos, Laguna de (Mexico), 18°35′N 91°40′W, 126
Tesuque (USA), 35°46′N 105°57′W, 215
Tetela (Mexico), 17°58′N 100°02′W, 146
Tetelco (Mexico), 19°12′N 98°58′W, 144
Tetzmoliuhuacan (Mexico), 17°34′N 98°59′W, 133
Texcoco (Mexico), 19°30′N 98°53′W, 133, 144, 146
Texcoco L. (Mexico), 19°29′N 99°01′W, 105, 133, 144, 146
Texcotzinco (Mexico), 19°30′N 98°50′W, 144
Tezli (Canada), 52°57′N 124°29′W, 81
Tezompa (Mexico), 19°11′N 98°58′W, 144
Tezoyuca (Mexico), 19°35′N 98°55′W, 144
Thiensville (USA), 43°14′N 88°00′W, 40
Thomas Riggs (USA), 44°31′N 100°34′W, 64
Three Kiva Pueblo (USA), 37°42′N 109°02′W, 69
Thule (Greenland), 77°30′N 69°29′W, 47
Tiahuanaco (Bolivia), 16°41′S 68°38′W, 174, 186, 189, 196
Tiayo (Mexico), 20°48′N 97°51′W, 133
Tiburon (USA), 38°00′N 122°29′W, 80
Tick Island (USA), 29°21′N 81°38′W, 40
Tierra del Fuego (Chile/Argentina), 54°00′S 67°00′W, 12, 152
Tierradentro (Colombia), 2°30′N 75°55′W, 166
Tihoo (Mexico), 20°58′N 89°39′W, 141
Tikal (Guatemala), 17°12′N 89°38′W, 91, 115, 126
Tilantongo (Mexico), 17°18′N 97°21′W, 105, 142
Tilcara (Argentina), 23°36′S 65°23′W, 196
Tiquisate (Guatemala), 14°19′N 91°23′W, 126
Titicaca L. (Peru/Bolivia), 15°50′S 69°20′W, 12, 152, 186, 189, 193, 196
Tizapan (DF, Mexico), 19°20′N 99°11′W, 144
Tizapan (Jalisco, Mexico), 20°09′N 103°03′W, 103
Tizayucan (Mexico), 19°49′N 98°59′W, 144
Tlachco (Tasco) (Mexico), 18°33′N 99°34′W, 146
Tlachquiauhco (Mexico), 17°15′N 97°40′W, 146
Tlacopan (Mexico), 19°26′N 99°11′W, 144, 146
Tlalcozauhtitlan (Mexico), 17°52′N 99°05′W, 146
Tlalnepantla (Mexico), 19°31′N 99°12′W, 144
Tlaloc, Mount (Mexico), 19°25′N 98°43′W, 144

Tlalpan (Mexico), 19°17′N 99°10′W, 144
Tlapacoya (Mexico), 19°18′N 98°55′W, 32, 91, 144
Tlapacoyan (Mexico), 20°10′N 97°48′W, 146
Tlapan (Mexico), 17°33′N 98°31′W, 146
Tlatelolco (Mexico), 19°27′N 99°08′W, 144, 146
Tlatilco (Mexico), 19°30′N 99°15′W, 91, 95
Tlatlauhquitepec (Mexico), 19°52′N 97°28′W, 146
Tlatlayan (Mexico), 18°31′N 100°07′W, 105
Tlaxcala (Mexico), 19°19′N 98°13′W, 146
Tlaxcallan (state) (Mexico), 19°30′N 97°40′W, 146
Tlaxialtemalco (Mexico), 19°14′N 99°04′W, 144
Tochpan (Mexico), 20°58′N 97°21′W, 146
Tochtepec see Tuxtepec
Togiak (USA), 59°05′N 160°30′W, 46
Toliman (Mexico), 20°56′N 99°54′W, 105
Tollantzinco (Mexico), 20°05′N 98°20′W, 105, 133, 146
Toluca see Tulucan
Tomaval (Peru), 8°27′S 78°43′W, 186
Tomebamba see Cuenca
Tommy Tucker Cave (USA), 40°34′N 121°52′W, 80
Tonalá (Mexico), 16°05′N 93°43′W, 91, 105, 115
Toniná (Mexico), 16°53′N 92°02′W, 126
Tonopah (USA), 38°06′N 117°17′W, 32
Tonto (USA), 33°33′N 111°12′W, 69
Toolesboro Mounds (USA), 41°18′N 91°21′W, 51
Topanga Canyon (USA), 34°11′N 118°29′W, 40, 80
Topoc Maze (USA), 34°42′N 114°29′W, 69
Topoxté (Guatemala), 17°00′N 89°26′W, 141
Tortuguero (Mexico), 17°37′N 92°38′W, 126
Totopec (state) (Mexico), 16°10′N 97°40′W, 146
Town Creek (USA), 35°02′N 80°00′W, 54
Towosahgy (USA), 36°43′N 89°10′W, 54
Trail Creek Caves (USA), 65°49′N 163°18′W, 46
Trancas Canyon (USA), 34°03′N 118°32′W, 80
Tranquillity (USA), 36°22′N 119°50′W, 40
Trapiche (Panama), 9°10′N 82°32′W, 174
Trempealeau (USA), 44°01′N 91°28′W, 51
Tremper (USA), 38°47′N 83°02′W, 51
Tres Zapotes (Mexico), 17°58′N 95°26′W, 91, 95, 105
Trinity Reservoir (USA), 40°36′N 122°29′W, 80
Tsurai (USA), 42°43′N 124°31′W, 80
Tukidi (Mexico), 15°46′N 96°31′W, 142
Tula (Hidalgo, Mexico), 20°01′N 99°19′W, 133, 146
Tula (Jalisco, Mexico), 20°38′N 103°43′W, 103
Tularosa Cave (USA), 33°53′N 108°28′W, 40
Tulpetlac (Mexico), 19°33′N 99°04′W, 144
Tulucan (Toluca) (Mexico), 19°17′N 99°40′W, 144
Tulum (Mexico), 20°11′N 87°30′W, 141
Tulyehualco (Mexico), 19°14′N 99°00′W, 144
Tumbes (Peru), 3°37′S 80°27′W, 16, 176, 196
Tunja (Colombia), 5°33′N 73°23′W, 166
Tupiza (Bolivia), 21°27′S 65°45′W, 196

Turner (USA), 39°09′N 84°15′W, 51
Turner Farm (USA), 44°08′N 69°01′W, 40
Turnstone Beach (Canada), 78°40′N 76°02′W, 47
Turrialba (Costa Rica), 9°58′N 83°40′W, 32, 161, 174
Turtle Mound (USA), 29°02′N 80°55′W, 54
Tusayan (USA), 35°58′N 112°07′W, 69
Tusket Falls (Canada), 43°50′N 65°59′W, 40
Tutishcainyo (Peru), 8°20′S 74°29′W, 176
Tutul Xiuh (state) see Mani
Tututepec (Mexico), 16°08′N 97°39′W, 133, 142
Tuxcacuesco (Mexico), 19°43′N 103°59′W, 103
Tuxpan (Mexico), 19°33′N 103°25′W, 103
Tuxtepec (Tochtepec) (Mexico), 18°08′N 96°08′W, 105, 146
Tuxtla Mountains (Mexico), 18°00′N 95°05′W, 95
Tuzigoot (USA), 34°50′N 111°59′W, 69
Tyara (Canada), 62°10′N 75°41′W, 47
Tzibanché (Mexico), 18°31′N 88°45′W, 141
Tziccoac (Mexico), 21°00′N 98°10′W, 146
Tzilacayoapan (Mexico), 17°31′N 98°10′W, 105, 142
Tzinapécuaro (Mexico), 19°49′N 100°48′W, 105
Tzintzúntzan (Mexico), 19°37′N 101°34′W, 133, 146

Uaacbal (Mexico), 18°19′N 89°46′W, 126
Uaxactún (Guatemala), 17°23′N 89°38′W, 91, 115, 126
Ucayali R. (Peru), 8°00′S 74°50′W, 152, 174, 176, 186, 193, 196
Ugashik Narrows (USA), 57°32′N 157°25′W, 46
Ulúa R. (Honduras), 15°00′N 88°25′W, 126
Unalakleet (USA), 63°52′N 160°50′W, 46
Unalaska Bay (USA), 53°51′N 166°35′W, 46
University (USA), 43°00′N 89°12′W, 51
Uolantún (Guatemala), 17°10′N 89°39′W, 126
Urabá, Gulf of (Colombia), 8°25′N 77°00′W, 161, 166
Uren (Canada), 42°51′N 80°22′W, 54
Urubamba R. (Peru), 13°25′S 72°30′W, 176
Uspanapa R. (Mexico), 17°12′N 94°11′W, 95
Usumacinta R. (Guatemala/Mexico), 17°50′N 92°05′W, 84, 115, 126, 133, 141
Utatlán (Guatemala), 15°00′N 91°08′W, 115, 141
Utz (USA), 39°19′N 93°00′W, 54
Uxmal (Mexico), 20°22′N 89°49′W, 126

Vail Ranch (USA), 33°35′N 117°09′W, 80
Valdivia Palmar (Ecuador), 2°04′S 80°49′W, 176
Valle de Bravo (Mexico), 19°10′N 100°09′W, 105, 133
Valliserrana (Argentina), 26°00′S 67°00′W, 186, 193
Valsequillo (Mexico), 18°59′N 97°39′W, 32, 91
Vancouver Island (Canada), 49°00′N 126°00′W, 81
Vaughn (Canada), 70°06′N 124°33′W, 47
Veale (USA), 38°01′N 122°10′W, 80
Venado Beach (Panama), 8°55′N 79°37′W, 161
Ventana Cave (USA), 32°31′N 112°17′W, 40
Ventura 70 (USA), 34°19′N 118°50′W, 80

INDEX

ANIAN.

Vlterius Septentrionem versus hę
regiones incognitę adhuc sunt.

TOLM.

Tuchana

QVIVIRA
Quivira   Sierra
nevada   Cicuic   Axa   Chucho.   Tiguas rio.

TOTO   TEAC.   Suala mons
Tiguex Totonteac   Ceubla   MARATA

Abacus nunc
Granata.

yª del ripa   P. Sardinas   P. de S. clara   ASTATLAN   Guaiaual rio.   TERLICHICH
Cazones inf. Costa blanca S. del papagaio Marata   R. Palmar
              Baia de fuego Granada Coans   HISPANIA NOVA
insi. Cedri. C. de seres   Ometlan XALISCO Chicil   Mesclan
Los diamantes   Culua- Chamet Yucapa TOPIRA   S. Mich
Baia de la   an Petatlan Guevos   Chinas
trinidad.   Roccha S. Thomas.   Caraconi Tala Vicilla
Las dos hermanos   Los bolcanes   parcida La Anubi   Culchucim MECHVACAN
Malabrigo   La farfana   ada.   Acapula
ARCHIPELAGO DI   Aguada
SAN LAZARO.   Icel
Restinga de ladrones
Zamal
Inf: de los corales.
OCCIDENS.   Los iardines   Inf: de los reys

Circulus Aequinoctialis
Los martyires   210   220   230   240   250   260
y de Crespos   Dai timo de mala gente
V. dos hombres blancos   La barbada
La Caimana
Los bolcanes

Ysola de los
tiburones

Hę duę insulę, infortunatę sunt dictę
à Magellano, quod nec homines nec
victui apta haberent.

NOVA GVINEA, Andre-   S.Petri
as Corsalus Florent: videtur eã
sub nomine Terrę Piccinnacoli
designare.

AMERICAE SIVE
NOVI ORBIS, NO-
VA DESCRIPTIO.